Oct., 1997

For Mary

my darling

Primo

Judgment in Jerusalem

Judgment in Jerusalem

Chief Justice Simon Agranat and the Zionist Century

Pnina Lahav

UNIVERSITY OF CALIFORNIA PRESS

Berkeley / Los Angeles / London

To Mort

The publisher gratefully acknowledges the contribution provided by the Art Book Endowment of the Associates of the University of California Press, which is supported by a major gift from the Ahmanson Foundation.

The publisher also gratefully acknowledges the contribution provided by the General Endowment Fund, which is supported by generous gifts from the members of the Associates of the University of California Press.

University of California Press
Berkeley and Los Angeles, California

University of California Press, Ltd.
London, England

© 1997 by
The Regents of the University of California

Library of Congress Cataloging-in-Publication Data

Lahav, Pnina, 1945–
    Judgment in Jerusalem: Simon Agranat and the Zionist century / by Pnina Lahav.
        p.   cm.
    Includes bibliographical references and index.
    ISBN 0-520-20595-2 (cloth: alk. paper)
    1. Agranat, Shimon, 1906–1992. 2. Judges—Israel—Biography.
3. Law—Israel—History. 4. Zionism—History—20th century.
I. Title.
KMKII0.A38L34   1997
347.5694'014'092—dc21   96-40381
                                                                              CIP

Printed in the United States of America
9   8   7   6   5   4   3   2   1

Contents

Acknowledgments

This book was in gestation for more than a decade. Harry Hirsch introduced me to the genre of judicial biography long before I embarked on this project. He and I had many discussions about the pleasure and pain of biography writing, and I benefited enormously from his insights. A 1984 fellowship from the Rockefeller Foundation enabled me to spend a year in Israel doing research, conducting interviews, and otherwise launching the "Agranat project." Without that initial support, I could not have written this book.

The Boston University School of Law consistently gave me material and emotional support. Without my good friends on the faculty, our former dean, Colin Diver, and particularly our present dean, Ron Cass, I would not have been able to complete this project. Alan Feld, Tamar Frankel, Fred Lawrence, Fran Miller, Bob Seidman, and Larry Yackle taught me that one can build true and enduring friendships even without a common background and similar professional interests. By making me feel at home in the United States they helped me experience some of those things that made Simon Agranat love his native land.

To the list of friends at the Boston University School of Law I should add Kenneth Westhassel, my loyal secretary of the past sixteen years, who offered deft, judicious, and patient help through the long years of work on this book. His skills at merging and polishing text and footnotes as the various chapters matured into a book were indispensable. I am indebted to him for helping me carry on the project of writing the biography of an Israeli judge while simultaneously teaching courses in American law and occasionally publishing on matters unrelated to the biography.

I also wish to thank my research assistants—Martha Berek, Sigal Blumberg, Mike Greenberg, Brook Holland, Mike Katzenstein, Coleen Klasmeier, Orna Kornreich, Tamar Krongrad, Meredith Savitch, Mike Siller, and Miriam Wugmeister—for their valuable help. Dalia Tsuk was indispensable in double-checking the citations and reviewing the manuscript as a whole.

I owe special thanks to Gaia Bernstein, Orly Erez-Likhovski, and Assaf Likhovski for their expert and skillful research on various segments of the book and for their wise and discerning comments on the manuscript. Assaf Likhovski also assisted with the glossary and transliteration, again proving his formidable efficiency as well as his brilliant command of the budding field of Israeli legal history.

I feel immensely fortunate to have had Douglas Abrams Arava as the sponsoring editor for my book. His enthusiasm and encouragement, as well as his deft and valuable advice, were crucial in bringing this book to fruition. I also wish to thank Scott Norton and Sarah K. Myers for excellent editorial help, which improved the book enormously.

Many people kindly agreed to be interviewed, among them Arthur and Dorothy Goldberg, Ben Sackheim, Mary Satinover, Esther Schour, and Leo Wolf, Agranat's friends in Chicago before he moved to Palestine. Jacob Halevy, Itzhak Kahan, Naphtali Liphshitz, and Jacob S. Shapiro helped me reconstruct Agranat's early years in Haifa. Judges Miriam Ben-Porath, Haim Cohn, Moshe Landau, Ayala Proccacia, Moshe Ravid, and Yitzhak Shiloh, Deputy Attorney General Judith Karp, and former Minister of Justice Chaim Zadok expanded my understanding of Agranat's twenty-eight years on Israel's Supreme Court.

I am also grateful for the help and encouragement of Chief Justices Meir Shamgar and Aharon Barak.

The Faculty of Law at Tel Aviv University provided warm hospitality during my years of shuttling between the United States and Israel. They treated me like one of their own, and for that I shall be forever in their debt. In particular I wish to thank Ruth Ben-Israel, Nily Cohen, Daniel Friedman, Eli Lederman, Asher Maoz, Menny Mautner, the late Ariel Rosen-Zvi, and Zeev Segal for our many conversations and for their encouragement and support. My gratitude also to Gad Barzilai, Lucian Bebchuk, Hanina Ben Menachem, Meir Dan-Cohen, Michael Keren, Motta Kremnitzer, Moshe Negby, Uriel Reichman, Yoram Shachar, Ronen Shamir, and Ilan Shiloh for insightful conversations.

Asher Maoz, Menny Mautner, Yoram Shachar, Michal Shaked, and Joe Singer read parts of the manuscript, and Yochai Benkler, Ephraim Kleiman, Avi Soifer, and Philippa Strum read the entire manuscript. All provided useful comments, and I thank them warmly, while acknowledging, as I do for everyone else mentioned on these pages, that the responsibility for all errors and misinterpretations is mine alone.

I met Laura Kalman in 1995, when the manuscript was almost complete. She asked to see it, and I soon discovered that she is one of those scholars who not only reads and comments on one's work but is truly generous with support. My friendship with her is a cherished consequence of writing this book. She gave me constructive comments and shared with me the long and sometimes painful process of bringing the book to publication. Thank you, Laura, for being such a good friend.

The Agranat family was graciously supportive throughout the years. Many thanks to Carmel, Israel, Yael (Didi), Orit, and Ayala for their generosity of spirit and unfailing cooperation. I also wish to acknowledge the noble, scholarly spirit of their assistance; though undoubtedly curious about my interpretation, the Agranats refrained from interfering in my work or trying to affect its course.

My mother tongue is Hebrew, and, despite my efforts, the effects of English being my second language are bound to show. English, however, is the mother tongue of my daughter, Alexandra, who was born and raised in the United States. Alexandra's editorial work in the initial stages of this manuscript was wonderful, and she was generous with advice and goodwill as I wrestled with a language not my own. I thank both of my children, Alexandra and Absalom, for making my life so rich, so fulfilled, so replete with fun and good humor. I also wish to thank their father, Moshe Lahav, for transcending the difficulties of divorce and shouldering the task of parenting fully and faithfully. His graciousness made life so much more livable. My warmest gratitude to my family—my mother, Ora Matalon; my aunt, Marcelle Nissan; my brothers, Yosef and Azriel; and their wives, Sarah and Shlomit—for their love and sympathy.

Mort Horwitz, my companion, patiently listened, wisely commented, advised, and heroically tolerated my swinging moods and many moments of self-doubt and frustration. It is to him that I dedicate this book, with love.

Prologue

Simon Agranat was to Israeli law what David Ben-Gurion was to Israeli politics. He was a visionary founding father, a passionate Zionist, and a true believer in the idea that a sovereign state is essential for the successful resolution of "the Jewish question." During his tenure on Israel's Supreme Court, from 1948 to 1976, Agranat had a hand in every important political issue facing Israeli society.

Agranat's story and the story of Israeli constitutionalism are also a reflection of the political struggles of Zionism during the century of its existence. A weak, hardly popular or influential movement at the end of the nineteenth century, Zionism nevertheless managed to muster enough power to achieve its goal of establishing the state of Israel fifty years later. Within twenty years of its creation, Israel was transformed from a small, poor nation-in-arms into the prosperous, powerful, and arrogant victor of the Six Day War. Its sense of well-being and security lasted only six years. In 1973 Israel was surprised and humbled by Arab military success in the early stages of the Yom Kippur War. Against these varied backgrounds, as Israeli identity was crystallizing, Agranat sought to resolve the constitutional conflicts that came before him. He was born and raised in the United States, and his American outlook affected the way he gauged these conflicts, which was in turn tempered and shaped by the dynamic political and social forces that had produced the Zionist century; his decisions molded the emerging political and legal culture of Israel.

The struggle, first to achieve and then to solidify Jewish sovereignty, and the anxiety over matters of national security fostered in Israel a brand of communitarian etatism known as *mamlakhtiyut*. This approach, in turn, encouraged suspicion of constitutionalism and intolerance of political and civil liberties. In his influential *Kol ha-Am* opinion, Agranat faced the question of what basic rights Israelis had against their government. As a judge, he also struggled with a methodological question: could the Court recognize rights, given the absence of a constitution? Agranat's insistence on the concept of limits on executive power and on the subordination of etatism to the concept of the rule of law had long-term effects on the Israeli polity.

The significance of statehood and "the state" in Zionist thought cannot be overestimated. The idea of the state as a preferred value is related to one of the cornerstones of Zionism—the negation of exile (*galut*). Zionism taught that exile was at the root of all Jewish predicaments and that only sovereign statehood held the key to Jewish well-being. It also taught that once exile was terminated and Jews were resettled in their homeland, a "new" Jewish person (in the early era he or she was called "the new Hebrew" person, discarding the term *Jewish* altogether) would emerge. The proud and accomplished home-grown sabra, the antithesis of the degraded Jewish person rooted in exilic life, was the Zionist ideal.

The negation of *galut* found expression in the early lessons Israelis were trying to learn from the Holocaust. While grieving over the catastrophic loss of millions of Jews, Israelis were trying to convince themselves that one reason for the calamity was the failure of the Jews in exile to behave like free men and women. Had they acquired the qualities of the sabras, they would not have "gone like lambs to the slaughter." This theme reverberated throughout the 1950s, culminating in the notorious trial of Rudolf Israel Kasztner, in which Agranat had to decide whether the Jewish leader had collaborated with Adolph Eichmann, chief architect of the Final Solution.

By the time Eichmann himself came before Agranat, two competing worldviews—universalism and particularism—were vying for Israel's soul. Should Israel understand itself as a victim, especially entitled to help and protection, or as a nation like all others? Was the Israeli enactment of the unique criminal offense known as "crimes against the Jewish people" justified, given the history of anti-Semitism and the Holocaust? Or did Israel, along with the rest of the nations, have to content itself with the more universalist ban on "crimes against humanity"?

This tension, which dominated the Eichmann trial, also appeared in the Yeredor trial, in which the political rights of the Israeli-Arab minority were contested. One of Agranat's first opinions as chief justice, *Yeredor v. Chairman of the Central Elections Commission,* asked whether the state could be justified in limiting the rights of Israeli Arabs to vote for a party of their choice. Should the state acknowledge the legitimacy of the Palestinian people's understanding of their own history? Should it strive to become an inclusive democracy, in which Arabs and Jews enjoyed the same rights and liberties? Or should democracy recognize the necessity of some limitations, deriving from the Jewishness of the state or from the real or imagined needs of national security?

Many a Zionist, especially in the founders' generation, associated the negation of *galut* with the end of Jewish religious life. The "reconstructed" Jew, they believed, would shed religion like unwanted skin and join the enlightened world, liberated, free, and secular. Other Zionists, however, insisted that without religion Israel could not be a "Jewish" state. This issue embodied the perennial tension in Jewish history between the universal and the particular, between the Zionist ideal of turning the "reconstructed Jewish people" into a "normal" "nation like all nations," and its rival, the ideal of becoming a "light unto the nations," pursuing justice in the spirit of the biblical prophets of Israel. Would Israel allow the apple of its eye, the "normal" sabra, to register himself as an Israeli and thereby to purge the "Jewish" element from his identity? The landmark case of *Who Is a Jew* exposed the depth of these agonizing questions in all of their complexity.

Zionism is a coat of many colors: it incorporates themes ranging across the entire political spectrum of nineteenth-century European thought and captures the polarities within Jewish discourse. These perceptions have been represented (not always successfully) by the polarity between catastrophe and utopian Zionism. For catastrophe Zionists, Israel serves primarily as a safe haven from repetition of the various catastrophes that have befallen Jews in the past. In contrast, utopian Zionism stands for the proposition that Israel should be constructed as a model state. This produced a second polarity between, on one hand, the Zionists' commitment to the reconstruction of all aspects of Jewish life and, on the other, the recognition that Israel might lack legitimacy if it failed to constitute a link in the chain of Jewish history. Zionism was an ideology fed by enormous reserves of both utopian and nationalist energy and passion, which splintered into numerous points of view about where and how the movement should proceed. At the same time, Zionists widely recognized that unity was essential to the movement's success. How did the push toward unity and the pull of diversity affect Israel's democratic aspirations? This theme resounded in all of Agranat's opinions but appeared particularly forcefully in the Agranat Commission's reports. Toward the end of his career, on the heels of the Yom Kippur War, Agranat stood at the helm of a commission appointed to inquire why Israel was caught off guard in 1973. In many ways his commission's reports, as controversial as they were at the time they were published, inadvertently helped unleash the forces that heralded a new era for Israel, starting with the Likud's rise to power and the historic peace with Egypt as the 1970s came to a close.

• • •

Agranat was unique among Israel's founding elite in that his cultural background was not the Eastern Europe of the early twentieth century but rather the United States of the Progressive Era. Israel is a nation of immigrants. Its leaders were mostly Russian or Polish; the American Golda Meir, or the British Abba Eban, were exceptions who proved the rule.[1] Likewise, in the first decades of statehood most of the justices were recent European immigrants: Russians, Lithuanians, Poles, or Germans.[2] Each brought with him (there were no women justices) the culture of his native land and the legal outlook of his law professors, elements that, consciously and subconsciously, were grafted onto his judicial work.

Agranat differed from his brethren both because he never felt persecuted in his native land and because of his admiration for the U.S. Constitution. One important and distinctively American feature of Agranat's worldview was his particular understanding of the nature of law. He was a strong believer in sociological jurisprudence: the theory that law was not a pure science but was grounded in culture and society. Many of his brethren were staunch formalists, who firmly believed in the separation of law and society. Thus the story told in these pages is also the story of how different cultures and outlooks, vying for power, combined to shape and form Israeli law and Israeli justice. Because of the prominence of Agranat's opinions, the canvas of Israeli legal culture is liberally sprinkled with American motifs.

Agranat was fifteen years old when the split between Chaim Weizmann and Louis D. Brandeis shook America's Jewish community. "There is no bridge between Washington and Pinsk," Weizmann declared, alluding not only to the incompatibility between himself and Brandeis but also to the estrangement between East and West, Europe and America. The Split was Agranat's first encounter with Zionism's need to create an "Other" in order to develop a sense of itself; it was embarrassing to Agranat to realize that Weizmann was making American Jews like himself into that otherness. Forty-two years later, in midcareer as an esteemed justice of Israel's high court, he delivered an opinion singing the praises of "America's beauty." At stake was the question of whether architectural aesthetics were to be judged by universal, transcendental standards or by aesthetic criteria relative to time and place. Quoting the American philosopher Santayana, Agranat held that beauty was a dynamic concept. As examples of modern beauty, he chose the Chicago Tribune building and the skyscrapers of New York City, stating that "even a bridge built of iron may contain attributes of beauty and proportion."[3] Bridges came to his mind as he insisted that America's modern functional architecture was as beautiful as Europe's classical monuments.

Agranat, who could not see the world as either good or evil, was always sensitive to the complexity inherent in every situation. His opinions and reports reflect his lifelong effort to build bridges: a bridge between collectivism and individualism, between Jewishness and modernity, between continuity and reform, between legal formalism and sociological jurisprudence, between law and justice, between the Jewish state and liberal democracy, and, last but not least, between Washington and Jerusalem. Present and future Israeli courts will have to wrestle with the antinomies embedded in his jurisprudence as Israel enters the twenty-first century.

• • •

The first time I saw Agranat was in 1969, when I was clerking in the district court, then located in the same building as the Supreme Court in the Russian compound in Jerusalem. He was a tall man, distinguished in his dark suit and thick, horn-rimmed glasses. Aloof and somber, he always had a pipe in his mouth. Fifteen years later, when I came to interview him, he retained a full head of silver hair. Although he was somewhat more stooped, his height still gave him a distinguished appearance. I learned that the pipe's stem and bit were thoroughly gnawed and corroded, suggesting that his well-known serenity was only a facade. I discovered a glimmer of mischief in his eyes, a boyish grin, and a dry sense of humor. Behind his serious veneer was an unpretentious man, open to self-criticism and capable of laughing at himself.

In 1984, after I had secured Agranat's consent to cooperate with me on this project, I spent a year in Israel, interviewing him and studying materials from various archives.[4] I would come to his home in Jerusalem, not far from the Israel Museum, two or three times a week, and there we would talk for three or four hours. At first we designated a particular topic for discussion. As he grew older and it became more difficult to control the drift of the conversation, I found myself listening to stories I had heard several times before, waiting for a different interpretation, a new twist, or trying to understand the connections he was making by free association.

When I started to work on this biography I did not give much thought to the component of immigration in Israeli legal culture. As my interviews with Agranat progressed and we grew comfortable with each other, I was struck by how much of the "American" was present in Agranat's persona. In Hebrew he was content to call himself Shimon, but in English he insisted on the American version, Simon, in speech and in writing.[5] Even though he spent sixty-two of his eighty-six years away from the United States, his accent was unmistakably Chicagoan. He would become excited about the technicalities of a baseball game; and, in his last year, enthusiastically watching Ken Burns's television documentary, *The Civil War,* he would vividly describe the minute details of every battle to anyone who consented to listen. Yet Agranat was not merely another "American abroad." Rather, he was the quintessential Israeli of the founding generation: an immigrant wholeheartedly committed to the task of nation building, using as guidance and inspiration the concepts woven into the identity he had ostensibly left behind.

Not everything I have written in this book would please him. My interpretation of Zionism is much more critical than his could ever be, and I occasionally disagree with the solutions he found for Israel's problems. He seldom had a bad word to say about anyone, and on the rare occasions when he did, he would put his negative comment ambiguously or in a double entendre. He was, therefore, uneasy with my critical portrayal of some of his brethren. Also, he was an intensely private man, ambivalent about the role of psychology in a judicial biography. On one hand, he wove psychological insights into many of his reflections. A favorite phrase was one he attributed to Justice Felix Frankfurter, concerning "the strong pull of the unconscious." On the other hand, he did not wish his opinions to be read as anything but the result of legal rules and legal reasoning. Thus my occasional references to a psychological motivation made him feel awkward. He wished the story could be told without such references, yet he conceded in conversation that an attempt to understand motive was an important part of the story.

I showed him early drafts of a few chapters; he was both complimentary and critical. When I reacted defensively, he said: "I don't always agree with you, but it is your book. You should go ahead and do what you think is right." This remark came from his deep understanding that even though this was a book about him, it was also an effort to understand Israeli law in the larger perspective of the Zionist century. His words had a liberating effect, freeing me to apply my own conceptions in shaping the book. I hope that I have done him justice. He was a noble and generous man; I feel fortunate to have known him.

The time has come to tell the story of Israel and Zionism through the prism of Israeli law, to see how the grand dreams for utopia, the catastrophes that befell the Jews in this century, the Arab–Israeli conflict, and the multiple immigrant backgrounds all coalesced to shape the legal culture. Legal scholarship, however, can be dry and inaccessible. Telling the story through the medium of intellectual biography keeps the life and drama of the tale from being stifled by legal technicalities.

When I first embarked on this project, I was captivated by the story of Zionism. The Zionist ideal, with which I grew up, was to rebuild the homeland and to base this revival on principles of liberty and justice. Nationalist authoritarian trends, always present in the Israeli polity, offered a competing conception of what Jewish revival was meant to be. In the 1980s, as the invasion of Lebanon and the *intifada* came to dominate Israeli politics, I became more and more fascinated with the power of Zionist ideology to construct Israeli consciousness, my own included, and more eager to understand the role of ideology in shaping Israeli legal culture. I also came to understand better the meaning of being an immigrant. Had I, a sabra, stayed in Israel, I would be less attuned to the subtleties of cultural transplantation, and in all probability this book would not have been the same. There is an irony in the fact that Agranat and I have traded places. Born in America to Russian immigrant parents, he made his home in Israel. I was born in Tel Aviv to parents from Iran and Egypt and made my home in the United States. This small detail is also a comment on the Zionist century.

PART I

FROM AMERICA TO PALESTINE

CHAPTER 1

America, 1906–1930

THE AGRANATS

Simon Agranat's first memory was that of tearfully imploring his father not to take the family to Palestine. He was three or four years old, frightened by the thought of crossing the ocean by boat. He remembered his father, otherwise doting and tender, asserting flatly that "Palestine was their true home" and that "they would be going there, soon."

Simon was born in 1906 in Louisville, Kentucky, to Aaron-Joseph and Polya (Pauline) Agranat, both Russian immigrants who had recently arrived in the United States. Almost a quarter of a century would pass before the family fulfilled the Zionist dream of leaving the United States to settle in Palestine. Simon's memory illustrates how insistent, throughout his childhood, was his awareness that Palestine was their true home.

The name Agranat carries two meanings. In Russian the letter *h* sounds like the English *g*; thus the name Agranat is Russian for Ahranat or Aharon. In Jewish tradition, Aharon, Moses's brother, was the great priest, the mediator between God and the people. His offspring, the Kohanim (Hebrew for "priests") continued to serve in this capacity until the destruction of the Second Temple. According to this version, Agranat traces a family lineage that goes back to the priesthood in the ancient Kingdom of Israel. Another interpretation leads to Spain in the Middle Ages. In 1492 Spain expelled its entire Jewish population. As the Jews moved east, to Germany, Poland, and Russia, their Spanish heritage faded. Agranat is a variation on Al-Granad—"the one from Granada"—and links the family to medieval Spain. The Agranats liked the first version better. Perhaps they preferred the attributes of priesthood over the Spanish connection, or perhaps they were more democratic, preferring the rather common Kohanim to the atypical Spanish extraction.

Simon's father, Aaron Agranat, was born in Chislavitch, Russia, to an "avid Mitnagged"—a member of the Jewish Conservative camp opposing innovation and reform.[1] He spent his childhood receiving religious Jewish education, aspiring to study in the great Lithuanian Yeshivah of Mir. Like many young Jews of his generation, however, Aaron's aspirations were decisively altered after he encountered the Haskalah movement, the Jewish equivalent of the Western Enlightenment. Haskalah meant more than the immersion of oneself in Western culture—it emphasized the revival of Jewish culture. Hitherto, religion was the essence of Jewish identity. Culture was incidental to, and embedded within, Jewish Orthodoxy. The Haskalah sought to reverse this process, to make Jewish culture the essence and religion incidental, to restore to center stage the secular manifestations of Jewish life: history, literature, the Hebrew language. The Haskalah signaled the disintegration of traditional Jewish life in Eastern Europe and the beginning of a search for new, human-made remedies for Jewish misery. Zionism, an ideology seeking a political-nationalist solution, was built on the foundations laid by the Haskalah.

Aaron Agranat was not a zealous ideologue. He wanted to acquire a profession before immigrating to Palestine. Because Russian universities did not welcome Jews, he dreamed of pursuing academic studies in Switzerland. Meanwhile, making a living by teaching Hebrew, he fell in love with one of his pupils, Polya Shnitzer. Polya's mother, a tough-minded widow, imposed one condition before giving her consent to marriage: that Aaron agree to join the family in emigrating to America. In 1904, as the bloody Kishinev pogroms signaled once again the fearful conditions of Jewish life in Russia, Aaron and Polya's brother, Yekhi'el, arrived in the United States and, for unclear reasons, headed to Louisville, Kentucky. The rest of the family joined them in 1905. Polya and Aaron were married, and Simon, the first of their two sons, was born the following year. Soon the family moved to Chicago, where Simon grew up. The move to Chicago was probably motivated by Aaron's desire for an education, but it was also precipitated by a rift between the opinionated young Zionist, committed to modernity, and the Orthodox Jewish establishment in Louisville.

Aaron earned his living in Louisville by teaching Hebrew. A ministorm erupted when Aaron was observed late one Friday afternoon at the barber shop having a haircut, in violation of the Sabbath. Aaron refused to be bound by rules that he regarded as rigid and out of touch with the times, and a heated argument ensued between Aaron and his employers about the viability of Orthodoxy in modern Jewish life. It is not clear whether Aaron was fired or was merely censured as a result of this incident, but he certainly felt humiliated. The story entered the family lore and made an impression on young Simon. From an early age he was sensitized to the struggle about the meaning of Judaism, the heavy-handedness of Orthodoxy, and the price one paid for daring to be different. The move to Chicago signaled Aaron's understanding that his aspirations could only be fulfilled in a modern environment.

During the opening decades of the twentieth century the city of Chicago experienced wild growth. From a small midwestern town it had expanded into a thriving metropolis, a center of industry and wealth that attracted immigrants. In 1920, 72 percent of its people were of foreign stock. Chicago had the second largest Jewish population in the United States.[2] Into this dynamic environment Aaron moved his family. He found a position as head of the Hebrew Department of the Marks Nathan Jewish Orphans Home and began to explore the possibility of academic studies. Those who saw *Hester Street*, a vivid historical film about the life of Jewish immigrants in America, may remember the stocky, vulgar manager of the sweatshop bantering that "in America the [ignorant] peddler is the boss and the Yeshivah bokher [learned student]—a mere employee." Most educated immigrants would welcome a modest teaching position, which would allow them to escape the harsh life of laborers. They would leave to their children the task of pursuing professional careers. Aaron was more ambitious than most of his fellow immigrants and regarded teaching Hebrew as a temporary job. Yet even he had to compromise. He wished to study medicine, but this seemed impossible for a poor Jew with a family to support. Dentistry emerged as an acceptable compromise. He enrolled in the College of Dental Surgery, and earned a D.D.S. Thus he placed himself among the 2.6 percent of American Jews who were professionals at the beginning of the century. Practicing dentistry, first at home in near-north Chicago and then from a rented office, he provided his family with a comfortable life and could look forward to a secure future.

Friends and relatives in densely Jewish northwest Chicago described Aaron as a short, flamboyant, and vivacious man who was rather meticulous about his appearance. Many commented on his perfectly pressed, knife-pleated trousers. Self-confident and witty, he was steeped in literature and passionate about the opera, to which he would listen while following the score.[3]

Aaron's years of struggle gave him a deep affection for America. During World War I, he was so overwhelmed by patriotic zeal that he wished to volunteer for military service, but for reasons of health he was not eligible. Still, his real passion remained Zionism. Irving Howe observed that "[b]y 1905 the total Zionist membership (mostly on paper) came to 25,000, representing a tiny fraction of American Jews. Of these, only a few hundred were at all active."[4] Most American Jews, traumatized by the long, painful, and uprooting journey from Europe, were not emotionally prepared to think of another major dislocation. That could be one reason why they remained unmoved by an ideology which proclaimed that only in Zion would Jews be at home. Indeed, it is quite possible that family stories about the hardships of travel frightened young Simon and made him dread a trip by boat on the high seas.[5] Aaron and Polya were among the few dedicated Zionists and among the fewer still who actually planned to merge theory with practice and move to Palestine.

Polya Agranat, who in the United States adopted the name Pauline and in Palestine took the Hebrew name Pnina, was a quiet, strong-willed woman, often described as pedantic and domineering. Simon described her as "tall, good looking, and practical minded." She had a beautiful voice (her husband claimed that she could have been an opera singer), and her son remembered her singing as she did housework during the morning hours. She supported her husband's gregarious nature by helping him turn their home into a center of social activity. They entertained almost every Zionist leader who came to Chicago, from Chaim Weizmann to Chaim Arlosoroff, and later, in Haifa, they opened their home to the local intelligentsia. Dorothy Kurgeans, who later married Justice Arthur Goldberg, recalled attending evening Hebrew classes with Polya, who was learning Hebrew in anticipation of their immigration.[6] Polya had an independent mind. Simon recalled that in the 1928 presidential elections, she refused to vote for Al Smith, the candidate favored by her husband and sons, for fear that "he would take orders from the Pope." In 1929 she sailed to Haifa by herself and set up the house and the dental clinic, in expectation of the family's arrival. After her husband's death, Polya experienced a transformation. The wife and homemaker turned into a political activist, and she chaired her local chapter of the Women's International Zionist Organization. She also blossomed into a feminist, critical, Simon recalled, of "this, a man's world," where "laws were drafted by men, for the benefit of men."

In 1949, the first Israeli elections, she campaigned for the Women's Party. Carmel, Simon's wife, recalled that Polya "persuaded" the entire family, including Simon, then already a justice of Israel's Supreme Court, to vote for her party. Aaron did not live to see either the birth of the Jewish state or the rise of his son to the highest judicial office. He died in 1946.

HOME AND FAMILY

First child and first grandchild in his extended family, Simon was much loved and cherished during his childhood, and he reciprocated this affection. The family moved often, leading Simon to change schools, which may have contributed to his shyness and probably made the family an even more important center of his life. Despite this instability and an affliction with stomachaches—which doctors kept promising would disappear as he grew older—he remembered his childhood in Chicago as a happy one, with occasional trips to the theater to see a beloved Gilbert and Sullivan show and exciting visits to the playing field to watch his favorite game, baseball. Unlike many of his peers, who had to share household chores, Simon was free to indulge his own interests. He attributed his freedom to the fact that his mother did not need the extra help because she did not hold a job. Her being a full-time homemaker, however, says as much about Aaron's traditional conception of family life. That Aaron did not wish his wife to work was a sign that, although he wished to revolutionize the condition of the Jewish people, he did not think that the status of women or of the family needed to be changed. This arrangement also suggests that Polya may well have raised her sons as the Jewish princes she probably considered them to be.

Simon's relationship with his father was close and warm. Aaron was deeply involved in his son's activities and supervised his education, making sure his public-school curriculum was supplemented by Jewish instruction and hiring private tutors to expand his horizons and hone his skills. Aaron was proud of Simon. He would often take him to public, mainly Zionist, meetings, where he would cheerfully boast about him. Father and son spent many hours together, discussing politics and other matters. Simon adored and trusted his father and often sought his advice. But even though Simon inherited a gifted mind and broad perspective from his father, he did not have Aaron's flamboyant personality or spontaneous manner. By all accounts, Simon was a reserved boy, more like his mother, whose physique he had also inherited.

In school Simon was an excellent student and active in public affairs—he was president of the Victory Club (the club of the graduating class). Twelve-year-old Simon's biographical statement in the *Von Humboldt Elementary School Record* contains the motto, "The earnest are not hindered by trifles." The anonymous author of a "Can You Imagine" column in the same publication asked rhetorically, "Can you imagine—Simon Agranat not serious?"[7] Girls described him as "a long-legged, tall, and somewhat stooped boy who was shy, aloof, detached." To the boys in his neighborhood, with whom he shared jokes, played baseball, and went to the movies, "Sy" was "just an ordinary, nice guy, totally unaffected, unassuming, natural."[8]

But his seriousness was always spiced by a light touch of humor and a sense of irony. Ben Sackheim, his closest childhood friend, recalled how Simon "could knit his brows like nobody else"—thereby mocking the heavy self-image. The origin of a lifelong friendship between the two provides a glimpse into Simon's personality. Ben's father extolled Simon's virtues, presumably contrasting Simon with the rebellious and defiant Ben. Ben, who had just returned home after a long battle with tuberculosis, immediately resolved to hate "this brilliant Hebrew student, this obedient and attentive son, this paragon of all virtues." But Ben, whose illness made him exquisitely insightful, soon managed to grasp Simon's vulnerability and sensitivity as well as his modesty: "[a]lmost instantly I was nonplussed and disarmed."[9] On his part, Simon was attracted to Ben's sparkling, buoyant laughter—a lightness that complemented his own heavy demeanor. They spent hours together, sipping tea in the kitchen and discussing books, politics, and themselves. In Ben's trusted presence, Simon revealed his yearning for harmony: his favorite pastime was pretending to be an orchestra conductor, making music with an imagined baton. Elias Canetti observed that "there is no more obvious expression of power than the performance of a conductor. . . . He stands on a dais [when all others are seated, standing reflects power]" and controls both the audience and the orchestra. For the audience, he is the leader; even though they cannot see his face, they are led by him and will not move until the music is finished. For the orchestra—"an assemblage of different types of men"—the conductor is "omniscient, for, while the players have only their own parts . . . he has the whole score in his head, or on his desk." Thus, "during the performance, . . . the conductor [is] the ruler of the world."[10] Of course, because Simon only fantasized about being a conductor, this fantasy may well disclose a sense of powerlessness in real life, and yet it also imparts an ambition to lead, to make a difference. His love of music, particularly the operas he admired—Donizetti's *Lucia di Lammermoor* and Wagner's *Tristan und Isolde*—also reveal the romantic, passionate self behind the serious, aloof appearance. This passion nurtured his interest in the Progressive movement, whose values were imprinted in his heart and mind.

GROWING UP AN AMERICAN: THE CRY FOR JUSTICE

> *If the human race is gradually to be lifted to higher and higher levels,*
> *if civilization is to be truly democratic and progressive, and if we are*
> *ultimately to come to as high a degree of perfection in government . . .*
> *it ought to be here in America . . . for we had here the best opportunity.*
> —ROBERT M. LA FOLLETTE, *The Political Philosophy of*
> *Robert M. La Follette,* comp. Ellen Torelle (Madison,
> Wis.: Robert M. La Follette Co., 1920), 147.

"Progressivism," Richard Hofstadter wrote, "was that broader impulse toward criticism and change that was everywhere so conspicuous after 1900 . . . [affecting] the whole tone of American political life." Progressivists wished to revive democracy and promote social justice by eliminating tenements, forbidding sweatshop labor, protecting the working class, and restoring economic entrepreneurship. "Vital to the search for social justice," Arthur Ekirch observed, "was the idea of wholeness— the concept that reform should be comprehensive and continuous rather than piecemeal and spasmodic."[11] Chicago was one of the major strongholds of the Progressive movement during the early decades of the twentieth century, and Progressivism dominated Simon's childhood.

He grew up in an atmosphere of optimism, of combative civic alertness that seemed to succeed. He breathed optimism at home, as he saw his father become a dentist and improve the family's socioeconomic status. He felt it in school. Von Humboldt, one of the public schools that Simon attended, looked blithely into the near future as it announced plans to become "larger and better," building "an assembly hall with a seating capacity of 1,000" and "the largest gymnasium in any grammar school in Chicago."[12]

As an adolescent, Simon, then associate editor of the *Tuley High School Review,* echoed the same spirit of collective pride and civic duty: "Therefore, Tuleyites, your duty, as regards school spirit, lies not only in your ready compliance with financial contribution, not only in your presence at school events, but mainly in your conduct towards your studies, in the enthusiasm with which you acquire your education, and in your earnest attempt to make the Tuley High School, THE High School of Chicago."[13]

Simon had already displayed an interest in public affairs as a grammar-school student. His ambition, competitiveness, and willingness to be publicly judged for his argumentative skills began to show as he chaired and personally participated in many debates. On one occasion, his opponent produced a newspaper clipping, read its contents to the audience, then walked over to Simon, and, with a theatrical gesture, placed it on his podium, as if to indicate that Simon had lost the argument. Quickly reading over the item thus handed to him, Simon realized that his opponent had omitted its final paragraph, which in fact supported his position. Simon slowly read it to the audience, then dramatically dropped the document on his opponent's podium.

A schoolmate, imagining the future of the Von Humboldt class of 1919 in the school's *Record*, wrote: "I visited a courtroom. The judge looked strangely familiar. It was Simon Agranat, and I thought he had expected to be a dentist."[14] It is not the prescience but the insight that is interesting here. The writer was able to see that, although very close to his father, Simon would not follow Aaron into a profession that was rather technical and mechanical. She perceived, as did his close friends, his reflective nature, his tendency patiently to sort out the ingredients of a dispute and seek a fair solution.

The topics Simon debated reflect his awareness of the political issues of the second decade of twentieth-century America: the death penalty; Charles Evans Hughes's plan for the reduction of naval armament; whether the city of Chicago should own and operate its transportation system. The last issue, in particular, represents a nutshell of all the great domestic problems of the Progressive Era: urbanization, monopoly, the question of political graft.[15] The massive concentration of people in the cities made mass transit indispensable. To the streetcar companies, monopoly meant higher prices. To the ordinary person, it meant paying a dime rather than a nickel for a ride. The Progressives exposed the contradiction between franchise renewal and local self-government. If government were of, by, and for the people, why was mass transit controlled by a monopoly? Simon, nevertheless, was not happy about arguing for public ownership. He worried that he could not persuade his classmates to vote for the radical proposition that "Chicago own its traction." The incident reveals the tension he would always experience between his commitment to social justice and his yearning to abide by the general consensus.

If in economic matters he was a moderate (like most Progressives, including Louis D. Brandeis, whom he admired), he was a radical, and remained one, concerning the death penalty. He abhorred the brute force, the affront to human dignity, in the spectacle of organized government taking someone's life. Like most Progressives, he believed that crime was the consequence of wretched social conditions and that reform, not capital punishment, would cure it. Even after he had retired and looked back on his public career, he singled out his debate against the death penalty with confident pride.

Robert La Follette, George Norris, Clarence Darrow, and Upton Sinclair were his heroes. Ben Sackheim remembered sitting with Simon for hours in the Agranat family kitchen, discussing *The Cry for Justice*. An anthology of the literature of social protest, the book was described by its editor, Upton Sinclair, as "a Bible of the future, a Gospel of the new hope of the race. It is a book for the apostles of a new dispensation to carry about with them; a book to cheer the discouraged and console the wounded in humanity's last war of liberation."[16] Divided into "Books," it addressed "Toil," "Revolt," "Mammon," "Children," "Struggle for Equality," and "The New Day" in poetry and prose. In the introduction to the first edition, Jack London wrote that he expected "this humanist Holy book . . . to serve the needs of groping, yearning humans who seek to discern truth and justice amid the dazzle and murk of the thought-chaos of the present day world."[17] The fascination of Simon and Ben with this book reveals the high level of social consciousness and the political involvement of the two youngsters. The question of social justice played an important part in the formation of Simon Agranat.

Simon's thoughts about a future career were rooted in these concerns. He vacillated between law and journalism. Sensitive to the printed word, perhaps stirred by the heroes of the Progressive movement—the muckrakers—he was drawn to journalism. Unlike the muckrakers, he recalled imagining himself not as the person who uncovered intricate corruption in government but, rather, as the writer of leading editorials, inspiring his readers to remedy social ills. He certainly expected, consciously or not, to become "somebody," to make a mark. The other avenue he considered, and eventually pursued, was a career in law. But during his childhood he did not imagine himself as a judge. Rather, he fancied himself a famous lawyer (a young Clarence Darrow?), delivering a fiery speech, urging the jury, persuading them—he recalled, raising his hand up—to acquit the defendant who may be "guilty according to black letter law, yet innocent according to principles of higher law." Higher law, values aspiring to transform reality, were the themes that nurtured the young Agranat.

If school encouraged his American identity and his Progressive instincts, home nurtured a Zionist commitment. Not surprisingly, the Progressive agenda of comprehensive social reform, rooted in the yearning to restore "a golden age," resonated well with Zionist ideology, the cardinal tenets of which were the liberation and reconstruction of the Jewish people on a restored homeland of Zion.

GROWING UP AN AMERICAN ZIONIST

Aaron Agranat was attracted to Zionism even before Theodor Herzl published "The Jewish State" in 1896.[18] In Russia he joined the Lovers of Zion—the late-nineteenth-century movement that anticipated Zionism and was close to the noted Zionist leader Menachem Ussishkin. Aaron believed in political Zionism—in the need to build international support for a Jewish National Home—but he went further, to consider the revival of Jewish culture as Zionism's essence. In this spirit he raised his sons.

In the United States Aaron did not encounter the zeal for Zionism with which he was familiar in his native Russia. In Chicago he joined the Knights of Zion, an organization with only a handful of Jews, mainly Russian immigrants, centered in the Midwest. He was also a member of the Federation of American Zionists. By 1914, a decade after Herzl's death and Aaron's arrival in the United States, "the Zionist organization in the United States was weak, in financial distress, and with no influence in the Jewish Community. A spirit of gloom and defeat engulfed the few dedicated leaders."[19] Simon grew up amidst this struggle, with his father instilling in him a commitment to Zionist ideology.

His afternoons were devoted to Jewish education. For a while he attended the Yiddishe Nazionalische Socialistische Schule, where he sang Yiddish songs and learned Jewish history from the perspective of Jewish cultural revival. Later, his father removed him from that school, to give him more time to study Hebrew. Hebrew, the sacred language now revived, was so central to Aaron that he even objected to Simon's pursuing violin lessons, despite Simon's overt interest, on the ground that the violin might come at the expense of the Hebrew.

Religion was an integral part of the Agranat family life: they observed the ritual of Sabbath dinners and attended the Orthodox neighborhood *schule* on the holidays (Conservative synagogues were still rare). The family's religiosity, however, was selective and flexible. Simon's mother never attended religious services, and his father worked regularly on Saturday mornings. Like many sensitive children, Simon had his "religious period" at the age of twelve or thirteen, when he prayed daily and, following Saturday services, arrived at his father's office to discuss the rabbi's sermon. "If you wish to pray every day, at least use a biblical chapter as your prayer," he remembered his father's advising. This admonition reflected Aaron's belief, in the spirit of the Haskalah, that one should deemphasize the rabbinical texts developed in exile and restore the centrality of the Bible— the book written when the Jews were an independent nation. The Agranats had a constructive approach to religion. They would neither subordinate their lives to religious rules and dogma, as the Orthodox had done, nor adopt a thoroughly secular lifestyle. Thus Simon grew up in a moderate home, one that acknowledged the value of religion without obeying religion's overbearing, fundamentalist commands.

As Simon entered adolescence, Jewish life in Chicago became more organized. The Conservative movement and Young Judea began to take root.[20] Both sought to adjust religion to modernity in general and to American reality in particular. In 1921 Sam Strauss, one of Simon's childhood friends and an active member of the Young Judea club, described the movement:

Stand outside of a public school, in a Jewish neighborhood, and think of the hundreds of Jewish children who crowd the school—how many are learning Hebrew? Very few. . . . [W]hat do these . . . boys and girls do? They roam the streets, play with the non-Jewish children in the neighborhood, and little by little they forget whatever they ever knew about Judaism. . . . Then Young Judea steps in. The older children join a Young Judea club. The scene is transformed. They begin to ask their parents questions on Jewish history and customs. Presently the parents' stock of knowledge is exhausted. The children begin to teach their parents! The parents begin to take an interest in their children's Jewish education. . . . They seek to better their environment. They become Jewish to the core.[21]

Aaron Agranat suggested that a Young Judea club be established in northwest Chicago, after Simon, then eleven or twelve years old, expressed an interest in pursuing some organized public activity. In the club, which met twice a week at the Talmud Torah of the United Congregation, the children discussed and celebrated Jewish holidays and engaged in debates with members of other Young Judea clubs, on such topics as "Purim is a greater holiday than Hanukkah," or "Public utilities [should] be nationally owned and controlled immediately upon the establishment of the Jewish state."[22] Simon was an active member of the club, first as a regular member and later as a Young Judean leader. Club members became his closest and lifelong friends: Harry Ruskin, later a prominent Chicago lawyer; Meyer Handler, later an international correspondent for the *New York Times;* and Ben Sackheim, later the owner of a successful advertising agency in New York. The youngsters adored their instructor—Isaac Schour—known for his propensity for reconciliation and compromise. In the Northwest Young Judea Club, Simon's ambition and talents bloomed. He decided to publish a monthly magazine, *The Herzlite,* therein to explore his world and the world of his peers. The ambitious project yielded only one issue, whose pages reflect the mix of American Progressivism and utopian Zionism that dominated Simon's world in those years.[23]

The Young Judeans took to the task of publication enthusiastically. They created a staff complete with an editor-in-chief (Simon), an associate editor (Harry Ruskin), an assistant editor (Meyer Handler), a staff artist (Leo Wolf), and a business department with a circulation manager, an advertising manager, and staff stenographers. They turned out a twenty-three-page publication complete with editorials, articles, comic strips, advertisements, and an aesthetic cover featuring a royal portrait of Theodor Herzl, the founding father of Zionism.

Leo Wolf, the staff artist, who later ran a commercial art firm in Chicago, remembered the excitement of assembling the magazine. Leo's father, a tailor, owned a large, long table on which he would cut cloth. The table was cleared, and the youngsters used it to spread out the sheets of paper and assemble the magazine. The Agranats' involvement in the project is clear from the "contributions" section, which featured the extended Agranat family: parents, aunts, uncles, and family friends.

The Herzlite reflects the efforts made by Simon's generation to come to terms with the meaning of being Jewish in America and with the impact of Zionism on their emerging identity. All of them either had been born in the United States to immigrant parents or had immigrated themselves at a tender age. Their parents struggled to make a living—as tailors, shopkeepers, day laborers. The cultural world of their parents was the shtetl. At home they heard Yiddish. At school they were initiated into the American world. It was a world that retained the familiar stereotypes of their parents' world, yet held so much hope for a better future. Simon himself did not recall any incidents of anti-Semitism in northwest Chicago in the Wilson era, but his fellow Young Judeans had many stories to tell.

For example, Mary Satinover, who lived not far from Simon, remembered verbal abuse and anti-Semitic epithets hurled at her as she crossed the "Polish" neighborhood on her way to buy ice at a discount place. But there was also a sunny side to America. These teenagers believed that the anti-Semitism was not official. As Americans, they were to be the beneficiaries of Progressivism. They possessed the firm confidence that talent and hard work would be rewarded. Indeed, all did enjoy successful careers as businessmen or professionals.

How, then, would they reconcile these contradictory aspects of their identity? What did it mean to hear Yiddish at home but feel more comfortable speaking English? The joke section of *The Herzlite* is a good-humored effort to make sense of the mystery of the conflicting languages and cultural traditions in the world of Simon's generation:

Mystery

I know who put the itch in Itchkovitz
And I know who put the awful booze in Bam
But the thing that's really worse
Than the names I've named at first
Is the fact that there's a ham in Abraham.

The Herzlite was published during Passover, the most powerful Jewish statement against exile. Was America another form of "exile"? Could one faithfully repeat the sentence that ends the seder, "Next year in Jerusalem," and yet be fully American?

These issues touched the nerves of both Zionism and American patriotism. If Zionism meant a radical denial of *galut* and insisted that Jewish liberation could be attained only through life in a Jewish state, did that mean that the sense of comfort Jews were experiencing in America was false? If American nationalism required a melting pot, did it reject the retention of cultural identity, or did it tolerate ethnic pluralism, a symphony of traditions?

The Passover Haggadah depicts four sons arguing about the significance of Passover: the wise, the wicked, the simple, and the one "who knows not to ask a question." *The Herzlite*'s leading article, entitled "The Four Modern Sons of the Hagadah," written by a fellow Young Judean, J. Licterman, but bearing the marks of Simon's influence, explores the dimensions of the Jewish dilemma. It provides an insight into the world of these youngsters, who were deft at making arguments in support of Zionism yet conflicted by their own love for America, who felt abandoned by the large majority of American Jews who rejected Zionism yet longed for a legitimating synthesis between their particular tradition and the ethos of the melting pot.

The Herzlite presents "self" as the modern rendition of the wicked son: a stereotype of the newly emerging, materialistic, American Jew, "interested in nothing but his own affairs." Clearly, this character is unattractive to the public-spirited youngsters. Even the drawing that accompanies the article depicts "self" in profile, whereas the other three sons face the reader. His dismissal sets the stage for the titanic wrestling between the Zionist (the "wise") and the assimilationist (the "simple") sons.

The assimilationist rejects the relevance of Passover to American reality: "How does it concern us now?" he asks, "It all happened long ago." And furthermore, "I am very comfortable here. This country suits me." The Zionist invokes the argument most compelling to European Jewish ears: that exile entailed catastrophe, pogroms, and persecution. But the assimilationist is not persuaded, for the argument fails to reflect his American reality: "We're not persecuted here"; "America is free to all. We have just as much rights as anybody else." In rebuttal, the Zionist resorts to anti-Semitism: "You are mistaken. We are only tolerated. Go to any college and try to join a fraternity. See if they will take you." It is interesting that the assimilationist does not rebut this argument. Apparently the youngsters could not agree about the impact of anti-Semitism on their future. Even the Zionist makes his argument about anti-Semitism only halfheartedly and immediately proceeds to his next argument—false consciousness. "Because here to [*sic*], in America, a free country, you are a slave. Not a physical but a moral slave, doing as all around you do, losing all your Judaism, trying to live up to your gentile neighbors, and I must admit, to my sorrow, that you for one are succeeding very well." Here the argument stopped. Not surprisingly, the assimilationist was not endowed with enough sophistication to turn this weapon against the Zionist and accuse him of "false consciousness."

The Herzlite ends the dialogue with the assimilationist cheerfully dismissing the subject as "a heap of nonsense" and joining "self" for a night at the movies. Before they leave, however, *The Herzlite* marks the assimilationist with the quintessential attribute of assimilation—self-hatred: "Yes, let's go. . . . Live in a Jewish country? I see enough 'Kikes' here." The assimilationist is a self-hating Jew who has internalized the prejudices of anti-Semitism and identified with the victimizers. Rushing to a happy end, the article has the "wise son" and the "one who knows not to ask a question" conduct their own brief dialogue, whereby the innocent son is "convinced of the necessity of Zionism" as well as of the desirability of joining the Young Judeans. A moral was added in capital letters: "WHERE THERE IS LIFE THERE IS HOPE."

Simon's contribution to the dialogue between assimilationist and Zionist is most emblematic of the dilemmas that Zionism posed to American Jewish youth. Simon suggested that the very first argument advanced by the Zionist be the need to have a country of one's own. At his suggestion, the Zionist introduced his position by quoting from Sir Walter Scott's poem, *The Lay of the Last Minstrel:*

> Breathes there a man, with soul so dead,
> Who never to himself hath said, —
> This is my own, my native land!

The message was clear: Zion was the Jews' own native land. Ironically, the context in which Simon had become acquainted with the poem was American patriotism, not Zionism. At school Simon participated in a play entitled *The Slacker,* based on Edward Everett Hale's story, *The Man without a Country.* The story, incorporating Scott's poem, was widely taught in American elementary schools, presumably to nurture patriotism and love of country in the immigrant children. The man without a country was a young military officer convicted of treason during the War of Independence, who cavalierly told the judge, "Damn the United States! I wish I may never hear of the United States again!" He was sentenced to have his wish fulfilled: never to set foot in the United States, nor receive any information about the country. The story describes the misery of the young man, exiled aboard U.S. navy ships for more than forty years, as he came to realize the barrenness of life without a country. His last wish was that a stone be placed in his memory, saying: "He loved his country as no other man has loved her; but no man deserved less at her hands." In Simon's mind the Zionist argument, that outside Zion Jews were persons without a country, was associated with the travails of Hale's expatriate. Palestine (Zion) was an abstract notion; the concrete country was America. He took the only "love to country" that he had actually experienced—love of America—and, through Sir Walter Scott's poem, transferred it to Palestine. There was a double irony here: the name of the ship aboard which the officer died was *The Levant*—French for the Middle East. In Hale's story the Levant was exile and America was home. Simon inverted the ingredients, making America exile and the Levant (Zion) the Jew's native land.[24]

The problem was that Simon and his friends did experience themselves as American. Love of Zion, certainly the claim that Zion was the true native land, raised the scary specter of disloyalty. Louis D. Brandeis, leader of both the Progressive and the Zionist movements and the first Jewish justice on the U.S. Supreme Court, showed them how to resolve the conflict.

LOUIS D. BRANDEIS, AMERICAN ZIONISM, AND THE BRANDEIS–WEIZMANN DISPUTE

By 1919 Brandeis had transformed American Zionism from a 12,000-person movement into an organization with 176,000 members. He achieved this stunning success by adopting a counteroffensive approach. The Reform Jewish establishment insisted that Judaism was a religion, not a nationality; Jews were thus not "hyphenated Americans" but, rather, Americans of the Jewish faith.[25] Zionism, with its emphasis on Jewish nationhood, threatened this conception, and the Reform Jewish leadership urged the immigrants to ignore it, for fear that it might taint all Jews with the stain of double loyalty. Brandeis rejected this conception. For him, true Americanism meant not the obliteration of ethnic origins in the name of uniformity but the opposite: the full exercise of the right to express ancestral endowment. Brandeis thus legitimated Zionism in a formula that enchanted Simon's generation: "To be better Americans we must become better Jews, and to be better Jews we must become better Zionists."[26]

But Brandeis did not remain the captain of American Zionism for long. Chaim Weizmann—then president of the World Zionist Organization and Brandeis's ally in persuading Great Britain to issue the Balfour Declaration—entered into a virulent clash with Brandeis. By June 1921 the discord ended with Brandeis's defeat in the convention of the American Jewish Congress in Cleveland, Ohio, and with Weizmann's declaration that "[t]here is no bridge between Washington and Pinsk."[27]

The event, known as the Split in the chronicles of American Jewish history, is of particular significance for understanding Simon Agranat. For the first time in his life he experienced the pull of two enormous forces: Weizmann represented everything about Jewish revival that his father stood for. Brandeis represented his own American world. The split between the two men reflected a split in his own soul, a split that would torment him and that he would always try to heal.

The immediate reason for the disagreement between Brandeis and Weizmann concerned a financial institution called Keren ha-Yesod. Weizmann and the European Zionist leadership decided to establish a special fund of 25 million English pounds to finance the development of the Jewish community (the Yishuv) in Palestine. Brandeis thought ill of this idea. He criticized the budget as inflated, the American share as too large, and the commingling of donations and investments as fiscally unacceptable and managerially unwise.[28] Weizmann, whose relationship with Brandeis had been rocky for some time, took the opposition as a casus belli. He decided to come to the United States and directly challenge Brandeis's leadership. The struggle over the path of the Zionist Organization was, as Weizmann acknowledged, "a revival, in a new form and a new country, of the old cleavage between 'East' and 'West,'"[29] between tradition and modernity. He was referring to the 1904 struggle between his own Eastern European group—the Democratic Fraction—and Theodor Herzl, which ended with Weizmann's victory. Brandeis and his followers had stirred in Weizmann the same old resentments against the well-to-do, urbane, and sophisticated westerners, like Herzl, who presumed to tell the Eastern Europeans how to conduct themselves. The rivalries were now revived on the American scene. Weizmann, who would ridicule Brandeis's Jewishness as "Yankee Doodle Judaism,"[30] painted Brandeis and his group as "plain Americans"—rule oriented, dogmatic, materialistic, calculating, and, above all, cold. By contrast, the Europeans presented themselves as men of vision, imbued with Jewish spirituality (*yiddishkeit*), generous, and (of course) warm. One of Weizmann's chief campaign speakers captured the distinction vividly when he claimed that Americans had *goyische kops* (gentile heads) whereas the Eastern Europeans possessed *yiddische herzen* (Jewish hearts).[31]

The voters in the Cleveland Convention, mostly immigrants, loved this juxtaposition. It allowed them to express their resentment of American culture and legitimized their own background as Europeans. For the first time they were permitted to feel superior to Americans, both culturally and temperamentally. Weizmann was a man they could both identify with and be proud of, and they gave him overwhelming support. The defeated Brandeis camp left the movement, feeling betrayed and humiliated.

Simon was unhappy about the Split. His father was a loyal soldier in the Weizmann camp. The controversy dominated their home for months. Aaron lobbied for Weizmann and, as a delegate to the Cleveland Convention, voted in his favor. Simon's close relationship with his father left him no choice but to support Weizmann's agenda. But his loyalty to Brandeis did not dissolve. He was grateful to Brandeis for having so masterfully resolved the conflict between American and Zionist loyalty. He adored Brandeis, the outspoken Progressivist. He was proud of Brandeis's elevation to the highest court of the land. The attack on the American character was also an attack on his own sense of self. America was rejected in no uncertain terms when Weizmann, elated with his victory, made his bridge proclamation.

The Split is mentioned only in the editorials of *The Herzlite,* penned by Simon. One editorial praised Keren ha-Yesod, the financial institution that became the point of contention between Weizmann and Brandeis. Placid and factual, the editorial hailed the Keren as a "noble institution" that would provide "for the reconstruction of . . . *our* country [Palestine]."[32] The content, Simon said sixty years later, was dictated to him by his father. Was he conflicted about this piece? The clue may lie in his second editorial, dedicated to Moses. Because the occasion was Passover, it would seem natural to praise the greatest of prophets, who led the people of Israel from slavery to freedom. Simon praised Moses, "educated in an Egyptian Court, taught a religion of idolatry," who nevertheless adhered "to his own Nation and People." Moses, Simon wrote, possessed the qualities of a great leader; for example, he had "a great and almost everlasting patience." Why Moses? Why patience? Brandeis's biographer Philippa Strum observes that when Brandeis gave his famous speech in support of Zionism in Boston's Symphony Hall, the corridors were filled with cries of "the New Moses, the New Moses."[33] The story is told that in Cleveland Felix Frankfurter was confronted with the charge that Brandeis lacked *yiddishkeit.* Frankfurter responded, "But so did Moses, raised as an Egyptian Prince."[34] Simon, who was thoroughly familiar with Brandeis's career, may have picked up this analogy between the founding father of Jewish liberation and the founding father of American Zionism. His editorial, dedicated to one great prophet, may well have been about another.

When I suggested to retired Chief Justice Agranat that the teenaged editor-in-chief may in fact have had Brandeis in mind, he pondered, then asked: "And what did I say there?" "You counseled patience," I said. "Ah, these were Brutus's words, 'Be patient till the last,' in Caesar's funeral." It is not surprising that Shakespeare's *Julius Caesar,* a tale of politics, the meaning of leadership, and treason, was on Simon's mind as he contemplated the Split. Nor was it unusual that Simon included Brutus, "the noblest Roman of them all,"[35] in his editorial. Like Brutus, Simon was "with himself at war,"[36] torn between Brandeis and Weizmann. Like Brutus, he grieved over the need to choose between country and friend. Did he feel he did not love Pinsk (his father) less, but Washington (his American self) more? Or did he feel "enslaved" by the foreign-born, with their *yiddische herzen,* who mocked American culture, deposed the prophet of democracy, and restored paternal authority? Simon, the editor-in-chief, urged his peers: "YOUNG JUDEANS: . . . If the YOUNG JUDEAN ORGANIZATION does not act . . . in accordance with your wishes . . . do not begin to lament over its 'foolish' step. Do not blame the Leaders. Cling to Moses' doctrine . . . BE PATIENT."[37]

Simon's reserved reaction to the Split reveals his way of dealing with conflicts: restrained, avoiding overt confrontations, deliberative, patient, bowing politely to authority, but not losing his inner conviction. Henceforth he dreaded splits with all of his heart and always strove to build bridges and pursue a balanced course, neither defying authority nor accepting its harsh judgment.

A FAILED MIGRATION TO PALESTINE, 1922

The *Tuley High School Record,* describing the graduating class of 1922, stated that Simon was "a three and a halfer"—completing his high school work in three and a half years instead of the customary four. Aaron, anxious to move to Palestine, supported Simon's accelerated pace. Aaron had no relatives in Palestine, but he was acquainted with a good number of the Zionist leaders through his activities in Russia and in Chicago. Like all fervent Zionists, he turned a blind eye to the costs of leaving behind extended family and many friends, the material security, and the physical safety of America for the instability of Palestine, where Palestinian resistance to the Zionist cause was already turning violent. His impatience to migrate, apart from his Zionist zeal, reflected the changing international status of Palestine. On 2 November 1917 Lord Balfour, the British minister of foreign affairs, issued the famous Balfour Declaration. It was the culmination of Zionist political activity, the first meaningful gain for Zionism. In the 1920 San Remo Agreement, England was given the mandate over Palestine. Negotiations were under way between England and the World Zionist Organization about drafting a charter, designed to implement a Jewish National Home. An eminent British Jew was appointed as high commissioner of Palestine. The Zionist dream appeared to be on the verge of becoming a reality, and Aaron ached to be present at the creation.

Aaron sold his dental practice, signed an agreement that he would not practice in his neighborhood for five years, and helped his wife pack their belongings and professional equipment. Leo Wolf, one of Simon's friends, probably reflected the mood at their departure. He recalled fear for the Agranats' safety in Palestine, the "backward land of the desert."[38] The family took a boat to Marseilles, France, and there boarded the *Sphinx* on its way to Alexandria, Egypt. In the early 1920s the only way to arrive directly in Palestine was through the Jaffa seaport, where ships could not reach the shore, and passengers had to disembark at sea and be hand carried to the pier. Alexandria had a more modern harbor. From there the Agranats took an Egyptian train to Kantara and then a Palestinian train to Tel Aviv. The tense, fatigued Aaron, on his way to the promised land, with no one to welcome him at their destination, received the first sign that his dream was coming true: the conductor's badge was printed in Hebrew. Exile was over. "I was impressed, but he was ecstatic," Simon recalled. As they arrived at Tel Aviv, his exaltation spiraled at hearing people actually communicating in Hebrew. They stayed at Hotel Eden, then rented an apartment in a house on Allenby Street, owned by an American Jew.

"Why Tel Aviv and not Jerusalem?" I asked.

Because that was *the* Jewish city. Agranat's face lit up as he emphasized "the." "It was a lovely city, clean. You can't imagine." Indeed, Tel Aviv was the jewel of the Zionist project. Named after the town in Herzl's utopian novel, *Altneuland,* Tel Aviv of the early 1920s was a residential suburb, with small houses surrounded by thriving gardens. The painter Reuven Rubin, who also settled in Palestine in 1922 and who had spent a few months in Jerusalem before deciding to settle in Tel Aviv, captured the difference between the two cities in terms of social character: "Jerusalem and Tel Aviv were completely different from one another, . . . phys-ically . . . [and] in character. . . . Jerusalem, with its stone buildings, old and new, and its population, made up mainly of government employees and Zionist officials, had nothing in common with the happy-go-lucky, worker population of Tel Aviv. . . . One had to live there and be part of its life to feel the vitality that was creating the future character of the Jew-ish homeland."[39]

The Agranats soon discovered that there were very few stores, with still fewer articles for sale, no regular supply of fresh fruit, vegetables, meat, or milk, and inconvenient public transportation to Jaffa, where real city life actually occurred. It was a massive adjustment for a family accustomed to life in metropolitan Chicago. But the lack of electricity was crucial. Aaron's health did not permit him to operate his dental equipment man-ually, and he was dependent on electricity: without electricity there was no clinic and no way to make a living.

While trying to decide how to proceed, the family began adjusting to everyday life. The Tel Aviv intelligentsia was predominantly of Russian stock, and they embraced Aaron as their lost brother. It was no small matter to have in their midst one who had tasted success in America and yet decided to uproot his family a second time and come to the land of Israel. Aaron's arrival confirmed what the intelligentsia longed to hear: that between America and Palestine, Palestine was the right choice for the Jews.

It was not easy for the children to adjust. They understood Hebrew and Yiddish, but they were Americans. The bright light of Palestine, so loved by native Israelis, so lamented by immigrant painters accustomed to the soft, gray shades of Europe, also affected the American children: it was not conducive to playing baseball. In that bright light it was impossible to fix one's eyes on the ball as it went up.

The centerpiece of Tel Aviv of the early 1920s was its high school, the Gimnasyah Hertsliyah. The school was the most impressive building in Tel Aviv. It towered over the small residential houses. Its facade, an imitation of no other than the Second Temple, was majestic. Its educational program was consciously ideological, designed to form the true Zionists, the perfect "Hebrew" men and women, sabras, raised free in their own homeland.

From Simon's perspective, however, the Gimnasyah Hertsliyah did not compare well with Tuley High School. The teachers made it clear that their European education was superior to the American system. They placed Simon in the eleventh grade, theorizing that it was the equivalent of a freshman year in an American college. For the second time in two years, Simon encountered the belief that European culture was superior to his. He later spoke about the incident with characteristic irony, thereby expressing disagreement. At the same time, he described himself as "stunned" by the lack of discipline, by the noise in the classroom, by the teachers' inability to control the class. Tuley's pupils waited for teachers to call on them. The Gimnasyah Hertsliyah's pupils thrust themselves aggressively to the forefront of the classroom discussion. This playful, sometimes impudent, defiance of authority was culturally significant. It was a reaction against the stereotype of the Jew in exile—weak, subdued, deferential to authority. Direct and contentious speech, disrespect for manners and rules, regarded as expressions of decadent "exile" culture, were all considered attributes of the "healthy" sabra personality. They came together with a deep commitment to the Zionist program: to rebuild the land at all cost, with personal sacrifice.

Simon was delighted to partake in the Jewish Renaissance, but his actions reflected the hardships of dislocation and the resistance he was developing to the pressure to shed his American self as if it were unwanted skin. The most salient manifestation of his ambivalence was his conscious choice to continue speaking English at home. Hebrew signified the new era, redemption, victory over exile. The teachers at the Gimnasyah Hert-sliyah were toiling to translate material from foreign languages into Hebrew, so that teaching and learning would be done in Hebrew exclusively. Tremendous pressure was put on children, especially, to speak only Hebrew and to force their parents to do the same. Yet Simon spoke English with his father. "We resolved to speak Hebrew. We both had good knowledge of Hebrew. But it didn't work. Somehow it seemed artificial." Until Aaron's last day, English remained the medium of communication between father and son. Simon was also attracted to the company of Americans. He befriended the only other American at school, Ed Bernstein, and the two established the Association for Life, designed to encourage young Zionist leadership and cultivate relations between Palestine and America. There is no evidence that the association acquired any membership beyond its two founders.

Within three months of their arrival in Palestine, the Agranats began to plan a return to Chicago. The family's favorite explanation for the abrupt move was the absence of electricity. It is not clear how much of this explanation is myth, as plans to bring electricity to Tel Aviv were already under way. Other possible explanations include the economic recession and the boys' education. Pursuing higher education in Palestine was impossible, for the country had neither a university nor professional training in law or medicine, the paths chosen by the Agranat children. It may well be that the Agranats concluded that the boys would be better off if they obtained an education in the United States, where neither language nor culture presented a barrier. Regardless of the motive, the decision was painful, an admission of failure as well as a desertion of the collective. The family found some solace in resolving to return. In Haifa, Aaron found a distant relative, Yehuda Itin, who had attended heder (Jewish primary school) with him in Russia. He bought a plot of land and left Itin in charge of building the Agranats' future home. The family then sailed back to America. As they arrived in New York, Aaron was so tormented by an ulcer that he needed hospitalization. One can imagine that his entire being grieved over the failed immigration and that his family grieved with him. They would stay seven more years in Chicago before finally settling in Palestine, this time for good.

DREAMS OF GLORY

On 1 April 1925 Jerusalem was an ecstatic city. Jews from all over Palestine, as well as distinguished dignitaries from Europe and the United States, assembled on Mount Scopus. Lord Balfour was the guest of honor. They came to lay a spiritual foundation for the Jewish National Home: the Hebrew University.

Jerusalem in 1925 was a small, almost medieval town. There were no facilities to accommodate a massive pilgrimage, let alone modern tourism; there was not even a hall to hold the guests during the opening ceremony. The organizers resorted to a natural amphitheater facing a deep canyon on the northeast slope of Mount Scopus. Tiers of seats were arranged along the rock formation. From a platform set on a bridge hastily built over the canyon, one could see the blue sky and the magical gold and copper tones of the Judean desert reflecting the setting sun. Here, a cultural center for Zionism was being inaugurated.[40]

The idea of a Hebrew University was emblematic of the basic Zionist program. Ahad ha-Am, the chief ideologue advocating the centrality of cultural rejuvenation, wrote to Chaim Weizmann shortly after the British occupation of Palestine, when permission to open a university was granted: "By . . . [a Hebrew University] . . . I mean . . . not a mere imitation of a European University, only with Hebrew as the dominant language, but a University which, from the very beginning, will endeavor to become the true embodiment of the Hebrew spirit of old, and to shake off the mental and moral servitude to which our people has been so long subjected in the Diaspora."[41]

In Chicago the event aroused "great excitement in the Jewish community and . . . was celebrated with great fanfare in an impressive public gathering."[42] For the Agranats, the event was particularly joyful. During their stay in Tel Aviv the family had taken several trips to Jerusalem to visit the site on Mount Scopus. The inauguration of a university was still more proof that the dream was becoming a reality, that Palestine was modernizing and joining the "civilized" world.

Simon and his father each commemorated the event with articles in the *Chicago Yidisher Kuryer*. This was Simon's first publication in a real newspaper, a mainstream Jewish daily published in Yiddish with a weekend supplement in English. His article, "Concerning the Hebrew University," was a juxtaposition of old and new in Jewish culture. Fifty years later, Agranat remembered it as an effort to synthesize political and cultural Zionism. Political Zionism, preached by Theodor Herzl, sought to cure the Jewish predicament by providing the Jews with a state of their own. Cultural Zionism, preached by Ahad ha-Am and his follower Chaim Weizmann, maintained that only cultural rejuvenation could rescue the Jewish people from stagnation and decay. In his article Simon tried to merge the two: "Today we witness a harmonization of Achad ha-Amism and Herzlism. The spirit is entering the 'flesh' of the haven of Palestine and is ready to accept the Hebrew University."[43] More important, the article contained a critique of Jewish culture in exile. In their homeland, Simon stated, the Jews produced the Old Testament, "a spiritual contribution that is as yet a non-pareil." In exile they remained productive, but their product, such as the Talmud, was "inferior in content to the Old Testament, and often full of dry 'dinim [legal rules]' and drier." Furthermore, whatever Jews produced "in Goluth [exile] . . . has become impressed with a gentile stamp. . . . And so I need not add that a Maimonides was under the spell of an Aristotelian philosophy." Most significantly, "exile culture" "has exerted hardly any influence on the peoples of this universe." Take the Talmud, Simon asked rhetorically. "Have any other nations considered it?" And the enlightened literature of the Haskalah: "There is our Hebrew literature of the past two hundred years. Do the other peoples take note of it—except probably to remark it as a passing phenomenon that may someday perhaps blossom into an influence?" Simon insisted that "exile" had not killed the Jewish creative genius: "It is ever present and ever functioning, . . . but under foreign banners: who indeed has not heard of Einstein, a 'German' scientist; Bergson, a 'French' philosopher; Brandes, a 'Danish' critic; and Antikolsky, a 'Russian' sculptor?"

The conclusion followed readily. In order to bloom, Jewish "genius" needed Jewish soil. Only in Zion would Jews liberate their talents, striving toward "the highest sort of perfection imaginable": "We are convinced that the future Hebrew culture will inspire the universe with such lofty ideals as it has never before experienced."

Simon's critique expressed the perennial theme in Zionist ideology—"rejection of *galut.*" This rejection of the "culture of the present" was accompanied by the romantic, utopian message that in their own homeland, Jews would build a model society. The model society also entailed "a model culture," and Simon dreamed of that glory while he extolled the establishment of the first university in Jerusalem.

Beyond the standard Zionist ideals, there could also be personal reasons for his eloquent yearning to see his future culture put on a pedestal. The young Chicagoan had to account for his commitment to rebuilding a faraway swampland when his contemporaries were basking in the materialistic delights of the Roaring Twenties—a commitment the wisdom of which was cast in doubt after the family's abrupt return from Palestine. Simon, having experienced Palestine and having decided that upon completing his studies he would indeed return to settle there, must have been rethinking the meaning of his American identity. The glorification of the future Zionist culture compensated for the perceived need to suppress the American part of himself.

Also, Simon's flat dismissal of "exile culture," the assertion that the "Jewish genius" in exile manifested itself best "under foreign banners," may be read as a veiled assertion of the superiority of Brandeis's way over Weizmann's. Indeed, "Concerning the Hebrew University" mentioned neither Brandeis nor Weizmann, who was the major force behind the Hebrew University. But "Brandes, a 'Danish critic,'" was included with Einstein, Bergson, and Antikolsky as examples of Jews of international acclaim. The nineteen-year-old college senior was telling his father's generation that *yiddishkeit,* judged by international standards, was a secondary subculture and that if a Jew were to live in exile, then his creativity would be much more valued if he followed Brandeis's way.

Clearly, Simon perceived himself as a soldier in the Zionist camp. Jewish revival, politically and culturally, had become a vocation, an aspiration that would guide him throughout his life. The deeper questions raised by the utopian dream were not addressed. Nor could they be addressed by a young ideologue: if *galut* culture were rejected, on what concrete foundations should the Zionists build their new culture? How much of a Jewish flavor would it retain, and how much Western influence should it absorb? Were the Jewish people to become a nation like all nations (in Zionist parlance, a "normal nation") or a light unto the nations? Only when Simon became a justice on Israel's Supreme Court, and in a position to influence the development of Israeli legal culture, would he begin to confront these problems.

• • •

Fifty-four years after the publication of "Concerning the Hebrew University," in the very same magnificent Mount Scopus amphitheater, the Hebrew University bestowed on retired Chief Justice Agranat the Solomon Bublik Award. The history of the university's campuses reflected the history of modern Israel. Built to reflect the modest aesthetics of the Yishuv at the time, the campus was evacuated during the Jordanian siege of Hebrew Jerusalem during the 1948 War of Independence. For almost two decades it remained in ruinous neglect. Another campus was built. After the unification of Jerusalem, on the heels of victory in the 1967 Six Day War, the university returned to its original home. Grand marble edifices were erected on the shaven mountain — monuments to post-1967 Israeli prowess. Agranat, coming to the new-old campus to accept his award, no longer the zealous youth of 1925, addressed the assembly. His recollection of his 1925 essay contained a twist: "All I remember today is the . . . final conclusion [of the article]. . . . [T]he event of inaugurating the Hebrew University . . . symbolizes the laying of the foundations for . . . the spiritual center of the Jewish people, . . . where the Jewish genius will be free to develop . . . *on the one hand;* and *on the other hand* . . . will influence the *[Jewish] communities in the diaspora, revitalize them and retain their general unity.*"[44]

Times had changed. The passion of Agranat's youth had turned into a sober assessment of reality. He no longer expected Israeli culture to be "the highest sort of perfection imaginable." Nor would he undervalue the role of the Jewish communities in Diaspora. In fact, during his last years in the United States, he was already striving to build bridges between the American Jewish community and the Yishuv in Palestine.

THE UNIVERSITY OF CHICAGO

Simon celebrated the future glory of the Hebrew University while a junior at the University of Chicago. For him, life as a college student was quite similar to life in high school: he lived at home, associated with his high-school friends, many of whom were also taking advantage of the excellent education the University of Chicago had to offer, obsessed about Zionism ("Could you, once, refrain from discussing Zionism in your writing?" he recalled his English professor asking), and immersed himself in the study of history, philosophy, and French. French he took for pragmatic reasons: it was the language of the educated classes in the Middle East, and his father persuaded him that it would be a useful skill once he had settled in Palestine.

But even though he lived at home and followed his father's advice, he progressively gained a measure of autonomy from his father's overbearing intellectual presence. His independent positions on politics were beginning to crystallize, and they were decidedly Progressive. He became an avid reader of the *New Republic* and an admirer of the French libertarian socialist Pierre-Joseph Proudhon. In 1924, still ineligible to vote, he supported Senator Robert La Follette's presidential bid as the Progressive Party candidate. That year he also had his first encounter with Chicago politics. His political science professor dispatched student volunteers to serve as observers in various precincts. In the second ward of Chicago, to which he was assigned, Simon queried the chairman, "a man with an Uncle Sam beard," about some procedural irregularities. "Almost immediately I was surrounded by thuggish-looking young men. I thought a retreat was the better part of valor. I was scared," he recalled. He spent the rest of the day at another precinct, "where the reality resembled somewhat more closely the classroom theory."

History and philosophy were Agranat's true love—and his strength. His college record shows that in 1925 he received an honorable mention for "Excellence in Junior College Work," and in 1926 he won a scholarship that gave him full tuition to continue his graduate work in history. It was a very tempting offer, which only his commitment to Zionism could make him refuse. The Jewish people were making history, the National Home was being rebuilt, and Simon was determined to acquire a profession that would contribute to this effort. Medicine, the field his father would have preferred for him, was not an option, for he had little interest in the sciences. Teaching history, he feared, would not make enough of a difference. In 1926 he enrolled in the University of Chicago Law School.

His first encounter with legal education felt like "being kicked in the stomach." It was a class in torts, taught by James Parker Hall, and the discussion centered around the fourteenth-century case of *De S. and Wife v. W. De S.*[45] The facts of the case revolved around one W., who aimed a hatchet at a woman "but did not touch her." Because actual harm was intended but not done, could she recover damages? Professor Hall used the case as an introduction to the difference between assault and battery. Assault did not require actual injury; battery did. Agranat recalled: "For me it was like a kick in the stomach. . . . [To me], who studied history and philosophy . . . it was so disappointing . . . so prosaic . . . nothing theoretical. . . . Now I am used to it, but in the beginning it was very hard."

Hall's teaching represented the case-method approach to legal education, in which "the teacher was a Socratic guide, leading the student to understand the concept and principles hidden as essences inside the cases. The teacher showed how these concepts unfolded, like a rose from its bud, through study of a series of 'correct' cases over time."[46] The case method was the predominant pedagogic device in legal education in the 1920s, and most of Agranat's professors adhered to its tenets. However, at the University of Chicago the case method had a serious contender in the figure and educational approach of Ernst Freund. Freund, one of America's first exponents of the integration of the study of law into liberal education, rejected the notion that legal science could be "pure," independent of social and political influences. He urged his students to adopt a broad approach that would attempt to comprehend the social base of legal rules, and he urged his colleagues to impart knowledge to the students through lectures rather than through the Socratic method.[47] Thus Agranat was exposed to the major drama in American jurisprudence before the New Deal: the rivalry between legal formalism and sociological jurisprudence, or what Agranat would later call "the closed and the open systems of law."[48] Legal formalists held that law was a science unto itself, independent of society, immune to historical changes and developments. Proponents of sociological jurisprudence insisted that legal rules reflected social and historical forces, had to be understood in their context, and could and should change to meet the new challenges of the bureaucratic and welfare state.

Agranat was only dimly aware that he was witnessing an intense drama. Most of his professors imparted a legal approach that reflected some synthesis of the two schools. For example, James Parker Hall, dean of the law school and practitioner of the Socratic method, also taught his students that balancing the various interests underlying any particular legal problem was an essential tool in legal reasoning. Balancing was a cardinal tenet of sociological jurisprudence. It may well be that Agranat perceived the struggle as merely a difference in emphasis among various teachers.[49] During his three years in law school he came to appreciate the rigorous case method and the emphasis on conceptual thinking favored by the legal formalists. But while his mind absorbed the technique of "thinking like a lawyer," his heart went after sociological jurisprudence. In interviews he pointed to Ernst Freund as the professor who had influenced him most. He found Freund's lectures on administrative law fascinating and thought provoking and loved the professor's effort to ground law in larger systems of political and social theory. He also recalled, sixty years after the fact, that the most exciting moment in his career as a law student was reading Benjamin Cardozo's *The Nature of the Judicial Process*, in which Cardozo elaborated his philosophy that judging included the fine tuning and adjustment of law to perceived social needs.

Agranat's academic achievement in law school, unlike his college record, was less than stellar (his average at graduation was 70). Even in the class he loved best, constitutional law, he received a grade of 71. A number of reasons might explain the difference between Simon's law-school performance and his excellent college record. Bad luck was one. Hurrying to take the constitutional law examination, on a snowy day, he recalled slipping on ice and injuring himself badly. He arrived at the examination with a severe headache, which affected his performance. Another examination period coincided with his mother's surgery, which in-

terfered with his ability to concentrate. It may also be that his natural in-
clination to ponder both sides of an issue, to peel off each problem until he reached its core, hindered the delivery of the one clever, quick, clear
answer valued by teachers of the case method.[50]

Moreover, this was the time when the Agranats were finalizing their
plans to move permanently to Palestine. In his final year in law school Simon was living by himself for the first time. He must have been troubled
by these events. The awareness that the American chapter of his life was
coming to an end must have introduced ambivalence about integration
into the life of the law school.[51] His status as a "confirmed Zionist"[52] and
his declared intention not to practice law in the United States failed to
garner sympathy from his peers. They must have come to view him as an
outsider, thereby reinforcing his feeling that he no longer belonged.[53] One
classmate, Leon M. Despres, offered this recollection of Agranat: "When
he was in law school, he gave no hint of the rich talent and intellect he
later displayed. He was very quiet, dull in manner, reclusive in class, undis-
tinguished in recitation. . . . When I was in Jerusalem, I went to visit the
Supreme Court principally for the purpose of seeing him. . . . I was
amazed to see how active and energetic he was in questioning the lawyers
and raising points. His obvious mental agility and acuity were a surprise."[54]
Some of this unflattering judgment could be attributed to the competi-
tive spirit of law school. It is not easy to watch a lusterless contemporary
reach the apex of the professional pyramid, albeit in a foreign land. But
there could be a kernel of truth in Despres's observations. Agranat's talents did not shine at the University of Chicago Law School. From the
perspective of his legal career, he was a late bloomer.

That impending relocation to Palestine absorbed and disturbed him
is evident from Agranat's interaction with Ernst Freund. Agranat so admired the Jewish professor, "Teutonic in manner and style," friend of
Louis D. Brandeis and Julian Mack, that he decided to seek his advice
about his Zionist plans.[55] Much to his disappointment, he found in Freund
an indifferent and unsympathetic ear. For confirmation that he was making the right plans, for support and solace, he had to turn elsewhere. The
student organization Avukah became the focus of his social life.

AVUKAH

American Jewish students of the 1920s were not particularly
interested in Jewish affairs, let alone in Zionism. Most were beleaguered

enough by the sheer effort to survive in the academic universe and to improve their lot. The socially conscious among them preferred a cosmopolitan stance. Who needed Zionism when democracy promised liberty and justice for all? If the world, at least the United States, were turned into one big community, then distinctions between Gentiles and Jews would wither away—and with them the "Jewish question." Identity formation also played a part: most students were either first-generation Americans or had been brought to the United States as young children. Zionism's emphasis on the national component of Jewishness was experienced as a barrier to full integration in America. Also, Brandeis's dramatic walkout after the Split left Zionism associated with immigrant culture. It is not surprising, therefore, that Jewish organizations on the American campus were rather anemic and that the Intercollegiate Zionist Association was practically defunct.

In Palestine, the leadership of the Yishuv was assessing how best to develop a socioeconomic base for a future Jewish state. In the unfolding Arab–Jewish dispute it was less likely that Britain would actively support the Zionist cause, and the rise of Fascism in Europe made the prospects of forging alliances on the Continent unlikely. Eyes turned to the United States. Its growing Jewish population could provide financial and political support; its government, instrumental in delivering the Balfour Declaration, could be of substantial help in the international arena. In the spring of 1925 a delegation traveled to the United States "to arouse interest among our youth in Zionism."[56] Two active Zionists, Max Rhoade, a young Washington lawyer, and Joseph Shubow, then a graduate student at Harvard University and later a noted leader of the Boston Jewish community, met with the Palestinian delegation. They formed a new Zionist student organization—Avukah (Torch)—aimed at organizing Jewish support for Zionism on American campuses.[57] In Chicago a student from Palestine, Yitzhak Chizik, volunteered to establish an Avukah chapter.

Chizik's family was a household name in the Yishuv. His parents were among the first pioneers to settle in the Galilee. His sister, Sarah, died in the battle of Tel Hai, a battle that instantly turned into the foundational myth of Israeli nationalism, underscoring the Zionist quest for peaceful coexistence with the Arabs as well as the Jewish determination to fight and die for the homeland.[58] It would soon become clear that the Chiziks' sacrifice for the homeland made a strong impression on Simon.

Chizik, a hard-core Labor Zionist, enlisted Simon in Avukah, and Simon soon became chairman of the local chapter. Among the other members were Arthur Goldberg (later a justice on the U.S. Supreme Court), then a student at the Northwestern University School of Law, and his wife, Dorothy Kurgeans. After Simon had immigrated to Palestine, Goldberg took over as chairman of Avukah. At their meetings the members discussed Zionism, its meaning for American Jews, and its social and political platform. Dorothy remembered the debates as "feverish and abstractly intellectual, above and beyond my grasp." Chizik introduced the group to Labor Zionism: the idea that Jewish liberation would fail if Jews confined themselves to the professional class. The secret of liberation was in the "conquest of labor"—the development of an educated, socially conscious Jewish working class. Jews should leave the ranks of the bourgeoisie —or abandon their aspirations to join the ranks—and become farmers or industrial workers.[59] Simon had already been exposed to Labor Zionist ideology during his brief sojourn in Tel Aviv, but only now did he begin to give it serious thought. So far, and under his father's tutelage, he was concerned mostly with the political and cultural theories of Zionism. Through Avukah he came to encounter the tension between his father's liberal Zionism and socialist Zionism, advocated by Chizik, and he found many of its aspects appealing. They fit well with the Progressive ideology he had supported in American politics.

As chairman of the Chicago chapter, Simon persuaded his comrades to dedicate the summer of 1927 to "an analysis of American youth and its 'Zionist potentialities'" and to the "history of the Palestine Youth movement," with "specially prepared papers." A proposal was drafted to enable American Zionists to partake in the concrete activity of Labor Zionism, even if they were unwilling to immigrate to Palestine. A nine-page report, authored by Simon, was published in an impressive format by the Chicago chapter and submitted to Avukah's national headquarters in New York.[60] Simon and Chizik hoped that the national leadership would adopt the project and channel Avukah's resources to its implementation.

The project sought "to establish between ourselves and Palestine a living liaison." "Palestine youth has decided to attach to the soil," Simon stated in the report, "since they have found in agriculture the medium for the assertion of their individuality." Avukah should assist a group of high-school graduates in Tel Aviv to form a kibbutz, or *kvutzah* (small communal settlement): "Engagement to aid the youth of Palestine in colonizing the land will bring us into definite contact with them for the next few years. The precise plans of the colony, the choice of its site, the evolution of its social forms, the composition of its personnel, and the various and manifold details that are involved with colony-making—all these will demand our joint attention."

The pamphlet had two distinctive characteristics, revealing Simon's state of mind at the time. Substantively, it was a pragmatic, level-headed approach to American Zionism, sidestepping as improbable the expectation that American Jewish youth would personally partake in "the conquest of labor." At the same time, the idea of a transatlantic partnership, in which decisions would be made "jointly," assured a high level of meaningful involvement in "colonization." The gist of the project was the effort to avoid the alienation likely to follow when one partner (the Yishuv) worked, while the other (the American Jews) paid. But the pamphlet also had an air of restlessness, a youthful defiance of authority, a demand for action to combat stagnation. The condition of the young generation, in both the United States and Palestine, was painted in gray: "apathy," "indifference," "standstill," "disintegration," and "staleness" described the members of Avukah. "Dissatisfied," "disgusted," "constrained," and "discouraged" were the sons and daughters of the Yishuv. Both were turned off by their parents' generation: "Our wholly different training, . . . varied experience . . . make up, contrasts sharply with that of the adult Zionists. . . . We should be stifled or lost in the meeting room of our parent organization." The pamphlet asserted that the youth of Palestine similarly felt that their "training and experience . . . [had] equipped them with an outlook on life that . . . broke too fundamentally with the . . . weltanschauung of the adult colonists." Settlement in existing colonies would be as stifling as sitting in the meeting room "of our parent organization": "existing colonies . . . have either swallowed them up, or forced them out . . . leaving them dissatisfied with life as a whole."

The pamphlet concluded that a breakthrough was needed, to rescue that "inherent vitality" held captive by the adult world: "The time has come for something very tangible, which is right in front of our nose, that we may see and feel."[61]

At the age of twenty-two, one year before he graduated from law school, Simon was asserting intellectual independence. He was no longer the teenager who would dutifully endorse his father's support of Weizmann in his editorial in *The Herzlite* or the college junior who had soared on the wings of his elders' dreams about a university that would create a culture "the like of which the world has never seen" (in his project, Simon deviated from Avukah's official policy, which made the Hebrew University the focus of its attention; his pamphlet alluded to the university only once as "other designs" not "so close and akin to our own spirit—as youth"). Simon was getting ready to be his own man, and Progressive Zionism suited him well, with its emphasis on self-expression and self-fulfillment, on the value of the community, on practical, concrete objectives (agricultural settlement), and on the promise of a model society based on distributive justice. It separated his brand of Zionism from his father's and founded it on more socially sensitive grounds.

Yet the depressive tone of the pamphlet could also convey anxiety about the future. Chicago was Agranat's home, English was his language, and American culture was his natural habitat. In Palestine, he already knew from previous experience, he would be an outsider, slowly making new friendships and painfully trying to adjust. Unlike European Zionists, under whose feet the ground was burning and who therefore saw Palestine as a haven from persecution, Simon's Zionism was thoroughly idealistic. American anti-Semitism, though existent, was not a serious menace to his prospects in Chicago. The devil of pragmatism must have been whispering in his ear. Why go to backward, preindustrial Palestine when people his own age were leaving Palestine in "alarmingly swelling numbers"?[62] Why join a Jewish community embattled by Arab violence and threatened by signs that Britain was cooling its support for the Jewish National Home? He, American-born, with a fine education and bright opportunities—why should he leave, when others would give anything to be in his shoes?

The Avukah project was an effort to lock Simon's American generation into a permanent, dynamic relationship with its peers in Palestine. Thus he would have the best of both worlds: he would fulfill Zionism while retaining his American ties. It may well be that this sense of urgency was the force that released the incredible energy and skill with which Simon promoted his project. With Chizik he raised funds at home,[63] campaigned to make the project the "outstanding topic of discussion" in Avukah's Third Annual Convention in Pittsburgh,[64] and lobbied frantically to secure support.

But they soon felt the cold shoulder of the national leadership. Max Rhoade, national president of Avukah, feared that fundraising could be demoralizing and poisonous to any prospects of true cultural endeavor: "Time enough for money raising after the college days are over," he wrote in his annual report presented at the Pittsburgh Convention of July 1928. Simon, anticipating opposition, devoted a special section of his pamphlet to "Possible Objections." But Rhoade was not persuaded: "The arguments of the cultural possibilities inherent in the project, while theoretically persuasive, are in practice an illusion. . . . [M]oney raising will reduce the cultural benefits to a vanishing point." Rhoade cleverly turned the ethos of Labor Zionism—individual self-sacrifice for the public good—against Simon's project: "Those Zionistically mature members who feel such a great personal need for the Project, must simply sacrifice their feelings in favor of their duty to dedicate themselves . . . to the task of leading the 'educational work' *per se* for their immature comrades."[65]

Simon and Chizik arrived in Pittsburgh ready to fight. The odds against them were great,[66] but one development fed their optimism: in Chicago they had met with Chaim Arlosoroff, and the influential politician had promised to support the project at the national convention. That endorsement, they felt, would swing the delegates in their favor.

Seven years older than Simon, Chaim Arlosoroff was a rising star in the Zionist movement. A widely admired intellectual with a doctorate in economics, Arlosoroff's Zionist theorizing emphasized the centrality of Socialism in Jewish national revival.[67] The Federation of Labor (Histadrut), established to provide the means for creating a productive infrastructure for the Yishuv, sent Arlosoroff to the United States to raise Zionist consciousness. In an effort to strengthen contacts with Jewish youth, Arlosoroff was made a member of Avukah's Executive Committee. During his visit to Chicago, Simon and Chizik enlisted his support for the project and hoped that his weight would tilt the convention in their favor.[68]

In Pittsburgh, tensions rose as the assembly turned to consider the project. Simon spoke, then Chizik. The Boston chapter supported Chicago. New York was adamantly opposed. Then Arlosoroff rose to speak. Simon and Chizik were flabbergasted to hear him propose another project, uttering not a word about the proposal he had promised to endorse. Chizik, the uninhibited sabra, could not contain his fury, rose, and shouted, "Traitor!" Simon, reserved and polite, swallowed the defeat in silence. Fifty years later, Simon recounted the unforgettable events with great excitement. It was his very first political campaign and his first failure. Anger at having been let down by the charismatic, influential Arlosoroff mixed with bitter feelings of disappointment at seeing his project doomed and with regret that all of his efforts had been in vain. On the eve of his immigration to Palestine Simon was a sad young man. It was one thing to accept that there was no bridge between Washington and Pinsk. But no bridge between Chicago and Tel Aviv?

A GUN AND A LICENSE TO PRACTICE LAW

Toward the end of Simon's third year in law school, his mother left for Palestine; his father and brother joined her soon thereafter. In his heart, Simon recalled, he did not feel as though he had had his fill of the student life. Nor was he ready for an independent life. He wished he could follow in the footsteps of his hero, Ahad ha-Am, sitting in the British Museum surrounded by interesting books. But he took no steps to fulfill this dream. Years later he recalled the riots in Palestine as the reason: "In these moments of danger I wanted to be with my family." The riots, however, erupted in August 1929, after he graduated from law school. Had he thought seriously of going to London, he would have taken steps prior to these events. More likely, Simon, even though quite independent intellectually, was not yet ready for separation from his family.

When separation came, it was so traumatic that he always wished to forget the experience. Renting a room of his own, caring for everyday necessities, and coping with loneliness were so stressful that he told me he "didn't want to talk about it." He remembered bidding his father good-bye at the Chicago train station. "He cried like a child, as if he would never see me again." It might have been twenty-three-year-old Simon, who "hated scenes, especially sentimental ones,"[69] who felt like a crying child, fearing that he would never see his father again.

A week later he failed the bar examination. "They wanted clear-cut answers," he recalled; "I gave complex ones." This awareness of complexity revealed a heart unprepared for the cruelty of Solomonic judgments. But to the bar examiners, it probably proved that he could not "think like a lawyer." Simon postponed his departure and immersed himself in preparations for retaking the bar examination. The second time found him calmer and better disciplined to give the examiners the answers they expected. He passed the bar and was qualified to practice law in Illinois.

While in Chicago preparing for the bar, Simon turned to his extended family for emotional support. Unhappy about living alone, he moved in with Mini, his mother's sister, and her husband, Louis. Simon later wrote to them affectionately (revealing the affection that he was so well aware he could not display in person): "I hate scenes, especially sentimental ones. I had no courage to tell you face to face . . . [of] the fullness of my heart, that is, akin to gratefulness and gratitude, when I think of the experience I have undergone in your house . . . the home that . . . [illegible] in substitute for the one that I had temporarily lost."[70]

A week after Aaron arrived in Palestine, Arab violence against Jews swept the land. In Hebron more than sixty Jews—men, women, and children—were slaughtered. The significance of the new wave of violence was unmistakable: the Palestinian Arabs would fight the Zionist attempt to colonize the land. The dimensions of the violence proved that the Arab community was powerful and organized: the entire Yishuv was threatened, not merely isolated spots.

In Chicago, Simon was frantic. In his hunger for every bit of news, he turned to the Yiddish newspapers. For two weeks the *Chicago Yidisher Kuryer* devoted its front pages to news from Palestine with such headlines as: "Horrifying slaughter. . . . [W]ild tribes from Syria are marching on Palestine,"[71] and "The entire Jewish population runs away from Haifa."[72] The Chicago rabbis declared days of fasting and mourning. Five thousand Jews gathered to protest the "message of horror, terror, and plunder and death."[73] Family members and friends were questioning the wisdom of leaving for that "storehouse of social dynamite" at that moment in history.[74] Did Jews leave the pogroms in Russia to beget pogroms in Palestine? The anxiety was so consuming that Simon, a loyal student of politics, hardly remembered the October stock-market crash. In his mind, the economic crisis that occurred at the same time was dwarfed by the events in Palestine, for it was on Palestine that his mental energy was focused.

But if Palestine was to be his home, why take an Illinois bar examination? Simon must have been torn—between America and Zionism, between the safety of the orderly world and the unknown fate awaiting him in Palestine. From Louisville, Kentucky, where he went to bid his grandmother farewell, he wrote to his aunt and uncle: "It was of course quite a change to leave a city of hustle and bustle, where I was in the thick of the maelstrom."[75] He was comparing Chicago with Louisville, perhaps thinking of Haifa. And so he felt conflicted in Louisville, the town of his birth. A rush of memory of rejection of his father, years ago when he was still an infant, upset his day. When he was asked to speak in the same Russische Schule in which his father had worked, he refused. When he was finally coaxed, he heard himself introduced as a "Louisville boy come home." The anger struck. "Somehow there kept recurring to my mind the story of how Pa left Louisville . . . impending poverty . . . feeling of discouragement . . . revolt at the hypocrites . . . the Jewry of Louisville."[76] Simon could easily be speaking of himself. His own "independent youth," "revolt at the hypocrites"—his friends who preached Zionism but stayed behind, Arlosoroff's failure to fulfill his promise. Addressing the audience, among them his grandmother, he said: "Tho [*sic*] I was born in Louisville; and tho [*sic*] I visited it periodically, I never resided therein and could not call Louisville my home nor myself a Louisville boy." Thus disowning his birthplace, Simon was almost prepared for his new life.

There were two more things left to do. In Louisville he bought himself a revolver, a 45mm Colt—"like the one cowboys had"—and bullets, the better to protect himself in Palestine. On 13 February 1930, in Springfield, Illinois, he paid a fee of five dollars and was admitted to the bar. Armed with a gun and a license to practice law—symbols of disorder and order; his security blankets for life in Palestine and in the United States—he left for New York and from there sailed on the RMS *Mauritania* to Palestine.

Simon disliked sailing, yet as soon as he embarked he felt relieved. Warm spring breezes filled the air and made the overcoat he had brought with him unnecessary. The calm Atlantic soothed him and inspired a cheerful letter to his aunt and uncle in Chicago.[77] The boat was full of Greeks and Jews who were returning to their respective homelands, he wrote. The Jews were "the usual variegated collection, ranging from the ultra pious to the ultra radical, containing rights, lefts, centers, left-centers, right centers and what-not." The fact that this cross section of the Jewish people shared an attachment to Palestine raised his spirits and fortified his confidence in Zionism: "To hear . . . their separate stories . . . is to become inspired all over again. Even tho [*sic*] I myself . . . have been through this . . . so many times before, [I] have considered myself satiated with it in the Galut." Once the flame of Zionism was rekindled, Chicago became *galut,* and Simon was leaving it to return to his true home: the land of Israel.

CHAPTER 2

Palestine, 1930–1948

HAIFA

Things had changed since Simon last visited Palestine. In 1922 the country had no commercial port; the Agranats had sailed to Alexandria and then taken a train to Tel Aviv. By 1930 the Haifa harbor was under construction, soon to become an international port with modern facilities. That the *Mauritania* could anchor in Haifa itself was a mark of the rapid development Palestine was experiencing under British rule.

Still, it was British, not Jewish, rule that awaited him in Palestine, and Simon was carrying a gun precisely because he realized that Jews and Arabs were already engaged in a fierce fight over the land. He became increasingly worried about his gun. It was illegal to import weapons, and Simon was a law-abiding fellow. Fear propelled him to throw the bullets into the Mediterranean, but pragmatism prevented him from discarding the gun. Impatient to see his son, Aaron came on board prior to disembarkation, and hearing of his son's predicament, offered to smuggle the gun himself. Simon refused. He would not shift the responsibility to someone else. Wary, he tied the gun with a rope around his waist and looked sufficiently innocuous to British customs officers to avoid a search.

At home, he found his family in good shape, well on its way to integration into life in Palestine. Aaron, who had not done so well in his practice in Tel Aviv, now tasted prosperity. His stationery, on which Simon wrote his first letters to Chicago, discloses interesting information about the Agranats and Haifa of the early 1930s. Dr. Agranat's post-office box number was 4 and his telephone number was 547—both indications of how few people used these "advanced" features of modernity. The possession of such luxuries also shows that the family's social status had improved as a result of immigration; they were now members of the upper class. Dr. Agranat's name and credentials appeared in Hebrew, English, and Arabic; evidently, despite the ethnic tension, Aaron expected to treat Arabs as well as Jews and Brits.[1] The stationery also presented Dr. Agranat as an "American Dentist," as did the sign outside his clinic. There was some irony in the reference to himself as "American," because he had always insisted that life in the United States was merely temporary. Undoubtedly that was a pragmatic decision: with American credentials one could attract more clients, especially among the British civil servants. But in a society of immigrants one is identified by one's place of origin, and by then Aaron was more American than Russian.

Simon spent the first weeks in his old-new homeland touring the country while waiting for his settler's visa. He visited Tel Aviv, Jerusalem, the Dead Sea, and the magnificent Valley of Yizra'el—the pride of labor Zionism and locus of the first kibbutzim—glowing in the bright blue sky amidst spring wildflowers. In Kibbutz Ein-Harod he wrote, I "had my eighth successive egg-meal during my three-day journey through the Emek [valley]" (the kibbutzim of the period were high on spirit and low on meat and poultry). The high morale was contagious, and Simon came out buoyed by what he saw: "the irresistible, irrepressible conclusion formulated itself, that Arab or no Arab problem, Inquiry Commission report or not, we Jews have nothing of which to be ashamed, a whole lot of which to be proud, and a great, legitimate hope of succeeding."[2]

EXILE AND REDEMPTION

Having sojourned so long amidst the gentile nations, having assimilated so much of their art of thinking and way of living, we too in the death of a Chizik feel more keenly and more vividly our passage, whether mental or physical—from "Galuth" [sic] to "Geulah" [from exile to redemption].
—SIMON AGRANAT, "A Modern Maccabean, The Life and Death of Ephraim Chizik," Avukah Annual 5 (1930): 104.

There was one more aspect to the alarm that shook Simon in Chicago when he heard of the 1929 riots in Palestine. He became personally acquainted with the toll extracted by the Arab–Zionist conflict. On 26 August 1929 Ephraim Chizik, younger brother of Sarah, who herself died in the battle of Tel Hai and of Yitzhak Chizik, Simon's partner in the Avukah project, was killed while defending the settlement of Huldah against Palestinian attack. His death brought home the menacing meaning of the Arab resistance to Zionism and cast a dark shadow on innocent dreams of constructing utopia in the ancient homeland. By 1929 the Yishuv had already realized that it could not rely on the Mandatory government to protect it against Arab threats. A voluntary organization—the Haganah —was established to provide for Jewish self-defense. Ephraim Chizik did not live in Huldah. He was sent by the Haganah to the agricultural set-tlement—located between Jerusalem and Tel Aviv—leading a force of thirty volunteers. As Simon told the story, the group encountered a thousand Arabs and was doomed before the battle even started. Chizik personally provided cover for his men as they retreated into the sand-bagged main house and was fatally wounded just as he was about to find shelter himself. When British forces finally arrived, after midnight, they refused to let the besieged pioneers evacuate Chizik's body. "It was left, wrapped in a white sheet, at the side of the tank-car."³

Now in Palestine, Simon decided to write a eulogy for Chizik, to be published in the 1930 volume of *Avukah*. It was his opportunity not only to reassess the meaning of Zionism but also to justify the not altogether rational decision to trade the safe environment of Chicago for turbulent Palestine. In a moving and at times deeply philosophical tribute to Chizik, whom he had not personally known, Simon expressed the emerging Zion-ist ethos concerning the Arab–Zionist conflict. He began by contrasting the martyr with the hero in Jewish history. Chizik, he wrote, symbolized Jewish Renaissance, the healthy effect of the land on its people. Indeed, in exile, Jews also showed courage and bravery, but it was the bravery of martyrs, passive, rooted in the abnormal circumstances of a people with-out a land. Zionism revived the Maccabean spirit, when Jews, outnum-bered by their enemy, fought for independence and liberty: "[T]he Chiziks . . . mark the return to the annals of our race of an old-new type of hero, of the 'Gibbor,' absent since the days of . . . Bar Kochba [the leader of a Jewish revolt against Rome in the second century A.D.]. It was the 'Gibborim' [heroes] who fought for the concrete evidences of the na-tional unity, for the tangible fatherland, for their country, for the national soil . . . and when they ceased to appear, we ceased to be discernible as a national entity."⁴

Ephraim was twenty-seven years old when he died. Simon was twenty-five years old when he wrote the eulogy. Ephraim was the antithesis of Simon: son of a Galilean village, fearless and combative. In his physical

vigor and farming background he epitomized the "new Jew" romanti-
cized by Zionist ideology. Simon, the boy from Chicago, highly educated
and reluctant to defy authority, was both paying respects to and identifying with Chizik: "His was not an abstract principle of Jewish Nationalism evolved rationally; nor yet a patriotic sentiment brought to the surface at the moment of the national crisis; but rather a deeply ingrained
intuition that his star was inevitably united with the destiny of the New
Israel."[5]

It is interesting to compare Simon's 1925 tribute to the Hebrew University with his Chizik eulogy. In 1925 he emphasized the cultural significance of Zionism—the belief that the return to the homeland would liberate the Jewish genius and launch an era of unprecedented intellectual
creativity. In the eulogy, the return to the homeland was still hailed as a
transformative experience, but in the realm of the physical rather than the
cultural. Jewish power, not spirit, had become the focus. Nationalism had
become the message: in exile, Jews lost the ability to fight for their country and thus "to the world . . . ceased to be discernible as a national entity."[6] Chizik-like acts of heroism heralded the arrival of the "New Israel"
and restored the Jewish place among the family of nations, lost since the
destruction of the Kingdom of Judea.

The "public" aspect of the eulogy, the fact that it was his "formal statement" to the world he left behind, led him to accentuate even more forcefully the nationalist theme. The eulogy displayed none of the ambivalence
he privately experienced about immigration and appears to have been the
equivalent of a rite of passage. He identified with the Zionist ethos, praised
the virtues of national heroism and the willingness to sacrifice oneself for
the land, and became a full-fledged member of the Yishuv.

LAW, POLITICS, AND THE ARAB–ZIONIST CONFLICT

Since his Avukah days, Simon had toyed with the idea of
joining a kibbutz—the correct move from the perspective of Labor Zionism. The thought was on his mind as he visited the kibbutzim in the Valley of Yizra'el. But despite his pride in the accomplishments of the kibbutzim, he returned home with the realization that "the kibbutz life was
not for me, [for] you are constantly a part of the group. There is no pri-
vacy. You eat together. Live together." His American individualism was
resistant to the Russian-inspired communitarianism of the kibbutz ideology. And there was more: beneath the phrase "we Jews" lay tangled

diversity. In his letter from the *Mauritania,* Simon had already alluded to the cornucopia of Jewish types: the left and the right, the ethnic diversity. Most kibbutz members were Eastern European. The tension between East and West, reminiscent of the Weizmann–Brandeis dispute, resurfaced. Clearly the kibbutz was not for him. He began to explore the possibilities of joining the legal profession.

To obtain a license to practice law in Palestine, Simon had to pass an examination for foreign lawyers, clerk for eighteen months, and pass the Palestine bar examination. He began to prepare for the foreign lawyers' examination while looking for a suitable place to clerk. The entire legal profession in Palestine numbered about three hundred lawyers, two-thirds of whom were Jews. Simon did prefer to train with a Jewish lawyer, but he was unhappy about what Haifa had to offer.[7] Although Haifa was a thriving town, its residents jokingly referred to it as a place "with neither a past, nor a present but a great future";[8] it did not yet have a lawyer of a national caliber. Simon wished to train with someone prominent, whose skills and range of practice would make the transition from the sophisticated American legal system to Levantine Palestine a little less shocking. He began to contemplate doing his clerkship in Jerusalem.

Moving to Jerusalem had its downside. Again he would separate from his family, a prospect he was not thrilled about, even though he was better prepared for it now that he had experienced living alone in Chicago and had traveled by himself to Palestine. More difficult was the realization that he would have to rely for financial support on his parents, as clerkship came without a salary. But his ambition prevailed. Mordechai Eliash agreed to employ him as a clerk, and Simon moved to Jerusalem, renting a room at the house of Yosef Sprinzak. Sprinzak was a noted leader of Ha-Poel Ha-Tzair (the Jewish Socialist Party, the left wing of the Zionist movement, founded in 1905), a founder of the Histadrut, and later the first speaker of Israel's Knesset. At the Sprinzak home Simon was embraced as one of the family, and he found himself in "the thick of the maelstrom" of Zionist and Mandatory politics. There, he frequently participated in heated political debates with people who wielded power and made policy. These were crucial times for the Yishuv. Since the 1929 riots, one important political event followed another. England was reassessing its commitment to the Jewish National Home, Palestinian Arabs were on the verge of rebellion, and the Zionist leadership was trying to come to grips with this, along with Hitler's rise to power abroad and the rise of right-wing Zionism at home.

Did Simon aspire to become involved in politics, to join the ranks of decision makers? Everything in his personal history pointed in this direction: his intense interest in politics since childhood, his aspiration to become a journalist, his involvement in Avukah. Indeed, his first steps in Palestine tell the story of a young man hesitantly testing the terrain to see what niche he would find for self-expression. He explored the possibility of becoming a political commentator. Shortly after the 1929 riots, *Davar*, the powerful Histadrut daily newspaper, began to publish an English supplement. Simon was interested in joining the supplement's editorial board. Yitzhak Chizik, who had connections in the Labor leadership, arranged a meeting with Moshe Sharett, the supplement's editor and later Israel's first minister of foreign affairs and second prime minister. But Sharett was a busy man and failed to show up. Disappointed and disheartened, Simon took the episode to signal a lack of interest and abandoned the idea.

He was following closely the British efforts at greater reconciliation with the Arab population. One of the means suggested was the creation of domestic governing institutions, to enhance self-rule. As a first step, a legislative council with limited authority was proposed (leaving considerable power with the executive branch, to remain in British hands), to be elected democratically by the entire population, Arabs and Jews. Because Palestine had far more Arabs than Jews, it was expected that the Arabs would enjoy a majority in the council. Britain hoped that such open recognition of the majority would quell Arab fears that the interests of world Jewry were preferred to those of the local population and encourage the moderate elements in Palestinian society.

The Yishuv was split on the proposal, which would inevitably reflect its numerical inferiority and recognize its status as a minority in its own land. The main speakers in the debate were Chaim Arlosoroff and Berl Katznelson, both noted leaders of MAPAI, the Jewish Socialist Party. Arlosoroff, by then head of the Political Department of the Jewish Agency (the "foreign minister" of the Yishuv), thought that reform was inevitable and imminent; hence, it would be a mistake for the Jews to boycott the plan. A boycott, Arlosoroff insisted, would only strengthen the Arabs and allow them to use their new legislative powers against the Jews. Arlosoroff urged cooperation, explaining that the proposed constitutional reform contained some advantages to Jews. Berl Katznelson and David Ben-Gurion opposed the plan ferociously. This brand of etatism, they claimed, would marginalize the Yishuv and cripple hopes for a Jewish National Home. They advocated autonomy and self-rule for both Arab and Jewish communities, as a means to safeguard Zionist interests.

Simon sided with Berl. As the war of words intensified, he entered the arena by sending a letter to the editor of the magazine *Ahdut ha-Avodah,* which had previously published both Arlosoroff and Berl on this issue. In fluent Hebrew (he had mastered the language during his previous stay in Tel Aviv, nine years earlier), Simon identified a major weakness in the British proposal for a legislative council: the plan reserved the powers over the budget to the high commissioner, thereby denying the legislature the power of the purse. Berl had already seized on this detail, in order to prove that the British did not intend to relinquish meaningful power. Arlosoroff argued that the executive power over the purse was benign and simply reflected the constitutional arrangements in England itself. Simon devoted four handwritten pages to refuting Arlosoroff. He argued that the analogy with Britain was misleading because the British executive was accountable to Parliament, which had the power to topple the executive, whereas in Palestine the executive was independent of the legislative branch. In the United States, he pointed out, where the principle of separation of powers obtained, the power over the purse was in the hands of Congress.[9]

Agranat's letter took a narrow approach. It refrained from entering the heart of the political debate: should the Jews oppose the democratization of institutions in Palestine, as long as they remained a numerical minority? He was hoping to assist the Yishuv in opposing the plan, while sidestepping the question of democratization. A Progressive and a reader of the *New Republic,* he was just beginning to learn about the full constitutional ramifications of the Arab–Zionist conflict and was only halfheartedly prepared to accept that the Zionist cause required the bending of cherished principles.

The letter was never published. There were a few weeks of anticipation. He even asked Arlosoroff about it during one of the eminent leader's visits at the Sprinzaks. Then came the cold realization that this was yet another failed attempt to engage in public affairs. It was not easy, even in the small Yishuv, to be taken seriously by the power holders, especially when one confined oneself to legalistic arguments.

Mordechai Eliash, for whom he was now clerking, was also a power holder. A man of letters, he was asked by the *Annals of the American Academy of Political and Social Science* to contribute an article to a special volume dedicated to Palestine. Simon was asked to prepare a draft.

The topic was "The Rutenberg Concession and the Dead Sea Concession." Rutenberg, one of the more colorful characters in the Yishuv, was a Russian revolutionary who had lost faith in revolution as the cure for anti-Semitism and developed a passion for Zionism. An engineer by training, charismatic, well connected, and enthusiastically backed by the Zionist leadership, Rutenberg persuaded the British to grant him a concession to establish electric and hydraulic power plants in Palestine. His Palestine Electricity Corporation eventually became Israel's Electric Corporation.[10]

It so happened that in 1914 the Ottoman government had already granted a similar concession to a Greek national, Euripides M. Mavrommatis. A legal battle ensued, concerning the respective validity of the two concessions.[11] Underneath the legalese raged a battle over control of Palestine's economy. Should it be vested in the hands of Jews, to further Zionist objectives, or should it be placed in the hands of the local inhabitants, mainly Arabs, who perceived the Jewish interest as inimical to their own welfare? Agranat's task was to review the history of the electricity concession with an eye toward validating the legality of the Mandatory power. By reviewing the Constitution of Palestine—the Charter of the Mandate—Agranat tried to show that the obligations of the British government under Article 11 of the Mandate—to "safeguard the interests of the Community in connection with the development of the country . . . " and its discretionary power to "arrange with the Jewish Agency . . . to . . . develop any of the natural resources of the country"— were perfectly harmonious. With conviction and dedication, he was deploying his budding legal skills in furtherance of Zionism.[12]

However, just as politics would not stay separated from law for long, so would it not leave scholarship secure in its ivory tower. The Palestine volume, conceived by Harry Viteles—an enthusiastic American Zionist—as a tribute to the emerging Jewish National Home in Palestine, was "discovered" by the Palestinian Arabs, who insisted on balanced representation. The war over public opinion or, if you wish, over political truth, reached everywhere—even the *Annals*. Viteles was compelled to solicit articles presenting the Arab point of view,[13] and what he read concerning the electric concession chilled his enthusiasm. Publication of the rejoinder, he concluded, would hurt the Zionist cause, yet omitting the rejoinder "would show discrimination."[14] "My dear Eliash," he wrote, "[Y]ou have again been offered as a sacrifice to the 'Cause'—probably not the last time. I was confronted with the question of either allowing Bury's article to be published (you have seen it), or omitting the subject from the Volume. Of course, the latter was the only possible course under the circumstances. . . . I hope that you will understand and not be too hard on me." Referring to the exasperation brought by the effort to have Arabs and Jews tell the story of Palestine, he concluded: "It was an ill-omened day when I thought of a Palestine volume."[15]

"Eliash was unhappy," Agranat quipped some fifty years later, "that his name did not appear on an article he did not write." Indeed, but so did Simon feel disappointed, after sweating over the thirty-one-page legal memorandum. Once again his efforts were thwarted because of external political considerations. He was experiencing the Zionist ethos: that one should always expect to sacrifice and be sacrificed for the greater goal of building the Jewish National Home.

PALESTINE'S LEGAL SYSTEM: BETWEEN LONDON AND ISTANBUL

If Ephraim Chizik was the epitome of the Zionist man of the future—the rough, direct, fearless sabra—Mordechai Eliash was the epitome of the modern, suave Jew. When Simon met him he was a middle-aged man with delicate features, gold-rimmed glasses, and a groomed goatee, noted for his meticulous dress and his broad-brimmed hats. Born in Ukraine and Yeshivah educated, he exuded Eastern European *yiddishkeit*— that which, in Weizmann's eyes, constituted the essence of Jewishness. In Berlin and London, where he had acquired his legal education, he learned to coat this *yiddishkeit* with fine social manners. Thus Eliash was at once Westernized and rooted in tradition. His Jerusalem home was the center of high society. He entertained high British officials, members of the Arab aristocracy, and leaders of the Yishuv. An enthusiastic Zionist, he served as legal counsel to the aspiring institutions of self-rule of the Yishuv and was involved in its politics.[16] He was known for his singing in the Yeshurun synagogue in Jerusalem, which he had helped establish. In short, he was very much like Simon's father and was the perfect mentor for the young man.

Simon had approached Eliash after he heard the famous lawyer deliver an oral argument in court. The brilliant eloquence of Eliash must have stirred the memory of another great lawyer, Clarence Darrow, whose legendary mastery of oral argument influenced Simon's decision to pursue a legal career. Eliash's office was located in the "Habashim" (Ethiopians) Street, a narrow road lined with stone houses. Typical of Jerusalem of the 1930s, the street was unpaved, and Simon recalled that "in the summer your shoes would be covered with dust and in the winter with mud." The place served Eliash as both an office and residence (distance was maintained, and the clerk was never invited into the residential quarters). The office had two rooms. One was reserved for the master, and the other functioned as a multipurpose room, accommodating "two typists, a Yemenite male secretary, a junior lawyer, the clerk, and clients waiting to see Eliash."[17] Turkish, Arabic, Yiddish, Russian, and Hebrew filled the air, while Eliash met with his clients over tiny cups of Turkish coffee or steaming sweet tea, as was the custom of the day. Simon remembered his clerkship as "akin to slavery"; for the sheer privilege of doing the clerkship and for little pay, a clerk was expected to run errands and perform various services for Eliash. Yet Simon managed to develop a good feel for the legal system, learn much, make contacts, and strike up a friendship with Isaac Olshan, the junior lawyer and MAPAI activist, who in time became one of the first appointees to the Supreme Court and whom Agranat would succeed as chief justice.

The culture shock Palestine's legal system inflicted on Western law graduates was described by Eliyahu Mani, who himself became a justice of the Supreme Court of Israel: "In the beginning of 1932 I came back to Palestine and . . . I felt engulfed in darkness. I was educated on the knees of English law. I have seen courts respected by all, courts the appearance of which inspired awe. And what have I seen here? Stables."[18]

The abysmal state of the facilities was not as startling as the practice itself. The first thing Eliash instructed Simon about was the chronic disease of Palestinian legal culture: corruption. Corruption was the legacy of the Ottomans, who had ruled until the British took over in 1917. It meant that practically everyone in the administration (with the exception, perhaps, of British officials, who were superimposed on the bureaucracy inherited from the Turks) expected and responded favorably to baksheesh. Simon was required to check all the files pending before the courts every other day, to ascertain that they were still in place and that neither the documents introduced therein nor the temporary court orders had been altered. While engaged in this daily routine, Simon learned another aspect of colonial life: because English was the master's language, Simon's fluency in it gave him an advantage, for some of the master's superiority rubbed onto him. At times, when frustration at disappearing files and mysterious changes in court orders were overwhelming, he would find that a stream of angry English prose provided some (temporary) relief. Documents would miraculously be "found," files straightened.

The judge could be an additional obstacle on the road to justice. In 1925 Bernard Joseph, a young lawyer of Canadian descent and later Israel's minister of justice, described in a memorandum to the Mandatory authorities the "normal modus operandi" in the Palestine courts: "The judge carries on business through the medium of some . . . intermediary . . . who is on the one hand sufficiently shady to do work of this character, but on the other hand sufficiently respectable to inspire confidence in all concerned, and the agreed bribe is deposited with this intermediary. If the judge can put through the business, the bribe is duly handed over to him. If . . . he fails to secure the desired judgement, the bribe is duly returned to the unsuccessful litigant."[19] Shmuel Y. Agnon, the Nobel laureate in literature, was less charitable: "Yesterday you gave the judge such and such a sum to rule in your favor, next morning before the court you see your nemesis winning, not because justice was on his side but because he had doubled the sum. Not only did you lose in court, you also lost your bribe money."[20]

The Mandatory government responded by protecting itself. Governmental litigation before the Palestine courts entitled the government to insist on judicial panels with a majority of British judges. It was not only an admission of mistrust but also an acquiescence in the situation, a recognition that the disease was too chronic for treatment.

From Joseph's memorandum we learn more about the legal system of Palestine in the 1920s. No public library in the entire country possessed a complete collection of laws or court opinions. Lawyers had private collections but, out of competition, were reluctant to share them. In 1931, before taking the preliminary examination for foreign lawyers, Agranat searched in vain for a copy of the Ottoman Commercial Code. He took the test without having the slightest idea about the contents of that code. Also, despite the fact that the courts adhered to precedent, no law reports were officially published. As a clerk, Agranat took advantage of the fact that his office, by virtue of Eliash's prominence, received carbon copies of Supreme Court rulings. He copied the opinions and brought "the treasure" with him to Haifa when he opened his own law office. But this system was not error proof. "Fighting back tears of rage," he realized that he lost the very first case he ever argued because he failed to know about a recent ruling, presented to the Court at the last minute by his adversary.

The solution for the sorry state of the law, sought by young attorneys — some educated in England, and some in the English law classes in Jerusalem — was aggressive British intervention: the replacement of "Ottoman law" with Mandatory (British colonial) law. Its partial implementation would create a perennial problem for Israeli law: a tapestry woven out of many legal traditions. A layered system had existed before the British took over Palestine. Moslem law governed Ottoman territories before the modernization of Turkey by Kemal Ataturk in the 1920s;

French, Swiss, and German law were imported into Ottoman territories as part of the efforts at modernization, sometimes replacing but often superimposed on the existing Moslem law as well as religious law (Moslem, Christian, or Jewish) regulating family matters. Now the English common law and principles of equity would join to create yet another layer.

By and large, the Jewish legal profession looked down upon Ottoman law as "antiquated" or "primitive."[21] Moshe Silberg, later a justice on Israel's Supreme Court, wrote in 1934: "The Law in Palestine is Janus faced: one face overlooks Damascus, the vast wasteland of the great desert, awakening periodically from its generational slumber to the slow rhythm of camels' bells, and the other is bowing and curtsying to European legislation, with its quick tempo of a car's wheels and airplane's wings."[22] In fact, not all of Ottoman law was premodern or useless. Much of it was rather advanced, and parts of it would in time prove much more in keeping with the communitarian philosophy of Labor Zionists than modern, individualistic English law would ever be.

The reasons for the Jewish profession's antipathy to Ottoman law should be found elsewhere: in the corrupt administration which gave it a bad odor, in the fact that it was inaccessible to most of the immigrants, who found it difficult enough to master the English language and who were reluctant to learn Turkish and French. Furthermore, the immigrants, some of whom had studied law in London, admired English law, which they associated—not always justifiably—with progress and modernity. Finally, and perhaps most importantly, Ottoman law was the legal system of the native population; it predated Zionism and the international recognition of the Jewish National Home. Equating Ottoman law with "a vast wasteland" and replacing it with another legal system would conveniently obfuscate the colonialist face of Zionism. Thus the battle over the normative content of the law of Palestine was informed by the tension between East and West, between tradition and modernity, and between the native population and the Yishuv.

British judges, recruited by the department of the colonies, were divided. Some leaned toward the importation of British law; others believed that changes in the local law should be minimal and await self-rule. Palestinian Arabs were generally unenthusiastic. Many experienced reform as an assault on their authentic culture. "Should I replace my snow white headdress of a Sheikh with this goat-hair?" a senior Arab judge scoffed when the British introduced the traditional wig into the courtrooms of Palestine.[23] The Arabs also understood that progress and modernity came hand in hand with the Jewish National Home, that it would be the educated, highly motivated, "Western" (in fact most of them were Eastern European, and thus "Western" only from a Middle Eastern point of view) Jews who would be the spearhead of progress. Inevitably, the dilution of native culture in service of reform would put the Jewish elite in control of the economy, to the advantage of Jews over Arabs. Those among them who understood progress as a tool to advance Zionism preferred to stall modernity: better backward and Arab than modern and Jewish.

As a clerk, Simon worked on one landmark case, in which the Privy Council in London ordered a reluctant Palestine Supreme Court to modernize Ottoman law in the spirit of English equity. It was a suit brought by the Ayoub family against Sheikh Suleiman Taji Farouqi. The Ayoubs sold land to Farouqi, a blind Arab poet and politician, who agreed to pay them 2,500 Palestinian pounds (at that time, the last phase of his clerkship, Simon was earning twenty pounds per month) if he failed to comply with any of the contract's provisions. When Farouqi failed to pay an installment of 400 pounds as stipulated, the Ayoubs took him to court. Eliash was their lawyer. Agranat encountered one of the basic differences between Ottoman and English law (and vicariously, the difference between the law of Palestine and American law): English law permitted only liquidated damages (proportionate to the transaction), not penal damages. Under English law, Farouqi would not be compelled to pay 2,500 pounds for having failed to pay an installment of 400 pounds. On the other hand, Ottoman law did not have the remedy of specific performance, available under English equity law, which enabled a court to order the delinquent party to comply with its obligations.

Farouqi was represented by another prominent lawyer in Jerusalem, Bernard Joseph, author of the 1925 memorandum describing bribery in Palestinian courts. At issue was Article 46 of the Palestine Order in Council, 1922, which provided that in cases of lacunae (failure of the law to provide for a solution) the courts in Palestine might resort to the principles of the British common law and equity.[24] This was a potent instrument to help shape Ottoman law in the English image. Through interpretation, the judges of Palestine could find endless instances of lacunae and turn the law of Palestine into a sponge that would absorb English law and thereby radically change its content. Until the 1930s the courts were hesitant to use this power. Agranat watched as the battle over the content of the law of Palestine raged.[25] The Privy Council instructed the lower courts to assess the Ayoub demand for 2,500 pounds: if it amounted to a penalty, it should not be awarded.[26]

For Agranat this was an interesting educational experience. He was personally partial to Westernization and sympathetic to the basic notions of fairness encased in the British law of equity. Nevertheless, as the Ayoubs' attorney, he remembered working diligently to defend their case as well as he could. Law, despite its close kinship to politics, still possessed some independent features that enabled one to do a professional job, even on top of the volcano called Palestine.

The case of *Farouqi v. Ayoub* is instructive for yet another reason. Despite the havoc created by the 1929 anti-Jewish violence and the fact that Eliash represented many Jews injured during the riots, as well as official Zionist institutions, the Ayoubs hired him as their attorney. Farouqi hired Bernard Joseph. In Palestine, the legal system was one of the few places where Jews and Arabs fully interacted as equals. Practice with Eliash provided Agranat with his first encounter with the Palestinian Arabs. It gave him an opportunity to meet Arabs of diverse social and political backgrounds: the landed aristocracy, law graduates of Cambridge and the Sorbonne who maintained lucrative practices, seasoned and experienced judges, and vociferous anti-Zionists who regarded the idea of a Jewish National Home as yet another imperialistic colonial ploy. He observed the social divide and made only a few Arab friends, yet he did not demonize Arabs, as many of his contemporaries tended to do. At this period in his life he still hoped that reconciliation, in the framework of a binational state, was possible and that Jews and Arabs could mutually recognize and respect each other's interests and aspirations.

Eliash appreciated the quality work done by Agranat and encouraged him to stay in his prestigious firm as a junior partner. As an incentive he offered a raise—by itself proof of the enthusiasm that the parsimonious lawyer had for his clerk—and permission to do independent appellate work. The latter prospect was particularly enticing, as it would give Agranat an opportunity to argue before the Court while benefiting from Eliash's seasoned advice. Agranat was tempted. His father came to Jerusalem, and the two met with Eliash and weighed the terms of the offer.

At long last he decided to decline the offer. He feared that at the Eliash firm he would remain in the shadow of the great master. He was not inclined to rely on Eliash's goodwill in offering occasional raises. Haifa, with its international port, its oil refineries, and its railroad, was rapidly becoming a thriving industrial center. His good friend, Jacob S. Shapiro, with whom he had studied for the bar examinations (and who later became the first attorney general of Israel and minister of justice), a vivacious and entrepreneurial young man, was moving to Haifa because of its economic prospects. There were also personal considerations. Simon's younger brother, Abel, had just left for the United States to study dentistry, and Simon felt that he should be closer to their parents. Most importantly, Simon had recently made the acquaintance of Carmel Friedlaender.

MARRIAGE

Carmel, a gentle, youthful, good-looking elementary-school teacher in the prestigious Ha-Re'ali School in Haifa, was similar to Simon in one important respect. Like him, she had been born in the United States to immigrant parents who were dedicated Zionists and who saw America as "the large corridor" to Palestine.[27] Her father, Israel Friedlaender, a noted authority on Semitic languages, was one of the first professors at the Jewish Theological Seminary in New York and a prominent leader in the fledgling American Zionist movement.[28] Her mother Lilian, née Bentwich, scion to an established Anglo-Jewish family with strong Zionist ties, was a formidable figure, active in Zionist affairs and patron of music and the arts.[29] In 1920, when Carmel was nine years old, her father was assassinated in Ukraine. He was on a mission on behalf of the Joint Distribution Committee to the war-ravaged Jewish communities of Eastern Europe. Lilian decided to fulfill Israel's dream and, with her six young children, defied the advice of most of her friends and emigrated to Palestine.[30] Thus Carmel shared Simon's American background and sensibilities—no mean feat in the sea of Eastern European and German immigrants who made up most of the Yishuv population. But Carmel also possessed an attractive difference—having spent her teen years in Palestine, she was practically a sabra, an attribute that must have had enormous appeal to the recently arrived Simon, who was eager to assimilate into his new homeland.

Carmel had been the apple of her father's eye,[31] and it should not be surprising that Simon's familiarity with Friedlaender's scholarship and awareness of his stature in Zionist American circles augmented his attraction to her heart.[32] A professor's daughter, she was attuned to and appreciative of the life of the mind, and that was precisely what the shy, reserved Simon had to offer in abundance.[33] They quickly discovered that they had more in common than an American background (his Israeli friends called him Shimon; she called him Sy—his American name), American accent, and Chicago (her brother was studying there). Both fiercely believed in Zionism, and although they were bilingual, they observed the cardinal tenet of Zionism and always spoke Hebrew at home. Both loved American and English literature, enjoyed classical music (she loved Mozart; he preferred Donizetti), had a tendency to speak in understatements, and were modest, even indifferent, to worldly goods and the trappings of social status.

They were engaged in November 1933 and married in May 1934. "Quite certainly," Lilian wrote, "Carmel's marriage is the climax of my life."[34] Indeed, Carmel's mother invested in this event all of her considerable organizational skills. The wedding took place in Zikhron Ya'acov, an exquisitely beautiful colony south of Haifa, overlooking the Mediterranean, where the Bentwiches owned a magnificent estate. The grand mansion, the ravishing garden, and the regal row of Washingtonians at the entrance gave the wedding "a fairy touch."[35] There is no doubt that Simon and his parents encountered a social lifestyle they could only have read about in novels about the aristocracy. The participants were extravagantly dressed,[36] the reception was luxuriously elegant, and after the wedding ceremony a trio consisting of Carmel's brother, aunt, and second cousin played classical music. The event stood in stark contrast to the ascetic culture of the Yishuv, based as it was on socialist ethics, and next to Agranat's retirement party was probably the most spectacular event in his personal life.

Agranat remembered the aftermath as anxious. An Arab driver was waiting in a taxicab to drive the newlyweds to their honeymoon. Arab violence against Jews was rampant, and the roads were unsafe. To be driven by an Arab (arranged by his mother-in-law) just as night was falling was not exactly a confidence-building measure. When they arrived at Judah Magnes's summer house (Magnes, a close friend of Israel and Lilian, was president of the New York Kehilah before he immigrated to Palestine to become chancellor of the Hebrew University), lent to them for the occasion, they found that it was not as empty as they had expected. Magnes's son—a surprise houseguest—would be leaving only the next morning. But the guest was discreet and unintrusive, and the young couple persevered. Theirs became a warm and solid marriage, of mutual love, devotion, and respect, which ended only with Agranat's death in 1992.

Marriage to Carmel opened before Simon the doors to her array of formidable relatives. Between the Bentwiches and the Friedlaenders he had access to anyone worth knowing in the intellectual community of Palestine. Among her uncles were Norman Bentwich, the first attorney general of Palestine, Joseph Bentwich, a noted educator, Eugene Meyer, an economist of distinction, and Louis Finkelstein, the eminent American Jewish scholar and president of the Jewish Theological Seminary.

These people embraced Simon as one of their own. They offered him hospitality, erudite conversation, and intellectual stimulation. For the first time Agranat encountered the Zionist left and Brit Shalom, a Jewish group that was critical of mainstream Zionism and insistent on Arab–Jewish cooperation.[37] He was sympathetic to their ideals, skeptical of their optimism, and admiring of their extensive libraries. He often came to rely on their collections when writing a judicial opinion.

Carmel and Simon Agranat had a traditional marriage: he was the breadwinner, she the homemaker. She described him as "working day and night," first as a young attorney and then as a judge. She, obliging his passion to research, write, and excel, left her job after their first child was born and devoted herself to running the household and raising the family. He, obliging her determination to have a large family, devoted all of his free time to her and the children. In an era when middle-class Israelis had at most two children, the Agranats had five.[38] Even World War II did not deter them from enlarging their family. In interviews, Agranat readily volunteered that Carmel was the "life of the home."[39] Generous, nurturing, and empathetic, Carmel kept their home lively and vibrant, full of children, grandchildren, great-grandchildren, assorted relatives, friends — and flowers. She was also opinionated and strong minded. Since my interviews with Agranat began, she insisted that this should be an intellectual biography, blind to the private dimension of their family life. I have tried to oblige. Even though she was a major figure in Agranat's life, she and the children rarely appear in this book.

PRACTICING LAW IN HAIFA

When Agranat joined the legal profession in Haifa as a solo practitioner, he was still living with his parents, associating with the few friends he had made while clerking in Jerusalem, and acquainting himself with the Haifa scene. He did not suffer from a lack of social interaction. His parents' house was the center of Haifa's Jewish community and gave him ample opportunity to meet interesting and influential people. In one such gathering he met Ya'acov Halevy, a young lawyer who had recently immigrated from Poland. Aaron liked the buoyant Halevy and encouraged his friendship with Simon, gently pushing the two toward a business relationship. He knew his son well. Simon was bright and motivated, but was not blessed with business acumen. Even though Aaron made an effort to channel his acquaintances and patients to Simon's office, he knew that Simon needed a practical partner. The Agranat-Halevy partnership lasted until 1940, when Agranat was appointed a justice of the peace.

Haifa, built on the slopes of Mount Carmel, overlooks the Mediterranean and is divided into upper and lower towns. The commercial section, predominantly Arab, was concentrated in the lower part, close to the seaport. Lawyers tended to establish their offices in that area, and with Aaron's help Agranat and Halevy rented a three-room apartment on Jaffa Street, in a building owned by a prominent Arab merchant, Aziz Chayat. The two found that even though Palestine had no income tax (that came only in 1940), the practice of law was not particularly lucrative. The pair struggled to make a modest living. Generally, an ordinary, small legal practice is based on tort litigation, but the legal system of Palestine, based as it was on Ottoman law, did not have a body of tort law. The British postponed the introduction of torts until the practice of insurance had taken root. Only in 1947 was a torts ordinance enacted in Palestine. Simon's practice, therefore, consisted mainly of small real-estate transactions and negotiable instruments.

His scholarly bent showed immediately. One of his first steps as a lawyer was to purchase a set of Halsbury's *Laws of England*, the centerpiece of English positive law. It required a down payment of 25 English pounds—a serious investment for a young lawyer—and a payment of 3 English pounds every three months. Haifa's lawyers, provincial and trade oriented, looked amazed and amused at the lengthy, scholarly briefs that emerged from Agranat's office. "Why," noted a bemused Yitzhak Kahan (Israel's sixth chief justice), Agranat's apprentice in the 1930s, "Agranat even cited the *Law Quarterly Review;* whoever heard of that in those days?"[40]

Simon's law partner described him as a young man who preferred the seclusion of his office, "thinking legal thoughts," to the hustle and bustle of commercial interactions. It also became clear that efficiency was not Agranat's strong suit. He would invest as much time in a case as was needed to crack the legal problems, unaffected by considerations of gain. In 1965, on the occasion of his appointment as chief justice of Israel's Supreme Court, he received the following letter:

You may not recall the case you handled when in private practice . . . in 1940. . . . My brother . . . [who was] mentally insane, was incarcerated in the Acre prison, and only a certificate from the High Commissioner could free him from [this] hell. . . . The matter involved lengthy correspondence . . . travel and many meetings, visits to the Acre prison and even private "lobbying."

You have taken upon yourself to do all this, without compensation (!) [*sic*] in consideration of my parents' difficult financial circumstances. Moreover —even the expenses that incurred in the process—you covered from your personal funds.[41]

The fact of the matter was that Simon remained a Progressive—or a *ha-lutz* (pioneer)—at heart. He needed more than his small practice could offer; he craved the feeling of actually partaking in alleviating social suffering and in fulfilling Zionism.

How does one fulfill Zionism within the contours of a legal practice? By developing a militant, instrumental outlook toward law as the long arm of the Zionist revolution. Lawyers could contribute by challenging the limitations placed by the Mandatory government on the Jewish National Home. The hot issues of the day were two: restrictions on Jewish purchase of Arab land, and restrictions on Jewish immigration. Agranat joined forces with lawyers who fought the British efforts to shut the gates of Palestine in the faces of Jewish immigrants.

ILLEGAL IMMIGRATION

Simon's arrival in Palestine coincided with the first serious British assessment of the consequences of the Balfour Declaration. Was a Jewish National Home compatible with the "rights of the inhabitants," or, more precisely, with rising Palestinian national aspirations?[42] For a while it seemed as though the Zionist cause were losing ground. The British government concluded that the absorptive capacity of the land had reached its limits and prohibited further Jewish immigration.[43]

The decision was a devastating blow to the Yishuv and to the Zionist movement. It undermined the Zionist raison d'être: the gathering of the exiles. Worse still, without immigration the Yishuv would have to resign itself to minority status and abandon its aspirations to achieve a majority that would legitimate self-governance. The Yishuv responded with a massive strike. From Haifa, Simon wrote his aunt and uncle in Chicago:

Today, the Jewish populace was on public strike, in emphatic protest against the recent edict of the British Government to close the gates of Palestine. . . . We here . . . consider . . . it to be . . . a slap in the face to the entire Jewish movement of Reconstruction. . . . [A]s one man all sections of the diversi-fied Jewish multitudes . . . whether extreme orthodox, or liberal middle class, or labor elements, or whether Seffardi, Askenazi, or radical Revisionist—went into strike. . . . It was impressed on the minds of everyone by the Jewish National Committee that the strike must be characterized by dignity and peaceful order. . . . [A]t twelve noon . . . all the Jewish shops—without exception—closed; all the Jewish busses stopped running; all Jewish building operations ceased. . . . How bitter and keen Jewish feeling is. . . . [It] is difficult to describe; . . . in all my experience I have never witnessed or read of an expression of public protest by so large a section of the population, that displayed as much dignity . . . calm and quiet—a calm that spoke of depths of silent determination and of inner strengths, a unified strength. I suppose you think I am exaggerating . . . but in truth I have hardly told the half of it.[44]

Intensive Jewish lobbying brought about a reversal of British immigration policy. The gates to Palestine reopened. Between 1933 and 1939 the Jewish population of Palestine doubled. The growing vigor of the Yishuv, in turn, increased Arab–Palestinian hostility. In 1936 the Palestinian Arabs launched an armed rebellion against the Mandatory government, demanding self-rule. The British quelled the insurgence while agreeing, again, to restrict Jewish immigration. At the same time, the ascendance of Fascism and anti-Semitism in Europe and the surging hostility against Jews in the Arab world intensified the Jewish search for a haven from persecution. The number of applications for immigration visas far exceeded the number of certificates issued by the Mandatory government.

Illegal immigration, in defiance of British authority, organized and encouraged by Jewish institutions, was on the rise. Long before ships like the *Exodus* were forcing their way to Palestine, Jews were being smuggled across the borders. They came through Lebanon or Syria, led by guides familiar with the terrain. Many were caught and brought before English magistrates. In court they were assisted by lawyers recruited by the National Jewish Committee, the executive body of the organized Jewish community.[45]

Agranat volunteered his legal services to the task. Once every two weeks he would take whatever transportation was available (he was not one of the few who owned an automobile) and go to the detention center in Safed to represent illegal immigrants before the court. Travel to Safed was itself a patriotic act. Vehicles were attacked regularly by Arab bands, intent on terrorizing the Yishuv and on driving out the British, whom they condemned as too friendly toward the Jews. In Safed, Agranat recalled, he would first meet with his local liaison, Itzhak Moshe Silber, an Orthodox Jew whose "eyes glowed like embers," who considered the rescue of illegal immigrants to be the fulfillment of the biblical commandment to ransom captives. Silber would brief Agranat about the files and, in anticipation of a conviction, would prepare the application for bail. The lawyer's task was to persuade the authorities to allow bail pending deportation. The deportee would self-bail, disappear from sight, and never be traced again. Silber, who would typically sign a collateral bail, would then seek legal help to escape his fiscal responsibilities.[46] The collaboration between Agranat and Silber symbolized the relationship between secular and religious Zionists. The two rationalized their motives differently but worked in tandem toward a common goal.

The encounter with British judges, in the context of the Zionist struggle, sensitized Simon to his position as a native under colonial rule, dependent on the goodwill of those in power. He recalled feeling humiliated when he was obliged to plead guilty for his clients, and even more so when he saw no other recourse but to appeal for judicial mercy. It was a far cry from the ideal image of the modern Maccabean who would stand up for his rights, by force if necessary. Agranat also recalled a defiant exchange in court, with his head high and his voice firm:

Agranat: Imagine a flesh and blood Englishman entering England without papers after years of absence. Even without papers, he is still an Englishman, is he not? Would he be sent to jail for such an offense?
Judge: What kind of an analogy is this?
Agranat: They consider themselves and we see them as citizens of this country.[47]

The port of Haifa was another site of the struggle over immigration. Agranat remembered being called to the harbor one morning, where a Jewish fugitive had been found aboard ship, trying to escape from Austria in the aftermath of the *Anschluss.* British policy was to send fugitives back on the same boat, unless they were too ill to travel. The ship was to depart in the afternoon. Agranat needed a doctor who might be willing to declare the fugitive unfit for travel. His only hope was Dr. Thomson, a prominent British physician and one of his father's patients. Agranat recalled the frantic wait in the surgery ward, desperately watching the clock ticking away, and a happy ending to the story. The good doctor emerged in time to make the appropriate finding.

In pursuit of relief for the illegal immigrants, Agranat came to recognize that the official Zionist policy of supporting all immigration did not always translate into goodwill on the part of individual Zionist officials. He recalled representing a group of seventy-five Polish immigrants who, held without bail in wretched conditions, launched a hunger strike. Agranat appealed to Yitzhak Ben-Zvi, head of the National Committee and later second president of Israel, urging him to set a meeting with the chief of police to release the prisoners. Ben-Zvi grudgingly agreed to attend a meeting, but only if Agranat could arrange one. Agranat was bitter. In Haifa, the pregnant Carmel was bedridden with malaria. In coming to Jerusalem, he had put the immigrants' interest ahead of his family. It was much more difficult for him, as a junior, anonymous lawyer, to set up a meeting with the chief of police than for Ben-Zvi, with his national authority and contacts. Through stubbornness and guile he managed to arrange a meeting, only to find himself trying to persuade both the British official and Ben-Zvi that raising bail in exchange for releasing the prisoners was the proper resolution of the crisis.[48]

The encounter with the illegal immigrants was an important event in the education of Simon Agranat. Hitherto, he had understood Zionism to mean the creation of a model society, founded on liberty and social justice, where the Jewish genius could bloom and Jews would be strong enough to defend themselves. Zionism as a solution to anti-Semitism and persecution did not play a significant part in his ideology. Now he was beginning to perceive the urgency of the Jewish need for political shelter. Catastrophe Zionism, that strand in Zionist ideology which saw the Jewish homeland primarily as a haven for persecuted Jews, was now tempering his worldview and modifying his utopian aspirations.

STRIFE FROM WITHOUT AND WITHIN

Haifa of the 1930s, a mixed city, was fraught with strife and violence. During the Arab Rebellion of 1936, a general strike by Palestinian Arabs was particularly hard on Haifa, where both the harbor and town hall ceased to function. Snipers made everyday life perilous. Agranat joined the Haganah and was assigned to guard duty on Bourge Street, between Hadar Ha-Carmel (the Jewish neighborhood) and the lower city, an area populated by Arabs. He carried a revolver while on duty, but he was awkward with the gun; he was driven only by his strong sense of solidarity and the wish to contribute his share to the collective defense.

He also resisted the ghettoization instinct that swept the Jews as Arab violence mounted. He refused to acquiesce in the urging of his partner's wife that they move their office away from the predominantly Arab downtown to Hadar Ha-Carmel. "I would not give them [the Arabs] the satisfaction," he recalled. "I therefore had to cross the streets with the knowledge that snipers were at work."

Arabs did not hold a monopoly on violence. The display of Jewish solidarity and uniformity of spirit and purpose described in Simon's 1931 letter to Chicago was indeed impressive, but it was a thin veneer over an essentially volatile terrain. The Yishuv was a painfully polarized community, explosive with ideological tensions that increased after the assassination of Chaim Arlosoroff in 1933.[49] Vladimir Jabotinsky, leader of the nationalist right, seceded from the World Zionist Congress and established his own Zionist movement. "I never forgave him for that," recalled Agranat, again disclosing the high value he put on unity: "One should fight from within, not by secession." A major divisive issue was the use of violence. The mainstream institutions of the Yishuv advocated "self-restraint." They calculated that world public opinion and British sympathies would favor their cause if self-restraint were displayed. The Irgun, the right-wing military underground, advocated a belligerent policy toward both Arabs and British, aggressive and uncompromising. Haifa was wrecked by several terrorist attacks, which rumors blamed on the Irgun. Simon knew firsthand of the Irgun's involvement. He was one of a two-member committee appointed by the Hadar Ha-Carmel Committee to investigate the matter.[50] Even though he thought himself fair and impartial in the investigation, his heart was not with the Irgun.

By then he had already formed his opinion about the Arab–Israeli conflict. He sympathized with the pacifist Brit Shalom,[51] with its vision of a binational state and Arab–Jewish cooperation, but he doubted that this was a realistic vision. He came to the conclusion that the road ahead could not be peaceful, that a bloody conflict was inevitable. He did not think of himself as a conventional person; he refused to join the Rotary Club, which promised diverse social connections, because "I refused to be a Babbitt."[52] But when it came to the use of organized force, he firmly believed that unity and support of the Zionist leadership were essential. His natural aversion to lawless violence, as well as his deep conviction that a split within the Yishuv would be socially detrimental, nourished his disenchantment with the Irgun.

Toward the end of the 1930s, Agranat was appointed executive secretary to the steering committee of the Haifa Jewish bar. Haifa's attorneys, recognizing his superior scholarly background and intellectual bent, also elected him as cultural secretary, in charge of organizing activities and lectures to broaden the horizons of the local lawyers. (The cultural menu included such topics as the law of negotiable instruments and copyright.) Agranat was never an engaging lecturer. His manner of speech was rather dry and scholarly; some characterized it as boring. Still, either the substance of his talks was sufficiently interesting or Haifa's thirst for culture was insatiable—the fact was that other organizations in Haifa also invited him to lecture. He spoke twice before the Rotary Club, once on the American political system (which he, not surprisingly, considered superior to the English), and once on Winston Churchill, a man he deeply admired. Louis D. Brandeis, whom he now began to appreciate not only for his Zionist activity but also for his legal brilliance, was the subject of yet another lecture.

Agranat was also mulling over his present and future career. He was gaining a reputation as a "lawyer's lawyer," and his colleagues held him in high esteem. He did not do very well, however, with the rough, commercial side of the small-town legal practice, the constant competition for clients, the pressure to win cases, the ingratitude of clients who lost their cases, the hassle over payment, the lack of appreciation for a fine legal brief. He was ready for a change.

His father engaged him in long conversations. A judgeship came to mind. It might agree better with Agranat's temperament, insulate him from the dependence on the market, and enable him to develop his talents. With his fingertips on the pulse of the system, Aaron waited for an opportunity to speak to Carmel's uncle Norman Bentwich, Palestine's first attorney general, then retired. When the Agranats escorted Bentwich, a man close to the Mandatory administration and a professor of international law at the Hebrew University, to the Haifa harbor on a trip abroad, Aaron mentioned the idea of judgeship for Simon, and the seasoned Bentwich responded instantly. He scribbled something on a piece of paper and handed it over to Simon, to pass on to the high commissioner. The practice of *protekstyah* (favoritism), apparently, was not inaugurated in Israel of 1948. Agranat recalled taking the note and stacking it in his files. It offended his sense of self-dignity, he said, to use *protekstyah,* even if the practice was as much a part of Palestine as was baksheesh. Two years later, at a meeting of the Jewish bar, he heard that a position for a justice of the peace in Haifa had opened. He submitted his application.

THE CRYSTALLIZATION OF IDENTITY: AGRANAT ACCEPTS PALESTINIAN CITIZENSHIP

The interview with the appointment committee in Jerusalem was smooth and easy. Agranat's credentials were impeccable, and his fluency in both English and Hebrew made him an attractive candidate for the Mandatory administration, which at that time was looking for a Jewish judge to join Moshe Landau, then the only Jewish magistrate in Haifa. As expected, the interviewers asked Simon if he had a hobby, and he, prepared for the question, responded without hesitation that, yes, he enjoyed playing tennis. Of course, he didn't. As a boy in northwest Chicago he occasionally played baseball, but tennis? That was the game of the upper classes. Moreover, reading, not sports, was his preferred activity. But he calculated that tennis would appeal to English sensibilities. He often saw British officers and civil servants play tennis in Haifa. Surely a colonial committee in quest of a native judge would look favorably on a tennis-playing candidate. His decades in Palestine had instilled in him some of the deference of the native—alienated from the government and yet aware that in order to join them, one must pretend to be like them. He felt unsafe being simply himself before the interviewers. By now he truly desired the job. At the same time, it could be his subconscious way of defying the process. By giving the obvious (and unlikely) answer, he was exposing the grotesqueness of it all, almost mocking the solemnity of the occasion. Be that as it may, the readiness to pretend to be another vanished within forty-eight hours. Summoned again before the committee, he learned that the position was his, conditional on his assumption of Palestinian citizenship. That meant losing his American citizenship. He balked.

"Will I become another Benedict Arnold?" The question leaped to his throat. He had taken himself out of America, but he could not uproot the American in himself. His inner world of associations and metaphors remained American. Benedict Arnold, the general who betrayed his country to the British during the American War of Independence, was the United States' symbol of treason. The image tortured him. Brandeis taught that to be a good American one must become a Zionist, but pledging allegiance to the British Crown? His American patriotic juices, long suppressed, began to flow. He was a son of the state of Illinois, Abraham Lincoln's home state, an admirer of Robert La Follette. He could not turn his back on the United States.

He sought advice from the American consul, who confirmed that pledging allegiance to Great Britain would, indeed, entail the loss of American citizenship. The consul also asked a provocative question: If Simon was a Zionist and wished to make Palestine his home, why not become a Palestinian citizen? Agranat hesitated. He needed to consult his father.

Aaron grew into the world with a different emotional package from that of his son. His memories were of czarist Russia, of persecution, of

America as a haven of safety and prosperity for Jews. Down at the Haifa harbor, boats filled with Jewish refugees were daily turned back by British troops. The future of the Jewish National Home was twisting slowly in the wind as Britannia, in anticipation of war, signaled its readiness to abandon the Balfour Declaration. Was this the time to renounce American citizenship? Could a Jew afford the luxury of believing that Palestine provided safety or that Palestinian citizenship carried meaningful protection? Aaron adamantly opposed the move, no matter what the cost.

The argument was heated. Simon recognized the sensibility of Aaron's position. That caution was the better part of valor was a norm he had already internalized. He now had a wife and two children. He himself had declined Palestinian citizenship before, even though it meant that he was disqualified from voting in the local elections. He remembered the observation of Britain's Peel Commission, appointed to investigate the causes of the 1936 Arab rebellion in Palestine, "that Palestinian 'citizenship' was . . . nothing but a legal formula devoid of moral meaning."[53]

It was his worst personal crisis to date. He wanted the job. He did not wish to continue in legal practice. He dreaded pledging allegiance to the Crown and severing his ties with America. But there was also something deeper. He felt that the American consul's remarks captured a truth: a decision to decline Palestinian citizenship implied a vote of no confidence in Zionism. "Your advice flies in the face of the entire Zionist education you have given me," he recalled telling his father. Simon admired and cherished Aaron; his devotion to Zionism was the very proof of his deep identification with his father. But by now he had a mind of his own.

The acquisition of Palestinian citizenship reflected the psychological maturity of Simon Agranat. He knew what he wanted. He was ready to take risks. He had decided to live in Palestine and was willing to accept it as it was. He believed he should do as he had preached. It was also an act of allegiance to Carmel and their own budding family. Carmel, American-born but Palestine-raised, was passionately attached to Palestine. Their children were sabras, this was home, and if all it could offer was a wobbly Palestinian citizenship, and if it meant forfeiting that precious American citizenship, so be it.[54]

A JUDGE IN PALESTINE, 1940–1948

Agranat's first day as a judge was ceremonious. Representatives of the Jewish bar made a special appearance to congratulate formally the second Jewish judge on the magistrate court. An Arab lawyer, waiting for his case to be heard, also rose to offer congratulations. Judges from the district court, housed in the same building—Arab, English, and Jewish—dropped by to welcome Agranat to the small judicial family of Haifa. In hindsight, the first week of judging seemed to have been his longest ever. He recalled feeling overwhelmed by the experience of heading this public forum, exposed to the scrutiny of lawyers, clients, policemen, the curious, pressured by the need to adjudicate case after case after case, and yet, "I immediately fell in love with the judicial work." Liberated from the "shackles of client interests," Agranat recalled feeling free to ponder the intricacies of the legal problem before him "objectively." The judicial task fit his temperament; he soon grew accustomed to the courtroom atmosphere and came to see judging as a vocation and the judicial chambers as his second home.

Like his first home, this second home was modest and humble. Arthur Koestler, in his book *Thieves in the Night: Chronicle of an Experiment*, written in Palestine during the early 1940s, described the chambers of the magistrate court in Haifa:

He . . . was surprised by the lack of ceremony in the proceedings, the bleakness of the court-room and the informal, almost familiar atmosphere prevailing in it. There were about twelve to fifteen rows of benches, on which policemen and civilians, Jews and Arabs sat mixed together, with the sleepy expression of school-boys when the sun shines outside. Facing them on a dais sat the Magistrate. . . . The dais was only a few inches high, but the table in front of the Magistrate had a marble top, which was the only solemn thing in the room. To the left of the dais were two separate benches at right angles to the others, representing the dock.[55]

In the Mandatory judicial hierarchy, a magistrate judge occupied the lowest position. The colonial civil service consisted of junior and senior divisions, with the magistrates at the bottom of the senior division. In addition to low pay, other attributes served to accentuate low status. Magistrates did not wear judicial robes, were not addressed as "Your Honor" (attorneys in court addressed Simon as "Mr. Agranat"), and had limited jurisdiction, especially if they were native judges.[56]

In everyday life in Palestine, the court was the place where Arabs, Jews, and Englishmen, generally segregated in their own semiautonomous communities, interacted most. Agranat now came into closer contact with Arabs than he ever had before, or ever would in the future. He would frequently hear cases involving Arab litigants or Arab attorneys. He also befriended some of the Arab judges on the court, and he remembered particularly Ahmad Bey Halil, who later was promoted to the position of senior magistrate. Halil, son of a wealthy family who had studied law at the University of Cambridge and occasionally served as liaison between the government and Arab nationalist groups, was the antithesis of the primitive Palestinian stereotype described in Zionist propaganda. It was at a party at Halil's house that Agranat was first introduced to whiskey. "How would you like your whiskey?" Halil asked. Agranat responded, "I never had any." Halil continued, "This will be your first time." For months afterward the English judges who were present at the party took a special delight in retelling the story. It probably fortified the stereotype of the Jew in British eyes, lacking in "cultivation" as compared with the "exotic" Arab urban classes.

World War II, which erupted shortly after Agranat joined the court, was an occasion to remind Englishmen, Arabs, and Jews that no matter what they thought of each other, they were tied to one another by a common destiny. The bombing of Haifa by Italian airplanes in 1940 subjected everybody to the terrifying realization that war was about arbitrary destruction, helplessness, and death and that it was oblivious to status or ethnic origin.[57] It was Agranat's first experience with war, and it hardened him to the events yet to come.

At the same time, the war reminded all of the deep abyss separating Arabs and Jews. Each had a different stake in its outcome. Terror struck the Jews as Rommel's German troops positioned themselves to invade Palestine at the gates of El-Alamein. Jews joined the Palestine Voluntary Force (PVF), organized to face the invasion. Most Arabs rooted for a German victory, which they hoped would terminate the idea of a Jewish National Home. Agranat joined the PVF, went through minimal training, and served on duty regularly.[58] It was a time fraught with anxiety, his first existential encounter with the Jewish vulnerability.

Within Mandatory judicial politics, the need to defend Zionist interests brought Agranat closer to the first Jewish judge on the magistrate court, Moshe Landau. Born in the free city of Danzig and, like Agranat's adored professor, Ernst Freund, Teutonic in manners and style, Landau was a fierce Zionist. The friendship and collaboration between the two would last a lifetime. One of their first endeavors was to preserve the status of Hebrew on the court. The two decided to write their judicial opinions in Hebrew. In 1942, ostensibly for reasons of efficiency and cost cutting, the president of the district court instructed them henceforth to write their opinions in English.[59] They staged a minirevolt. In a meeting with the president, Agranat recalled delivering a lecture on Zionism in which he insisted that "Hebrew and the Jewish People go together." The two hinted that if and when the Jewish bar, perhaps the Yishuv as a whole, heard about this policy shift, there would be a public uproar. It was, possibly, Agranat's very first political triumph. Within days the chief clerk informed them that the president had decided to postpone implementation of his order. The demand was never raised again. It is instructive that Agranat did not know whether a similar directive was sent to the Arab judges. When it came to Zionist interests, Jews preferred not to explore the possibility of a Jewish–Arab alliance against the British.

But despite the fundamental disagreements and adversity, there was enough in the necessities of everyday life to require Arab–Jewish cooperation. At the end of the war, when the English chief justice of Palestine decided to meet the dire shortage of judges by recruiting "temporary judges," enticing them with offers of pay higher than that offered the tenured judiciary (but no benefits), the judges of Palestine—Arabs as well as Jews—united to demand a raise. Ahmad Bey Halil and Agranat found themselves members of the same delegation, representing Haifa before the Mandatory government in Jerusalem and threatening a judicial strike should their demands go unmet.

A few of the cases before the magistrate court involved the criminal law, but most were cases about commercial papers or housing.[60] The war, the influx of immigrants and refugees in the 1930s, and the territorial segregation between Arabs and Jews caused an acute housing shortage, and eviction litigation was common. For Agranat, these were akin to criminal proceedings: "From the point of view of the fate of the individual, they were almost like murder trials." What should a judge do when an apartment owner, who had previously rented a room or two, expanded her family, needed more space, and wanted to evict her tenants? For Agranat, the question of "Where will the tenant go?" was not legally irrelevant. He would often personally inspect the premises before he issued a ruling, and frequently he opted for solutions that partitioned property in order to accommodate all parties. Thus he preferred a balancing approach and a compromise over a strict application of the right to private property. More and more his judicial experience confirmed the insight he had read in so many critiques of legal formalism, that a judge intuits the result before he begins to write the opinion. He recalled that "I never wrote an opinion without knowing in advance what the result would be. I never started with the facts to see how it would go."

These were the years when Agranat's judicial philosophy was crystallizing. As a law student he had been introduced to the idea that every legal rule was the result of the balancing of interests, that balancing was the preferred approach to legal problems, that the text of legal norms was not enough to make a good decision, and that context had to be taken into account. Now, with several years of legal experience behind him, he felt increasingly aligned with this approach, known as progressive jurisprudence.[61] Its rival approach, mechanical jurisprudence or legal formalism—the idea that a legal solution followed automatically from the application of the legal rule—appeared to him more and more as pedestrian and narrow minded. He was now reading Holmes and Brandeis, Cardozo and Pound, with extra care and with ever-growing appreciation.[62] The more he reflected on the nature of the judicial process, the more critical he became of the Mandatory system, which appeared to him as excessively formalistic, and the more he tried to show, in as discreet and inoffensive a way as he could, that a legal opinion need not be full of what Felix Cohen called "transcendental nonsense."[63]

His opinions tended to be uncommonly long. Early in his judicial career he had developed what came to be known as the Agranat trademark: elaborate opinions, endlessly weighing arguments and counterarguments, meticulously listing and pondering precedents, exposing the historical roots of legal doctrine. Why did he write at such length, if he had already determined what the result should be? Later, when he joined Israel's Supreme Court, he explained this tendency as the need to elevate the level of legal discourse in the new state by setting an example, educating bench and bar about the value of legal analysis. But the fact that he developed the habit when he was still a magistrate suggests that this could not be the only explanation. As a magistrate he was not in a position to set an example or to educate, yet he adopted the elaborate style. One reason was ambition. He was hoping that a display of legal virtuosity would earn him a promotion to the district court. That explanation is fairly plausible.[64] Another explanation surfaced in interviews with me: he was writing for himself. Sensitive to the indeterminacy of legal doctrine, to the two sides of each coin, he needed to persuade himself that his result was justified. He felt compelled to expose the process of legal deliberation in order to feel at peace with the result.

The Haifa bench and bar, however, were puzzled by his style. Mostly provincial and formalistic, viewing law as something one did for a living, not as an intellectual pursuit, the legal community felt that Agranat's opinions were a hindrance to an efficient resolution of legal problems and an unnecessary obfuscation of clear doctrine. The deputy president of the district court, particularly allergic to Agranat's opinions, would often sardonically begin an appeal with, "This is another lengthy judgement from the learned magistrate." Yitzhak Kahan, then a practicing lawyer in Haifa, remembered these remarks as demeaning and humiliating. Only a few understood the fine legal quality of Agranat's work. Jacob S. Shapiro, later Israel's first attorney general, was one. Chief Justice Frederic Gordon-Smith was another. In 1943, sitting on appeal, Gordon-Smith broke the tradition of silence regarding the work of the lower tribunals to praise Agranat openly: "The judgement of the Magistrate goes into the facts and law at length, is lucidly expressed and, irrespective of whether the decision is right or wrong, is an admirable judgement which reflects great credit on the Magistrate (Mr. Agranat)."[65] The praise was balm for Agranat's wounds, but when the promotion failed to arrive and the pay no longer covered the expenses for a family of six, he began to contemplate returning to private practice. In 1947 Acting Chief Justice Bernard Vidal Shaw urged the frustrated magistrate to wait. He was loath to lose one of the judiciary's most talented judges. Indeed, the 25 November 1947 issue of *Ha-Arets,* the Yishuv's mainstream newspaper, informed its readers that Agranat was recommended for promotion to the district court. Four days later, however, the United Nations passed the Partition Resolution, and all governmental activity came to a halt.

AARON PASSES AWAY, SPRING 1946

Aaron Agranat was a fortunate man. He was a successful dentist. He was a public persona well known and respected in Haifa's social circles. He had lived to see Zionism rise from an ideology espoused by a few fanatics to a full-fledged movement supported by a substantial population. He witnessed the triumph of the Allies in World War II. His sons were married and established. Three days after he had suffered a stroke, Aaron passed away. Simon grieved. Aaron's untimely death signaled the end of an era. After the traditional shivah (seven days of mourning), Simon did not heed the halakhic (Jewish legal) rule of remaining unshaven for an entire month. Tradition, according to Agranat, could be and should be tempered by secular modernity.

THE STRUGGLE FOR INDEPENDENCE

As soon as the German threat to invade Palestine receded, relations between the British and the Yishuv took a turn for the worse.

The Zionist leadership insisted on the implementation of the Biltmore Program: the establishment of an independent Jewish commonwealth in Palestine.[66] Tension kept mounting once victory over the Axis powers became final. In November 1945, Jewish resistance flexed its muscles by launching a major attack on railroads all over Palestine and sinking several coastal patrol boats. In June 1946, all the bridges connecting Palestine with neighboring countries were blown up. In an effort to break the back of the resistance, the British enacted the Defense (Emergency) Regulations,[67] suspending civil liberties in Palestine. Choosing the one day when even secular Jews were expected to stay home—Saturday—the British army imposed a general curfew and arrested about 3,000 members of the Yishuv leadership.[68] In Haifa the wave of detentions began at dawn, and the first arrests took place at 4:15 A.M. At about 6:00 P.M. police cars cruised Agranat's neighborhood announcing the curfew. The city sank into a state of siege. Armored cars and British soldiers filled the streets. The oppressive feeling was further aggravated by secrecy. Military censorship had effectively blocked all information about what came to be known as the "black Sabbath." *Ha-Arets* called it "the gravest and most sinister of the cabals schemed against our national home in the last twenty-six years."[69] The next morning an armored army vehicle arrived at Judge Agranat's apartment building. He was taken to a downtown hotel, to administer the trials of curfew violators.

What does a judge do when he perceives justice and law to be set on a collision course? For Agranat, justice was on the Zionist side; the legal machinery deployed by the British to crush the political aspirations of the Yishuv was unjust. But as a judge, he believed he had to apply the law as it was. He was acutely mindful of the moral content of law. A philosophy advocating the separation of law and morality, which would make the application of unjust law less painful, was not a part of his worldview.[70] Would he now assist the British, his employers, in enforcing a curfew designed to crush the political aspirations of his people? True, he could resign, return to legal practice, and use his legal skills to defend the Yishuv. But one less Jewish magistrate in the Haifa courts might mean less everyday justice for Jews; it would certainly mean a change for the worse in the balance of power between Arabs and Jews in governing Palestine. This was not the first time Agranat had been caught in such a moral dilemma. He had had occasion earlier to try Jews charged with stealing ammunition from British military bases or with smuggling refugees across the border. In those instances, he recalled, he sided with the law.

Again he avoided open defiance. He convicted the curfew violators but imposed only nominal fines.[71] He did not experience this as a betrayal of the Zionist cause. In an interview, he insisted that his loyalty to the Yishuv was explicitly stated when he had joined the Haganah, never resigning from its ranks even after he had been appointed a judge and when the organization was outlawed and went underground. Also, he was a regular payer of the voluntary tax known as *kofer ha-yishuv.* But he recalled feeling helpless and subdued as he discharged his judicial duties in the aftermath of Black Saturday.

• • •

It was an autumn night in Haifa on 29 November 1947 when the General Assembly of the United Nations considered the recommendation that the British Mandate be terminated and that Palestine be partitioned into Jewish and Arab states. Agranat recalled standing in the hall between his apartment and that of his neighbor, tensely listening to the debate, which was broadcast live from New York City. The Agranats had purchased their first small radio a few months earlier, but the neighbor's transmission was better, and Agranat was determined to hear everything. He had changed his mind since the first suggestion of partitioning Palestine was considered by the Peel Commission in 1937. For a long time he had favored a binational state, perhaps because of his strong sentiments against secession associated with the American Civil War. Now he believed that partition was inevitable. The two peoples, albeit each tied to the land in its own way, were incapable of jointly governing it. Simon's elation mounted as the votes were counted. When the result was announced, 33 to 13 in favor, with 10 abstentions, many Jews took to dancing in the streets, seeking togetherness to express their joy at being recognized by the international community. With four small children to care for, the Agranats celebrated at home. They were coming close to the dream they had cherished since childhood.

The Palestinian Arabs, however, immediately rejected the idea of partition. Britain, refusing to take sides, announced it was terminating the Mandate and evacuating its forces on 15 May 1948. Since the 1980s, with the benefit of hindsight, young historians have been able to demonstrate that the outcome was predictable, that the Jewish military organization was superior to the Palestinian forces, and that Jewish forces could even stand against the organized armies of the Arab states.[72] But to ordinary Jews in 1947 the reality looked ominous. Panic struck many of Simon's friends, who doubted the ability of the tiny Jewish population to survive without British protection and yearned for the continuation of the Mandate. Their European experience led them to fear that another Holocaust was imminent. A dispatch from the American Consulate in Jerusalem, concerning American citizens in Palestine, corroborated the sense of doom: "The question of protection of American citizens . . . is problematical. . . . [A] large number of the American citizens here are Jewish. Any Arab uprising will not distinguish between American and other Jews. . . . Americans of Palestinian Arab origin are making arrangements to leave the country as far as possible. A similar Jewish trend may be prevented by their inability to reach this Consulate in safety."[73]

Agranat recalled drawing sustenance from the American War of Independence. He knew it was possible for the few to overcome the many and was hoping that, against all odds, the same would happen in Palestine. One more time, his positive American experience and his ability to identify with American history served as a source of strength and optimism.

Haifa had more than its share of violence and strife. From the adoption of the Partition Resolution in late November 1947 until the Jewish conquest of Haifa in late April 1948, 140 Jews and 184 Arabs were killed. Everyday activities were fraught with danger. Agranat's judicial session was once interrupted by bullets fired right into the courtroom. No one was hurt, but the judges were sufficiently alarmed to cancel the trials for the day. Because of the rising tensions, Agranat resumed service in the Haganah and again stood guard at the Bourge, the street connecting Jewish Haifa to the downtown, mainly Arab section.

Terror pervaded the atmosphere. Judge Landau suspected the young Arab clerk they had shared. The clerk seemed restless. Could they trust him? And the Arab litigants—would they not confuse a natural hostility litigants harbor against a judge ruling against them with their animosity toward Jews in general? Agranat and Landau acquired permits to carry pistols. Agranat took the pistol out of its leather pouch, filled it with bullets, and attached it to his belt under his coat, "like the Wild West," he recalled, only half joking.

Neither stories of the Wild West nor even a pistol tied to his belt can prepare a man for an actual encounter with violent death. One morning, early in 1948, as Agranat was crossing the street to enter the courthouse, a commotion froze him in his shoes. A man, hit by a sniper, was dying in a pool of blood in the middle of the street at the entrance to the court. A few yards away a British police car was parked, the soldiers inert, symbolizing the collapse of law and order. The dying man was alone. No one dared approach him, lest he or she be a live target for the unseen sniper. No scene could better describe the chaos that descended on Palestine during the dusk of the British Mandate. A man shot in front of the courthouse—the symbol of the law—the police watching, determined not to get involved, the civilians petrified by fear and helplessness. Agranat was faced with a terrible dilemma: should he take the risk and approach the man? "I said to myself: I have a wife and four children. It is not fair to them to risk my life. Retreat is the better part of valor."

"What do you think of me, now that I told you this story?" he asked me. "Not too complimentary for my character, is it?" He puffed his pipe.

No. But it made him more human. It does take training, a certain hardening, to overcome fear in the face of death. Agranat did not have to tell the story, and, had he not done so, in all probability it would never have reached the printed page. He may not have been the most courageous member of a community terrorized by violence and strife, but he recognized that and did not spare himself. I remember him saying, in another context, that as a judge he would always warn himself: "There, but for the grace of God, go I."

Life went on even behind the roadblocks, barbed wire, and trenches that now marked the line between Jewish and Arab Haifa. Judicial work proceeded almost as usual. Businessmen, worried about the future of their vested interests, pressed for prompt decisions before the British evacuation. The Mandatory government decided that postponement of trials for reasons of extreme danger on the roads would not be permitted. Only official curfew would justify postponement.[74] It must have felt strange to try cases without knowing whether the decrees would be enforced, without knowing whether one would still be a judge a few months hence. The British judges were scheduled to evacuate Palestine with the termination of the Mandate. Would there be a Jewish state? Would the new state invite Mandatory judges to continue their service? And what if the Jews lost the war?

Arab judges (the majority on the court) and Jewish judges were eyeing each other with anxious indignation. Each group was actively involved in the political struggle. Slowly the majority of the Palestinian middle class began to pack up and leave. The battle of Haifa took place during the third week of April, on the eve of Passover. On 21 April, Ahmad Bey Halil, the chief magistrate of the Haifa courts and the only remaining representative of the Arab High Committee, the executive body of the organized Palestinian-Arab community, left for Lebanon by sea.[75] His departure signified the end of an era. Within two days the city of Haifa would be in Jewish hands. Of the 70,000 Arabs in Haifa in 1947, only 3,000 remained to witness the birth of the state of Israel on 14 May 1948.

It was a tragic irony of history that in celebrating the re-creation of the Jewish state after the forced exodus two millennia earlier, the Yishuv had helped bring about the exodus of the Palestinians. The fact that this was Passover evening, when Jews celebrate their own exodus from slavery in Egypt, only deepened the irony. The Agranats, however, experienced the joyful reality of Jewish victory. A civil war had raged, in which one lived or died. They had expected Arab victory to mean not only the end of the Zionist dream but also physical decimation. Like most Jews in Haifa, they were delirious over their victory and hardly thought about the misery of the defeated. Agranat, who himself harbored fear of but not animosity toward the Arabs, understood the Arab flight from Haifa to be voluntary, not coerced. He strongly insisted, until the end of his life, that "no one forced them to go. They left."

Victory in battle did not mean victory in war. Agranat was full of worries about the political future. The press reported that the United States preferred another trusteeship. The Arab states threatened to invade Palestine if a Jewish state were declared.[76] Yet Agranat supported the bold move of declaring independence. When David Ben-Gurion declared the establishment of the state of Israel on Friday, 14 May 1948, Agranat pushed away his worries and rejoiced in the fulfillment of his dream. On Passover of 1922, as an adolescent of sixteen, Simon had argued passionately with his friends in Chicago about the necessity of a Jewish state. In 1948 the state came to be, and Simon felt privileged to partake in its creation.

PART II

LAYING THE FOUNDATIONS FOR A JUDICIAL BILL OF RIGHTS

CHAPTER 3

Israel, 1948–1953

FROM THE DISTRICT COURT TO THE SUPREME COURT

What happens at twilight, after a colonial power has left but the sovereign government is barely installed? The British behaved like shopkeepers closing a store: they locked the court buildings and kept the keys. The shutdown symbolized not only the British refusal to choose between Arabs and Jews but also the suspension of law and order.

Overnight Palestine had become Israel and its citizens Israelis. When Judges Agranat and Landau, one week after Independence, arrived at the court, they found the chambers shut and deserted. Landau remembered Agranat's personally kicking the door open, giving a little push to set the wheels of justice in motion again.[1] Agranat remembered instructing the clerks to kick the door. Elated by the sweet taste of Independence, they were not prepared, in Agranat's words, to "let an Israeli court be closed even for one day." The episode serves as a metaphor for the condition of Israeli justice in 1948. The doors of the legal system had to be forced open, and the very act of breaking through was imbued with the symbolism of a new era. Still, the structures wherefrom justice was to be dispensed remained the same.

The question of the future of the judiciary now became acute. With the departure of the English and Arab judges, the courts of Haifa shrank to a small fraction of their previous size. Five judges remained to serve the population. Other judicial districts in Israel experienced a similar collapse; only Tel Aviv, the one wholly Jewish city, was not affected. An entire judicial corps had to be assembled — and quickly. The burden fell on Pinhas Rosen, minister of justice in the provisional government.

Rosen's appointment as minister of justice is itself revealing. In the coalition government he represented the tiny Progressive Party, and putting him in charge of the justice portfolio indicated that law was not a priority for MAPAI, David Ben-Gurion's ruling party. Rosen, a prominent lawyer and an active Zionist, was thought fit for the job because, among other reasons, of his German background.[2] In the hierarchy of the ethnic groups that composed the 650,000 members of the Yishuv, German Jews ranked highest in terms of refined legal culture and respect for law and order. In Tel Aviv, headquarters of the provisional government,[3] Rosen and his staff were laying the foundations for Israel's judiciary.

Rosen's attorney general was Jacob S. Shapiro, a short and savvy man whose reputation soared when he represented the Yishuv in trials related to illegal Jewish immigration by sea. In previous years Shapiro had handled the Haifa business of Rosen's law firm and had used its Jerusalem offices. Apart from a close professional relationship, which must have made the choice more appealing, Shapiro had another important asset: he ranked high in MAPAI circles and enjoyed the confidence of Ben-Gurion. Rosen and Shapiro complemented each other well. If Rosen represented the German component, the Russian-born Shapiro represented the less formal, more peppery, Eastern European *yiddishkeit*. Also, whereas Rosen did not conceal his clear preference for the continental legal model, Shapiro was overtly partial to the English way of doing things.

A longtime Haifa resident, Shapiro planned Rosen's visit to Haifa in June 1948, to acquaint the minister of justice with the bar and to initiate judicial appointments. Agranat had been Shapiro's close friend since they prepared for the bar examination in 1933, and the two had discussed the impending changes prior to Rosen's visit. Years later, Shapiro remembered Agranat's threatening to resign if he were not appointed president of the district court. "For the first time, I saw that Shimon had an appreciation of himself," Shapiro mused to me in a interview. In a way, Shapiro was right. Agranat was an ambitious man, but he was too proud to make explicit demands. It may well be that the volatility of the situation propelled him to overcome his inhibitions and to insist on a grand promotion. Shapiro, who had admired Agranat's learned opinions as a magistrate, had even grander plans for his friend. He lobbied Rosen to include Agranat among the five appointees to Israel's Supreme Court. One item on Rosen's agenda during his visit to Haifa was to assess Agranat's candidacy for that position.[4]

Agranat liked what he heard from Rosen that afternoon as Haifa's Jewish judges and lawyers assembled to greet the minister. Rosen spoke of extensive legal reform, of plans for a constitution and for the fulfillment of the Zionist aspiration to create a just society. He also spoke—thereby endearing himself to Agranat—against the excessive formalism of the bar. "There was a lawyer among us," Agranat recalled Rosen's telling his audience, "who sought to invalidate a contract on the ground that it lacked the required stamps. What a great legal argument," Rosen added, sarcastically. "The man's gravestone will read 'here is buried the man of stamps.'" After a personal discussion with Agranat, Rosen was sufficiently impressed to inform him that he would be a nominee to the impending Supreme Court.

For once, Agranat felt the intoxicating sensation of having one's wildest dreams fulfilled—the end of foreign domination, the creation of the new Israeli state, and now ascension to the highest post a judge could have. He was the happiest of fathers, as he celebrated the bar mitzvah of Israel, his older son. The press announced the provisional government's list of five candidates for the Court, including Agranat.[5] Congratulations poured in. At home, a mini-insurrection raged as the Agranat children announced that they would not leave their hometown. The sensation of success was spreading when a telephone call summoned Agranat to meet with Rosen in Tel Aviv.

The Ministry of Justice did not yet have its own headquarters. Official business was conducted in hotels; and over coffee at the Dan Hotel, Rosen delivered the bitter news. The government had decided to drop Agranat's nomination. For political reasons, it was important to obtain the broadest support for the nominations from the Provisional State Council (which preceded the Knesset). The General Zionists threatened to oppose any list that failed to include its own candidate, Shneur Z. Cheshin.[6] Rosen felt compelled to sacrifice Agranat in order to obtain the unanimous vote. Agranat recalled his frustration. The seeming insulation of the judiciary from political considerations could not shelter him from the ugly hand of politics. Indignant, his immediate reaction was to cut all ties to the courts. He offered his resignation. But Rosen would not hear of it; even being considered for the Supreme Court was a great honor, Rosen said, trying to soften the blow. The district court was Agranat's; and in the near future, Rosen gently hinted, if the cabinet approved the expansion of the Court, Agranat would be the sixth nominee. Rosen's warmth and empathy helped calm Agranat. "Stay," Rosen implored. "Let us go to hear the Philharmonic tonight." Israel's Philharmonic Orchestra symbolized the bond between the West and the reconstructed Zionist civilization. An invitation to listen to its music together was both a reminder of the sensibilities Rosen and Agranat shared and an assurance of personal friendship despite the pain and public embarrassment Rosen just inflicted on Agranat. Agranat stayed. The sound of *Peter and the Wolf* helped him regain his perspective. Armed with his appointment as president of the district court, he returned to Haifa.

INAUGURATING THE DISTRICT COURT

One argument for preferring Cheshin over Agranat was seniority. Cheshin had been a district court judge since 1944, whereas Agranat had only served as a magistrate. Considerations of seniority, however, did not prevent Rosen from bypassing the two Jewish district court judges in Haifa in favor of Agranat. Judge Aharon Shams, widely considered an anti-Zionist, was undergoing quasi-official disciplinary proceedings for allegedly having helped his son avoid military service. Why Judge Ya'acov Azoulai, another Sephardi, was bypassed is less clear. The Ministry of Justice had insisted that the preference was motivated by considerations of merit alone.[7]

Presiding over men who only yesterday were his superiors was an awkward task. Agranat's modesty and gentle nature enabled him to provide a smooth start. Intuitively he knew that teamwork would diffuse the resentment his elevation must have generated. He sought Azoulai's advice about the pending inauguration of the court; he also suggested that the two visit Judge Shams, whose illness had confined him to bed. Azoulai also rose to the occasion, and the first district court in Israeli Haifa was ready for inauguration.

The police offered a special guard of honor. A taxi was arranged to drive the judges, because Agranat believed that arrival by bus would undercut the solemnity of the occasion. Because, as a magistrate, he did not have the privilege of wearing a judicial robe, he rummaged through the judicial chambers and was relieved to find a gown, red ribboned around the collar and sleeves, left behind by a British judge.[8] In full attire and with modest pomp, President Agranat led the judges past the saluting guard and into the judicial chambers. The court was officially open for judicial business.

The Agranats now discovered the privileges associated with public office. A telephone—a very scarce commodity in Israel of 1948—was installed in their apartment. As a senior judge, Agranat was able to persuade the army to postpone the induction of the family's maid into military service. With four small children, domestic help was crucial for Carmel. Otherwise, Agranat continued his old lifestyle. He remained a workaholic, and his life continued to revolve around his judicial opinions. Now, however, he was in a position of leadership, and his opinions could make more of a difference.

One of his early opinions, reported by *Ha-Arets,* invalidated a conviction issued by his Mandatory predecessor. Two weeks before the end of the Mandate, the English president of the district court had convicted a man of violating the price-control laws. The conviction was entered on the basis of a guilty plea by someone who had claimed to represent the accused. Agranat invalidated the conviction, seizing the opportunity to assert the commitment of the new state to justice and to ground this commitment in the Jewish ethos. A cardinal principle of justice, he announced, was that a guilty plea should come only from the accused himself. This rule should be zealously guarded, Agranat said, particularly because in Jewish law even a guilty plea by the accused himself would not suffice for conviction.[9] Agranat also tried to disconnect the emerging Israeli system from the Mandate by avoiding the death penalty prescribed for certain crimes by the criminal code. In the next two years he would lobby the Knesset to abolish the death penalty. The excitement of the establishment of the state had rekindled his deep commitment to social and legal reform. He was preparing to contribute his share to turning Israel into the model state he had always dreamed it would become.

THE INAUGURATION OF THE SUPREME COURT

Four months after the establishment of Israel, Agranat attended the ceremony inaugurating the Supreme Court. In August 1948, when the Ministry of Justice announced that the Supreme Court would occupy the building that had previously housed the Supreme Court of Palestine, Jerusalem was a divided city, its Jewish Quarter and Western Wall under Jordanian control and its population shaken and distraught. The long siege and the ferocious war had taken their toll. The building designated for the Court was located in the Russian Compound, less than a five-minute walk from the cease-fire line. On lease from the White Russian Church, the hostel-turned-court was deficient in both decor and facilities. Why such a humble home for the highest court of the land?

In the summer of 1948, Tel Aviv was the indisputable center of governmental affairs. The justices had their eyes on a certain building on Tel Aviv's posh Rothschild Boulevard, not far from the site where the Jewish state had been declared. Although the provisional government was proud to establish the Supreme Court, to further symbolize sovereign Israel's place in the family of enlightened nations, such mundane matters as judicial facilities were rather low on its priority list. Tel Aviv suffered from an acute housing shortage, and the building originally targeted by the justices went to the Soviet Embassy instead. Protracted negotiations followed, and the justices became increasingly disheartened; a few threatened to resign. Only then was the idea of reoccupying the old building in Jerusalem raised. Later, long after the City of David had been officially annexed to Israel and embraced as its eternal capital, the establishment of the Court in Jerusalem was hailed as symbolic of the revival of Jewish political life. The actual reality, however, was much more prosaic. The Supreme Court of Israel was established in Jerusalem more out of necessity than out of choice.[10]

Making his way from Haifa to Jerusalem to attend the inaugural ceremony, Agranat was torn between elation and sadness. Palestine was now divided between Jordan and Israel. Latrun, the crossroad to Jerusalem, which he had passed endless times in the past, was now enemy territory. A few passengers made their way through the "Burma road," a path carved in the mountains by Israel's army, in order to break the Arab blockade of Jerusalem. An occasional charred vehicle served as a stark reminder of the 6,000 youths, one full percent of Israel's Jewish population, who died in battle for Israel's Independence. The road was not fit for travel. At one point, the travelers were instructed to disembark from their vehicle and proceed by foot to facilitate passage through a particularly bumpy piece of road. They arrived at a sadly ravaged Jerusalem, wary of its future.

It was 13 September 1948 in Ellul, the last month on the Jewish calendar, devoted to soul searching in anticipation of Rosh Hashanah and Yom Kippur. Present were a few reporters, representatives of the Israeli judiciary, the minister of justice, the attorney general, the justices, and Colonel Moshe Dayan, military governor of Hebrew Jerusalem. It was a humble occasion, yet the assembly bravely suspended its worries and its resentment at the rough treatment inflicted by the administration, in order to rejoice in the fulfillment of the Zionist dream. To the music of sporadic bullets, Minister of Justice Rosen rose to inaugurate the court. "Honorable judges, like a nanny carrying the baby I hand over to you today this child of joy, precious of precious, which was raised and developed for many difficult and tiring months. May it stand on its feet and carry it-self and shine like heaven." The Child of Joy who shines like heaven in Jewish sources is Ephraim, and Ephraim, according to tradition, is the name of the "Messiah whose light shines from one end of the world to the other." The minister of justice was thinking of redemption (*geulah*) as he inaugurated the Court.[11] Chief Justice Moshe Smoira continued in the same vein: "For almost two millennia the Jewish people were pray-ing three times a day, 'Restore our judges as at first'; trembling we ap-proach today the fulfillment of this vision."[12]

The creation of the state of Israel rekindled the flame of utopian Zion-ism. Everyone expected that Israel would soon have a constitution.[13] The judges expected to partake in the miracle of Jewish revival, pursuing jus-tice under law.[14] And yet, grim reality kept chilling the grand expectations.

AN EQUAL BRANCH OF GOVERNMENT?

Rosen kept his promise, and Agranat was appointed to the Supreme Court in January 1949, six months after its inauguration.[15] He found his five brethren operating under dire circumstances. The eupho-ria had faded, and the hardships of everyday life were taking their toll. The winter of 1949 was bitterly cold, heating oil was scarce, and the jus-tices were freezing in their chambers. Smoira arranged for electric heaters to be placed in the court's chambers (not an easy task, given the regime of rationing and the fact that heaters were a luxury), only to find that the electrical system in the building was insufficient to meet the demands. Short-circuits occurred with maddening frequency. The rain, the winds, and the high ceilings and stone walls all conspired against warmth and comfort. Paper was scarce. The opinions of the first few years of the Supreme Court of Israel were written on the reverse side of completed Mandatory forms left in the wake of the British evacuation. The cheap ink stained the cheap paper. There was no library and no way to verify the legal citations relied on by the lawyers pleading before the Court.

More stinging was the wind blowing from the government. Revolu-tionary times usually inflate the significance of the executive branch. Is-rael's leaders had good intentions about, and high expectations from, the rule of law. But it is one thing to appreciate the theory behind separation of powers and checks and balances, and quite another to experience these limitations in practice. The executive rejected liberal principles as soon as they appeared to contradict necessity. The Knesset, well aware of the

potential abuse inherent in a strong executive, swiftly secured its own status by granting itself parliamentary immunity, broader than any known
in the Western world.[16] A bill providing for full independence of the judiciary would be enacted only after much struggle and a number of crises,
in the summer of 1953.[17] Stories from this period abound, describing a
mean-spirited attitude toward the judiciary. The justices were not included
in the list of regular invitees to formal ceremonies and public events.
Negotiations concerning salary and benefits were always adversarial and
frequently humiliating. The Ministry of Foreign Affairs, in an inexplica-
bly niggardly mood, refused to issue the justices diplomatic passports
for travel, despite agreement that they were equal in status to cabinet
ministers.[18]

This state of affairs can only be explained by an ambivalence toward
the idea of legality. The political culture of the Yishuv contained deep
streaks of lawlessness. As revolutionaries constantly fighting convention
and the powers that be, both within and without Judaism, the Zionists
were not, could not, be law abiding. The acceptance of illegality as a legitimate mode of behavior gained particular ascendancy during the
1940s, when the Mandatory government outlawed the Haganah, prohibited the purchase of Arab land by Jews, and, most importantly, prohibited Jewish immigration into the country.[19] At the same time, MAPAI's
leaders rejected the liberal notion that law was independent of social im-
peratives. If reality was socially constructed and people were responsible
for shaping its content and institutional forms, as they had firmly believed,
then law was nothing but a tool to advance the particular ideology that
dominated society. The legal system in general, then, and the courts in
particular were expected to pursue and implement the needs of the nation as articulated by the government.

Looming above this complexity was chronic anxiety about survival.
There was a sense that national security was at stake in almost every important legal issue raised before the Court, that every adverse move would
weaken the government, hence the state, and that deference to the needs
of the executive was imperative to the survival of the fledgling nation.
Not surprisingly, these elements seemed to strengthen catastrophe Zionism—the idea that history is a chain of calamities perpetrated against the
Jews. Simultaneously, this condition conspired to tame the great hopes
of utopian Zionism for a just legal system, worthy of the vision of the
great prophets of Israel. Nothing illustrated this state of affairs in the
nascent Israeli political culture better than the events that occurred within
two weeks of the inauguration of the Supreme Court.

THE ASSASSINATION OF COUNT BERNADOTTE

In 1950 Agranat was appointed chairman of the investigative commission to look into the assassination of Count Folke Bernadotte. Bernadotte, the U.N. mediator for Palestine, was assassinated on 17 September 1948 in Rehavia, Jerusalem, then under Israeli military control. The assassination occurred four days after the inauguration of the Court. Israelis were almost uniformly hostile to the Swedish count. His plans to end the war included a substantial shrinkage of Israeli territory, an unconditional return of Palestinian refugees, and a denial of Israeli sovereignty over Jerusalem. But whereas Ben-Gurion's government was pursuing its offensive against Bernadotte through diplomatic channels, extremists of the far right deployed the tactics they had mastered during British rule—terrorism. The assassins were members of Lohame Herut Yisrael (LEHI; Fighters for the Liberation of Israel, known abroad as the Stern Gang).[20]

The assassination touched the deepest fears in the provisional government. Not yet accepted as a member of the United Nations, yearning for international legitimacy and recognition, the government feared it would be judged by international public opinion either as condoning terrorism or as unable to control its own turf.[21] Even worse, the assassination fanned fears of an internal putsch.[22] The government reacted swiftly. The existing emergency powers were ruthlessly applied,[23] further emergency regulations for the prevention of terrorism were promulgated,[24] and, as if these were not enough, the government asked the Provisional State Council to enact the same regulations into law.[25] The statute, quite similar to the Defense (Emergency) Regulations already in force, reflected the stress Israel's leadership experienced as a result of the assassination.[26] These maneuvers also disclosed the government's impatience with conventional principles of due process and disdain for political and civil liberties. In the debate in the Provisional Parliament, responding to Liberal objections that the proposed bill violated due process, Prime Minister Ben-Gurion reflected on law and lawyers: "The question is this: have we been made for the legal principle or has the legal principle been made for us? Every jurist knows how easy it is to weave juridical cobwebs to prove anything and refute anything. . . . [A]s a [former] law student I know that no one can distort any text and invent farfetched assumptions and confusing interpretation like the jurist. . . . [W]e need recognition of the reality and knowledge of the facts, and this should be decisive, not juristic, legalisms."[27]

While it resolutely crushed dissidents at home, the government sought to show its uprightness abroad. The Swedish government, conducting an independent inquiry, concluded that Israel's failure to supply the count with armed escorts was reckless and that the Israeli police investigation lacked the necessary rigor and desire to find the assassins. On 22 March 1950 Ben-Gurion's cabinet appointed a commission to study the Swedish report and make recommendations to the government. Agranat was its chairman.

The sixty-two-page Agranat Commission report rejected some of the Swedish conclusions. The commission found that "the failure to supply an armed escort should not be placed at the feet of Israel's government." It agreed with the Swedish report, that the investigation by the Jerusalem Police Department was "negligent and incompetent." However, the commission rejected the Swedish assertion that there was an Israeli policy to avoid bringing the assassins to justice and attributed the flawed investigations to the political chaos in Israel in general, and in Jerusalem in particular, at the time of the assassination. The commission declined to recommend a new police investigation into the matter but said that the file should remain open and that if the assassins were found they should be brought to justice. The report, kept secret for more than forty years, did contain some criticism of the government and ended with a recommendation that Israel apologize to Sweden for the deficient investigation.[28]

In hindsight, it is quite evident that Ben-Gurion did not do all he could to find the assassins, partially because he feared fanning political passions and preferred to quell the LEHI and Irgun forces by other means.[29] The language of the report amounts more to a defense of the Israeli government than to the findings of an impartial arbiter. The Agranat Commission, it appears, bent over backward to assist the government in what it perceived to be a major international crisis.[30] More than thirty years after the events, Agranat recalled the commission's anxious effort to "prove to the world that the State did all it could to prevent terrorism" and particularly to persuade the Scandinavian countries, which had suspended their recognition of Israel pending the investigation, that Israel's government was innocent of wrongdoing and could be trusted as a law-abiding sovereign.

The entire episode captured well the multilayered attitude toward law, order, and the role of the judiciary that dominated Israeli culture in its formative years. On the surface was the government's commitment to a democracy under law, manifested in the establishment of a judicial system, the enactment of the Prevention of Terrorism Ordinance, and the appointment of a commission of inquiry. Underneath lay the perception that the concept of justice lacked a well-defined core and that law was an instrument to further social goals. Still deeper lay the perception on the part of Israel's ruling elite that the normative order, particularly as it was administered by members of the legal profession, was nothing but a sterile set of cobwebs, an obstacle rather than a means of obtaining justice. At bottom lay the belief, widely shared by both members of left and right, that what really mattered was "what the Jews do." Not values, norms, or words but action made the difference, and everything else diminished before the main, colossal task of surviving as a sovereign state.[31]

The Bernadotte affair captured the impossible dilemma faced by the legal profession in matters of national security: on one hand, judges and lawyers wished to restrain the executive branch, maintain the rule of law, and expose manifestations of illegality. On the other hand, they were constantly aware of the government's fragility, the dangers from without and within. There was always a sense that the state was holding on by the skin of its teeth; that the world was arrayed against "us," applying a magnifying glass to Israel's slips and errors; that citizens had a duty to protect the government against the chorus of ill-wishers. This dilemma, the tension between utopian and catastrophe Zionism, would accompany Agranat for decades to come.

CHAPTER 4

In Quest of Progressive Reform

*The State of Israel . . . will be based on freedom, justice
and peace as envisaged by the prophets of Israel; it will
ensure complete equality of social and political rights to all
its inhabitants irrespective of religion, race or sex; it will
guarantee freedom of religion, conscience, language, education
and culture.*

— Declaration of the Establishment of the State of Israel.

In the month following the inauguration of the Court and the assassination of Bernadotte, the government decreed LEHI "a terrorist organization," and two hundred of its alleged members were administratively detained. Akiva Brun, a LEHI leader, challenged his detention on the grounds that the law did not explicitly vest the government with power to detain administratively and that the decree failed to specify the reasons for concluding that LEHI was a terrorist organization.

For the first time the Court was asked to take a stand on the question that would haunt Israel for decades: what political and civil liberties do Israelis have? Can the executive branch suspend all or any liberties for reasons of national security (in this case, the fear of internal subversion)? And what role, if any, should the Court play in protecting individuals against governmental action? Denying Brun's petition, Chief Justice Smoira spoke for the Court: "When the security of the state and the public peace are in grave danger, ordinary legal tools might not be sufficient, and it is necessary to prefer the needs of state security over the protection of individual liberties. *In such a case the public mandates that every citizen sacrifices his rights for the benefit of the public.*"[1]

Three elements emerge from this statement. First is the acute perception of a grave danger. Like most Israelis, the justices felt extremely vulnerable, and their decisions were emblematic of this experience. Second, the opinion demonstrated an approach to civil liberties that is typical of institutions under stress. The Court characterized individual liberty as antithetical to the stability of the state, perceiving itself as able to protect either the individual or the state, but not both. The Court did not take seriously the option of mediating the two through notions of due process. Finally, and most importantly, the motif of self-sacrifice reveals how deeply the Court identified with the predominant political philosophy of the day.

Self-sacrifice has been a perennial theme in Jewish history. Abraham was ready to sacrifice Isaac in order to prove his unconditional loyalty to God. Self-sacrifice was the yeast of the Zionist program. Collectivism, the subordination of the individual to the public need and the public will, was the predominant ideology within which self-sacrifice was justified and encouraged.[2] The ethos of self-sacrifice marginalized the values of individual rights and the "conventional legal tools" to protect them (for example, due process). Both were elements from liberal ideology, and in this context, from utopian Zionism. Given the absence of a bill of rights, the Court could combat the disregard for individual rights by lending normative force to Israel's Declaration of Independence. The opportunity arose in one of the first petitions to come before the Court, concerning a challenge to the practice of confiscation of private property. The government was in the process of confiscating scores of Jewish-owned apartments to provide housing for its growing bureaucracy. It was an unabashed attack on the bastion of liberalism—the principle of private property—and the government executed the policy administratively and often heartlessly.[3]

In *Zeev v. Gubernik* the petitioners argued that the confiscations violated Israel's Declaration of Independence, thus metaphorically inviting the Court to follow the American decision in *Marbury v. Madison* and recognize the power of judicial review. The argument, which the Court itself called "heartening," was that the confiscation was invalid because the Mandatory law authorizing the policy expired with the inauguration of the state. In *Marbury v. Madison* Chief Justice Marshall interpreted the American Constitution as conferring on the Supreme Court the power to invalidate legislation, even though the Constitution itself was silent about such power. Now Israel's Supreme Court was asked to interpret the Declaration of Independence in a similar vein. But the Court declined the invitation. It conceded that the Declaration of Independence indeed expressed the "people's vision" but held that it had only political, not legal, authority. One major reason for rejecting the petition was that the Declaration itself stipulated that a constitution would be enacted, thereby implying that it was not a constitution. Still, the opinion reflected the Court's generally positivist and formalist philosophy. *Marbury v. Madison* drew a distinction between the will of the people and the will of the legislature and designated the Constitution as the authentic expression of the people's will, subordinating Congress to the constitutional command. Israel's Supreme Court explicitly stated that the Knesset alone was competent to express the people's will. It was a majoritarian conception of democracy, which vested enormous power and trust in the legislature.[4] It left open the possibility that should the legislature decide to suspend rights, the Court would be powerless to provide relief. Perhaps more could not be expected of judges who were as yet untenured, who felt unappreciated by the political powers, and who were told that protection of the individual would jeopardize survival.

As it turned out, the Knesset never enacted a constitution.[5] The Court found itself presiding over a system devoid of express legal guarantees of political and civil liberties and replete with emergency regulations permitting any imaginable suspension of rights.[6] Without a written constitution, the Israeli legal system by tradition (the Mandatory), ideology (catastrophe Zionism-etatism), and necessity (the war, the task of nation building) gravitated toward enormous executive discretion. In all fairness to Israel's leadership in the early 1950s, it must be emphasized that this Socialist leadership did lead the Knesset in enacting a vast array of social-welfare legislation that ensured the rights of working persons.[7] But given the government's Socialist bent and security-minded ethos, it had little interest in conventional civil liberties and great use for a centralized, powerful executive. Because most laws literally vested wide discretion in the executive, the Court's deference to the legislative judgment in fact indicated its acceptance of concentrated and authoritarian administrative action. The Court's acquiescence further solidified the power of the executive branch. Occasionally, of course, the Court did protect individuals, but only by confining its reasoning to the narrow boundaries of the black-letter law. Thus the flame of a commitment to justice and fairness, raised during the inauguration of the Court, though burning, failed to grow into a torch.[8] The potential for future activism, which Agranat realized a few years after he had joined the Court, remained unknown to the majority of Israel's judiciary.

AGRANAT'S LEGACY: THE PERIOD
OF EXPERIMENTATION

In his first two years on the Court, Agranat barely distinguished himself from his brethren. His opinions reflected a common formalistic style: addiction to stare decisis, legalistic interpretive moves, and a rhetoric of judicial deference. Although he did reveal a sensitivity to civil liberties in emphasizing the importance of respect for the individual in the emerging legal system, the intense rhetorical power that would characterize his later opinions was missing. Agranat appeared to be biding his time. He was a junior justice, and for a while he held a temporary appointment. He was lonely in Jerusalem—his family had remained in Haifa—not yet accustomed to the modus operandi of his brethren, none of whom, except for Olshan,[9] he had known before; and he probably was torn between his lofty expectations and his realization that reality was not ready to embrace his progressive agenda. Perhaps he was waiting for his inner confidence and sense of direction to grow and crystallize.[10]

In Agranat's second year on the bench, *Al-Couri v. Chief of Staff* came before the Court.[11] Naif Al-Couri, a Palestinian Arab, had served as an officer in the Mandatory Police Force. In late 1947, as a police officer in the Gaza area, he had intentionally withheld police protection from members of Kibbutz Negba during an Arab attack.[12] The Mandatory authorities began criminal proceedings against Al-Couri, but the prosecution lapsed with the termination of British rule. Al-Couri joined the Arab forces in the war against Israel and was captured by Israel's military forces. On 26 September 1949 the chief of staff signed a detention order for a period of one year against Al-Couri. When Al-Couri brought a petition for habeas corpus, State Attorney Haim Cohn defended the order on the ground that the man did pose a danger to the public peace even though the evidence against him might not suffice for a criminal conviction. Al-Couri presented three arguments: that the detention order failed to identify the detainee; that it failed to specify the location for detention; and that the chief of staff did not exercise independent discretion but, instead, relied on the recommendations of the detention committee. Speaking for the Court, Agranat held the order null and void on the ground that it failed to specify the location for detention. He rejected the State's position that the omission was merely technical and insisted that the specification of the place of detention was a constitutive part of the order, without which it would be incurably defective.[13] He also emphasized the prophylactic nature of administrative detention and the illegality of using it for punitive purposes or because the person was of dubious character.[14] But more interesting was the theory of rights that informed his opinion.

The State invited the Court to see the dispute from the perspective of the Palestinian–Israeli conflict. Al-Couri was responsible for the murder of Jews, because they were Jews. He abused his position as a police officer by denying help to the Yishuv. He contributed to the concerted Arab effort to terrorize and demoralize the Jewish community. From the Israeli perspective, he was the epitome of lawlessness. Also, he had been an active participant in the Arab military effort to defeat the young state in the battlefield. Under these circumstances, the defects of the detention order appeared trivial. The government was urging the Court to join forces with it in the struggle for Israeli independence. From this perspective, the Court faced the difficulty of defining the Jewish state. Should the state extend universal rights to all of its inhabitants, regardless of their position on its very legitimacy, or should it take the particular context into consideration?

Speaking for the Court, Agranat emphasized the right to personal liberty. It was a common-law right, incorporated into Israeli law by virtue of Mandatory legislation.[15] He proceeded, however, to anchor the right in Israeli soil. The right was a part of Israel's legal system, not only because Israel incorporated English common law but also because it "resonated with the spirit of the Declaration of Independence, which stated . . . that the state of Israel shall be based [inter alia] on the foundations of liberty."[16] In so doing, Agranat implied his disapproval of the position taken earlier, in *Zeev v. Gubernik*, that the Declaration of Independence was devoid of legal meaning. His disagreement, however, was qualified insofar as it only supported a right that, in any event, had been incorporated into Israeli law through conventional legal channels.[17]

Agranat also insisted that Israel was a state of all its citizens, and therefore Al-Couri's identification with the enemy could not take away his entitlement to liberty under the law. This was so not because the Court should be neutral to such matters but, rather, because the Court should be mindful of the moral values of the state, for which the Yishuv had been fighting. However, the statement about the relevance of Israel's Declaration of Independence was followed by the "realistic" observation that "statements about the existence of individual liberty are one thing, and the implementation of such a right, another."[18] Agranat was prepared to go as far as to invalidate an order signed by Israel's chief of staff; yet he refrained from attacking the validity of the Defense (Emergency) Regulations, which vested the military with extensive powers, and stopped short of offering any criteria that would limit executive discretion.

The crux of the opinion revolved around the duty of the military commander to decide on a case-by-case basis where specific individuals should be detained. In this sense, the opinion was formalistic and narrow. Except for the passing reference to the Declaration of Independence, there was no effort to justify the right with anything but statements appearing in English case law.

Al-Couri hardly signified a breakthrough in the Israeli conception of rights and liberties. Agranat adhered to a formalistic model of rights and to the basic judicial position, rooted in English jurisprudence, that such matters should be analyzed through the lens of administrative, not constitutional, law.[19] From the broader perspective of Israeli legal history, this means that the Court had barely advanced any vision of its own as an alternative to the emerging Socialist vision actively developed and implemented by Israel's Knesset. The judicial reference to liberties was reactive and hesitant, and it rested on the notion that law was independent of society. The justices failed to anchor "due-process" rights in a larger moral vision of the Israeli polity.[20]

MORE EXPERIMENTATION: THE IMPORTATION OF HOHFELD'S THEORY OF RIGHTS, 1952

On 28 December 1949, before the Court began tending to the business of the day, Chief Justice Smoira and the attorneys present in the courtroom congratulated Agranat on having received a permanent appointment as a Supreme Court justice. An emotional Agranat confessed: "I know that the attorneys are prepared when they appear before us and I also know that the justices are prepared. I am hardly prepared today." After thanking those present, he added: "I feel the heavy responsibility of a supreme court justice, especially at this time, a time without a constitution."[21] Agranat was increasingly disappointed by the absence of a constitution, realizing that if the Knesset failed to fulfill the promise of the Declaration of Independence, it would fall to the Court to craft a judicial bill of rights. A jurisprudence of rights was necessary to curb the strong utilitarian tendencies of the government and the insensitivity of the bureaucracy to basic notions of due process.[22]

As Agranat grew more comfortable with his peers and more confident of his abilities, he became more inclined to write long, scholarly opinions. He returned to the judicial style that had characterized his opinions in the Mandatory period. He could now rationalize this tendency as a means of simultaneously educating the legal profession and elevating Israeli law to the high ground of an intellectual discipline. In the case of *Podamsky v. State of Israel* he found the right opportunity to marry the two goals.[23] In a twenty-one-page opinion he discussed the theory of rights and duties as it had been developed in 1913 by American legal scholar Wesley N. Hohfeld and incorporated into a noted English treatise on jurisprudence by Sir John Salmond.[24] Agranat hoped thereby to encourage a more active judicial involvement in the protection of rights in Israel.

PODAMSKY V. STATE OF ISRAEL

On 15 October 1950 two men arrived at the detention quarters of the district court of Tel Aviv, each brandishing two pistols. They demanded the release of prisoners arraigned earlier by the police. When one of the two policemen standing on guard resisted, the perpetrators threatened to "fill his stomach with bullets," whereupon the policemen opened the door. The prisoners escaped, but they were later caught, along with their "liberators," and brought to trial.

It turned out that the arrest order pursuant to which the prisoners were detained had expired prior to their arraignment and that, therefore, they were being detained illegally at the time of their escape.[25] Could the perpetrators be convicted of coercing the guards to free the men, whom the guards thought were legally detained, if the arrest order had been invalid?

Agranat faced an intricate dilemma. The prosecution emphasized the theme of law and order. The events had occurred when the state was barely eighteen months old and the building of a police force still in its initial stages. Incidents of disrespect for the police and the law were widespread.[26] Failure to convict, therefore, might send the wrong signal and demoralize the fledgling police force. On the other hand, a conviction under these circumstances would mean that the rules of criminal procedure were an empty promise. If orders, invalid under the law, would nevertheless beget judicial recognition, then citizens could claim no protection of personal liberty. Such a result, in a country where the executive branch already exercised vast powers of administrative detention, would turn the concept of law and order on its head. Law would become what the police said it was. Also, what message would such a decision send to the lower court that carelessly issued the order? Why hew carefully to the letter of the law if in any event the Supreme Court validated unlawful orders?

THE MODEL OF RIGHTS: IMPORTATION
OF THE HOHFELD-SALMOND EDIFICE

The district court had convicted the prisoners under section 100(c) of the Criminal Code, which provided that: "Any person who . . . with intent to cause any person to do any act which that person is not legally bound to do, or to omit to do any act which that person is legally entitled to do, threatens another with injury to his person, reputation, or property, or to the person or reputation of any one in whom that person is interested, is guilty of a misdemeanor."[27] The district court found the perpetrators guilty of violating the first part of the statute, in that they intended to coerce the policemen to act (open the prison door) — something that they "were not legally bound to do."[28] On appeal, counsel for the perpetrators challenged this finding, arguing that the right of the prisoners to liberty led to a corresponding duty of the police to set them free. Hence, when the perpetrators coerced the policemen to let the prisoners go, they merely made them perform an act that was, in any event, their duty to perform. In the alternative, the defense argued, the policemen could not have a right to resist escape, because the prisoners were not under a duty to remain incarcerated.

Speaking for a unanimous Court, Agranat sustained the conviction. But he seized the opportunity to elaborate on the correspondence between liberties and duties and the meaning of rights, which the appeal presented.[29] In terms of the result, he opted for a "surface" conception of law and order; that is, supporting the police by punishing those who attempt to obstruct their routine operations. On a deeper level he developed a conception of law that was much less sympathetic to the police and was based on a theory of rights.

Agranat began the opinion by observing that an understanding of the meaning of the criminal offense of coercing someone to perform "an act which that person is not legally bound to do" requires an inquiry into the meaning of the "various aspects of the concept of a 'right.'"[30] This observation produced, for the first time in Israeli decisional law, a serious discussion of the meaning of "rights." Agranat began by dividing the concept of rights into categories:

1) legal rights entailing legal obligations;
2) legal liberties or privileges;[31] and
3) legal powers.

The first category, he observed, encompassed rights that promoted interests guaranteed by the state. Such rights carried a correlative duty not to infringe on them. Interference with the right could result in civil or criminal sanctions against the violator.

The second category presupposed the "*absence* of any law prohibiting such activity."[32] The meaning of that liberty was that "I am free, within certain limits, to do for myself different things—or to refrain from doing them—without any interference by the state."[33] The main characteristic of this activity, he said, was its legal content: "[T]he state will not punish the holder of such a liberty, for exercising his liberty, in any way."[34] Agranat then listed two exceptions to this rule of validation: first, sometimes the law would not protect liberty, in the sense that a violation of liberty would not carry any legal consequences; and second, "two different people may possess, simultaneously, liberties which collide with each other."[35]

Agranat then moved to the third category of rights, namely, legal powers. Legal powers meant "a legal entitlement to change, by an act of will, the legal relations existing between the power-holder and another, or between third parties."[36] Such legal powers, he continued, were divided into private and public. For the description of legal powers, Agranat offered an example from property law.[37] About the public powers he said: "These are identical with all the powers given, for the purposes of executing their official functions, to the legislative, judicial and executive branches of the government."[38]

Agranat then distinguished between the second category, liberties, and the third category, powers, by elaborating a hypothetical example: "The fact that a man acted without power does not always mean that he deserves punishment, criminal or civil. . . . If members of a city council enact a by-law which violates the Municipalities Ordinance, then clearly that by-law will be considered null and void. However, no-one will argue, absent malice or dishonesty on the part of the council members, that they should be punished for having voted for that by-law. As we shall see, the distance between this hypothetical and our case is not far."[39] This last move signaled his mode of resolving the case. The police certainly had no right to detain the prisoners (first category). Neither did they have the power (third category) to deny them their freedom. But because the police acted pursuant to what they believed to be a valid court order, they were at liberty to resist the escape. Hence, by coercing the police to open the door, the perpetrators violated section 100(c), which prohibited the coercion of a person to perform an act that the law did not compel.

THE SIGNIFICANCE OF *PODAMSKY*

Although Agranat's opinion had the same result as the district court,[40] its reasoning is uniquely significant. Clearly, Agranat felt that the time had come to introduce rights discourse into Israel's legal language in a more comprehensive way. The judicial honeymoon with the executive was coming to an end. Frustration with the administration was growing. There was a feeling that the ruling elite had itself become repressive and authoritarian. There were competing explanations for the rise of political intolerance. The zeal to fulfill Zionism, the sincere effort to benefit the collective as a whole, perhaps the dizziness produced by the experience of power after years of suppression and subordination, or even the blinding ethos of individual sacrifice for the sake of the homeland—all of these militated against tolerance. Whatever the reason and however well intentioned, the climate stood in stark contrast to the utopian vision of Zionism. The time had come to restore the balance that had tilted so heavily toward the collective and away from the individual.[41] But the discourse on rights could not be political, or the judiciary might be blamed for interfering with legislative prerogatives. It had to be done in a strictly "legal" way. The "correct" way of talking about rights would create the impression that individual rights emerged from the "pure science of law." Hohfeld's model of rights, based on the discipline of analytical jurisprudence, seemed perfect for the task. It rested on principles of logic, seemingly insulated from politics and ideology, and was therefore immune to the charge of judicial politicking.

This insulation appears to have been the main reason for Agranat's choice of Hohfeld's model. Sensitive to human dignity and the role of the individual in the community, Agranat understood that in Israel it fell to the judiciary to develop a culture of political and civil liberties. Perceiving Ben-Gurion's ambivalence about the meaning of law, he believed that he could only legitimize the concept of rights if he discussed it in strictly analytical and scientific terms.

To accomplish this purpose, Agranat began his discussion of the concept of a right by emphasizing that the model he used was not his but, rather, consisted of a summary of the views of "authoritative legal schol-ars."[42] He thus sought to articulate the principle that rights and liberties were inherent in the legal system. They might be determined and struc-tured by the legislature (not the executive), yet they had a life of their own and had to be taken into account. The distinction between liberty and power was central to this agenda, insofar as it emphasized that the prisoners were in fact free men, entitled to their liberty, irrespective of their legal status.[43]

Agranat's analysis emphasized the doctrine of constitutionalism: that all branches of the government were vested with limited powers and that, therefore, any action outside their constituted boundaries was null and void. In strictly legal terms, the reason for ruling in favor of the police was not the power to keep the prisoners under arrest. Rather, the reason was the prerogative of the police to resist the violation of what they had considered (albeit mistakenly) a valid arrest order. The police were vested with this prerogative, Agranat explained, not to facilitate their own op-erations but to prevent an executive authority from passing judgment on judicial decisions: "The public interest requires that the policeman will implement the orders of the court . . . and that he will not pass judge-ment upon the validity of the court order."[44]

The final phase of the analysis, stressing that in this case two liberties collided with each other, was also significant to this scheme. Agranat's reasoning reduced the apparatus of the state to the level of its citizens. The scheme Agranat envisioned placed the citizen and the policeman on an equal footing: each had liberties he or she could fully and lawfully ex-ercise. The relationship between the prisoners and the police was not that of subjects and masters but, rather, that of citizens and civil servants.

One can only appreciate this opinion against the Eastern European background of czarism, Bolshevism, and authoritarianism that shaped the consciousness of Israel's ruling elite and contributed to the rise of etatism (*mamlakhtiyut*) in the early 1950s.[45] Through *Podamsky,* Agranat intro-duced an unfamiliar idea to Israel: that the state existed for its citizens, not the citizens for the state. Indeed, Agranat's model of rights proceeded from this very principle. The analysis, resting as it did on private rather than public law,[46] served to "privatize" the state. The agents of the state, and therefore the state itself, could have a right, a liberty, or a power—but whatever the legal relation, it was created and confined by law. No special rules privileged the rulers.

There was an irony in the importation of this analysis into the Israeli situation. Behind the analytical model of rights was the effort to legitimize state power to implement Progressive reform. Both Hohfeld and Salmond, by emphasizing that a liberty could not be justified through the classical Liberal premise that it concerned merely self-regarding acts, sought to legitimize the view that "[w]hether to grant a liberty to do a specific set of acts [should] . . . be seen as a choice between competing interests and policies."[47] Hence, under the Hohfeld-Salmond theory, the scope of liberties possessed by the citizens was a political or collective decision. The insulation of certain human activities from legal regulation, because permitting a person to "do anything that does not hurt others" was a self-regarding act,[48] could not be justified. This was so because human activity always had the potential of hurting others; therefore, the decision as to which rights should be granted was always political. This insight, in turn, opened the gates to Progressive reform.[49]

But this theory was not necessary in the Israeli context. In the early 1950s, social-rights legislation was progressing forward in full force. Israel's leaders, well versed in Marxism and Socialism, needed neither Hohfeld nor Salmond to expose the fallacy of classical liberalism. On the contrary, it was their excessive zeal for reconstructing social reality, backed by immense public powers, that had to be cabined. A spirit of liberalism could nurture the value of human dignity, individual autonomy, and limited state powers. Hohfeld's critique of classical liberalism, ironically, served to introduce some of the ideology into the etatist climate of 1950s Israel.

Hohfeld's model suffered two shortcomings in the Israeli legal context.[50] Its implicit permission for the legislature to restructure rights could only serve to strengthen the government's perception that individual autonomy could be readily sacrificed for the benefit of the collective. Also, it was too detached and abstract. Hohfeld's discussion of rights lacked the spark that would ignite the imagination.[51] These may be the reasons why Agranat, in the aftermath of *Podamsky,* kept looking for something else.[52]

Podamsky rested on pure majoritarianism. There was no concept of rights immune from majority rule that would justify judicial intervention. This model fit perfectly with the expectations of the legislative branch and resonated with the formalistic tendencies of the Court.[53] But it seems that after *Podamsky,* Agranat became increasingly aware that in the context of Israel of the 1950s, it was too timid.

A further explanation for the ambivalence that characterized *Podamsky's* schizophrenic effort to build a model of rights on a result that upheld the power of the police can be found in the constitutional crisis that shook the judiciary as Agranat wrote the opinion. The resolution of this crisis in the summer of 1953 and Agranat's visit to the United States in the spring of that year opened the door to a more open and bold discourse on political and civil liberties.[54]

CRISIS: ATTACK ON THE JUDICIARY

The Knesset was quick and efficient in protecting itself and in enacting social-rights legislation, but it took its time when it came to the judiciary. The rules of the Mandate remained in force, neither recognizing the judiciary as an independent branch of government nor vesting the judges with tenure.[55] There was a vague expectation that judicial independence would be honored, but this expectation was nowhere written into the law.

The Court heard oral argument in the *Podamsky* case on 18 February 1952. Three weeks earlier, Minister of Justice Bernard Joseph had proposed a bill providing for mandatory minimum sentences for persons convicted of assaulting police officers.[56] In the Knesset, Joseph explained that incidents of attacks on the police were on the rise and that "[t]he public must know that it should respect the law, the government, and the representatives of the government."[57] The mandatory aspect of the sentencing, he further stated, was necessary because the "judges are too lenient" and their discretionary sentencing practices amounted to "an insult to the rule of law."[58] In the uproar that ensued in the Knesset, Joseph defended his criticism: "[I]t is my right and my duty to express such thoughts. Are they [the judges] winged saints who descended from heaven, in the confidence of the Lord, who know right from wrong? They are humans like myself, they can err like I can and I may criticize their decisions. I am worried about the fate of law in this country."[59]

The pending case of *Podamsky* was precisely about an attack on the police. One indication of Joseph's notion of the relationship between the state and its citizens may be gleaned from the fact that his attack on the judiciary was accompanied by an attack on the press. Joseph had unleashed his wrath on what he termed "the vulgar level of the press" for discussing the government's financial difficulties.[60] Thus Joseph targeted both judicial decision making and the press as villains who obstructed the smooth operations of government.

A week before the Court heard *Podamsky*, Chief Justice Smoira sent a letter to the Speaker of the Knesset. It is generally agreed that the letter was sent with the advice and consent of all the justices.[61] Smoira conceded that his letter "may be unprecedented in the history of constitutions" but insisted that Joseph's attack so upset the balance among the branches of the government and had such a potential to undermine the legitimacy of the judiciary that a dialogue about these issues was imperative. The chief justice reminded the Knesset that "judges cannot publicly defend themselves."[62] Implicit in his message was a sense of alarm: if the minister of justice, the "political" channel through which communication was maintained between the government and the judiciary, attacked the courts publicly, who would defend the judges? The judiciary felt abandoned. Its only recourse was a plea to the Knesset itself.

The right-wing Herut and the left-wing United Workers Party (MA-PAM) presented a joint motion urging the Knesset to hold a special session to discuss Smoira's letter as well as the independence of the judiciary. But Ben-Gurion stood by his minister of justice and as head of the coalition government mustered enough votes to defeat the motion.[63] The chief justice's letter was returned to the Court—a symbolic gesture meant to emphasize the doctrine of separation of powers and the sovereignty of the legislature in its deliberations but also meant to be a slap on the wrist for an already shaken Court.[64] On 5 March 1952 *Ha-Arets* informed its readers that the minister of justice and the attorney general had paid a visit to the chief justice. Presumably the meeting was meant to bring about a reconciliation. No public announcement followed that meeting.[65] These events took place while Agranat was writing *Podamsky*. In 1984 he wrote that "[Joseph's] words—particularly his scathing remarks—upset the justices and caused . . . agitation."[66] Agranat delivered the opinion exactly one month after the Knesset had rejected a motion to discuss the crisis.

Podamsky should be read in light of these events. While Agranat grew more and more conscious of the need to develop rights theory in Israel, he was also mindful of the Court's vulnerability. The crisis did not bode well for the untenured judiciary. Agranat's retreat to "a pure science of law" thus acquired a special gloss, as did his insistence that the executive and legislative branches were limited to their "official functions." Significant, too, was the hidden premise that rights and liberties were inherent in the concept of law and that a policeman was no different from any other citizen in society. The result in *Podamsky*, however, also acquires an added meaning in light of the events: this was not the time to supply Bernard Joseph with more proof about the "leniency" of the judiciary.

It took more than a year, and the replacement of Bernard Joseph with Pinhas Rosen, for the Knesset to pass the Judges Law that formally recognized the independence of the judiciary.[67] The Knesset approved the

28.08.1953

Judges Law on 20 August 1953. Two months later Agranat delivered the *Kol ha-Am* opinion, which radically transformed the status of political and civil liberties in Israel. One can only speculate about the probable connection between his newly acquired security and the daring opinion recognizing freedom of expression in Israeli law.

One more crucial event sheds light on Agranat's pathbreaking opinion in *Kol ha-Am:* his visit to the United States in the spring of 1953. The trip reawakened his ties to his native culture and strengthened his instinct that substantive notions of justice should be integrated into the judicial process.

TRAVEL TO AMERICA, SPRING 1953

Simon was twenty-three years old when he left the United States. He was forty-seven when he returned. On his first night in New York, he called the head waiter after dinner and asked, "I am a stranger in this country. Could you tell me how much [tip] I should leave?"

Agranat came to the United States on an official, though not very important, visit. It would have been easy for him to turn the invitation down. Smoira, the ailing chief justice, objected to one of his most valuable associate justices taking a leave while the Court was still in session.[68] Had the invitation been to England, Simon would have probably declined, but the chance to return to the United States was an opportunity he could not refuse. He was determined to go, even if the chief justice objected.

And yet, arriving home, Agranat declared himself a stranger. Certainly, there is an easy literal interpretation of his question in the restaurant. He felt more Israeli than American; and as a family man who rarely dined out, he was a stranger to the etiquette of restaurants. But Agranat's choice of words may hide a deeper meaning. Simon was returning triumphant, an emissary of the Jewish state, a justice on its Supreme Court. He was thrilled to reunite with his family and friends in Chicago and excited about the prospects of finally watching another baseball game. He could only suppress the feeling that he was coming home by sternly declaring to the world that he was a stranger. Still, a few of his activities while in America, as well as actions after his return to Israel, suggest that the relevance of American constitutionalism to the nascent law of Israel was very much on his mind.

Agranat insisted on going to Washington to see his old friend Arthur Goldberg. At the time a labor lawyer, Goldberg was to become secretary of labor and justice of the U.S. Supreme Court. Arthur and Dorothy gave a party in his honor, in which he was introduced to Judge David Bazelon.

Both Goldberg and Bazelon spoke energetically about the role of the law, particularly of judicial decision making, in building a better society. In Bazelon, Agranat met an impressive judge, full of exuberant confidence in the ability of the court to affect the law and improve society. Later, Bazelon sent Agranat his opinion in the *Durham* case, in which he had broken new ground in the area of the insanity defense.[69] Agranat also accepted an invitation by Justice Harold H. Burton to visit the U.S. Supreme Court, and he expressed his admiration for the scholarly work done in preparation for the opinions. He was determined to build a library for the Israeli Supreme Court. When Bartley Crum, a noted New York lawyer, asked what he could do for him, Agranat requested that a full set of the *Harvard Law Review* be sent to Jerusalem.[70] As he was leaving, he learned that he could not return the unspent expense money he had been given at the beginning of the trip. He rejected the suggestion that he make personal use of it and instead asked his hosts to spend the money on law books and good-quality ink for his Court.[71]

Agranat's reconnection with the Progressive tradition of American law rekindled his faith in the program of his youth and heightened his awareness of the possibilities inherent in the judicial processes. But this was only one face of 1953 America. McCarthyism pervaded the atmosphere, oppressive and demoralizing. Agranat's Israeli perspective enabled him to understand the fearful dimensions of intolerance in America. His American perspective shed a different light on the situation in Jerusalem. From Washington, Ben-Gurion's treatment of the opposition looked more like a zealous crusade than a rational defense of national security. The experience resolved the ambivalence he was feeling about the tension between civil liberties and national security, between restraint and activism, between formalism and sociological jurisprudence. Shortly after he returned to Israel, secure in the independence of the judiciary, he started working on the *Kol ha-Am* opinion.[72] Using the test announced in *Dennis v. United States,*[73] in which the U.S. Supreme Court sustained the convictions of the leadership of the American Communist Party but infusing it with the true spirit of the Holmes-Brandeis dissents,[74] he rejected the McCarthyism of his native land, set the standard for tolerance and openness in the legal system of Israel, and recognized the right to freedom of expression as an integral part of Israel's constitutional law.

· · ·

In 1949 Justice William O. Douglas of the U.S. Supreme Court came to Jerusalem and invited the Israeli justices to lunch at the King David Hotel.

He told them about his recent opinion in *Terminiello v. Chicago,* in which he held that a hateful anti-Semitic speech was protected by the First Amendment.[75] "Don't you think you went too far?" asked Agranat. "We can afford it," Douglas retorted, "can you?"

Agranat recalled that Douglas's remark left an impression on him. His *Kol ha-Am* opinion was a message to Israelis that "we, too, can afford a meaningful protection of speech."

CHAPTER 5

The Foundations of Progressive Reform

THE RIGHT TO FREEDOM OF EXPRESSION, OCTOBER 1953

Almost as soon as Israel was established, David Ben-Gurion announced which parties were in and which were out for purposes of building a coalition government. He declared both Herut, Menachem Begin's right-wing party, and Israel's Communist Party to be beyond the pale of acceptability.[1]

The Communist Party, initially rebuked because of its rejection of Zionism's nationalist component, loyally trumpeted Stalin's line at a time when the Soviet Union was becoming increasingly anti-Semitic and anti-Israeli.[2] This did not endear the party to Israel's decision makers. One target for harassment was the party's newspaper, *Kol ha-Am* [The People's Voice], and its Arabic counterpart, *Al-Itihad*.

The government had inherited from the Mandatory regime vast powers to whip the press, and they were put to use against the Communist Party. In March 1953 the daily newspaper *Ha-Arets* reported that Abba Eban, then Israel's ambassador to the United States, had announced that in the event of a war between the United States and the Soviet Union, Israel would dispatch 200,000 soldiers to assist its American ally. A few days later both *Kol ha-Am* and *Al Itihad* denounced the "anti-Soviet incitement" of the "American warmongers" and the "bankruptcy" of the Ben-Gurion government, which "meekly follows its American masters." Ben-Gurion appeared before the Knesset and declared *Ha-Arets'* story to be "a piece of journalistic imagination."[3] At the same time, the minister of the interior invoked his powers under the Press Ordinance of 1933 to suspend the publication of both Communist newspapers (but not of *Ha-Arets*) for more than ten days. Responding to a parliamentary question, the minister announced that if the Communists were upset with the implementation of the law, they could go to court. There was a whiff of conceited righteousness in that advice. A few months earlier, in a similar case, the Court had declined to interfere with the discretion of the executive to apply its suspension powers against the same newspapers.[4]

Given the course of these events, it is quite clear that when the petition came before the Court, the justices were well aware that the government viewed the suspension as a necessary means of defending Israel's reputation abroad and preventing social disruption at home. The Court heard the case at the end of June 1953 but did not resolve it before it adjourned for the summer.

When the Court reconvened on 16 October 1953, Agranat, on behalf of a unanimous Court (Justices Moshe Landau and Joel Sussman concurred), announced that the right of free speech was the cornerstone of Israeli democracy, that it had been abridged in this case, and that the suspension order was invalid. One fascinating aspect of Agranat's opinion in *Kol ha-Am* is his extensive usage of United States law.[5] The opinion incorporated a substantial portion of American First Amendment doctrine available in the early 1950s: the Blackstonian doctrine against prior restraint; the aversion to prohibitions against seditious libel and its concomitant rejection of the bad-tendency test; the clear and present danger test and its progeny, the "gravity of the evil discounted by its improbability" test; and the technique of balancing.[6]

Agranat's reliance on American law is significant for several reasons. First, Agranat transplanted the American doctrinal protection of expression into Israeli law, thereby providing Israelis with the legal framework for protecting their right to freedom of speech against the government. Second, Agranat celebrated American political and legal culture. Louis D. Brandeis, Zachariah Chafee, Learned Hand, Oliver W. Holmes, and Thomas Jefferson appeared among the authorities quoted in *Kol ha-Am* and thereby joined the gallery of thinkers whose influence would inspire Israeli law. Third, the jurisprudence utilized by Agranat in *Kol ha-Am* was distinctively American, rooted in an upswing in Progressive thinking and politics. *Kol ha-Am* rejected legal formalism and rigid positivism and recognized law as a social system and the judicial process as an enterprise engaged in balancing political interests. In short, Agranat's opinion in *Kol ha-Am* vindicated sociological jurisprudence.[7] Thirty-two years after

Chaim Weizmann declared that "there is no bridge between Washington and Pinsk," Agranat built a bridge between Washington and Jerusalem.

There was more in this landmark opinion, which has since become the cornerstone of Israeli constitutional law. It developed a theory of individual rights in a constitutional democracy, emphasizing the significance of personhood, deliberation, and the liberty to speak openly and defiantly about matters related to security.

DEMOCRACY AND THE INDIVIDUAL

Agranat began by contrasting democracy with authoritarianism. In an authoritarian regime, he observed, the ruler is treated as a superior being, whose understanding of right and wrong the subjects are compelled to accept. Criticism of the rulers, if undertaken at all, should be discreet and expressed with respect and deference.[8] A democracy, in contrast, presupposes self-rule. The people are the true rulers, and the government is merely their temporary agent. In the authoritarian polity, therefore, the individual has no rights; does it follow, Agranat wondered, that in a democracy citizens have unlimited rights? For example, are they totally free to speak against the government? Such a view, Agranat said, is too simplistic. No polity can accommodate absolute rights. Rights have to be shaped in accordance with considerations of the public good and the interests of the state. But—and here came Agranat's crucial point—the considerations shaping the contours of rights are not confined to collectivist or utilitarian calculations. The self-realization of individuals and their role as political actors constitute an integral political value. These interests, therefore, should influence the contours of rights.[9] Although rights cannot be absolute, neither should reasons of state supersede them. It is imperative for the state to facilitate open deliberation, albeit distasteful, because open deliberation is an important part of the moral value of the state itself.[10]

Agranat next analyzed the significance of open deliberation for the realization of the good society. What weight should be assigned to considerations of national security under such a theory? What powers did the state possess to defend itself against dangers internal and external?

THE SIGNIFICANCE OF OPEN DELIBERATION

Political participation, Agranat began, is not the privilege of the elite. In a democracy, deliberation and the shaping of political opinion should not be the exclusive domain of the few. The "simple citizen" participates in the political process not only by voting or through the parties and the legislature but also by the daily monitoring of politics. However "simple" ordinary citizens are, they should be expected to form an opinion about current events and "understand what needs correction."[11] Open deliberation has a tremendous educational value for the citizenry. Public debate is crucial for building the consensus that distinguishes the democratic polity from a regime based on the "power of the fist." Agranat added that the process of open deliberation also contributed to "the search for truth" and allowed the individual "to give full expression to his characteristics and personal attributes; to nourish and develop, to the extent possible, his self . . . so that life will be worthwhile for him."[12] Thus, he continued, free expression is not merely a "private" interest but a part of the public interest itself.

THE POTENTIAL USE AND ABUSE OF THE INTEREST IN NATIONAL SECURITY

Agranat was willing to accept a broad conception of national security. The interest embraced "everything related to the prevention of enemy invasion . . . ; the frustration of every effort to overthrow the regime with force and violence . . . ; the maintenance of public order and the securing of the public peace."[13] Indeed, he observed that during a national crisis it would be legitimate to use the interest in security in order to limit the right to free speech.[14] However, Agranat proceeded, this interest might be easily abused. Historically, governments tended to overreact to conditions of crisis and strike at expression "even when it does not constitute a threat to the peace . . . or the nation."[15] In support of this proposition, he cited Lord Sumner's observation that England had gone too far in suppressing expression during World War I and an article in the *Encyclopedia of Social Sciences* concluding that such abuse typified governmental behavior under stress.[16]

Agranat then pondered the philosophical difficulty of tilting the balance toward national security, which brought him back to the theory of the polity. The significance of national security should not skew the calculus in favor of the collective to the detriment of the private interest of the individual. One should beware the conclusion that the sacrifice of the individual is justified by the good of the collective. The interest in preserving free speech is a "collective interest," no less crucial than national security for the realization of the state as the moral polity. The danger lurks not in threats from within and without the boundaries of the state but, rather, in the misguided act of sacrificing the very freedom that the state was set up to safeguard.[17]

Here Agranat resolved his ambivalence about subordinating all interests to national security. Having devoted his life to the idea that the Jews were entitled to a state of their own, he could not agree that security automatically justified the sacrifice of liberty. Blind devotion to the tender Jewish state, he came to understand, might well result in throwing out the baby with the bathwater.

ISRAEL'S DECLARATION OF INDEPENDENCE: A NORMATIVE MEDIATOR

Still, Agranat needed normative authority in order to facilitate the incorporation of rights theory into Israeli law. The task was difficult because there was neither a written constitution nor a jurisprudence that could comfortably support his theory.[18] He could rely only on a few court opinions addressing "basic rights," but those opinions contained no theoretical elaboration of the justifications for the recognition of such rights. In the absence of higher norms, he invoked Israel's Declaration of Independence. Early opinions rejected the idea of using the declaration as a legal source.[19] But in a bold leap, Agranat reinterpreted the previous opinions in order to open the gates for reentry of the declaration into Israel's legal system: "Insofar as it [the declaration] 'expresses the vision of the people and its faith,' we are bound to pay attention to the matters set forth in it, when we come to interpret . . . the laws of the state."[20] From then on, reference to the declaration became the cardinal method of giving meaning and direction to Israel's system of laws. Its commitment to democracy, political participation, equality, freedom of conscience, and, most importantly, "the principles of liberty, justice and peace in light of the vision of the prophets of Israel," when infused into the interpretation of laws, had the capacity to transform the entire landscape of Israeli political and civil liberties.[21] Indeed, *Kol ha-Am* itself served as an example of the radical potential with which the declaration could be invested.

LIMITATIONS ON EXECUTIVE DISCRETION AND THE SCOPE OF JUDICIAL REVIEW

Israel's legal system contained two basic devices for the nullification of individual rights: the broad, often absolute, executive discretion to violate basic human rights,[22] and the absence of judicial review. The Press Ordinance applied in *Kol ha-Am* vested full discretion in the minister of the interior to suspend a publication for "such a period as he may think fit."[23] Agranat imposed limits on this broad discretion. A newspaper could be suspended only if the minister concluded, after having taken into consideration the "high public value of the principle of freedom of the press," that "as a result of the publication, there is a probable danger to the public peace."[24] Moreover, the Court would review the minister's substantive considerations. In the case of *Kol ha-Am,* Agranat held, a probable danger was not likely to occur, and the order of suspension was therefore invalid.

This result was crucial for ensuring proximity between the theory and the practice of enforcing rights. The opinion not only boldly disrupted the government's crusade against the Communist Party, it also served as a model for judicial review of the vast pool of discretionary powers vested in the executive. The probable-danger test was developed in this case; other formulations would limit governmental powers in future cases. The crucial point was the guarantee of substantive judicial review. It was exercised in full power and vigor in *Kol ha-Am.*

Kol ha-Am was the most important judicial breakthrough in Israel's formative years and is one of Israel's most-quoted and better-known opinions. With *Kol ha-Am,* the press gained protection against the arbitrary deployment of the sanction of suspension. Reporters began to enjoy considerable freedom to criticize governmental operations, and observers of the legal scene could cite an authoritative decision of the high court as proof of Israel's commitment to political and civil liberties. Finally, judges were provided with a theoretical model and a methodology for integrating fundamental rights into the legal system.[25]

Shortly thereafter, Agranat started working on another seminal opinion, regarding the insanity defense. After retirement, he singled out *Kol ha-Am* and *Mandelbrot,* the insanity case, as the best, most significant opinions of his judicial career.

CHAPTER 6

Law, Morality, and Judicial Review

MANDELBROT V. ATTORNEY GENERAL

One year after Agranat returned from the United States, Zalman Mandelbrot's appeal reached the Court.[1] Diagnosed as a paranoid, Mandelbrot had shot and wounded a woman and killed a man in a textile factory in Haifa. The Court faced a dilemma. On one hand, Mandelbrot's paranoia was sufficiently advanced as to negate his willpower. On the other hand, he understood that what he had done was prohibited by law.[2] Israel's Criminal Code Ordinance treated the issue of insanity in section 14, which incorporated England's M'Naghten rules: a person who understood that his actions were legally proscribed could be held criminally responsible.[3] The doctrine of irresistible impulse was not considered a part of Israeli law. The district court held that because Mandelbrot understood that his actions were legally prohibited, he should be convicted.

The Court had several options. It could affirm the conviction. It could reinterpret the facts so as to "find" that Mandelbrot did not understand that his behavior was forbidden. It could engage in creative judicial lawmaking, recognizing irresistible impulse as a defense, and send Mandelbrot to a mental institution. The three justices sitting on the panel could not agree on one solution. Agranat opted for incorporating the defense of irresistible impulse. He had long been interested in the theory of criminal law and was teaching the subject at the Hebrew University.[4] With Professor Sheldon Glueck of Harvard Law School, he believed that criminal law should recognize the effects of the social environment on crime and the criminal—a distinctively Progressivist view. He admired Judge David Bazelon's opinion in *Durham,* which invited advanced psychological knowledge to influence criminal-law doctrine and broadened the defense of "irresistible impulse" in American law. Agranat used the *Mandelbrot* case to do the same for Israel.[5] Silberg reinterpreted the facts, thus overturning the conviction while remaining within the framework of the black-letter law. David Goitein delivered a fierce dissent. Accusing Agranat of exercising raw judicial power and describing his opinion as "a little too daring . . . one which finds no support in the language or import of the law,"[6] he urged the Court to remain loyal to the doctrine of judicial restraint.[7]

Indeed, Agranat's opinion was a daring affirmation of the judicial role in shaping the value system of a society. In addition to a forty-page critique of the M'Naghten rules and the brilliant deployment of technical means to locate the defense of irresistible impulse in section 11 of the Criminal Code,[8] Agranat's opinion expanded on the understanding of civil liberties.

At issue were the rights of the mentally insane. Agranat used the occasion to discuss the theory of rights in criminal law. He analyzed the relationship among the individual, civil society, and the state. Also, he addressed the choice embedded in judicial decision making: either to engage in judicial activism by shaping society's value system and norms of substantive justice or to take a deferential stance and avoid a decision, thereby leaving the status quo intact.

THE INDIVIDUAL IN SOCIETY

The M'Naghten rules emphasized will and reason as the predominant factors in guiding human behavior. The rules required a strict distinction between the cognitive and emotive aspects of the personality and insisted on the irrelevance of the emotions to the process of shaping legal rules.[9] In this sense, the M'Naghten rules reflected a Cartesian conception of the personality, which "assumes that the individual will is the cause of all actions."[10] Agranat rejected this conception: "It is very evident that those [M'Naghten's] rules . . . contain one weak point . . . namely, the formulists' assumption that man lives in fact by his reason alone . . . that that element in his personality alone guides his behaviour and directs it; whereas we know today . . . that man's 'ego' constitutes a unit combining . . . the will and the emotions, without any possibility of separating them."[11] Agranat's idea of the individual was at odds with the classical Liberal conception of the self as an atomistic being, the independent carrier of a bundle of rights. He proposed a more contextualized and textured conception of the self, more akin to American Progressivism than the Cartesian-Kantian conception underlying the M'Naghten Rules. Agranat's opinion portrays the individual as a being largely motivated by emotions, whose condition may not be evaluated apart from his social context. Early in the opinion Agranat emphasized, in addition to the hereditary paranoid streak in Mandelbrot's immediate family, the hardships the man had experienced that had exacerbated his condition. As a child Mandelbrot had been placed in an orphanage, and he later served as a guard and a soldier in "difficult external conditions which prevented him from achieving rest and reward."[12] A jurisprudence of rights had to take into consideration the person as a social being, to understand the influence of emotion on human experience, and to recognize how society affected individual activity.

How should the law, as an organ of the state, treat the insane? Agranat advocated a position that was informed first and foremost by "a sense of justice and morality."[13] Rather than remain neutral to the individual's predicament and leave him to his own devices, thereby separating law from morality, law should display compassion and understanding. Substantive justice should inform the law in shaping the content of rights. This "sense of justice and morality," Agranat explained, was different from and preceded utilitarian calculations. Even though utilitarian considerations dictated that on balance the prospect of punishment might deter an insane person from performing the criminal act, a sense of substantive justice militated against punishment: "Finally, even if we assume . . . that one cannot be entirely certain that the threat of the criminal law might not succeed, in a certain case of 'sick impulse,' in influencing behaviour, even then the conclusive consideration is bound to be the one tied up with the sense of justice which all feel, and not in the consideration that perhaps the fear of punishment may, for all that, have the effect of turning the scales . . . in favor of deterrence and restraint."[14] A question remained, however, that Agranat's brethren impressed on him: should the judiciary infuse the law with norms of substantive justice in cases where the positive law was relatively settled against the just solution?

JUDICIAL REVIEW

In *Kol ha-Am* Agranat had already made clear his position on judicial review. He accepted that, absent a constitution and a bill of rights, the judiciary did not have the power to invalidate statutes. But he did not endorse the deferential position that limited the interpretive role of the judge (as had been announced in *Zeev v. Gubernik*),[15] though most justices still thought that deference followed from the absence of a constitutional normative structure. *Kol ha-Am* did not explicitly address the function of the judiciary as the guardian of rights, but its core assumption was that the courts ought to recognize Israel's fundamental values and interpret statutes in their spirit. Like his friends Arthur Goldberg and David Bazelon, Agranat now took it to be a part of his judicial duty to participate in shaping the nation's value system through law.

Mandelbrot adopted this position. It rejected the approach Agranat himself had advanced in *Podamsky,* when he justified his Hohfeldian model of rights with the observation that law was "found" in old cases and scholarly articles and that, hence, the charge of judicial activism was logically false.[16] In the spirit of Progressive jurisprudence, he now insisted that the democratic nature of the regime in *Kol ha-Am* and the sense of morality and justice in *Mandelbrot* should inform the judicial decision-making process. It was not as if he understood the judicial role to be similar to that of the lawmaker. He recognized the limitations on judicial decision making and made a serious effort to show that his normative program was rooted in the statutory language.[17] At the same time, he had a sense of vocation about judging, based on both his utopian Zionist background and his American Progressivism. He believed that the judge should not merely apply the law, he should apply it justly.

In *Mandelbrot* Agranat faced difficulties more formidable than those in *Kol ha-Am*. In *Kol ha-Am* he was backed by his two colleagues on the panel. He was not alone. In *Mandelbrot* he faced two strong opinions accusing him of trespassing on the domain of the legislature. But without wavering, he advanced arguments in support of his chosen path. He earnestly tried to respond to the charge of usurpation by locating his position within the mainstream of common-law jurisprudence and by painstakingly showing that his solution could be squared with the statutory language. He then faced the classical warning: that because his position was not based on a neutral principle, it was bound to slide toward the exercise of raw judicial power. Summarizing the English opposition to the irresistible-impulse test, based as it was "on the impossibility or extreme difficulty of distinguishing an irresistible impulse from an unresisted one," Agranat responded: "I do not deny that, from time to time, 'borderline' cases are liable to come before the court, and that in such cases, it may well have difficulty in arriving at the true nature of the impulse and be bound indeed to tread most warily before deciding on its final diagnosis. However, this difficulty involved in the task of judging does not justify . . . 'the application of the same, harsh law' to the [healthy] offender . . . and the sick person."[18]

This was the statement of a mature, experienced judge, confident in his ability to handle even borderline cases. Because judging had become a vocation for him, a way to participate in the fulfillment of Zionism, he could not accept the judicial model of the mechanical application of law. He understood judging to be one way of responsible participation in building the good society, and his *Mandelbrot* opinion was an effort to show that it could be done *within* the parameters of acceptable legal analysis. It was here that the different parts of his personality coalesced: his American Progressivist legacy and his Zionist ideology came together. It was, probably, for this reason that he came to rank *Kol ha-Am* and *Mandelbrot* as his best contributions to Israeli law.

• • •

Only in hindsight were Agranat's opinions of this period fully appreciated as the very foundation of Liberal, Progressive jurisprudence in Israel. In the turbulent 1950s they failed to make a mark. Israel was poor, small, and frightened in those years, torn between right- and left-wing ideologies, with very little room for the Liberal spirit to unfold. Israel's political leadership was obsessed with nation building, an awesome task given the ongoing trauma of the Arab–Israeli conflict. People were implored to ask what they could do for their country, not what rights they had against the government. The press saw itself as the long arm of the state and dedicated itself to the furtherance of collective, not personal, goals. Rights discourse at that time was practically nonexistent, and the intelligentsia, therefore, could hardly understand the significance of Agranat's opinions.[19] Nor did the judicial docket of the mid-1950s give Agranat too many opportunities to devote his intellectual energy to the development of rights jurisprudence. The dark presence of the Holocaust, translated into a sensational libel trial, sapped the public energy, and all too soon Agranat himself became embroiled in the controversy.

PART III

CONFRONTING
THE HOLOCAUST

CHAPTER 7

Blaming the Victims:
The Kasztner Trial

[S]acrificed, abandoned, and betrayed, delivered to the invader and left to face him alone, we were ignored by everyone but the enemy. He alone paid attention to us.

—ELIE WIESEL, describing the liquidation
of the Sighet Jewish community, a provincial town
in Hungary, in *All Rivers Run to the Sea.*

KASZTNER'S LIST

"This trial takes us back to the days of the Holocaust." The simple words that opened Agranat's *Kasztner* opinion concealed the most explosive material in Jewish history since the destruction of the Second Temple. A dramatic *j'accuse* shook Israeli society and exposed a tortured, pained, divided, and confused people. Between 1953 and 1958, Jewish activity during the Holocaust occupied the front pages of newspapers and the deliberations of the Knesset, the cabinet, and the courtroom.

Rudolf Israel (Rezho) Kasztner was a journalist involved in Zionist affairs in the provincial town of Kluz, Hungary. His political ambition and Zionist activity brought him to Budapest, where he lived throughout World War II. In March 1944, four months before the Allies invaded Normandy, Adolph Eichmann, commander of the Gestapo Department Four, in charge of the organized mass murder of Jews, arrived in Budapest. His targets were 800,000 Hungarian Jews. Eichmann had ordered the reactivation of the Auschwitz crematoria, prepared the cattle cars, and locked the Jews in ghettos. As elsewhere, he used the local Jewish leadership to facilitate the operation. Kasztner, a hitherto small functionary

in the communal life of Hungarian Jewry, either found himself, or or-
chestrated, a position as the chief negotiator with the Nazis on behalf of
Hungary's Jewish community. During his negotiations with Eichmann
he enjoyed privileges that set him apart from other Jews. He kept his automobile, he was allowed to travel, his telephone was not disconnected,
and he was not required to wear the yellow Star of David. In less than a
year, almost two-thirds of Hungarian Jews would be murdered. Among
the survivors was a group of 1,685 Jews that became known as the Bergen-
Belsen transport. Like Noah's ark, the group constituted a cross section
of the Hungarian Jewish community—termed by the Nazis the Jewish
Biological Nucleus. But the list of survivors also included a dispropor-
tionate number of Kasztner's friends and relations. In the summer of 1944,
after nerve-wracking negotiations between Kasztner and Eichmann, all
persons whose names were on the list left for Switzerland. By that time,
most of Hungary's rural Jews had been turned into ashes.

After the war Kasztner presented a report to the Zionist Congress in
Basel. It soon became clear that his was only one version of the events
and that some viewed him as a cynical opportunist who had deceived,
misled, and ultimately sacrificed the multitude in order to save himself
and his family. The congress established a committee of inquiry, but it
failed to reach any conclusions.[1] Kasztner's accusers were survivors and
relatives of those who had perished, as well as Hungarian Jewish leaders
who believed that he had usurped their power in negotiating with the
Nazis.

Kasztner and his family immigrated to Israel and settled in Tel Aviv.
He climbed the political ladder in MAPAI, was included in the party list
of candidates in the second elections,[2] and by 1952 served as spokesman
for the Ministry of Trade and Industry.

Malchiel Gruenvald was seventy-one years old when the trial began.
A native of Hungary, he had been a devoted member of the Ha-mizrahi,
the religious wing of the Zionist movement. In 1938 he settled in Jerusalem
and became active in the right-wing circles of the Jewish underground.
A highly controversial figure, he was possessed by a zeal for cleansing the
government of corruption, even if it took some tarnishing of individual
reputations. His weapons were pamphlets, which he would write, publish, and circulate himself. Kasztner, a member of the ruling party—
Gruenvald's political nemesis—was an irresistible target. Gruenvald also
had a personal ax to grind with Kasztner—only six of his fifty-eight immediate relatives survived the Holocaust. The last in the series of his pamphlets against Kasztner opened with the following paragraph:

FRIENDS, MEMBERS OF HA-MIZRAHI FROM HUNGARY:

Dear Friends:

The smell of a corpse scratches my nostrils!
This will be a most excellent funeral!
Dr. Rudolf Kasztner should be eliminated!
For three years I have been awaiting this moment to bring to trial
and pour the contempt of the law upon this careerist, who enjoys
Hitler's acts of robbery and murder. On the basis of his criminal tricks
and because of his collaboration with the Nazis (see my letter no. 15
[*sic*]). I see him as a vicarious murderer of my dear brothers.[3]

The pamphlet proceeded to expose Kasztner's crimes, denounce MAPAI,
and demand Kasztner's purge and the appointment of a commission of
inquiry to investigate the events that led to the decimation of Hungary's
Jews. At first Kasztner maintained his silence, but soon his superiors informed him that the attorney general insisted that he either sue Gruenvald for libel or resign from his government post.

THE ATTORNEYS: COHN AND TAMIR

Haim Cohn, Israel's attorney general through the 1950s,
was Gruenvald's complete antithesis. Young, educated, savvy, and charming, he was a fixed star in Israel's political and legal establishment. Born
in Germany in an ultra-Orthodox home, he arrived in Palestine in the early
1930s as an anti-Zionist and joined the Yeshivah of Rav Kook, who was
then developing a synthesis of religion and Zionism. Slowly he "converted
from Orthodoxy to Zionism,"[4] and eventually he turned into a firm secularist and a close associate of Prime Minister Ben-Gurion.

Why Cohn insisted that Kasztner either sue Gruenvald for libel or resign, why he later decided to prosecute Gruenvald for criminal libel, remains unclear. It could have been simply lack of political and legal culture from which he could draw guidance. After all, the state of Israel was
only four years old, and its leaders may not yet have been aware that fighting zeal with more zeal is not always the best strategy. Perhaps Cohn, too,
believed that the essence of Zionism was the rejection of *galut* and perceived old Gruenvald as a symbol of everything Israel should reverse in
Jewish history. The mistrust of government, the refusal to recognize the
achievements of official institutions, the whining—always emphasizing
the downside—seemed embodied in the person of Gruenvald. Perhaps

Cohn's *hoch kultur* background made him allergic to Gruenvald's vulgar accusations. Perhaps he believed that a prosecution for libel would purge such calumny from the new society. Perhaps he indeed believed that this would be a simple case expeditiously processed, in which it would be categorically proved that the public officials of the new state were honorable men.[5]

In any event, Cohn, who a few years later would join the Supreme Court and acquire a reputation as a civil libertarian, was at that time a loyal servant of the government, filled with high-minded intolerance and loyalty to a single cause. Even though he was never prepared to admit that he had erred in prosecuting Gruenvald, it is clear that Cohn had at least failed to foresee the pandemonium Shmuel Tamir was planning as a part of Gruenvald's defense.

In Tamir, Cohn had found his equal. Younger than Cohn, Tamir was a relatively unknown lawyer and politician, burning with hostility toward Ben-Gurion and MAPAI, which he called the "regime of darkness."[6] Unlike Cohn, Tamir immediately understood the scandalous potential of the trial. His deal with Gruenvald gave him a free hand in developing the trial strategy. Tamir's defense trumpeted the common theme in the Israeli understanding of the Holocaust in the early 1950s — that there were only two ways of reacting to the Nazi assault: the way of the Judenrat (the Jewish councils established by the Nazis), which meant cooperation, collaboration, and ultimately destruction, or the way of resistance, epitomized by the Warsaw ghetto uprising. The defense also insisted that, in collaboration with the British, Ben-Gurion and his associates deliberately withheld help from the Jewish community in Hungary.

If Cohn was the antithesis of Gruenvald, Tamir was the antithesis of Kasztner. Kasztner, balding and bespectacled, epitomized the stereotypical Jew in Zionist literature — conscious of his vulnerability, deferential to Gentiles, always in search of a gimmick to help him get by. Tamir (the word means *tall* in Hebrew and replaced the original family name, Katznelson), the sabra, fair, blue-eyed, and exuding self-confidence, represented the "new" Jew. A loyal adherent to the teachings of Hadar (Jewish glory) expounded by Jabotinsky (founding father of right-wing Zionism), Tamir would neither defer nor make concessions, he would fight back. In the 1940s, when Kasztner was negotiating with Eichmann, Tamir was organizing acts of sabotage against the British in Palestine, as a member of the right-wing underground. He was subsequently deported to a detention camp in Kenya. The contrast between homeland and *galut* reached its symbolic peak during cross-examination, when the young

Tamir's fluent, rich Hebrew, spoken in a perfect Israeli accent, mercilessly exploited Kasztner's confused and self-contradictory testimony, delivered in broken Hebrew and in a thick Hungarian accent.

And so the two attorneys, one representing the state, the other representing the political opposition, locked horns before the district court about everything that mattered to a Jew and a Zionist. Both thrived when a crusade was at hand. Both nurtured a fervent commitment to the national honor and would relentlessly pursue those who dared defile it. They differed about who the villains were and what patriotism actually inspired.

On 22 June 1955 Judge Benjamin Halevy, sitting as the sole judge in the case,[7] held that by choosing the way of negotiations Kasztner "had sold his soul to Satan." With some premonition about the meaning of this trial, Halevy alluded to Kasztner throughout his 234-page opinion as *K*, thereby making the Jewish leader anonymous and indistinguishable from other members of the Judenrat throughout occupied Europe. If Halevy entertained a doubt about his judicial course, it could only be found in the unconscious link between the *K* of Kasztner and that other famous *K*—Kafka's antihero in *The Trial*.

Outside the courtroom, the defeated Kasztner declared that the injustice done unto him was no less than that visited on a fellow Jew: Alfred Dreyfus. It was a potent analogy. The Dreyfus trial confirmed Theodor Herzl's conviction that anti-Semitism would not be cured unless the Jews had a state of their own. Herzl founded Zionism as a response to anti-Semitism. Could Israeli Zionists, in their zeal to explain the Holocaust, fall into the trap of an anti-Semitism no different from that of the French court?

In March 1957, thirteen years after he had started negotiations with Eichmann in Budapest, while his appeal was pending before an all-Jewish court in Jerusalem, Rudolf Kasztner was assassinated. Three men, linked to the right-wing, ultra-nationalist circles of LEHI, would be convicted of Kasztner's murder.[8]

"KASZTNERISM" AND THE ELECTIONS TO THE THIRD KNESSET, 1955

Agranat was aware of the drama. The district court was in the same building as the Supreme Court, and one could scarcely ignore the army of reporters and crowds of curious citizens eager to watch the trial. One could not read a newspaper without encountering the amazing twists and turns in the trial, where Holocaust survivors testified along-side the top leadership of the Yishuv and the international Zionist move-ment. It is difficult to believe that the justices did not raise an eyebrow at the spectacle as political passion shook the district court.

The judgment—that Kasztner "had sold his soul to Satan"—was de-livered a month before the 1955 elections. For the first time in the eight years of Israeli history, the judicial system became the focus of national attention. The country was torn between those who hailed the judgment and demanded that Kasztner be immediately prosecuted as a Nazi col-laborator and those who observed with dismay that the judge seemed to have fallen prey to Tamir's intoxicating rhetoric.[9]

Immediately after the trial, a contentious debate in the cabinet ended with a decision to leave the question of whether to appeal to the minis-ter of justice and the attorney general. In the Knesset, both the right-wing Herut and the Communist Party asked for a vote of no confidence in an Israeli government "which defends collaborators." There followed an ac-rimonious parliamentary debate. Charges that the official decision to ap-peal was designed to cover up MAPAI's involvement in the collabora-tion met with indignant assertions of good faith and insistence on due process of law. A record ninety members were present as the centrist Gen-eral Zionists, among them Tamir's mother, abstained from the vote, even though their party was a partner in the coalition government. The Knes-set defeated the move to topple the government, yet Ben-Gurion tendered his resignation. A few days later a new coalition was formed, excluding the General Zionists. Cynics observed that the abstention of the General Zionists was the first shot in the election campaign. The Center Party was trying to avoid a situation in which it would become a scapegoat for Herut.

The five weeks between the decision of the district court and the elec-tions were consumed with issues related to the Holocaust. Herut's cam-paign advertisements portrayed Kasztner as the devil; the posters warned voters not to support a party that espoused "Kasztnerism." The Left par-ties, whose ranks included some of the partisans who had led the Jewish resistance against the Nazis, joined the Right in denouncing Kasztner as the symbol of the Judenrat and collaboration. MAPAI found itself de-fending the policies of the Jewish Agency in the 1940s and the rule of law, both symbolized by Cohn's decision to file an appeal. Holocaust history, not Israel's future, loomed large in the election of 1955.[10]

That same year Agranat was appointed chairman of the Central Elec-tions Committee, in charge of overseeing the elections to the third Israeli Knesset. For the first time he actually associated with politicians.[11] He also recalled developing a more sober view of MAPAI's machinations to retain power, which reminded him of the practices of Chicago's political bosses he had encountered in the 1920s. But there was no escaping the Kasztner affair. Two days before the elections a bomb exploded next to the home of Israel Rokah, a leader of the General Zionists Party who, as minister of the interior, had opposed the appeal of Kasztner's verdict.

The day before the elections, in a radio speech—Israel had no television— Agranat proudly emphasized that the third elections proved Israel's commitment to the democratic process and that the campaign showed that the opposition parties were free to criticize the government. He urged his listeners to treat voting as a duty, not a right.[12] They did. In the end, MAPAI won forty seats in the Knesset, down from forty-four, and Herut doubled its vote, gaining fifteen seats. Kasztner had lost in the court of Israeli public opinion.

When the appeal reached the Supreme Court sometime in 1956, Chief Justice Olshan appointed a panel of five (instead of the usual three) judges, among them Agranat. Hearings began in January 1957 and lasted six months. On the heels of Kasztner's assassination, the police began to fear for the lives of the justices. For the first time in his life, much to the delight of Ronnie, his youngest son, Agranat found himself escorted by an armed police guard.

APPEAL

The year following the election campaign was a mixed one for Agranat, from which he emerged strengthened and confident. In 1955 his mother, Polya, died in Haifa after a long battle with cancer. With both of his parents dead, Agranat was now the senior member of his family. In March 1956, the twenty-sixth anniversary of his immigration to Palestine, his sadness was mixed with joy as he became grandfather to Orit, firstborn to his oldest son, Israel. Simon was fifty years old.

Shmuel Tamir, urging the Court to sustain the judgment against Kasztner, was about the same age as Simon had been when he arrived in Palestine a quarter of a century earlier and published his Chizik eulogy. That eulogy emphasized the distinction between old and new Jewish heroes, the passive martyrs—products of *galut*—and the new fearless fighters—modern Maccabees.[13] Like Agranat, Kasztner was born in 1906. Three years after Kasztner was conducting his controversial negotiations with the Nazis, Agranat was a magistrate in Haifa, petrified by the sight of the bleeding victim of Arab snipers early one morning at the entrance to the court. "Caution is the better part of valor," he then advised himself and stood still.[14] By what standard should Kasztner, operating in Nazi occupied Budapest, be judged?

Agranat remembered his months of studying the record as some of the most traumatic of his life. Personally he was not affected by the Holocaust; all of his and Carmel's relatives had left Europe before Hitler launched his war against the Jews. As a young lawyer Agranat had occasionally tried to obtain immigration certificates for clients whose families were left behind. He particularly remembered a Haifa kiosk owner whose wife and son were trapped in Poland. Agranat had tried, unsuccessfully, to persuade the British to issue the life-saving certificates for the two. That man never saw his family again. But the hair-raising details of the Nazi persecution—the hunger and the thirst, the trains and the crematoria, the terror, the helplessness, the depths of desperation—Agranat encountered in 1956 for the first time. The shock was so numbing, the burden of deciding so heavy, that he retreated more and more into himself. He became like a ghost in his own home, silent and aloof. His young daughter-in-law, a house guest until she and Israel moved to their own home, thought he disliked her or was simply antisocial. But he was agonizing over the need to give legal meaning to the terrible facts. What was a Jew to do?

Mindful of Agranat's intellectual bent and analytical skills, Chief Justice Olshan asked him to be the first to write an opinion, even though Agranat was not the most senior member of the Kasztner panel. At the end of six months, he produced a 194-page opinion. He found that in three out of the four counts Gruenvald had indeed libeled Kasztner. A majority of the Court, Chief Justice Olshan, Deputy Chief Justice Cheshin, and Justice Goitein, joined Agranat in his conclusions. Justice Silberg, whose parents had perished in the Holocaust, dissented, partially endorsing the district court's conclusions.

Like all of Agranat's major decisions of the period, his *Kasztner* opinion was ahead of its time. His version of the history of the Holocaust of Hungarian Jewry, which he carefully detailed, declined to echo popular opinion. Today Agranat's version is widely considered standard history.[15] His opinion differed from that of the lower court and of Justice Silberg in another important aspect. Whereas the condemnation of Kasztner injected adrenalin into the veins of an already highly agitated public, Agranat was on hand with some Valium. His prescription was low-keyed, avoiding passionate rhetoric and providing a sense of perspective and civilized respect for all the parties involved. He even refrained from stating that Kasztner was assassinated and referred to him as "having passed away."[16] Although he reversed the lower court in almost every respect, Agranat began and ended his opinion by praising the "reasoned, detailed and most impressive" opinion delivered by Halevy. Similarly, he thanked attorneys Cohn and Tamir for "the great effort they invested in this complex appeal and the extensive and talented way in which they presented their arguments."[17] Only the length of the opinion, coupled with the almost compulsive repetition of some points, revealed the tension within him. His categorical rejection of the Tamir-Halevy version showed what he really thought of the entire affair.

It was bitterly cold in Jerusalem, and the elaborate security arrangements reminded the press of the British trials of the Jewish underground in the mid-1940s. Every person who entered the building in the Russian compound was searched. Armed policemen could be seen on the rooftops surrounding the courtroom. In accordance with custom, Agranat started reading the Court opinion. He read for seven hours.[18]

The opinion contained three parts. First, Agranat recounted the history of the destruction of Hungarian Jewry, stating that "it is imperative to judge Kasztner's behavior critically within the framework of the events in Hungary at the time, since these were the events which affected the lives of the Jews in that state in general and were reflected in Kasztner's public behavior in particular."[19] Agranat thereby implicitly rejected the position that one may divorce a legal question from its context and render judgment in a historical vacuum. This position became explicit in the second part of his opinion, in which he set forth the basic premises that had guided him in evaluating the record. In the third part he examined the charges and found that Kasztner could not be characterized as a Nazi collaborator, that he could not be charged with laying the groundwork for the mass murder of Hungarian Jews, and that he did not collaborate in the embezzlement committed by Nazi official Kurt Becher. Only on one count did the Court find that Gruenvald had spoken the truth: Kasztner did attempt to rescue Becher from justice after the war.

THE LEGAL FRAMEWORK

Much of Kasztner's legal fate depended on which rules would apply to his situation. In criminal trials, the prosecution must prove guilt beyond a reasonable doubt. In civil litigation, the standard is less stringent. Plaintiffs are expected to show that a preponderance of the evidence favors their side, no more. As the prosecutor, Cohn urged the Court to apply the criminal standard. He said that Kasztner had been the true defendant in this trial, accused of no less than "indirectly assisting in the mass murder of Hungarian Jewry." Tamir urged the Court to see the trial for what it technically was: a civil libel suit. True to the American Progressive tradition that he had already highlighted in *Kol ha-Am*,[20] Agranat sought to resolve the dilemma by balancing the interests represented by the two opposing approaches: the interest in flexibility in civil litigation and the interest in defending individual reputation. The *Kasztner* case, he said, did not fall neatly into either category. Hence the Court should be creative and design a rule of its own. The gravity of the charges, he ruled, required that Gruenvald submit "strong and clear" evidence, capable of persuading the Court that Gruenvald's allegations were in fact true.[21]

Another important legal rule concerned the role of the appellate court. In common law, appellate courts were expected to defer to factual determinations made below, both for purposes of efficiency and out of deference to the judge who had the first impression of the witnesses. Upholding this rule would necessarily require deference to Judge Halevy's finding that Kasztner "had sold his soul to Satan," a finding Agranat declined to endorse. "It was never impossible for this Court to intervene in the evaluation of the evidence, when such evaluation is founded on ungrounded considerations," he wrote.[22] Here the district court had failed to give weight to certain significant factors. Furthermore, Agranat said, the Israeli Law against the Nazis and Nazi Collaborators explicitly permitted deviations from the ordinary rules of evidence, if such deviation were necessary to discover the truth and do justice.[23] Even though this trial was not governed by that statute, he held, its spirit should serve as guidance. Justice, not formalities, should serve as a compass in the Kasztner trial.[24] But how could justice be distilled barely a decade later from this murky history of the Holocaust?

TRUTH AND HISTORY

"The greater the truth the greater the libel" was the premise of the medieval English law of defamation. With the advent of the Enlightenment, truth became a major value and an important defense in libel law. If a defendant proved that statements were true, the plaintiff lost the case. Because the case was technically about Gruenvald libeling Kasztner, the issue of truth became central to the trial. Tamir wanted to "open the wound and apply bitter, hard, cruel" medicine in order to teach the nation *the truth* about the Holocaust.[25] Indeed, he managed to persuade the district court to expand the trial beyond the contents of Gruenvald's pamphlets, even beyond the activities of Kasztner himself. In the aftermath of the affair, one of Israel's prominent journalists declared: "[T]o the extent that the trial contributed to the exposure of a part of the cruel truth, to the extent that it shook the nation and forced it to search for the entire truth—it was inevitable."[26] There was a naive, almost primitive belief that a ruthless act of exorcism was necessary and would put to rest, once and for all, the demons of the Holocaust. To Agranat, studying the record with the eye of an experienced judge, Tamir's version of the truth was so ideological, so partisan as to blur the conventional distinction between truth and libel.

Rarely does one find a judicial opinion in which the judge candidly acknowledges the danger of ideology lurking behind the seemingly objective application of legal rules. It was unfortunate that Agranat buried his insights into the tension between truth and prejudice in the middle of the lengthy opinion, for these insights provide a fine example of humane jurisprudence. Agranat identified three factors that might affect the judge's task in pursuing the truth: one emerging from the philosophy of history, one deriving from the limits of the judicial enterprise, and a third related to the specific difficulties associated with treason trials.

The task of the historian, he explained, citing G. M. Trevelyan and Isaiah Berlin,[27] is to collect, select, and interpret historical facts. The process of determining which facts are particularly significant demands a certain bias—the worldview of the historian always affects his work. Indeed, although a professional historian, carefully sifting and evaluating the evidence, can reduce the effect of the bias on his interpretation, a thoroughly objective rendition of historical events remains impossible. Agranat wished to make a subtle point: setting straight the historical truth is not within human power. Even historians, in command of their materials and conscious of the process of evaluating the past, do not arrive at the truth, only to a particular version of it. The truth about Jewish behavior during the Holocaust, then, would resist reduction to the activities of one or another individual.

In the *Kasztner* case, Agranat proceeded, the difficulties that would lead historians to different interpretations were compounded by the very nature of the judicial process. The judge in the courtroom differs from the historian in one fundamental aspect: he is not in charge of the research. The parties decide which materials are presented. The attorneys, as professional and ethical as they may be, are driven by the desire to win. Thus they are bound to present only those arguments that support their own position. Agranat was confident that the Kasztner affair, as well as the larger issue of the international Jewish leadership's involvement in the effort to save Jewish lives in the Holocaust, was not dispassionately and methodically explored by the litigants. Hence, he concluded, a court could not possibly render a truthful version of the Holocaust. Given the fervent ideological flames that surrounded the trial, he said, "we should be extra careful about drawing conclusions" related to Kasztner's public activities.

Agranat's analysis of the viability of inviting a court of law to determine historical truth had ramifications that extended beyond the *Kasztner* case. It amounted to a challenge to the claim of judicial objectivity and an attack on the sacred cow of the adversarial process and its ability to yield "a truth"—both very daring steps in Israel of the 1950s. The inspiration for his insights into the subjectivity of the legal and historical processes was American legal scholarship, but it was daring for Agranat to have made these statements in legally formalistic Israel.[28] Agranat introduced his observations on objectivity in order to lower the expectation that "legal science" could bring the issue to rest. He was trying to raise awareness of the value judgments underlying the decision, thereby sensitizing the public to the enormously complex problem at hand.

Having exposed the limited perspectives of the parties, Agranat turned to himself. "We should beware not only of the prejudices of others, but also of our own prejudices," he wrote. In dealing with contemporary history, one must necessarily "suffer from the lack of perspective." It is therefore extremely difficult for a judge not to view the event through the prism of his own views and emotions. Agranat concluded that the main flaw of the lower court's opinion was Judge Halevy's use of historical hindsight, his own subsequent knowledge of how the events in Hungary of 1944 had unfolded, in order to evaluate Kasztner's actions. Halevy's prejudices, feeding on such hindsight, hindered justice. A judge, Agranat said, must strive to "put himself in the shoes of the participants themselves; evaluate the problems they faced as they might have done; take into consideration sufficiently the needs of time and place, where they lived their lives; understand life as they understood it."[29]

Finally, Agranat addressed the feverish climate in which the trial took place. People tend to associate collaboration with betrayal and treason, he warned. But treason trials, by their very nature, excite passion, encourage an atmosphere of totalistic prejudice, and lead the public to expect a clear-cut conviction or acquittal. Again he drew on his roots in American jurisprudence. Invoking the authority of yet another great American, Chief Justice John Marshall, he cautioned both the Israeli press and the judiciary of the perils inherent in succumbing to such passions, "lest we ourselves become its victims."[30]

It was, probably, Agranat's finest hour as a judge. He penetrated the psychological and philosophical difficulties of delivering judgment and exposed the hardships of taking a stand. Avoiding reductive relativism, the sort that would justify anything, he based his analysis on the foundations of humble wisdom. His analysis rested on his effort to come to grips with the tension between the social construction of reality and the struggle to achieve objective justice. It was wise in its recognition that, within these limitations, one must strive nevertheless to achieve a comprehensive understanding to the best of one's abilities. Then, with his awareness heightened and his human vulnerability acknowledged, he proceeded to examine the charges.

PACT WITH SATAN?

Kasztner made contact with the Nazis within days of their arrival in Budapest. Initially he and Joel Brand, his partner in the negotiations, offered Eichmann 2 million dollars in return for the lives of Hungary's Jews. Eichmann took the ransom money, indicated a willingness to discuss sparing of 100,000 lives, and proceeded to hammer the nails into the Jewish coffin. Toward the end of April a desperate Kasztner realized that rapid ghettoization was under way and that mass deportation to Auschwitz would soon begin.

From the viewpoint of the trial judge, the crucial date was 2 May 1944, when the alleged signing of a pact with Satan occurred. On that day the Nazis offered a concession: 600 Jews would be allowed to leave Hungary for a safe haven (the number eventually was raised to 1,685). Was this a shrewd and cynical ruse designed to deflect the energy of the Jewish leadership away from the likelihood of death awaiting the multitude and onto the narrow escape awaiting the chosen few? Had Kasztner fallen into the trap set for him by the experienced Germans? Did he become so obsessed with the possibility of saving his kin that he was willing to sacrifice the majority of Jews? Or was he pursuing the reasonable and sane course: take whatever offer the Germans would give and keep negotiating, in the hope that more lives would be saved in the process. The district court, endorsing Tamir's interpretation, held that by accepting the offer Kasztner had fallen into the trap of collaboration; from then on he was at Eichmann's mercy.

The fate of the 18,000 Jews of Kluz, Kasztner's hometown, became the major proof of Kasztner's collaboration. In Tamir's version, the masses of Kluz were kept ignorant of the meaning of deportation and were encouraged to believe that they were being transferred to a labor camp, because their leaders were among the 388 "prominents" to board the Bergen-Belsen train. If Kasztner were not in the debt of the Nazis, he could have organized resistance. He could have encouraged more attempts to smuggle refugees across the nearby Romanian border. He could have agitated for every possible means to sabotage the Nazi plan. Kasztner's initial choice, as well as his behavior throughout that period, made him the "greatest Jewish agent in Nazi service in 1945 Europe."[31]

It dawned slowly on Agranat that this was a grossly slanted perspective, reflecting moralistic rectitude rather than a balanced view of the reality of the time. For months he studied the facts, the concept of collaboration, the history of the period, the philosophy of history, and the body of criminal and libel law. His opinion wove together his American jurisprudential orientation, his deepening expertise in criminal law, and his Zionist ideology.

From a strictly legal point of view, the theory that Kasztner entered into a pact with Satan rested on a series of fictions. The major premise was that Eichmann the Nazi commander and Kasztner the chairman of the Jewish rescue committee were equal partners in a freely conducted negotiation. Two minor fictions proceeded from that major premise. The first was that Kasztner's knowledge of the impending catastrophe was tantamount to criminal intent to assist the Nazis in murdering the Jews. The second was that Kasztner's failure to share his knowledge with his fellow Jews made him a collaborator, because "a person is presumed to will the consequences of his actions" and because the consequences of withholding information meant death to the majority of Jews.

Tamir portrayed Eichmann and Kasztner as two free agents, standing on equal footing: Kasztner "signed" the "contract" with Eichmann out of free will and in full comprehension of his options. American legal philosophers of the 1920s and 1930s would have called this interpretation "mechanical jurisprudence" or legal formalism.[32] It was a conception of law as a phenomenon independent of society and of the individuals inhabiting the legal world as atomistic beings, rational, possessed of free will, unaffected by circumstances and time. American scholars of criminal law criticized this view of human affairs: "Historically . . . our substantive law is based upon a theory of punishing the vicious will. It postulates a free agent confronted with a choice of doing right and wrong and choosing freely to do wrong."[33]

In analyzing Kasztner's behavior, Agranat reasserted his rejection of legal formalism and his insistence on adopting its rival perspective, sociological jurisprudence. He introduced a more subtle, less judgmental, and fuller understanding of Budapest in the spring of 1944. He attempted to enter Kasztner's psyche during these crucial months, in order to reinterpret, soften, and contextualize the set of legal fictions that together formed Kasztner's alleged intent to negotiate with the Nazis. Thus Agranat came to paint an alternative picture of a Jewish leader at the gates of hell.

The major premise, that Kasztner and Eichmann were equal partners, was repeatedly rejected in Agranat's opinion. Agranat took his cue from an exchange between the Nazi and the Jew. In one of their meetings, Eichmann reportedly said: "You seem extremely tense, Kasztner. I am sending you to Teresienstadt for recovery; or would you prefer Auschwitz?"[34] It is important to remember, explained Agranat, that a Jew, albeit a leader and in possession of privileges, could never feel like an equal partner in these negotiations. Kasztner was under the control of the Gestapo, who subjected him to abuse and even to occasional imprisonment.[35] Sensitivity to the terror growing within Kasztner—Kasztner's awareness of his own vulnerability between April and June—was essential to the resolution of the case. Agranat's insistence on giving meaning to legal events in the context of the time and place opened a fresh evaluation of Kasztner's state of mind.

Legally, Agranat could analyze Kasztner's intent from two different perspectives. The "hard" perspective would focus on the extreme gravity of the charges, thereby requiring that Kasztner's behavior be judged by the standards of the criminal law (even though Gruenvald was the defendant) before the truth of Gruenvald's charges was validated. The "weaker" perspective would forgo the technical categories of criminal law and ask whether an ordinary person might have considered Kasztner a collaborator. The district court blurred the two perspectives, and Agranat decided to separate them and subject each to careful scrutiny.

If Kasztner were to be considered an accessory to the crime committed by the Nazis,[36] an offense of which he was blamed by the lower court (he was not legally convicted, he was not formally indicted), then there must be proof of his intent. But not even Gruenvald had claimed that Kasztner had actually intended to have Jews murdered. Thus criminal intent had to be artificially construed, determined by an application of a legal fiction unrelated to the complex motives that actually propelled action. Here Agranat walked a tightrope. On one hand, he had already expressed skepticism about the adequacy of such a legalistic analysis when he insisted that Kasztner could not be viewed as a free agent. On the other hand, he was reluctant to abandon the world of legal fictions, lest his exoneration of Kasztner be linked to a radical, rather than a mainstream, view of the law. Legal scholars suggested that if an accessory knew with certainty that the principal had a foul goal,[37] that knowledge would count as intent. Agranat focused on the requirement that the knowledge of that foul goal be certain. In the first week of May, after the alleged pact with Satan took place, did Kasztner have "full and certain knowledge" of the impending deportations? When answering this question, Agranat warned, the Court should be careful not to attribute the knowledge acquired in hindsight to Kasztner in May 1944.

Agranat had these facts: on 3 May, after realizing that deportation might be imminent, Kasztner hurriedly obtained a permit to visit his already cordoned-off hometown of Kluz, in order to meet with the Nazi officer Dieter Wisliceny. On his way, he saw a trail of Jews en route to concentration centers. Wisliceny refused to confirm the "Auschwitz news" and, while expressing pessimism, suggested that he could not communicate any information before conferring with Eichmann in Budapest. It was not until 8 May, when the visit with Wisliceny finally took place, that the truth was confirmed. Under these circumstances, Agranat concluded, one could only say that Kasztner understood that deportation was a high probability, not that it was certain. Hence the certainty required to transform knowledge into intent was not present, and in a criminal court Kasztner could not have been convicted of a crime.

By 8 May, Kasztner had learned that Auschwitz was the destination of the trains leaving the ghettos. Did Kasztner possess criminal intent from that day onward? Again, Agranat combined sensitivity to Kasztner's circumstances with mastery of the legal materials. In the case law he found an exception to the fiction that identifies knowledge with intent: if "the accessory assisted the criminal with utter reluctance and under the pressure of the circumstances and—and this is the crucial factor—while hoping or expecting that the criminal will nevertheless fail to achieve his foul goal," then the knowledge of that accessory cannot be equated with intent, and he should not carry criminal responsibility.[38] On 8 May, as Wisliceny confirmed the Auschwitz news, Joel Brand received Eichmann's offer of "trucks for blood," exchanging Jewish lives for Western trucks. On 15 May, Eichmann promised Brand "to keep the deported Jews on ice" (to postpone their execution) until Brand had returned from Turkey, where he was to negotiate with the British. Meanwhile, Hungarian officials kept promising that they would not permit the deportation of "their Jews." The Russian army was pressing against the Hungarian border. The Allies were flexing their muscles. German defeat was inevitable. In the vortex of despair, could Kasztner hold to the Brand mission as a thread of hope, at once ephemeral and real? Was it totally unreasonable, under these circumstances, to keep negotiating, hoping against all odds that something might happen and that lives would be saved? Viewed through this lens, Agranat decided, even after 8 May Kasztner could not have possessed the required intent.

Agranat believed that he had to emphasize Kasztner's lack of intent. Public agitation was strong to prosecute Kasztner under the Law against the Nazis and Nazi Collaborators rather than to appeal the judgment in the libel case. It was imperative to hold that such prosecution could not have been successful.

Yet this analysis was a Band-Aid applied to a minor cut compared with the ugly wound that Agranat knew he had to treat with all his skill and mental powers: the poisoned heart of the Jewish people.[39] For the Kasztner affair sprang from an overwhelming sense of betrayal. The Jews had been betrayed by the Germans: who would have believed that the children of Mozart and Goethe would starve, torture, shoot, gas, and burn the children of Mendelssohn and Heine? The Jews had been betrayed by their neighbors: who would have believed that the Hungarians, hitherto good neighbors and fellow citizens in an enlightened society, would hand the victims over to their murderers? Had the Jews also been betrayed by their own leaders? The chorus of Gruenvald, Tamir, and Halevy was chanting, "Et tu, Kasztner!" When you failed to share the Auschwitz news, when you failed to organize a resistance, to encourage escape, when you begged for one more permit and yet another, while Jews were being slaughtered at the rate of 500 persons per hour, you, Rudolf Israel Kasztner, betrayed your people who put their trust in you.

Was Kasztner a collaborator?

A GAME OF ROULETTE AND MORAL DUTY: WAS THERE "A RIGHT WAY"?

Surely "not every act of cooperation should be termed collaboration, and not every person who had maintained contacts with the Nazis, and extended assistance to them, could be denounced as a 'collaborator.'" Thus began Agranat's analysis of this fearful question. He accepted the position that the trial was concerned not with the question of whether Kasztner violated the criminal code but, rather, with the question of whether he was commonly perceived as a collaborator. Still, Agranat insisted on an examination of the meaning of collaboration. His starting point was that the fulfillment of objective elements—the subordination of the local population to Nazi occupation, the extension of actual assistance to the occupier and the resultant harm to one's own people—would not suffice to make a person a collaborator; proof that his motives were commonly considered evil or illegitimate had to precede a determination of collaboration.[40]

The hidden dilemma, unmentioned in the text, was the standard against which the "commonly considered evil or illegitimate motives" should be judged. Should popular perception serve as a guide, or should detached moral meditation apply? The opinion suggests that this question never occurred to Agranat. From his perspective there was no dilemma. The question of what would commonly qualify as an "evil or illegitimate motive" was not to be answered by counting heads in the squares of Jerusalem but by considerations from moral philosophy.

"When Reuben shoots Shimon and kills him, his very action testifies . . . of Reuben's will to bring about [Shimon's death]. On the other hand . . . if Levy, standing on the banks of the river, sees that Judah is about to drown and does not hasten to his rescue—then [Levy's] inaction does not necessarily prove his intent to see Judah die."[41] This was a law professor's attempt, in as detached and analytical a manner as he could muster, to make the statement that the *Kasztner* case was analogous not to Reuben's shooting Shimon but to Levy's failure to save Judah. Agranat wished to emphasize that the core of Kasztner's alleged collaboration lay not in his actions but in his inaction: his failure to disseminate the Auschwitz news.

Agranat's distinction between action and omission amounted to an application of advanced American criminal-law scholarship to the problem.[42] At that time American scholars were insisting that law should display extra sensitivity to the state of mind of one who had failed to act, because "failure to act often is not accompanied by external manifestations which allow accurate conclusions on the defendant's state of mind. The motives for his inactivity may spring from an interplay of forces."[43] In the absence of "external manifestations," how could the Court decipher a state of mind? American scholars advised an inquiry into the defendant's moral duty to the victim. Agranat proceeded to reflect on the nature of Kasztner's moral duty to his community. In his report to the Zionist Congress after the war, Kasztner commented on the politics and morality of his plan to negotiate with the Germans in order to buy lives with money: "This was not a matter of merely saving a few hundreds of Jews from the countryside. If here and now Eichmann would not be forced to give up [on his plan to cancel the Bergen-Belsen transport] then the Rescue Committee, which has put its card on the German number in this game of roulette in human lives, would be the innocent loser, just like many before us in occupied Europe. Then the millions we have paid were a crazy action. The loser in this game would be also called a traitor."[44] From this Agranat gathered that Kasztner had understood the enormous political stakes involved in his choice of policy and that he concluded that it was reasonable to continue the negotiations with the Nazis.

The district court was ready to declare Kasztner—the loser—a traitor. For Judge Halevy, Kasztner's collaboration was captured not by the metaphor of the gambler but by the metaphor of the watchman. In the small hours of the night the watchman is surprised by the enemy:

The enemy informs the watchman that the compound is surrounded by a powerful force, determined to destroy the entire camp, and all attempt to alert the soldiers is doomed to failure. The enemy gives the watchman an offer: a few of the guard's chosen friends will be saved if the guard does not alert the remainder of the camp and makes no effort to save them. The watchman gives the enemy a list of his best friends and refrains from alerting the rest. The enemy destroys the entire camp, sparing only the watchman's friends. The watchman has committed treason against his fellow soldiers and has betrayed his duty. His action amounts to a collaboration with the enemy and to assistance in destroying the camp.[45]

"[T]his metaphor is . . . completely irrelevant,"[46] said Agranat, choosing to place his reaction to the watchman metaphor at the end of his lengthy analysis of the charge of collaboration. Kasztner's duty to his community was not analogous to the watchman's. Under no theory could the guard have discretion as to whether to alert his fellow soldiers to the attack. The watchman's duty, in legal terms, was ministerial, not discretionary.

What was the nature of a leader's discretion? Agranat rejected the position of the district court on that issue. For Judge Halevy, a leader's duty to treat equally all members of his constituency translated into an obligation to each member individually. Kasztner therefore was expected, in keeping with this theory, to disseminate the Auschwitz news to as many individual Jews as he could reach, letting each determine for himself or herself whether to board the trains, resist, or risk escape. Agranat did not accept this theory of leadership. A leader does not owe a duty individually to each member of his constituency. Rather, a leader owes a duty to the community as a whole. This, he hastened to add, does not necessarily mean that "a leader is permitted to sacrifice . . . the lives of the 'few' in order to save the 'many.'"[47] Rather, "if a leader is to choose between two opposing ways of action, one likely to save the majority, but not all, of the community, the other geared to save each and every one but likely to save only the few—then his public office requires—and this is also his moral duty— . . . that he follow the first way."[48]

In hindsight, Agranat's conception of the leader's duty amounted to utilitarianism with a human face, reflective of Socialist Zionism and contrasting with the district court's atomistic conception of society. From this perspective, Kasztner acted reasonably in withholding the Auschwitz news from the Jewish masses. It was not unreasonable for Kasztner to assume that gambling on the "German number" and continuing the negotiations, coupled with a general warning to the ghetto leadership that the situation was very grave and that escape should be encouraged, were more likely to save lives. For Agranat, the following exchange concerning negotiations with the Nazis, between Kasztner and representatives of the American Jewish Joint Distribution Committee, captured Kasztner's state of mind when he decided to withhold the Auschwitz news:

Joint Representative: Do you really believe it [the plan of buying Jewish lives with money] will work?

Kasztner: Why shouldn't I believe? What else is left to us? Do you have any other, better ideas of rescue?[49]

Kasztner was hoping the negotiations would either succeed or be rendered moot by the Allies' victory. From this perspective, the Bergen-Belsen transport was only one plan among several negotiated by Kasztner during the spring of 1944.[50] What animated him throughout the period was the same spirit that had kept the Jewish people alive: hope. "Ha-Tikvah [The Hope]" is the title of Israel's national anthem. The lyric, "Our hope is not yet lost," is its heart. Agranat echoed this Jewish disposition in his description of Kasztner's state of mind during the awful months of April and May: "[T]he hope was not yet lost, to stop, through negotiations with the Germans, the impending deportation and annihilation."[51] He thus resisted the conclusion that Kasztner's behavior could be morally justified.

Agranat's opinion did not exculpate Kasztner. He only held that, within the context of Nazi occupation, it was not unreasonable for a Jewish leader to do what Kasztner had done. One question persisted: from the perspective of Zionist ideology, what was a good Jew to do?

THE POISONED HEART

The context of the trial, held in Israel shortly after Independence and with all the participants adhering to one or another version of Zionism, was based on the premise that a good Jew was also a Zionist. Had Europe's Jews heeded the Zionist warning and immigrated to Palestine, there would have been no Holocaust. Tamir fired the first shot in this battle when he portrayed Kasztner as the rotten product of *galut*. There was poetic irony in Tamir's position, because if any of the characters in this drama resembled the stereotype of a *galut* Jew in Zionist literature (borrowed from anti-Semitic descriptions), it was the man Tamir himself was representing, Malchiel Gruenvald. With his beard and yarmulke, old, heavy, and shabby-looking, Gruenvald could serve as a model for any anti-Semitic casting of Shylock. Kasztner, on the other hand, was the quintessential modern Jew, educated, secular, well dressed, and well mannered. But then, Kasztner fit precisely into the Zionist perspective that informed Tamir. The corrupting conditions of *galut* could not be reduced to external attributes. *Galut* shaped Jewish consciousness and was evident in the Jewish worldview. *Galut* ossified the Jewish arteries by breeding what Tamir denounced as "the anti-militarist mentality." At best, *galut* produced naive and cowardly Jews who walked like "lambs to the slaughter"; at worst, *galut* produced collaborationists. In Tamir's analysis, Kasztner was turned into a collaborator, not so much by the reality of Nazi occupation as by the conditions of Jewish life in exile. This was why he chose to gamble on the German number in the game of roulette in human lives.

Tamir's strategy, however, was aimed at much larger fish than Kasztner: the entire MAPAI leadership, Israel's ruling party, were his targets. He accused the Zionist leadership—David Ben-Gurion, Moshe Sharett, and the Jewish Agency, the organization they headed during the calamitous years prior to Israeli statehood—of failing to come to the rescue of Jews in Europe. As Tamir saw it, MAPAI's loyalty to the British, conditioned as it was by their subservience to colonial authorities, hardened their hearts to the plight of their brethren in Europe. It led MAPAI's leaders to silence news of the Holocaust and encouraged them to oppose the Irgun's resistance in Palestine. After Independence it led them to instruct the attorney general to cover up the truth. This was the reason they insisted on defending Kasztner at all costs.[52] For Tamir, the story of the Holocaust was a drama with good Jews and bad Jews. Against Kasztner and the leadership of the Yishuv he juxtaposed both the Israeli members of the Irgun and LEHI, who pursued violent resistance in Palestine and the Jewish partisans in occupied Europe. The uprising of the Warsaw Ghetto had already become a glorious symbol of Jewish resistance.[53] Tamir urged the court to uphold the rebellion at the Warsaw ghetto as the model of "correct" Jewish behavior under Nazi occupation, as the only way that, if it did not save lives, would at least save Jewish honor. His rhetoric struck a powerful chord with the Israeli public.

It was typical of the Israeli political scene of the 1950s that the right-wing Tamir found a staunch ally in the left-wing MAPAM leadership. MA-PAM, from whose ranks had come many of the Jewish partisans, also hailed violent resistance as the only option open to Jews during the Holocaust. The glorification of the Warsaw uprising was not only about the past, about crafting an alternative Jewish history that would tie the heroic partisans to the Maccabeans. It was also about the present and the future. It enabled Israelis to cure the shame of their own flesh and blood "marching obediently to their deaths." The populist rhetoric in which that version of the events was cloaked, the claim that but for villainous leaders like Kasztner the Jewish masses would have revolted, thereby saving both themselves and Jewish honor, was attractive. Most importantly, Tamir's version was pregnant with a crucial lesson for the young: Jews should live by the sword, to defend themselves against a hostile, anti-Semitic world. Auschwitz was the alternative to self-defense, and Auschwitz must never happen again — that was the crucial significance of the lesson to be drawn.[54]

The district court accepted Tamir's version. One could envision the ghetto Jews, "among them strong and healthy men who had good hands to hold a gun, a knife, an ax, a stone . . . veterans of Zionist and Socialist movements, children and grandchildren of experienced revolutionaries and rabbinical martyrs," defending their right to live had they only known the truth.[55] It was a paradoxical rejection of *galut*. For according to this version of events, not all *galut* Jews were meek and servile; only the leadership was. How could one argue, then, that the culture of *galut* itself shaped the Jewish psyche in a negative way? Despite the contradiction, it was a comforting version of history.

On appeal, Justice Silberg, representing the religious-nationalist school of Zionism, fortified the district court's position with a twist of his own. In a paragraph strategically placed at the very end of his opinion, Silberg provided the ultimate proof, from his perspective, of Kasztner's lowly character. Kasztner, said Silberg, valued everything, human life included, only in pengos (the Hungarian currency). Silberg summed up Kasztner in three words, borrowed from Kasztner's own report: "[W]e paid less." Kasztner was referring to the fact that during the war many nations had to make financial concessions to the Nazis in order to retain their territorial integrity. Wrote Silberg: "'[W]e paid less'—less than the Turks and less than the Swedes. They were coerced to sell . . . their chrome and steel. We—No! . . . [Kasztner] knows—and certainly his heart aches—that during this very period Hungarian Jewry lost 600,000 lives . . . and nevertheless 'we . . . paid less,' our [sic] operation was also successful from the financial perspective. . . . [H]erein lies the key . . . to understanding Kasztner's personality and public activities."[56]

The reduction of the Jewish psyche to pecuniary considerations is the historical heart of anti-Semitism. In the whirlwind of condemning Kasztner and the Judenrat for facilitating the Holocaust, even Zionists like Silberg could not resist Shylock's allure.

Agranat was immune neither to the Zionist ethos of rejecting *galut* nor to the reverence for Jewish physical power. In his 1931 eulogy for Chizik he had made clear his preference for the "new Jew."[57] He always expressed admiration for the young men and women who formed the backbone of Israel's Defense Forces. But he was now the head of a large family. Experience had shown him both the paralysis that springs from fear mixed with responsibility for loved ones and the hope that somehow the very worst would not happen. He developed a theory that contrasted Jewish action in the Diaspora and Zionist action in the homeland:

The heroism of the rebels of the Warsaw ghetto added . . . a glorious chapter to the history of the Jewish people; it became an inseparable part of our national saga; it will return to influence the national spirit and strengthen, among those who need it, the sense of national honor. But . . . the position that even in Galut—*and not only in the homeland*—Jews should be willing to "sacrifice lives for purposes of self defense"—and do so "without intricate calculations"—this position is relevant only to the general Jewish welfare in the long run; . . . it is only within this perspective—that one may ask the clearly political question—whether Hungarian Jewry should have followed in the footsteps of the Warsaw ghetto uprising. The question before us was much narrower in scope.[58]

Agranat expressed the theory tentatively. Earlier in the opinion he had already asserted, as a matter of fact, that Hungarian Jewry had been terrorized into submission and was not in a position to resist. Perhaps at this stage in his life, Agranat had come to accept the notion that the fervent Zionist goal of "becoming a normal people," if translated into the admiration of sheer physical prowess, was itself a sign of abnormality. The emphasis on honor, physical power, and valiant resistance came at the price of insensitivity to the tragedy of the human condition and to the vulnerability of Jews in the face of Nazi terror. Perhaps the best sign of normality was a coming to terms with the past, an empathizing with rather than a judging of the millions of victims. Humility, not fiery rhetoric, was needed. Agranat attempted to provide all of these in his long, repetitive, and careful opinion.

Yet, even in the 1950s, Israelis were exhibiting signs of normal national behavior. The sovereign Jewish state had its own soccer team, just like England and France, and, "like every normal nation," was competing in the 1958 World Cup series. On the morning of 17 January 1958 Agranat read his opinion before a packed Court. After lunch, when he returned to resume reading, the courtroom was almost empty. A soccer fan himself, he was only mildly surprised. In Wales, that afternoon, Israel's team was playing against the Welsh team, and the country's ears were glued to radios that transmitted the game live. It was evidently a sign of "normality" that the press preferred to follow the game rather than the learned arguments in the Kasztner affair. Israel lost, 0–2. "Two defeats," quipped a member of the Tamir legal team, "but both well reasoned."[59]

It was dark and bitterly cold that evening, when a messenger from Kasztner's widow delivered a bouquet of roses to Agranat's home, in gratitude. The chapter of Jewish self-blame for the Holocaust had come to an end.

CHAPTER 8

Blaming the Victimizers:
The Eichmann Trial

JEWISH ANGUISH, JEWISH JUSTICE: ESTABLISHING THE "CORRECT HISTORICAL PERSPECTIVE"

May 1960 was festive. Israel had survived for a full twelve years and was celebrating its bat mitzvah, the age signifying passage from childhood to maturity in Jewish tradition. The bat mitzvah happily coincided with the 100th anniversary of the birth of Theodor Herzl, founding father of Zionism. In the Knesset, parties of all ideological colors were outdoing each other in singing the praises of the man who had proposed the creation of a Jewish state as the resolution of the Jewish Question. Two weeks later Ben-Gurion announced that Adolph Eichmann, executioner of the Final Solution, was on Israeli soil, being interrogated by the Israeli police.

Adolph Eichmann was the Satan to whom Kasztner had sold his soul, according to the opinion of Judge Halevy of the Jerusalem district court. Between 1957 and 1958, as Israel's Supreme Court overturned the verdict in *Kasztner*, its Secret Service, the Mossad, had been authorized to locate Eichmann and deliver him to Jerusalem.[1]

Eichmann was head of Department IV B 4 of the Reich Security Services, in charge of Jewish Affairs and Evacuation. He proved his excellent managerial skills by successfully expelling Vienna's Jews from Austria and went on to engineer the systematic transportation and murder of the larger part of European Jewry. In 1944, shortly before the Red Army marched on Budapest, he reactivated the Auschwitz crematoria to add

Hungarian Jewry to his 5.5 million victims. After the war he escaped to Argentina and assumed a false identity.

For two years after Eichmann's capture, Israelis rode the most high powered of roller coasters, delighting in pride, shrieking in horror, immersed in self-vindication, revenge, anxiety, pain, fear, torment, shame, guilt, anguish, satisfaction, horror, pride. Thus Justice Cheshin's admonition in the *Kasztner* appeal—that Jews stop blaming each other and focus on those who had visited the destruction on them—became a reality.[2]

In May 1960 the Court could barely allow itself to share with most Israelis their feelings of excitement at the thought that Jewish justice would finally be meted out to a Nazi criminal. Almost overnight the Court found itself at the center of an international controversy.[3] Until 1960 Israel had showcased its army or kibbutzim; neither the government nor the world found Israel's judiciary worthy of attention. Now the judges found themselves in the limelight. The *New York Times* and the *Washington Post* condemned the idea of trying Eichmann in an Israeli court. These newspapers reflected the consensus of the mainstream international legal community that Jewish judges would be too biased to render justice.[4] Thus, as Eichmann prepared to stand trial before Israel's Court, the Court was preparing to stand trial before world public opinion. Would it rise to the occasion?

As recounted years later by then Chief Justice Olshan, the judges took it for granted that justice would be done; they wanted to make sure that justice would be seen. The performance had to be prepared quickly. For the first time, the government took a good look at the Court building and realized that even if it were a place to show the world, which it was not, the world would not fit in it. In the 1960s it would not do to hold a major international event in the ascetic Russian hostel, turned into a court by a colonial power in 1930s' Palestine. Because Jerusalem did not have any fancy palaces (the old palaces existed only in the form of archeological excavations, and even those were across the border, under Jordanian rule), the government decided to accelerate the construction of the new auditorium known as Bet ha-Am—the People's House—and hold the trial there. To accommodate the international media, the Court waived the conventional rules of the common law, which prohibited cameras and microphones at the trial. A post office was installed on the premises, and simultaneous translation was provided. A formidable security machine was constructed, including a bullet-proof glass booth in which the accused could be seen but not reached. To prove that it was taking seriously the task of holding a fair trial, Israel offered to pay for Eichmann's attorney of choice. He chose Dr. Robert Servatius, a German lawyer. These logistics, albeit demanding, were the easy part. The question of who would preside over the trial proved more difficult to handle.

The law provided that Eichmann would be tried first by the district court. The president of the district court was Benjamin Halevy, whose thinking about Eichmann was clear from his *Kasztner* opinion. Would his presence cast a shadow on Israeli justice? Worried about the world's reaction to Halevy, Chief Justice Olshan repeatedly implored Halevy "to put the interests of the State above his concern for personal reputation and honor," to no avail. And so, in order to protect the appearance of justice, Olshan found himself doing what all rulers do when the law stands in their way: he negotiated an amendment to the statute, which provided for a Supreme Court justice to preside over the district court when Nazi crimes were adjudicated. Justice Moshe Landau, one of the senior justices on the Supreme Court, was appointed chairman of the panel, with Judges Benjamin Halevy and Yitzhak Raveh at his side.[5]

Justice Landau, a good friend of Agranat since the 1940s, was the perfect man for the job. Born to a bourgeois family in the free city of Danzig, Landau was steeped in high German culture and was known in Jerusalem as a gifted pianist and a frequent player in amateur quartets. His English legal education, his career of more than thirty years on the bench, and his reputation as an even-handed, solid, and temperamentally reserved judge ensured that Western journalists would not find the trial very different from what they were accustomed to at home.[6] Furthermore, this tall and dignified-looking man, who had come to Palestine in the early 1930s, had been an ardent Zionist since childhood. Few people knew that he had declined, as a matter of principle, to accept German reparations offered to Nazi victims. He would surely project the glory of Jewish empowerment realized in the state of Israel as it came to judge the representative of Nazi destruction.

David Ben-Gurion and Attorney General Gideon Hausner, who served as Eichmann's prosecutor, wanted the trial to fulfill all their dreams. On this stage "the canvas soaked in blood and tears" was to unfold,[7] and two intertwining tales would be told: one of Jewish misery, the other of gentile frigidity. A minor benefit of thus exposing the passivity of the Allies in the face of Jewish destruction was the perspective the tale would lend to the questionable behavior of the Yishuv leadership during the war, which had tormented Israel since the *Kasztner* case. But the major purpose was to prove the insight embedded in Zionist ideology: that the Enlightenment had failed to resolve the Jewish problem and that only a

Jewish state could guarantee the survival of the Jewish people. It was to this larger agenda that Attorney General Hausner alluded when he insisted that the purpose of the trial was to establish "the correct historical perspective."[8] Both Ben-Gurion and Hausner were convinced that this symbolic and ideological content should and could fit within the framework of a conventional criminal trial. No wonder, then, that Susan Sontag wrote in 1964 that she considered the trial to be "the most interesting and moving work of art in the past ten years" and observed "a fundamental paradox in the Eichmann trial: it was primarily a great act of commitment through memory and the renewal of grief, yet it clothed itself in the forms of legality and scientific objectivity."[9]

The year Eichmann was captured was particularly gloomy for the Agranats. In one year, the family lost both Simon's sister-in-law in Haifa and Carmel's aunt in the United States. Both were tragic and painful losses to the close-knit family. In addition, the Agranats had just moved to a new home, in an area remote from the Court and at the time quite inaccessible to people who, like Agranat, did not own an automobile. The hardships of commuting and of adjusting to the new environment intensified the tension.

Agranat dreaded confronting the Holocaust again, but there was no escape. From the moment that Hausner announced that 6 million accusers were standing next to him on the prosecutor's stand until the appearance of the last witness, Agranat's household, together with every home in Israel, listened, mesmerized, to the radio, absorbing the detailed descriptions (there was still no television) as if possessed.[10] The witnesses were skillfully chosen; together their stories told the saga of European Jewry, from the thriving communities of the 1920s, through Hitler's rise to power, *Anschluss, Kristallnacht,* the Wansee Conference, the ghettos, the Gentiles who did help, the search for ever more efficient methods of mass killing, the medical experimentations, the gas chambers, the Jewish resistance, the mountains of eyeglasses, gold teeth, shoes neatly piled.

Agranat appears to have been increasingly torn between his Jewishness and his judicial instincts. As a judge he felt compelled to insist on legal principles: that an accused is considered innocent until proved guilty, that only relevant testimony is admitted, that true stories are not always valid evidence. As a Jew (and he did not perceive a difference between being a Jew and being an Israeli), he felt that simple human need to share the emotional travails of the trial, to experience catharsis. Still, in 1961 he was merely an observer. He knew the task was much more difficult for those on the bench, who were struggling to force the drama to conform to the rigid rules of criminal procedure.

Eichmann's conviction by the district court on 15 December 1961 brought proud relief to Israelis. The trial was a success. Its goals had been accomplished. Israelis had lived through the entire saga and had committed it to memory. They had "forced the world to confront its yesterday."[11] They had vindicated Zionism, the need for a state of their own. Unlike the *Kasztner* case, here they were united in the experience. They delighted in their judges, who had demonstrated the viability of Jewish justice. Eichmann had been convicted of crimes against the Jewish people and sentenced to death. A confirmation of the sentence on appeal appeared certain. Ready to resume normal life, most people lost interest in the trial.

For the Supreme Court the ordeal had just begun. In the fall of 1961 Michael A. Musmanno, justice on the supreme court of Pennsylvania and former judge in the International War Crimes Tribunal at Nuremberg, stated that "[i]t is startling to recall how many respectable journals, eminent lawyers, and renowned commentators beat the drums of censure and reproof against Israel for arresting, transporting, and indicting [Eichmann]."[12] The widespread criticism was somewhat tempered by the general concession that the trial had indeed been fair. Still, most opined that Israel erred in convicting Eichmann for crimes against the Jewish people, a category then unknown in international law. International commentators further insisted that international law was violated by the fact that Israel, a state that had not existed during the Holocaust, abducted Eichmann against his will and tried him for crimes he had committed in faraway Europe, not on Israeli soil.

FROM PURIM TO PASSOVER: APPEAL

Eichmann's appeal began on 22 March 1962 and was denied eight weeks later. The feast of Purim, celebrating Jewish survival in the ancient Persian Empire, coincided with the opening of the hearings. Reports had it that Attorney General Hausner, who was scheduled to represent the State on appeal, compared Haman, the Persian detractor of the Jews, to Eichmann while participating in a service at a Jerusalem synagogue. The symbolism was striking: the Jewish people had survived yet another conspiracy to annihilate them. But Eichmann, as one newspaper explained, was already a dead man. When the appeal opened, both the justices on the bench and Eichmann in his glass booth faced a practically empty hall.[13]

Five justices were chosen for the panel on the basis of seniority: Chief Justice Olshan and Justices Agranat, Silberg, Sussman, and Witkon. The panel decided to write the opinion per curiam, to reflect the unanimity of Israeli justice. Thus the *Eichmann* opinion does not bear the signature of any individual justice. The justices also decided to divide the issues and assign the task of writing to three justices; in Court each justice read his own portion of the assignment, implicitly stating his individual share. Olshan, himself never a prolific writer, wanted Agranat to write the part justifying Israeli jurisdiction, and so it was. Silberg, born in Lithuania and educated in Central Europe, undertook to write the factual part and the part related to Eichmann's argument in his own defense, that he was but a small cog in the Nazi machine. Sussman, who had left Germany after Hitler's rise to power, wrote the procedural part, responding to Eichmann's effort to introduce new evidence before the Court.

Although the auditorium of Bet ha-Am was luxurious by Israeli standards of the early 1960s, it was not air-conditioned, and the heat affected the justices. One journalist described Agranat as "hardly moving in his seat, chin held in the palm of his hand, staring into space so that one wonders whether he was listening." To quell all doubts, the journalist added that Agranat's questions and comments were "right on point."[14] Agranat had good reason to be anxious. In Washington, Arthur Goldberg, his friend of more than thirty years, was now a member of the Kennedy cabinet. Goldberg was widely admired in the United States as well as in Israel. For the first time in his life Agranat, too, would come to the world's attention. He would be watched by the international legal community, his work evaluated by persons he had respected and whose professional judgment mattered. Not only his own reputation but those of Israel and the Supreme Court were at stake. He wished to present arguments that would meet with universal approval.

Agranat also understood that more than appearance was at stake: the soul of the Zionist project was reshaped by the brutal confrontation with the Holocaust. The old tension within Zionism between universalism and particularism now tilted in favor of particularism.[15] Israelis were perceiving themselves as special: a special target for genocide and special in their right to ignore international norms in pursuit of justice. Popular hubris was growing, nurturing a victim mentality, a sense of self-righteousness and excessive nationalism, threatening to weaken the already shaky foundations of universalism in Israeli political culture.

While the appeal was pending, skirmishes on the Israeli-Syrian border peaked with an Israeli raid on the Syrian military stronghold of Nukeib in the Golan. In keeping with its policy of retaliation, Israel was thereby sending a message to the Syrians to stop shooting at Israeli fishermen in the Sea of Galilee, "or else." Israelis were elated by this show of military might, but in the United Nations the Security Council unanimously condemned Israel for the attack. The international community looked at Israel and saw a lawless state.[16]

Agranat understood that the legal reasoning he chose would affect the resolution of the tension between particularism and universalism. The Supreme Court could either let the conviction stand on the basis of crimes against the Jewish people, thereby lending force to the contention that Israel operated by its own rules, impervious to the laws developed by the community of nations, or it could try to show that Eichmann's trial was compatible with international norms of justice and fairness.

Again Agranat experienced sleepless nights. Even though nothing had been explicitly said, the Court was expected to deliver its judgment expeditiously. The general strategy was designed collectively, but he was to put his own spin on it: let the district court's rather particularistic version of Jewish justice stand, while emphasizing a different approach, that of universal justice. He recalled how the tension grew as he struggled with mountains of materials on international law. That was one legal discipline he had neglected over the years, and he now had to digest it quickly.

The Court concluded oral arguments on 29 March 1962; the opinion was delivered on 29 May. Agranat, seated between Olshan and Sussman, began by reading the four-part indictment against Eichmann: crimes against the Jewish people; crimes against humanity; war crimes; and membership in hostile organizations. Agranat then struck a chord of unity: "The District Court has . . . dealt with . . . [the] contentions in an exhaustive, profound and most convincing manner. We should say at once that we fully concur, without hesitation or reserve, in all its conclusions and reasons. . . . Moreover . . . were it not for the grave outcome . . . we would have seen no need whatever to formulate our opinion separately and in our own language."[17]

What "grave outcome" was he alluding to in the passage? An obvious answer would be the pending death penalty against Eichmann. But deeper layers of gravity could be detected. Agranat recalled being worried about the international perception of Israel as a lawless state "feeling free to do what it wants to do"; the victim's mentality that threatened to sweep the nation, leading to a policy that emphasized Jewish self-interest and dismissed criticism as anti-Semitic. The reputation of the state was on Agranat's mind. He said so. The rise of particularism in Israeli political culture at the expense of the universalist element in Zionism pervaded the structural logic of his *Eichmann* opinion. Ten pages into the

opinion, he disclosed that he was dividing his arguments into those stemming from "a negative perspective" and those stemming from "a positive
one."[18] Literally, the "negative perspective" referred to a legalistic interpretation of the question of jurisdiction; the positive, to the universal principles embedded in international law. The negative and positive mental-
ities of Zionism lurked close to the surface of these legal arguments.

NEGATIVE AND POSITIVE PERSPECTIVES: JEWISH
JUSTICE VERSUS UNIVERSAL JUSTICE

Most of the legal arguments advanced by Eichmann were
designed to prove that Israel lacked jurisdiction to try him. Two of these
arguments received extensive attention from the international community. The first was that the 1950 Israeli Law against the Nazis and Nazi
Collaborators,[19] which vested jurisdiction in the Israeli courts, was an ex
post facto criminal law and as such could not apply to foreign nationals;
the second was that, because the crimes were "extra-territorial offenses"
committed by a foreign national, Israel could not prosecute Eichmann
according to the territoriality principle of international law.[20]

In rejecting these arguments, the district court stressed the superiority of Israeli law in the sovereign state of Israel. The Law against the Nazis
and Nazi Collaborators, the district court held, was a part of Israeli positive law and, as such, was binding on the courts of the land. It did hold
that the law agreed with international norms, but emphasized the impact
of the Holocaust on the evolution of the law of nations. This holding
contained a symbolic message: Jewish national pride and self-assertion
ruled the day. There was poetic justice in this interpretation. If the Final
Solution was about the lawless murder of Jews, the *Eichmann* case was
about the subjection of the perpetrators to Jewish justice, conceived and
applied by the very heirs of those murdered.

There was ambivalence in Agranat's handling of this theme. On one
hand, he endorsed the district court's analysis; on the other, his own reasoning went in a different direction. He sought to prove that the validity of the Law against the Nazis and Nazi Collaborators stemmed not from
its superiority to the law of nations but from its compatibility with international law. Jewish justice was thereby not different from or superior
to the law of nations; rather, it was a part of it.

Agranat began his analysis with the "negative perspective." Citing
scholarly works and judicial opinions, he asserted that international law

did not prohibit ex post facto laws and was not dogmatic about the territoriality principle. Thus Israel's decision to prosecute, far from being a violation of international law, was simply a perfectly legitimate reluctance to recognize principles not fully endorsed by the community of nations. The "negative viewpoint" rested on solid legal grounds, yet Agranat devoted twenty pages in a thirty-page discussion to "positive thinking" — silent proof of the weight he attached to its significance. He wanted to show that Israel's law was not an aberration but an affirmation of the law of nations.

The Law against the Nazis and Nazi Collaborators created a new category of crimes: crimes against the Jewish people. As such, it was a unique ex post facto law. The crime was specific to Jews and created a category hitherto unknown in any legal system. It was precisely for this reason that the crime formed a coherent part of Zionism. After all, it was Zionist ideology that insisted that "a Jewish people" existed, and it was Jewish detractors who protested that Jewishness was merely a religion.[21] Zionism portrayed the Holocaust less as the vile fruit of totalitarianism and more as the culmination of two millennia of anti-Semitism. The Jews had been defenseless because they did not possess political power. Even in Nuremberg the Allies refused to recognize that the Jews as a nation were especially targeted by the Nazis.[22] The offense, "crimes against the Jewish people," was designed to correct that myopia and to assert, ex post facto and forever, the Jewish point of view. Indeed, Eichmann was also charged with crimes against humanity, and abundant evidence was presented that other groups, such as the Gypsies, had also been victimized, but the insistence on the legal category of "crimes against the Jewish people" seemed crucial. Israeli public opinion, the government, the prosecution, and the district court each emphasized its validity and significance.

Speaking for the Supreme Court, Agranat raised a different voice. He reviewed the four categories of the indictment,[23] and he concluded that they had a common denominator, a "special universal characteristic."[24] About "crimes against the Jewish people" he had this to say: "Thus, the category of 'crimes against the Jewish people' is nothing but . . . 'the gravest crime against humanity.' It is true that there are certain differences between them . . . but these are not differences material to our case."[25] Therefore, he concluded, in order to determine whether international law recognized Israeli jurisdiction stemming from this ex post facto statute, the Court could simply collapse the entire indictment into "the inclusive category of 'crimes against humanity.'"[26] This "simple" technique enabled Agranat to devote the bulk of his opinion to the universal aspects of the *Eichmann* case.

In twenty pages replete with scholarly quotations and case citations—all non-Israeli—Agranat argued that the indictment incorporated actions which were always known as crimes by the international community and therefore could not be viewed as crimes invented by Israel ex post facto. As he would occasionally do in his opinions, he invoked his hero, Justice Oliver Wendell Holmes Jr., in arguing that law (in this case, customary international law) was not about logic but about experience.[27] Experience showed that crimes which shared the following features were prohibited by "enlightened humanity," even though international law had not recognized them as such: "they constitute acts which damage vital international interests; they impair the foundations and security of the international community; they violate universal moral values and humanitarian principles which are at the root of the systems of criminal law adopted by civilized nations."[28] Conceding that there were no international mechanisms to enforce these norms, he attributed that to the "primitive" state of international law at the moment. Therefore, "for the time being, international law surmounts these difficulties . . . by authorizing the countries of the world to mete out punishment for the violation of its provisions. This they do . . . either directly or by virtue of the municipal legislation which has adopted and integrated them."[29] At the end of this analysis the Law against the Nazis and Nazi Collaborators seemed to be nothing but a reflection of international law. Israel was not a state with a unique conception of justice but, rather, a loyal member of the community of civilized nations (a term repeated almost obsessively), adhering to its collectively recognized principles.

And what about the territoriality principle, the rule that a state cannot prosecute foreign nationals for crimes committed beyond its borders? Agranat conceded that territoriality was an important principle in international law, but he found an exception to it. That exception related to crimes against humanity. Any state could claim jurisdiction to prosecute the perpetrators of these crimes, regardless of where or by whom these crimes had been committed.[30]

Eichmann had still another argument: Israel was under an obligation to seek his extradition as a German national, to Germany, on whose territory these crimes had been committed. For the second time in the opinion Agranat addressed this sensitive issue. He recalled doing this at the request of Chief Justice Olshan, who felt that this argument weighed particularly heavily against Israel in the court of international public opinion.

Agranat rejected the extradition argument on two grounds. First, Eichmann did petition the government of Germany to request his extradition, and Germany refused. Hence there would be no "pragmatic utility" in having Israel seek his extradition, because it was known that Germany was not interested. Second, the requirement of trying persons in their country of nationality was not based on any legal principle. Rather, it stemmed from pragmatic considerations of expediency. A trial should be held in the place where documents and witnesses pertaining to it could be found. In this case, Agranat observed, the bulk of the documents were stored in the museum of Yad va-Shem in Jerusalem, and the majority of survivors resided in Israel; therefore expediency required that Eichmann be tried in Israel, not in Germany. As for other countries on whose territories Jews were murdered, "it is to be observed that we have not heard of a single protest by any of these countries against conducting the trial in Israel."[31] Thus, because no other jurisdiction stood ready to prosecute, Eichmann's release would leave him free by default, a result strikingly at odds with any concept of justice.

The descent from the metaphysical world of principle to the ground of pragmatism and the reference to the utter silence of the "other countries" aroused the awareness of that other silence—the silence of the community of nations during the Holocaust. As if this reminder of the anguish of Jewish helplessness tilted the pendulum of reasoning from the universal back to the particular, Agranat ended his "positive thinking" with a reaffirmation of the district court's approach. Yes, Israel was an agent of the civilized world, enforcing universal principles. But Israel was also acting on behalf of the Jews, because it alone stood for Jewish nationhood, even before it declared itself a sovereign state: "We wish to add one further observation. In regard to the crimes directed against the Jews the District Court found additional support for its jurisdiction in the connecting link between the State of Israel and the Jewish people, including that between the State of Israel and the Jewish victims of the Catastrophe, and the National Home in Palestine. . . . It should be clear that we fully agree with every word."[32] This relapse hints at Agranat's ambivalence about the dominating theme of his opinion: that these were crimes against humanity, universally recognized by the community of nations. Agranat returned to the universalist theme as he responded to Eichmann's third challenge, that the acts he was accused of were acts of state and that his role in performing them was the role of a "small cog."

A SMALL COG?

Even if Israel had jurisdiction, Eichmann argued, he still had a good defense. The Final Solution was a project undertaken by the

German state under Nazi rule. In keeping with international law, Israel could not pass judgment on the legality or criminality of these "acts of state" by Germany, because such judgment would amount to interference by one country (Israel) in the internal affairs of another (Germany). Also, Eichmann was merely a small cog; all he had done was to obey the orders of his superiors.[33]

Relying mainly on American sources,[34] Agranat rejected the defense of acts of state. Sovereignty is a relative concept, he observed, presupposing that the sovereign state will not flagrantly violate basic principles of international law. Thus, under customary international law, sovereign states were always understood to be bound by the prohibition of crimes against humanity; the Nuremberg Charter merely solidified, rather than created, this principle. Agranat concluded by quoting the district court: "[t]he very contention that the systematic extermination of masses of helpless human beings by a government or regime could constitute 'an act of state,' thereby absolving the executioners, appears to be an insult to reason and a mockery of law and justice."[35]

Agranat was now coming to the "small-cog" defense: that Eichmann was bound by the oath he had taken when he joined the S.S. (Schutzstaffel) —to obey Hitler unconditionally—and that his implementation of the plans for mass murder was simply a loyal execution of Hitler's orders in keeping with that oath. Israel's Law against the Nazis and Nazi Collaborators had explicitly denied the validity of this defense. Eichmann challenged the statute as a violation of international law and urged the Court to accept his "small-cog" defense. Agranat was eager to respond to both arguments. Criminal law was his field, the subject he had taught at the Hebrew University for the past decade.

Why does conventional criminal law recognize the "small-cog" defense? he asked somewhat didactically and proceeded to explain: if you wish to maintain discipline in military organizations and to protect a soldier who is unsure whether an order is legal, you need to absolve those who violate the law while obeying orders. This explanation presupposes that a defendant was not fully aware that the order was illegal. But if one fully understood the illegality of one's actions, and if one had a choice to refuse to obey, then he could not be exonerated. Both conventional criminal law and international law would allow for a "small-cog" defense only if the perpetrators expected that disobedience would result in their own death. Therefore, even if the Law against the Nazis and Nazi Collaborators did recognize such a defense in the *Eichmann* case, it would be to no avail. Eichmann, said Agranat, "performed the extermination order at all times and in all seasons *con amore* . . . with genuine zeal and devotion to that objective."[36]

Twice in this section Agranat mentioned that his discussion was limited to the legal aspects of the defense, that the questions of fact pertaining to Eichmann's "small-cog" defense would be discussed later. He did this because the initial agreement between the justices was that Agranat would write about international law and Silberg about the facts. Silberg, who had lost his entire family in the Holocaust, was still grieving, and he probably perceived the opportunity to write a part of the opinion as yet another way of saying kaddish for the dead. He imbued his role with symbolism and thus was particularly jealous of his turf. Agranat recalled that on reading his colleague's opinion, Silberg furiously accused Agranat of "invading his territory." Agranat knew that Silberg was right, but he would not omit his discussion of these facts.

Why the insistence? Agranat himself, in interview, was reluctant to discuss motives. Some of it could be related to Agranat's pride in his own expertise in criminal law and its application to the case. Some could be attributed to a deeper need to reconcile the point with his approach in the *Kasztner* case. In reviewing Kasztner's negotiations with Eichmann, Agranat urged humility. A man must be understood in the context of his time. But if so, why should Eichmann not be judged in the context of his time? Why not give Eichmann the benefit of the doubt? To this question, never explicitly raised among the justices, Agranat had to respond himself, to satisfy his own sense of justice. In interview, he insisted that Kasztner, the Jew, was operating under tremendous pressure; by contrast, Eichmann, the Nazi, did what he did *con amore*—with love, dedicated to the project of genocide.

There could be another reason for this trespass into a colleague's turf: it was expected that Silberg's opinion would emphasize the Jewish, not the universal, point of view. Silberg was an open wound. First and foremost, he saw Jewish tragedy calling for Jewish redress. Of all the justices, Silberg wrote the most eloquent prose, and Agranat knew, even before he saw the opinion, that Silberg would unleash his pen at Eichmann, making words the vessel of his wrath. Indeed, Silberg dismissed Agranat's arguments (not referring to his colleague by name) as too soft, charging that they did not capture the full truth: "Determined though we be not to enter the wide field of research into the history of the Holocaust, we shall nevertheless not assist in any historical distortion of the personalities. . . . We shall not underestimate the standing of Eichmann or belittle his great 'merits' in achieving the Nazi's [*sic*] cherished objective, *viz,* the extermination of the Jewish people. We shall assign to him his proper place in the Nazi hierarchy as it emerges from the evidence."[37] The rift was clear on the face of the opinion. Whereas Agranat tried to generalize, to sweep all issues into the universal category of crimes against humanity, Silberg insisted on the particular and left no fact unturned, demonstrating Eichmann's special role in destroying European Jewry. Only the decision to deliver the opinion per curiam could hide the tension within the Supreme Court's reasoning.

Thus understood, Agranat's discussion of the "small-cog" defense was one way to deflect attention from Silberg's approach and to offer an alternative to the particularistic point of view. The contrast between the two approaches is striking. Agranat emphasized Israel as a member of the community of nations, as humanity's agent in prosecuting universal crimes; Silberg emphasized the Jewish point of view.

Could anyone earnestly believe in the impartiality of this judicial process? Most foreign commentators agreed that the trial had been dignified and that all the judges, both at the district and high court levels, had made a conscious effort to preserve the principles of fairness and legality.[38] Yet it had been more than that, a trial staged in a public auditorium, with evidence presented not to prove the guilt of a man presumed innocent but, rather, to commit events to memory and thereby to restore the "correct historical perspective." Was Eichmann's attorney right when he claimed that "the judges of the district court, being Jews and feeling a sense of affinity with the victims . . . were psychologically incapable of giving the Appellant an objective trial"?[39]

VICTIMS JUDGING THE VICTIMIZERS

The charge was serious. With the exception of Agranat, all of the judges involved in this trial had been born and raised in Eastern or Central Europe. They had known enough people who died in the Holocaust, had met enough survivors. Agranat himself had called Eichmann "a monster" in his opinion in the *Kasztner* case.[40] Like most Israelis, the judges understood the Holocaust not in terms of totalitarianism (as Hannah Arendt understood it) but, rather, as the demonic epitome of obsessive anti-Semitism. Could one look at a demon, then fairly judge it? Was it possible for Jews to give Nazis a fair trial? Eichmann did not deny that they would try. He doubted that they psychologically could. Nor did Eichmann confine his argument to the district court, as Agranat stated in opening his opinion. He insisted that no Jewish judge was capable of objectivity. Agranat rejected this contention by quoting the district court: "[T]he judge, when dispensing justice in a Court of Law, does not cease to be a human being, with human passions and human emotions. Yet he is enjoined by the law to restrain and control such passions and emotions, else there will never be a judge qualified to try a criminal case. . . . It is true that the memory of the Holocaust shocks every Jew to the depths of his being, but once this case has been brought before us it becomes our duty to control even these emotions when we sit in judgement. We shall abide by this duty." He then sealed his contribution to the opinion with the following words: "the learned judges did abide by their duty—fully and to the end."[41]

It was unlike Agranat to discharge an important issue so summarily and by means of quoting others. After all, this was one of the crucial points raised by the international community against trying Eichmann in Israel. It could be that he was simply exhausted. He had already completed seventy typewritten pages, and his energy was ebbing. But it could also be his ambivalence. How else could one explain his use of "they," not "we," in his final sentence, as if he were not implicated?

DEATH

Within weeks of Eichmann's trial, as Agranat was writing his report on the powers of the attorney general (see the next chapter), he experienced acute physical exhaustion. It is unclear whether the exhaustion was caused by personal circumstances, by the tension emanating from governmental crisis related to the attorney general, or by the fact that for the first time in his life he was called on to abandon one of his most cherished principles, his opposition to the death penalty. One thing is clear: even though the part confirming the death penalty was left to Silberg, Agranat understood full well that for the first time in his life he was sending a human being to the gallows.

Silberg captured succinctly the anguish—"[W]e know only too well how utterly inadequate this death sentence is as compared to the millions of bizarre deaths he inflicted on his victims. Just as there is no word in human speech to describe . . . such . . . deeds . . . , so there is no punishment in human laws sufficiently grave to match the guilt"—and the height of pride—"The fact that the Appellant—by a variety of ruses, escape, hiding, false papers, etc.—succeeded in evading the gallows prepared for him and his friends at Nuremberg, cannot afford him relief here, when at long last he stands his trial before an Israeli Court of Justice."[42]

Most Israelis agreed. Every Israeli child has memorized "On the Slaughter," written after the pogrom in Kishinev in 1903 by Israel's national poet, Hayim N. Bialik: "Cursed be the man who says: Avenge! No such revenge—revenge for the blood of a little child—has yet been devised by Satan."[43] But now revenge did seem compatible with justice. The difference lay not only in the fact that they had Satan himself at hand. Bialik had spoken when Jews were powerless and in exile; now they had a state and gallows of their own. Israelis also learned that the Enlightenment, on which Bialik had put his hopes, had failed to deliver. Theirs was a world in which might made right. Justice consisted not of lofty metaphysical arguments but of death to Adolph Eichmann. Decades later, Agranat could not remember any consultations among the justices. It was clear that there was no other option.

Agranat later rationalized his vote: "Mind you, it is not we who imposed the death penalty. We merely upheld the district court," and "the objection to the death penalty was grounded in the possibility that the accused was innocent. With Eichmann there was no doubt." Or, "Silberg would not conceive of any punishment but death." But Agranat also provided deeper insights: "Remember the victims, the victims. . . . [T]hese were barbarians, barbarians." "Mind you, at that time [1962] we were still a small people, a small state. . . . [P]eople must know that their state will defend them."

Simon Agranat was at a crossroads. His was the Zionism of reconstruction, of universalism and humanitarian values. This school of Zionism was almost the identical twin to the other intellectual tradition of his formative years: American Progressivism. Agranat's opposition to the death penalty harkened back to the 1920s and was associated with Clarence Darrow, La Follette, Brandeis. As soon as Israel gained sovereignty he started lobbying the Ministry of Justice and the Knesset to abolish the death penalty. When the Knesset, in the spirit of Progressive reform, proudly abolished capital punishment in the early 1950s, he was elated. It was one more instance of Israel's serving as a light unto the nations. In 1962 very few Israelis objected to the death penalty for Eichmann. Among them were the philosophers Martin Buber and Hugo Bergmann, both founders of Brit Shalom. Another opponent was Norman Bentwich, Carmel's uncle, who in the 1930s had put in a good word on Simon's behalf when he was applying for a judgeship. Buber, Bergman, and Bentwich were urging the government not to abandon the Progressivist track of utopian Zionism.

But the saga told in the district court dwarfed these Progressive traditions. The moral arguments against execution stood limp before the mass graves, the gas chambers, the crematoria. That, in my view, was the meaning of Agranat's emphasis, in interview, that "these were barbarians, barbarians." The lofty dreams of turning the Jews into an exemplary nation were deformed by the nightmare of genocide. Surrounded by enemies, with a history of persecution, this small people and small state were developing the mantra of "never again." "Never again" meant that the state was under an obligation to meet violence with violence in order to prove to itself that Jews were no longer defenseless. Agranat, now agent of the Jewish state in his capacity as deputy chief justice, was performing his duty and sending that message. The price was the considerable weakening of the Progressive spirit.

AFTERMATH

Adolph Eichmann's plea for a pardon was denied. A media blackout surrounded the execution. Only on the morning of Friday, 1 June, did Israeli radio announce that on the previous night, Eichmann had been hung and cremated and that his remains had been scattered over the Mediterranean. The evening newspaper, *Yediot Aharonot,* captured Israel's shtetl mentality when it described the last bottle Eichmann had asked for as "sour red wine"—a designation reflecting the common Jewish division of wines into sweet and sour. Its headline was also telling: "Operation Final Solution to the Eichmann Problem." In the process of doing justice, the victims were internalizing the vocabulary of the victimizers. The Holocaust became a chapter of Israeli history for good, but also for bad. The trial allowed for catharsis. It ennobled and dignified the act of commitment to memory. But it also legitimized anxiety and nourished the suspicion of "the other," the non-Jew. It turned "never again" into a fetish and legitimized any means necessary to preserve that precious of precious: a Jewish state. The morning papers reflected another facet of the emerging Israeli persona: a high sensitivity to "what the world says." The front-page headlines of *Davar,* MAPAI's newspaper, and *Herut,* the right-wing newspaper, declared, "The Reaction in the World: Justice Was Done."[44]

Agranat's opinion in the *Eichmann* case contains both morning and evening themes. The morning newspapers captured the task as Agranat had perceived it while writing the opinion: to persuade the world that

Israel was a law-abiding state, a member of good standing in the community of nations. This was not the first time that Agranat was reasoning with an eye toward international public opinion.[45] Did he feel used? He did not. It was second nature to every Israeli, when dealing with outsiders, to find arguments in favor of the State's position. In this case the task was rather easy, for he was expounding on a theory that had been his credo since childhood: the idea of utopian Zionism, of a humanistic and progressive Jewish state. In doing so he continued the battle he had begun in the 1950s, with his opinions anchoring freedom of expression, due process, and a concept of human dignity in Israeli law. It is true that even then he fought themes from catastrophe Zionism, but in previous cases these themes could also be understood as expressions of MAPAI's authoritarianism, not deriving from the tension between utopian and catastrophe Zionism.

Here the dilemma confronted him with all of its cruelty: How committed to universal values and humanitarian principles should Israel be after the Holocaust? How did the Enlightenment and Progressivism contribute to Jewish survival, let alone Jewish welfare? Why shouldn't "never again" mean the subordination of every and any value to the requirements of national security? Why adhere to the rule of law when it had failed to guarantee survival? On the other hand, was an Israel without the universal message still his Israel? The preoccupation with "what the world will say" revealed the internal insecurity of Israelis: their yearning to be recognized. Agranat would have liked to persuade himself and the world that Israel was merely employing the principles of international law. But in his heart he must have known that he was defending the State because it was the only Jewish state. As he silently and without argument gave his approval to Eichmann's execution he must have felt the ominous burden of this encounter. His convictions were shaken, his innocent trust in the good destroyed, his insistence on universality and humanism tempered by the cruel recognition of their limits. He would never be the same again.

Figure 1.   Simon Agranat in Chicago. Circa 1910.

Figure 2. The Agranats in Chicago. From left to right: Polya, Aaron, Abel, and Simon. Circa 1918.

Figure 3. Simon Agranat under Abraham Lincoln's statue in Springfield, Illinois, where he received his license to practice law. 13 February 1930.

Figure 4.　Simon and Carmel's wedding in Zikhron Ya'acov. 3 May 1934.

Figure 5.　Simon Agranat listening to oral argument during Adolph
Eichmann's appeal. 22 March 1962.

Figure 6.   Adolph Eichmann's appeal. From left to right: Joel Sussman, Simon Agranat, Isaac Olshan, Moshe Silberg, and Alfred Witkon. 22 March 1962.

Figure 7.   The Supreme Court justices at the home of the president of Israel, on the occasion of Simon Agranat's appointment as chief justice. From left to right: Alfred Witkon, Moshe Silberg, Simon Agranat, Joel Sussman, Haim Cohn, Moshe Landau, and Zvi Berinson. 18 March 1965.

Figure 8.   Chief Justice Agranat with Chief Justice Earl Warren of the U.S. Supreme Court during Warren's trip to Israel. July 1968.

Figure 9.   Golda Meir's departure for the United States. From left to right: Simon Agranat, Haim Barlev, and Moshe Dayan. 24 September 1969.

Figure 10.   The Agranat Commission. From left to right: Yigael Yadin,
Moshe Landau, Simon Agranat, Yitzhak Nebenzahl, and Haim Laskov.
December 1973.

Figure 11.   Simon Agranat at the end of his career as chief justice. Summer 1976. (Photograph by David Rubinger)

PART IV

POLITICS AND THE RULE OF LAW

CHAPTER 9

Who Is the Guardian of the Law:
The Minister of Justice or the Attorney General?

THE RULE OF LAW

The same week that Adolph Eichmann was executed, a social commentary appeared in *Davar,* titled "Restlessness in Israeli Society — Why?" The 1961 volume of *Ha-Praklit,* the bar's law review, was full of complaints about the "weakening of the rule of law."[1] At the same time, the long-simmering tension between the minister of justice and the attorney general exploded. Within weeks the government appointed Agranat chairman of a commission to decide who was in charge of law enforcement in Israeli democracy.

Israelis perceived the Eichmann trial as the epitome of justice. But no one felt completely at ease with its kernel of lawlessness: Israel had abducted Eichmann from Argentina and transported him, against his will, to stand trial in its courts. Was there symbolism in the fact that as Eichmann's plea for pardon was pending, it was revealed that one of the leading attorneys for the prosecution was guilty of making false representations and, in fact, was not qualified to practice law?[2]

In the background rumbled the angry echo of the "Lavon Affair." In the early 1950s, Israelis and Egyptian Jews executed an ill-conceived and disastrous clandestine operation, aimed at sabotaging Western and Egyptian relations. A cover-up followed. The questions of what the minister of defense knew and when he knew it (or, in the Israeli parlance, "Who gave the order?"), had haunted the Israeli leadership ever since. In 1960, while the Eichmann trial was in progress, a committee of seven ministers chaired by Minister of Justice Pinhas Rosen concluded that Pinhas Lavon, then minister of defense, did not give the order. Furious, Ben-Gurion resigned, and his resignation led to the dissolution of the Knesset and to new elections. The new government, established after the election of the fifth Knesset, in 1961, did not include the Progressive Party.[3] For the first time in ten years the Ministry of Justice went to MAPAI. Bernard Joseph, the man who had precipitated the 1953 crisis with the judiciary, again found himself in charge of the Ministry of Justice.[4]

Ben-Gurion's fury had complex roots. A battle over the control of MAPAI, and therefore over the leadership of the country, was under way. Many saw Ben-Gurion's crusade as a last-ditch effort to remain in power. The struggle was also perceived as a clash over the nature of the polity: should Israel continue its emphasis on etatism (the Eichmann trial could be perceived as a part of this trend), or should it strive to become a more pluralistic, more tolerant democracy?[5]

Meanwhile, tension developed at the Ministry of Justice. When Joseph took over as minister of justice, he was determined to exercise more influence over the decisions of the attorney general. Ben-Gurion actively supported his efforts. The more Hausner resisted, the more their relations deteriorated. Rumor had it that Joseph shunned Attorney General Hausner (appointed by his predecessor) and frowned on the latter's insistence on professional independence. The media reported that the attorney general was no longer invited to cabinet meetings, that MAPAI bosses were apprehensive about the reputation Hausner had acquired as Eichmann's successful prosecutor, and that they were looking for an opportunity to be rid of him.[6]

The institution of the attorney general was indeed constitutionally peculiar, "somewhat fish, somewhat meat, and somewhat milk, but in any event not kosher."[7] In England and the United States the attorney general serves as both a political confidant and as a legal professional. Israel split the position into two: the minister of justice, a politician and a member of the cabinet, and the attorney general, a professional lawyer.[8]

The matter came before the cabinet, and the cabinet's inability to decide led to the appointment of the Agranat Commission. On 26 June 1962 Ben-Gurion asked Agranat, along with Justice Berinson and attorney Avraham Levin, to determine who had the power to decide what at the Ministry of Justice.[9]

That summer Chief Justice Olshan was away on vacation, and Agranat, as deputy chief justice, was in charge of the Court. It fell to him to play host to the chief justice of Peru, then visiting in Jerusalem. In last-minute preparations he hurried to buy shoes; Carmel was busy elsewhere, his own shopping skills were minimal, and he soon realized that he had bought shoes one size smaller than he needed. The painful sensation of the pinching shoes served as a metaphor for his general state of mind. He felt exhausted: the Eichmann trial, the details of the carnage, the international limelight, the decision to violate a cardinal component of his worldview and sentence a man to death, and now the need to choose between Ben-Gurion and the attorney general. In some way the dilemma evoked the Weizmann–Brandeis Split of the 1920s. Ben-Gurion, the widely admired, visionary, yet pragmatic founder of the state, stood against the attorney general who represented Progressivism and the rule of law in Israeli political culture. Could Ben-Gurion's request conjure Agranat's old exasperation at being forced to choose?

On one hand, Agranat remembered that he initially preferred the American arrangement, in which the attorney general is both a political confidant and the guardian of justice. On the other hand, he tended to agree with the former minister of justice that, given the pressure cooker of Israeli politics, it was wiser to isolate the attorney general from politics.

The general malaise concerning the rule of law received further confirmation by the Robert Soblen affair, which erupted in early July 1962, just as the crisis of the attorney general was reaching a fever pitch. Soblen, a Jewish Holocaust survivor and former Troskyite, was convicted by American courts and sentenced to life in prison for conspiring to obtain secret defense information.[10] Probably one of the last casualties of McCarthyism, Soblen jumped bail and arrived in Israel with a forged passport. The U.S. government (could it react to Israeli rhetoric during the Eichmann trial that had ended two months earlier, hailing Israel as a haven to all persecuted Jews?) was unequivocal in its demand that Soblen be returned immediately. Despite a pending court order enjoining the deportation and despite the fact that Israel had no extradition treaty with the United States, Soblen was handed over to agents of the Federal Bureau of Investigation (FBI) and flown to the United States without notifying his attorney.[11] On the way he attempted to commit suicide, and his aircraft made an emergency landing in London, where he died. Prior to his death, English courts issued a writ of habeas corpus, which was honored by the British government.

The contrast could not be more disconcerting. Britain would not bend its legal procedures to accommodate American dictates. Israel would. In Jerusalem, Agranat grudgingly denied a petition to reverse the hasty deportation and to allow Soblen to exercise his rights under the Law of Return. Agranat justified the denial on the grounds that Israel's courts lacked jurisdiction, because Soblen was no longer on Israeli territory. The press reported that the minister of justice did not consult with the attorney general before instructing the police to hand Soblen over to the FBI.[12]

THE POWERS OF THE ATTORNEY GENERAL

Agranat was familiar with the issue of the powers of the attorney general. Five years earlier, the Court had refused to overrule a decision by the attorney general, to dismiss the private criminal suit a woman had initiated against her lawyer.[13] Agranat's opinion in *Frieda Schor* became the landmark case on the power of the attorney general to halt criminal proceedings. But it was one thing to opt for deference when the discretion of the attorney general was challenged in court and a different matter to hold that the minister of justice should defer to the attorney general's discretion in matters of law enforcement.

Joseph's strongest claim was for accountability. The minister, as a member of the cabinet, and the cabinet collectively, are accountable to the Knesset for the activities of the ministry. The democratic tenet of executive accountability, Joseph argued, should be the guiding principle. The officer who is most accountable should also have the final say. The pending visit in early August of Earl Warren, chief justice of the United States, may have sharpened Agranat's ever-present awareness of subtle cultural barriers. Rooted as he was in the American system of separation of powers, in which the executive was independent of the legislature, he asked himself whether he failed to understand something about the parliamentary system, in which the executive depended on parliamentary approval. He had long talks with Justice Berinson, another committee member, in an attempt to get to the bottom of the accountability claim. Writing the first part of the report, concerning the attorney general's powers to start and stop the engines of justice, was easy. But as he came to the question of whether that jurisdiction was exclusive to the attorney general or whether the minister of justice had the final say, Agranat balked.[14] He felt restless and upset, slowly realizing that he simply could not write. He, reputed for diligence and productivity, could not deliver. He knew what he wanted to say, yet the words eluded him.

The family doctor prescribed sleeping pills, but these only worsened his condition. Next came a consultation with an expert, who pronounced that he suffered from "fatigue." Agranat's ironic tone and the twinkle in his eye as he recounted the story signaled Agranat's willingness to share the euphemistic nature of the medical term "fatigue." He was advised to take a "complete rest," preferably away from Jerusalem.

Indeed, after a week or two in a luxurious villa owned by the parents of his daughter's friends in Herzlia and long walks with Carmel, Agranat was ready to complete the report. Dictating to his clerk, he was confident that he could complete the task "between Yom Kippur and the Feast of the Tabernacle."

Did the attorney general possess exclusive powers? Yes, came the unanimous answer of the commission. The attorney general must be free to exercise his discretion independently. Brushing aside the minister of justice's argument that continuity with the Mandatory arrangement required the subordination of the attorney general to the minister and emphasizing that the democratic nature of the state required that the law be superior to the judgment of the executive branch,[15] Agranat explained the significance of an independent attorney general. At its base lay a distinction between politics writ small and Politics writ large. The attorney general, he maintained, was "the custodian of the public interest"; his was a "complex role," requiring the attorney general to preserve the rule of law while advancing the cause of justice.[16] Agranat did not pretend that the public interest had legal content or that the reason for the attorney general's independence was his superior legal training. His report emphasized that the concept of the public interest required balancing the contending principles of the public good and demanded more than narrow legalistic considerations.[17]

The spine of Agranat's argument was the need to check partisan considerations masquerading as the public interest. The fierce nature of Israeli politics, the conviction of each party that it alone understood Israel's best interests, and the nation's lack of a democratic tradition all combined to enhance the vulnerability of the principle of the rule of law. A minister of justice could hardly resist partisan considerations for long. The need for an insulated attorney general was obvious.

The attorney general should serve as a barrier and protection against executive attempts to pursue political-partisan goals by unjustly invoking the criminal process against the citizen. . . . It is important that justice be "seen" (not only "done") so that when the Government initiates criminal proceedings for reasons grounded in the public interest, the public will not erroneously attribute the decision to a lack of bona fide and partisan motives. *We are dealing here with an important guarantee of civil liberties and the maintenance of good order in the state.*[18]

Indeed, Agranat observed, the attorney general must consult with the minister, "particularly where actions related to public or political security are at stake,"[19] and must keep him informed of the ongoing work. But, he emphasized, "to the extent that there is disagreement between [them] . . . the attorney general must decide . . . in keeping with his own understanding and conscience."[20]

A more difficult question lay ahead: if the attorney general were autonomous, what was the purpose of making the minister of justice head of the ministry? When frustrated, was there anything the minister could do to guide his ministry? Surely the attorney general could be dismissed. But because he was appointed by the cabinet (as he was legal adviser to the government as a whole, not merely to the minister), he could only be dismissed by a collective cabinet decision. Short of dismissal, what recourse was left to a minister? For example, could he arrogate to himself powers that the law vested in the attorney general and thereby step into his shoes?

The question troubled Agranat deeply. A unilateral arrogation of power by the minister would undermine the rule of law and might even amount to usurpation of powers. For if the minister could simply arrogate powers to himself, thereby stripping the attorney general of his powers, and then proceed to indict or halt a pending criminal process, then the entire effort of sheltering the public interest from partisan calculations would prove to be a house of cards.[21] The very presence of the option, it seemed, guaranteed that partisanship, not the public good, would prevail. In the end, and not without trepidation, the commission decided that the minister could unilaterally arrogate powers to himself.

One reason Agranat chose this solution was because Joseph and Hausner also endorsed it. Why fight over something on which both agreed? But a deeper force informed his choice. The scheme looked neither neat nor logical, but it did give some muscle to a very weak tissue in the Israeli body politic: checks and balances. Under the parliamentary system of government, the only check on the executive is a parliamentary vote of no confidence. In England this state of affairs is somewhat fortified by a tradition of respect for the rule of law. The principle that "certain things are simply not done" has been an important part of British politics. But both the Lavon and Soblen affairs were painful reminders that Israel had yet to develop such a tradition. Drunk with Jewish political power, Israel's political leadership considered parliamentary control (majoritarianism) as adequate to check the executive. But were accountability to the Knesset and the concomitant availability of a no-confidence vote sufficient? In emphasizing the autonomy of the attorney general and simultaneously allowing for arrogation of his jurisdiction, Agranat introduced an idea of checks and balances that was distinctly American. It was an intricate, hydraulic, and pragmatic solution, one that avoided the insular independence of any one branch of the government.

What about the danger to the rule of law posed by the minister's arrogation of responsibilities or the government's decision to dismiss the attorney general? The possibility of abuse remained real. But under Agranat's plan, any invasion of the attorney general's powers would be publicly seen. Any disruption in the delicate balance of power would occur in plain view, and the people and the Knesset would have the responsibility of holding the executive accountable.

Agranat conceded that his solution affected the relationship between the executive and legislative branches. The collective responsibility of the government to the Knesset in matters within the jurisdiction of the attorney general was limited,[22] and consequently the supervisory powers of the Knesset over the attorney general became limited as well. But this was a price well worth paying for defending the rule of law against partisan politics.[23]

Agranat's report thus constructed a system in which the attorney general, and therefore the administration of justice, was generally autonomous of the Knesset, the cabinet, and the minister of justice. It left the government two remedies—dismissal or arrogation of powers—and the Knesset the remedy of a vote of no confidence, but all three were harsh medicine, not to be casually prescribed. Thereby, Agranat encouraged the move toward professionalization and away from partisanship in the administration of justice, while allowing the government to prevail, provided that it did so publicly.

Once the report was submitted to Ben-Gurion, it became the most discussed item in Israel. The press interpreted it, not without justification, as a major victory for the attorney general. The cabinet, a student of these events has noted, "was stunned":[24] it voted to adopt the commission's report, after much deliberation, despite Joseph's vociferous opposition and Ben-Gurion's reported opinion that the conclusions lacked logic.

From the bench, Agranat observed the rapid developments. Within weeks, Hausner resigned. In early 1963 Moshe Ben-Ze'ev, a district court judge from Haifa, was appointed attorney general. Ben-Ze'ev, a competent jurist, was a man after Joseph's heart, modest, gentle, and unassuming. It presumably did not hurt that he had been close to MAPAI circles in the early 1950s[25] or that, as a district court judge, he was accustomed to having his decisions reviewed and sometimes overruled by a higher authority. In accordance with tradition, the chief justice was expected to give his consent to the appointment, and Olshan conditioned it on Joseph's guarantee that the commission's recommendations would be followed. Later, however, Olshan learned that the new attorney general did not wait for the chief's approval before he accepted the appointment.[26]

The effectiveness with which the government managed to quell repeated Knesset efforts to restructure the position of the attorney general during this period of upheaval and the successful secrecy in which Joseph shrouded his nominee prior to appointment reconfirmed Agranat's worries: in Israel the locus of power was in the cabinet, not in the Knesset. Neither accountability nor Knesset supervision could safeguard the rule of law from the constant interference of partisan politics. Only an insulated attorney general and an alert public could do the job.

Agranat considered his recommendations to be not an approval of the status quo ante but an important barrier against the real danger of the corruption of the rule of law by partisan politics. The commission's report became the cornerstone of a professional ministry of justice.

With the benefit of hindsight, it is clear that the report gave an important boost to the idea of the rule of law in Israel. However, one may also detect the seeds of Conservatism, the preference for pragmatic solutions whose reformist message was not too radical. Agranat was now a senior justice. Within two years, he expected to replace Olshan and become chief justice himself. In the aftermath of his encounter with personal "fatigue," the fervor of his belief in the capacity of utopian Zionism to transform Israel was also cooling down.

PART V

BETWEEN PAST AND FUTURE

CHAPTER 10

Chief Justice Agranat

THE ROAD TO THE HIGHEST POSITION

A photograph taken on 18 March 1965 shows a beaming Agranat shaking the hand of President Zalman Shazar on the occasion of his appointment as the third chief justice of Israel's Supreme Court.[1] The promotion followed the principle of seniority. Since 1959 Agranat had been second in seniority to Olshan; his ascension to the high position was foreseeable once Olshan reached the mandatory retirement age of seventy.[2] But even though the principle of seniority was designed to insulate the judiciary from politics, Agranat's transition to the highest judicial position was not entirely smooth.

No sooner had Olshan's retirement become imminent than rumors of political schemes to reshape the rule of seniority began to spread. The press reported that Olshan, unhappy about retirement, was encouraging his friends in the Knesset to amend the Judges Law and push the retirement age up to seventy-five.[3] Privately, people voiced concern about whether the reserved and contemplative Agranat would make a proper captain for the judicial ship, given the rough seas of Israeli politics. It is quite likely that this uncertainty prompted the justices to convene and unanimously affirm both the principle of seniority and the choice of Agranat as the next chief justice. Agranat must have felt relieved and vindicated by the vote of confidence given to him by his brethren.[4] If he knew about the doubts entertained behind his back, he had managed to forget them by the time we came to discuss these events.

He anticipated his new position with some trepidation but also with enthusiasm. True, Olshan had far better managerial skills than Agranat would ever have, and he had proved to be a zealous guardian of judicial interests, but he was also a temperamental and brusque man whose passion for control wore heavily on the justices.[5] Agranat looked forward to a new judicial order, with a kinder, gentler style of leadership that would make judges feel more like autonomous members of a community devoted to the cause of justice and less like soldiers in a judicial army marching to the music of the law. Moreover, Olshan lacked intellectual rigor; his opinions were terse and legalistic. Agranat believed that, by leadership and example, he could steer the Israeli judiciary away from legal formalism and toward a more substantive understanding of the meaning of law.[6]

His first move as chief justice was to organize a Judges Conference. He wished to assemble all of Israel's judges in one place, in order to foster a sense of community that would transcend the hierarchy of higher and lower courts and launch an ongoing process of deliberation about judicial decision making.[7] The conference was held on 13 October 1965. Two crises, both of which erupted during the first two weeks of October, challenged his leadership, strengthened the Conservative instincts awakened in the aftermath of the Eichmann trial, and set him on the course of guardian of the status quo. Indeed, Agranat was growing wings, but rather than use them to soar upward, toward an expansive implementation of his vision of social justice as it had unfolded in the 1950s, he found himself spreading them to protect his Court against the embroiling politics of the mid-1960s. Of course, the Court did not stay out of politics. But in the years to come, Agranat's position became more Conservative, reflecting the great compromises of Zionism, particularly in the sensitive areas of the separation of church and state and national security. These great compromises were already embedded in Agranat's resolution of the two crises of October 1965.[8]

One crisis was related to the alleged cover-up of corruption by MAPAI's coalition partner, the National Religious Party (MAFDAL). The other concerned the right of an Israeli Arab group to run in the November 1965 elections. Church and state collided in the first; democracy and national security, in the second. A bizarre—yet not altogether illogical—development tied the resolution of the first crisis to that of the second. The place of "Jewishness" in Agranat's image of Israeli law came to affect the scope of Palestinian nationalism in Israeli democracy.

BETWEEN JUDGES AND RABBIS, OCTOBER 1965

"The Scandal of Tel Giborim" was conceived in the early 1960s, when the Ministry of Health was run by its deputy minister, Yitzhak Raphael, a prominent MAFDAL politician.[9] The ministry decided to build a major public hospital south of Tel Aviv and designated Yehuda Spiegel, another MAFDAL politician and an associate of Raphael, to handle the project. In his negotiations with potential contractors, Spiegel intimated that a generous contribution to MAFDAL institutions was expected of those who would obtain the lucrative contract; he also said that he was speaking with the express consent of his boss, Raphael.[10] Spiegel was reported to the police, indicted, and convicted of bribery. Throughout his trial, Spiegel insisted on his right to remain silent, refusing to testify. Out of court, however, he asserted that he had been "sacrificed" in order to shelter the MAFDAL leadership. Extensive press coverage and intense public pressure propelled the government to investigate the charges of a cover-up. Prime Minister Levy Eshkol appointed a district court judge, Moshe Golan, to investigate the matter.[11] Golan concluded that Raphael knew about Spiegel's request for a contribution and that, furthermore, Raphael was responsible for additional improprieties related to the Tel Giborim project.[12] Because the main figures were prominent MAFDAL politicians, MAFDAL was implicated in the affair.

All through the hot summer the matter dominated the election campaign and the front pages of newspapers. In July the Knesset removed Raphael's parliamentary immunity. He was tried and, on 16 September 1965, acquitted on the basis of Spiegel's refusal to testify. After his acquittal, as Israel was preparing to celebrate the High Holidays, an elated Raphael delivered a stinging attack on Judge Golan and the Israeli judiciary. He declared that "religious people had no confidence in Israel's justice system," that Judge Golan's investigation was prejudiced and grossly flawed, and that the time had come to partition Israel's justice system into secular and rabbinical courts—secular courts for the secular, rabbinical courts for the religious.[13]

Raphael's speech triggered the crisis that first tested Agranat's leadership. The press and the legal community treated Raphael's speech as if it were a car bomb exploding in their midst. The bar issued a statement indignantly reasserting its confidence in Israel's courts and denouncing Raphael's speech as a subversion of the rule of law.[14] The judges of the lower courts assembled, vented steam, and sent a delegation to Chief Justice Agranat to demand vindication and redress. MAFDAL was an important partner in the coalition government. Governmental silence might be interpreted as acquiescence to Raphael's denunciation of the impartiality of Israel's judges. In an emotional meeting with Agranat, between Rosh Hashanah and Yom Kippur, the delegation insisted that he confront the prime minister and demand redress.

"I tried to calm them down; I said that I would take care of the situation . . . but I failed to tell them that I had already sent a letter to the prime minister. I don't know why. . . . It was childish on my part." Previously, and after consultations with his brethren, Agranat had written and dispatched by a special emissary a letter calling on the government to defend the reputation of the courts and demanding full public disclosure of the Golan report. Obviously, the sad specter of the crisis of 1953, when a letter from Chief Justice Smoira was returned unopened to the Court on grounds of separation of powers, did not deter Agranat.[15] Indeed, the Ministry of Justice was again in the hands of Bernard Joseph, but Agranat was confident that he could convince the status-sensitive minister to support his move. He remembered calling Joseph, informing him of his intent to send a letter, and offering to show it to him in advance. Joseph agreed, and Agranat, waiving the protocol that required the minister of justice to come to see the chief justice, traveled to Joseph's home to show him the letter. With Joseph's support thus secured, it was much easier to gain the ear of the cabinet.[16]

Why Agranat decided to withhold information about his letter from the delegation of judges, when he could expect it to become public knowledge soon enough, is not clear. Agranat's admission, "It was childish on my part," may indicate that he somehow wished to project an impression of leadership, not of subordination. But surely the judges could not doubt his leadership if he told them that he had acted even before they urged him to take action. It may well be that Agranat withheld the information out of courtesy toward the cabinet, not wishing to leak the news before the government had had a chance to react to it, or that he feared a repeat of the 1953 fiasco. His reaction certainly did not help to foster that sense of a judicial community which he aspired to launch in the forthcoming Judges Conference.

In any event, the press exaggerated the content of Agranat's letter, reporting in lead stories that the entire Supreme Court was threatening to resign in protest if the government failed to act.[17] In fact, there were no threats. Following an acrimonious cabinet debate, Eshkol issued a statement in support of Golan, and the damaging report was immediately released. The courts emerged triumphant, basking in the widespread public expression of confidence. Agranat was pleased with the results, feeling that the ship of court weathered its first storm under his leadership. Still, he must have been shaken by the deeper conflict between religion and state that the Golan crisis exposed.

Zionism was born of a confrontation between traditional Judaism and secularism. Traditional Judaism expected redemption to be engineered from heaven. Zionists believed that they should take their destiny into their own hands. Traditional Jews believed that observing the rules of the Torah was the essence of being Jewish. Zionists believed that the reduction of Judaism to religion was the result of a loss of national sovereignty and of life in *galut* and that back in their homeland Jews would be liberated from archaic rules and behave as modern nations do. Early in the twentieth century, a part of the religious sector joined the Zionists in their struggle for national sovereignty, while rejecting secularization. As its name makes clear, MAFDAL, the national religious party, became the spokesgroup for this sector. Since the establishment of Israel, MAFDAL had insisted that religious law become the law of the land, while secular Israelis had urged the separation of religion and state. Hence the animosity between the two camps.[18]

The unraveling scandal of Tel Giborim was precious ammunition for the secular camp in its fight against MAFDAL. Those were the years of innocence, before the great disclosures of MAPAI's elaborate schemes to divert public funds to its own coffers. It was easy, therefore, for large parts of the public to identify the religious sector as the "other"—lacking civic virtue, preferring the partisan over the public interest, replicating "dirty politics" typical of *galut,* but unbefitting the noble enterprise of Zionism. Raphael's call for the partition of the judiciary played right into these sentiments. It was the ultimate proof that religious people were wanting in *mamlakhtiyut*—the idea that one should subordinate all sectarian interests and considerations to the interests of the state.[19]

But Agranat was also capable of seeing the other side. The Spiegel conviction, the Golan report, and other Supreme Court holdings that Israel was committed to the separation of religion and state caused deep alienation in the religious sector.[20] Religious people could easily conclude that there was little Jewish about the Jewish state.[21] By siding unequivocally with the secular camp, the Court transformed itself into a divisive, rather than a healing, institution.[22] As Yom Kippur came to a close, building a bridge between the secular and the religious must have become almost an obsession for Agranat. As I shall argue in the next chapter, his dictum in the *Yeredor* opinion, that the "Jewish state . . . is a fundamental constitutional premise," may well relate to his yearning to demonstrate that, despite Raphael's accusations, it was possible to be both secular and Jewish. His speech during the Judges Conference corroborates his yearning for the reconciliation of competing values.[23]

The conference took place on 13 October, one day after the Court's *Yeredor* decision and a week after the culmination of the Golan report crisis. In his attempt to dignify the conference with the aura of a stately occasion, Agranat had invited the prime minister and other dignitaries, including the two chief rabbis. None of the three made an appearance; the prime minister could be said to have been represented by the minister of justice, but the rabbis' absence, in the context of the Golan crisis, could be interpreted as a statement of disapproval. Agranat's interruption of the proceedings to read messages of congratulations from all three showed his eagerness to prove that the highest rabbinical authorities were not denying recognition to the Court. In their messages, both chief rabbis emphasized that the conference interested them mainly because of the scheduled lecture by Justice Silberg on "Impartiality in Jewish Law," thereby implying that what really mattered was Jewish, not secular and Israeli, law. Agranat responded: "I wish to assure the chief rabbis—that not only do Israel's judges apply Jewish law in matters of personal jurisdiction, but we are also aware of the great importance of interweaving the values of Jewish law whenever they fit contemporary needs. . . . Jewish law is our heritage."[24]

Agranat was now concerned about reconciling continuity and reform. Reluctant to erect a wall separating religion and state, he strove to reconcile Orthodox Judaism with secular Zionism. Continuity, not reform, was the theme of his opinion in the case of *Yeredor*.

CHAPTER 11

Arab Representation in the Jewish State

THE ARAB QUESTION

Less than a week after Agranat withstood his first crisis as chief justice, he faced his second. A group called the Arab Socialist Party, banned from running in the elections, petitioned the Court for relief. It was a case of first impression. Never before had a party been barred from participating in elections. Israeli Arabs had been enfranchised in 1948 and had voted in all previous elections.[1] Could they be prevented from voting for the party of their choice? In *Yeredor v. Central Elections Commission,* Chief Justice Agranat, joined by Justice Sussman, sustained the ban. Justice Haim Cohn filed a powerful dissent.[2] An appreciation of the dimensions of the crisis from the perspective of Israeli-Palestinian relations requires a short detour. The rest of this section contains a historical profile of Palestinian radicalism in Israel until 1965. The next section discusses Agranat's encounters with Israeli Arabs, particularly his opinion in the 1960 *Qardosh* case. Both discussions will help anchor the *Yeredor* case in the legal history of the Arab–Israeli conflict.

The Palestinian Arab population of Israel was devastated by its defeat in the 1948 war, by the concomitant loss of its leadership and its middle class, and by the harsh military regime imposed on it by Israel's government.[3] During the 1950s only the Communist Party, at that time composed of both Jews and Arabs, actually represented Arab interests and aspirations. In 1958 a handful of young Arab intellectuals began to organize. Theirs was the voice of Palestinian nationalism. They broke ranks with both the Communists, whom they regarded as insensitive to Arab nationalist aspirations, and with local leaders, whom they dismissed as feudal, corrupt, and meek. They were moved by the engine of pan-Arab nationalism, fueled by the rhetoric of Egypt's charismatic leader, Gamal Abdel Nasser. They considered themselves an integral part of the "sleeping Arab giant" now about to awaken.[4] They took the Egyptian-Syrian unification of 1958 — so threatening to Israelis — as a clear sign that the future was theirs. Their enthusiasm attracted young Israeli Arabs who were growing up in an oppressive, demoralized and demoralizing, segregated Arab Israel. They formed their own movement and called it Al-Ard [The Land].

The disruptive potential of Al-Ard's rhetoric sounded the alarm throughout the Israeli security machine. Between 1958 and 1965 the government led a ruthless campaign against it, culminating in the *Yeredor* case. In the Supreme Court, Agranat had encountered Al-Ard several times. In April 1960 the group filed an application with Haifa's companies' registrar to form a corporation. Their purpose, they said, was to "engage in printing, publishing, translation, journalism, book importation and other matters related to printing."[5] By then they were already bruised by their first skirmish with the government. A few months earlier they had been convicted of publishing a newspaper without first obtaining a license.[6] The registrar denied a permit to incorporate, relying on the attorney general's finding that the group was subversive. Al-Ard petitioned the Court, and Agranat, with Justice Witkon concurring, invalidated the denial, thereby allowing the group to form a corporation to disseminate its views.[7]

The aftermath proved that the market worked, to an extent. The prosperity of Al-Ard, Inc., confirmed both its potential and its appeal.[8] The government became even more determined to crush the group. Al-Ard's leaders were repeatedly placed under house arrest, subjected to administrative detention, and exiled to remote, Jewish-populated towns.[9] In 1964 the government denied Al-Ard's request to register as an association. Yet another petition reached the Court, but this time the tide had turned. The Court unanimously found the denial valid.[10] At about the same time, Al-Ard was declared illegal under the Defense (Emergency) Regulations of 1945.

Al-Ard then decided to form a political party and run in the 1965 elections. It stands to reason that its leaders hoped that Knesset representation would win the group both public exposure and parliamentary immunity.[11] They named themselves the Arab Socialist Party, fulfilled all the requirements of the elections law, and submitted an application to the Central Elections Committee. Their list included all the leaders of Al-Ard, and it was easy for the attorney general to persuade the committee that this was the outlawed Al-Ard in another garb.[12] For the first time in Israel's history, a party was forbidden from participating in the democratic process, and the electorate was denied the opportunity to consider its platform.[13] The message to Israeli Arabs was unambiguous: a political organization based on Palestinian nationalist aspirations would not be tolerated.[14]

DEFENDING THE ARAB RIGHT TO INCORPORATE: AGRANAT'S 1960 *QARDOSH* OPINION

Throughout his life, Agranat had displayed a tolerant attitude toward Arabs. Since his arrival in Palestine, he had encountered Arabs from all walks of life, had represented a few in court, had adjudicated cases in which litigants were Arab, and had cooperated with fellow Arab judges in the common struggle to improve the working conditions of the judiciary in Mandatory Palestine. His goodwill survived the War of Independence. In the early 1950s, as a junior associate justice, he had erected the first barriers against the army's heavy-handed use of the Defense (Emergency) Regulations against Arabs.[15] In 1955, as chairman of the Central Elections Committee, shortly before the Sinai Campaign, Agranat sympathized with the plight of the Arab population, which had been subjected to military rule since 1948. Refusing to avert his eyes from the abuse and harassment inflicted on them by the military governors who quelled dissent while engineering Arab voting patterns, Agranat insisted on a more tolerant policy.[16] In the celebrated *Kol ha-Am* case he invalidated the suspension order of both the Hebrew Communist newspaper and its Arabic counterpart, *Al Itihad,* thus insisting on the equal protection of the laws whenever fundamental liberties, such as the freedom of the press, were at stake.[17]

When in 1960 Al-Ard challenged the government's decision to prohibit its registration as a corporation, Agranat applied the same liberal attitude.[18] The statute that invested power in the companies' registrar was typical colonial legislation. It allowed the executive branch "absolute discretion" in deciding whether to allow groups to incorporate. The registrar argued that the term "absolute discretion" meant no or minimal judicial review of his action. Justice Haim Cohn, who as attorney general defended the army in the *Al-Couri* case, agreed. No matter how arbitrary the decision, he opined, the Court could not intervene.[19]

Agranat had a different view. For him, the concept of the rule of law was richer than mere adherence to the letter of the law.[20] The fact that administrative agencies were vested with "absolute discretion" did not mean that their powers were standardless. Agranat feared that Cohn's purist positivism would turn "the government of laws" into "a government of men," because it would give officials a free hand to limit civil liberties. Agranat took the jurisprudence he developed in *Al-Couri* and *Kol ha-Am* one step further, holding that "[t]he general principle is that every administrative agency should act within the four corners of the purpose for which it was vested with powers by the law," regardless of whether the statutory language created absolute or limited discretion.[21]

In order to grasp the significance of this result, it is important to understand the strong appeal of the government's argument. The registrar had based his decision on considerations of national security—the need to dismantle the base that enabled Al-Ard to accelerate its grass-roots campaign—and had been supported by both the police and the attorney general. Agranat could easily have concluded that the argument from national security, coupled with the government's solid conviction that Al-Ard had subversive potential, legitimized the decision. He declined this option, preferring a more Liberal course of action. In essence, he said, the ban amounted to censorship in that it purged a certain voice from the public discourse. Censorship, he said, was "a difficult, complex and delicate matter," even when national security concerns were clearly at stake. Quoting at length from his *Kol ha-Am* opinion, he reiterated his warning that fear for security might subvert the democratic spirit: "It would be a failure of the first order if the enemies of democracy were to force us to abandon our belief in the power of deliberation built upon credible information . . . and thereby lowered us to their own level."[22]

Because of Israel's democratic nature, Agranat held, censorship should be exercised only by officials who were explicitly vested with the power to censor. It was not necessary to add yet another means to the repressive arsenal already available to the government. The powers of the registrar should not be interpreted to include ideological monitoring. Agranat made a classic point in administrative and constitutional law, but his choice of words gave it added panache. Evidently, he had reservations about the government's habit of using Mandatory legislation to consolidate its own hegemony.

Putting the government's characterization of Al-Ard's ideas as dangerous in quotation marks, twice describing censorial powers as "harsh," twice posing rhetorical questions, and ending with an expression of bewilderment accompanied by an exclamation mark, Agranat brought his opinion to a powerful finale: "In view of the detailed and drastic measures, available [in] the Defense (Emergency) Regulations, one should pose, again, the question: is it conceivable that the wish to prevent "dangerous" opinions . . . is within [the Registrar's] . . . jurisdiction . . . ? Is there room for the view—given the proliferation of the censorial means, and their harsh nature—that the [Registrar's] power . . . was meant to serve as yet another means? I wonder!"[23] The fact that the petitioners were Palestinian Arabs was not mentioned in Agranat's opinion, as if to state that the Court was ethnically blind.

Stunned, the government asked for a further hearing. The Court convened a five-justice panel, with Chief Justice Olshan and Justice Sussman joining the original panel composed of Agranat, Witkon, and Cohn. A majority of 3–2 sustained Agranat's result. Agranat could not have been surprised by Olshan's dissent or by Olshan's wry observation that although he "could not disagree with Agranat's progressive views," he still thought the result smacked of too large a dose of judicial activism.[24] Olshan, who identified with the government in matters of national security, appreciated "progressive views" as long as they stayed clear of national-security policy. One wonders whether that was the reason why Agranat, then deputy chief justice, was not included in any of the successive panels adjudicating Al-Ard's petitions to the Court between 1961 and 1965.[25]

It may well be that Al-Ard harbored hopes that, with Agranat as chief justice, the Court would be willing to defend the group's political rights. But this time Agranat upheld the Central Elections Committee decision to ban Al-Ard from the ballot. The core of Agranat's *Yeredor* opinion revolved around the fundamental values of the Jewish state. For the first time in Israeli history, the "Jewishness" of the state was declared a core constitutional value, to which political and civil liberties were subordinated.[26]

YEREDOR: LIMITS ON THE POLITICAL RIGHTS OF ISRAELI ARABS

Because the impending Festival of Succot coincided with the imperative of reaching a judicial determination within four days, the three justices convened at Agranat's home during the Court's recess. Justice Haim Cohn, prolific and efficient, was ready with a written opinion invalidating the ban. Cohn argued that the Elections Law did not authorize the Central Elections Committee to ban parties on substantive grounds. The rule of law, he elaborated, required explicit statutory power to ban a party.[27]

Sitting in his living room, listening to Cohn's arguments, Agranat pretended he did not feel hurt. The Court's unwritten code of conduct required that the justices not write opinions before judicial consultations had been completed. By preparing a written opinion, Cohn had violated the rules, thereby challenging Agranat's authority. Agranat was also surprised that Cohn, who had previously held that Al-Ard should be denied the right to form a corporation,[28] now gave the group a chance for political survival. Perhaps Agranat added Cohn to the judicial panel (the choice of Justice Sussman could be explained on the basis of seniority) expecting that he, who had a solid national-security background by virtue of having served as attorney general, would be the appropriate substitute for the retired Olshan. He might have expected that Cohn, like Olshan, would take the lead in urging the Court to defer to the judgment of the government in matters of national security.

The government insisted that the group was subversive. If Agranat were to join Cohn, there would be a majority against the government's position. Would that not jeopardize the state? It was one thing to let Al-Ard operate as a private corporation, quite another to let it promote its agenda under the umbrella of parliamentary immunity. And then, if the group indeed engaged in subversive activities, would not the Supreme Court, which had given it license to exist, be perceived as a negligent guardian of the national interest? Agranat understood *Yeredor* to be a test of his leadership as the newly appointed head of a co-equal branch of the government. He recalled being concerned not only with upholding the rule of law, not only with the status and reputation of the Court, but also with the best interests of the state. He needed time to reflect.

The private judicial conference took place on the eve of the Sabbath. Ever since he had joined the Court, Agranat had adopted the habit of refraining from writing on the Sabbath.[29] On the heels of this Sabbath came the holiday of Succot. Only after the holiday ended and the family guests had left did Agranat start to work; he spent the night writing. He decided to uphold the ban. No platform that advocated the destruction of the Jewish state should be permitted representation in the Knesset. He did not know whether his opinion would be in the majority or in the dissent, for Justice Sussman had not yet indicated his position. Only the next morning in Court did he learn that Sussman concurred in the result.[30] Cohn remained the lone dissenter.

One legal hurdle to affirming the ban was that the elections statute said nothing about banning parties that fulfilled all of the technical require-ments enumerated by the law. Agranat's opinion conceded that Cohn was right, holding that, in general, the powers of the Central Elections Com-mittee were merely ministerial, not discretionary. But unlike Cohn, Agranat would never agree that the rule of law could be reduced to the strict application of statutory language. Agranat insisted on considering the statute in context; a judge was permitted, even obliged, to reinterpret the law in a way that made it responsive to contemporary problems. *Yere-dor*, Agranat announced, was a unique case, and its resolution required analysis beyond the black-letter law. Agranat considered imperative a re-turn to the basic constitutional premises on which the state had been established.

Israel's Declaration of Independence asserted the "natural and historic right of the Jewish people to live like any nation." Agranat asserted in the opinion's central statement that this meant that the "continuity—and if you wish: 'the immortality—of the state of Israel—is a fundamental con-stitutional premise'" which no organ of the state may ignore.[31] Hence the Knesset could not put the issue of destroying the state on its agenda, the Central Elections Committee "had no option but to ban Al-Ard," and the Court was obliged to uphold the ban.[32]

Agranat set two "facts" on a collision course: the survival of the Jew-ish state, and the intent of Al-Ard to destroy it. Each "fact" was charged with complexity. Together, they offer a clue to Agranat's state of mind at this important juncture in his judicial career.

INTENT TO DESTROY THE STATE OR AN EXPRESSION OF PALESTINIAN NATIONALISM?

Agranat based his factual finding that the Arab Socialist Party aimed to destroy the state on two grounds: the judicial upholding in the previous year of the government's proclamation that Al-Ard was an illegal organization,[33] and the finding of the Central Elections Com-mittee that the Arab Socialist Party was, in fact, Al-Ard. Justice Landau, chairman of the Central Elections Committee, relied on the same prece-dent in recommending the ban. Landau conceded that the burden of proof required to satisfy the committee was "much less" than that required by a court of law.[34] Indeed, as Justice Cohn pointed out in *Yeredor*, the com-mittee had no proof, except the judicial holding and the subsequent ex-ecutive declaration that Al-Ard was an illegal organization.[35] The proof, then, was embedded in the Court's holding from 1964. That holding was based first and foremost on an interpretation of Al-Ard's constitution provided by the military authorities. In a concurring opinion in the 1964 case, Justice Landau relied on a broadcast from Radio Cairo and an article from the Jordanian newspaper, *Falastin*, both praising Al-Ard. The members of Al-Ard had only one prior conviction, for publishing a newspaper without a permit. No further evidence of any conviction for violation of Israel's law was presented. The conclusion that Al-Ard was, in fact, determined to destroy Israel rested on an analysis of Al-Ard's written statements, fortified by statements from Arab media outside Israel.[36]

Al-Ard's constitution, however, was much more ambiguous than the interpretation given it by the military and adopted by the Court. Its first two articles vowed to "raise the [social] level of its members" and to "establish full equality and social justice among all social groups in Israel."[37] The land mine appeared in article 3, which called for "finding a just solution to the Palestinian problem — viewing it as an indivisible unit — in accordance with the will of the Arab Palestinian people . . . which restores its political existence . . . and [which] sees it as holding the first right to determine its destiny by itself, within the framework of the superior aspirations of the Arab nation."

One did not have to be a security expert to see that this article constituted a ringing affirmation of the Palestinian national narrative, the narrative that Israelis hoped had evaporated with the Arab defeat in the 1948 war. Viewed from this perspective, Al-Ard's constitution reflected the menacing reality that the Palestinian narrative had returned to challenge the legitimacy of the Zionist narrative. Further consultation with the "contemporary political dictionary" revealed more alarming layers of meaning.[38]

The security experts invited the Court to treat Al-Ard's text as a code that, once cracked, revealed an ominous subtext. The term "Palestine problem" stood for the restoration of the status quo ante, preceding the War of Independence. "An indivisible unit" meant a rejection of the idea of partition. "Restoration to political existence" meant a Palestinian state, in lieu of the state of Israel. "The first right to determine its destiny" asserted Palestinian primacy in defining and implementing a political solution, the right of return (to homes left during the 1948 war), and the restoration of land confiscated from Palestinians and given to Jews. The "framework of the superior aspirations of the Arab people" meant inviting Egypt's Nasser, Israel's nemesis, to have a say in the resolution of the conflict and served as a reminder that Jews were a mere drop in the Arab ocean.[39]

This interpretation, combined with the name they chose for themselves — "The Land" — could be perceived as a declaration of war. From the Zionist perspective, "the land" (in Hebrew, *Ha-Arets*) belonged to the Jews, who had returned to reclaim it after 2,000 years of exile.

The failure of the drafters of Al-Ard's constitution to recognize explicitly Israel's legitimacy and right of existence touched the raw nerve of Israeli survival anxiety. That silence was interpreted as yet more resounding proof of Al-Ard's evil intent. Thus interpreted, Al-Ard could only be perceived as a movement that required a simple and clear-cut existential choice: us or them.

Of course, Agranat did not have to accept this interpretation. He could reflect on Al-Ard's own gloss on its constitution, which was that the Palestinian Arabs wished to live in dignity, side by side with the Jews; that although Israel was not explicitly recognized, it was implicitly acknowledged as a given. He could choose to evaluate the document as a whole and bring its other, more innocuous parts to bear on the interpretation, or he could take another course and separate fantasy from reality. The Palestinian fantasy, indeed, was the destruction of Israel. The reality was life as a miserable minority under military rule. Israel fantasized itself as a diminutive David fighting a giant Goliath. In reality David was far from being a powerless wimp. Agranat could distinguish belief from conduct and assign legal consequences only to the latter. He could require some concrete proof that illegal conduct either took place or was being planned. He could ask whether actual representation would not foster goodwill and responsibility. Finally, he could view the fact that some Jews were included in the list as a brake on Palestinian harshness, perhaps as an encouragement of ethnic interaction. All of the above were equally plausible options. But Agranat chose the factual gambit—"which should not be reflected upon"—that Israel's survival was at stake.

In his mind, there was no bridge between Zion and Falastin.[40] National sovereignty, embedded in the charged term "The Land," could animate only one nation, and the question had been resolved in 1948 in favor of the Jews. Al-Ard's Palestinian narrative cast a dark shadow on the Zionist narrative. This shadow, it appears, propelled Agranat to insist on the Jewish state as an axiomatic "constitutional premise." Israel, he said, was "here to stay, and its continuity and immortality should not be reflected upon."[41]

"A FUNDAMENTAL CONSTITUTIONAL PREMISE": THE ZIONIST NARRATIVE

Agranat took his guiding principle from the Declaration of Independence. That was not the first time he had invoked the declaration.

In the 1953 *Kol ha-Am* case he had abandoned precedents that denied the declaration normative value. Invoking a model borrowed from Progressive Harvard Law Professor Zachariah Chafee Jr.,[42] holding that the laws of a nation should be interpreted in light of the national vision and its core values, Agranat conferred on the declaration normative validity. In *Kol ha-Am* he used the link between domestic law and the national vision to validate a shift from the authoritarian regime of Mandatory Palestine, with its repressive legislation, toward a more Liberal regime, consistent with enlightened Zionism. In *Yeredor* Agranat used the same model, this time to assert the supremacy of the Zionist narrative.

Clearly, *Kol ha-Am* and *Yeredor* were in tension with each other. In *Kol ha-Am* the "national vision" inspired a judicial commitment to political and civil liberties; in *Yeredor* that very vision called for a commitment to the Jewish state that would trump political liberties.[43] In *Kol ha-Am* Agranat applied the probable-danger test to evaluate and reject the government's contention that speech posed a danger to the nation's security. *Yeredor* cited *Kol ha-Am* but ignored its doctrine of probable danger and overlooked its warning against overzealous security arguments.[44] Agranat explained the reason for his rejection of rights jurisprudence in favor of his commitment to the idea of the (Jewish) nation-state: "For if you would not say so [that the Jewish state is a fundamental constitutional premise], it would mean complete ignominy toward the two wars Israel has fought, since its establishment, in order to prevent its annihilation by the hostile Arab states; it would mean utter negation of the history of the Jewish people and its aspirations, including the contradiction to the fact of the Holocaust . . . before the establishment of the state . . . and which proved anew . . . the necessity of resolving the [Jewish] problem."[45]

This statement is a ringing reaffirmation of the Zionist narrative: the calamities and persecutions visited on the Jews in exile; the return to Zion; the blood spilled and the tears shed for the attainment of political sovereignty. Invoking the Holocaust in this context echoed the "correct historical perspective" distilled by the Eichmann trial: that a Jewish state was absolutely necessary for the resolution of "The Jewish Problem."

Eichmann nourished and fortified the Zionist banner of "never again": never again should the Jews remain without the means of political power—a state of their own. A constitutional principle that put the Jewish state above and beyond all other values would serve as yet another weapon in the defense of "never again." Adopting the harsh approach toward Al-Ard, Agranat's *Yeredor* opinion projected the collective vision of catastrophe Zionism, of a common Jewish destiny of victimization and persecution, in which the Arabs had now emerged as the "other," the enemy that threatened Jewish life.[46]

An additional reason for the overwhelming weight Agranat now assigned to the Jewish state related to the resolution of the Golan crisis that he confronted during the same week. That crisis resulted in asserting the supremacy of judges over rabbis. It concerned the rabbinical assertion that Israel was not sufficiently Jewish, perhaps not Jewish at all. Agranat's characterization of "Jewishness" as "a fundamental constitutional premise which could not be challenged," was a response to the rabbis. Israel was Jewish, Agranat seemed to be saying to the rabbis, even if its citizens were secular, because Jewishness was much more than a religious way of life. Perhaps he was trying to unite the secular and the religious by reference to the common enemy—the Palestinian Arab.

Nowhere in the opinion did Agranat demonstrate overt awareness that his position suppressed the Palestinian narrative in favor of the Zionist one. His reference to the threat of "annihilation by the hostile Arab states" presumably alluded to a version of Zionist ideology that denied the existence of Palestinian nationhood and viewed the conflict as one between Israel and the Arab states. His awareness that Al-Ard was about Palestinian collective rights flowing from nationhood could be discerned only from his claim that denying the "fundamental constitutional premise" would amount to the "utter negation of the history of the Jewish people." Yet only his perception of the unbearable incompatibility between the two narratives would lead him to abandon his lifelong dedication to bridge building as well as his attachment to the bright side of Zionism: the utopian vocation of Israel.

Utopian Zionism was never immune to catastrophe Zionism. Both played a role in shaping Agranat's worldview. But his work up to and including the *Qardosh* opinion reflected a constant search for the balance between the needs of national security and the universalist vision of a Progressive society. In *Yeredor* this effort stopped. Survival anxiety had become so overwhelming that it paralyzed his Progressive convictions. That his reasoning was animated by deep fears was evident from his adhesion to "facts," which actually were ideological constructs, and from his assertion that these "facts" should not be doubted or, in his words, "should not be reflected upon." He had to still his doubts and flatten his deep-seated Liberalism, thereby creating a rigid structure within which he could do what he thought was now imperative in order to protect the state.

But because he did not recognize the struggle as one between Zionist and Palestinian narratives, he could not simply reject one in favor of the other and thereby conclude his opinion. In his mind, the contradiction was between the essence of Israel as Jewish and Israel's commitment to a democratic form of government. He therefore felt obliged to reconcile the commitment to democracy with the suppression of a certain point of view.

THE JEWISH STATE AND THE COMMITMENT TO DEMOCRACY

A commitment to democracy and a guarantee of political and civil liberties were embedded in the Declaration of Independence and constituted the pillar of Agranat's jurisprudence. The heart of democracy, he knew, was the right of representation. How could he deny it to one political party and still retain the democratic character of the state?[47] Agranat believed that he found a "decisive answer" in the notion of self-defense, democracy's need to defend itself against its enemies.[48] He chose three historical events to substantiate this point, each revealing his evolving worldview in the 1960s: the defeat of the Weimar Republic by the Nazis, the cold war, and the American Civil War.

First, the fall of the Weimar Republic: "Occasionally, fascist and to-talitarian movements arose against the democratic states and used all the rights of freedom of speech, press and association . . . in order to con-duct their destructive activities under their shelter. Whoever witnessed it during the days of the Weimar Republic would not forget the lesson."[49] The quotation came from Justice Witkon, who had been forced out of his native Germany by Hitler's Third Reich and who authored the pas-sage to justify the 1964 banning of Al-Ard. His experience with the Nazis shaped his judgment of the Arabs. The analogy between Arabs and Nazis was common among Israelis.[50] The Eichmann trial, fresh in Witkon's memory as he wrote this passage, also served to make the lesson more acute and immediately relevant. Tolerance of the Nazis by the Weimar government facilitated their ascendance to power. Tolerance of Al-Ard might end in yet another calamity for the Jews.[51] Agranat had now come to assimilate this view. The trauma of *Eichmann* made him focus on na-tional survival in ways he, a native of America, had never done before. Further, political events in 1963 fed the fear of an Arab-Nazi conspiracy: the press was full of stories about German scientists, mostly former Nazis, building an arsenal of atomic, chemical, and biological weapons in Egypt for use against Israel.[52] It was therefore the duty of Israel's government, its Court included, to avoid the mistakes of Weimar and to kill the serpent of Al-Ard when it was still in the egg.

Agranat next invoked the cold war: "[A] party owing a foreign allegiance, and only acting in the democratic system in order to overthrow the system, can hardly in justice claim the benefit of the system." The quotation, from the pen of political scientist Ernst Barker, was based on the cold-war theory that the Soviet Communist Party controlled and guided sister parties in Western democracies, as a part of its goal to destroy the free world.[53] In 1953 Agranat had rejected this theory as an insufficient justification for suppressing Israel's Communist Party. In *Kol ha-Am* he had endorsed the "probable-danger" test announced in the American *Dennis v. United States* case but had rejected the conclusion that the Communist Party could be constitutionally suppressed.[54] Now Agranat was using this justification to suppress Al-Ard. It is quite conceivable that the events of the 1950s and the early 1960s (the Cuban Missile Crisis comes to mind) made him take the Soviet menace more seriously. His thinking must have been affected by Israel's entanglement in the cold war and the staunch anti-Israeli and pro-Arab stand taken by the Soviet Union.[55] The verbal support offered to Al-Ard by Egypt and Jordan convinced Agranat that the case fell into the model, described by Barker, of "a local party owing foreign allegiance." The Palestinian party was to Israel what the Communist Party had been to America, and the defense of democracy required the suppression of both. Having thus introduced the relevance of the American experience, he was ready to summon the quintessential crisis in American history, the Civil War, as a justification for the suppression of Al-Ard.

Agranat quoted from Abraham Lincoln's address to Congress after the secession of the Confederacy: "It forces us to ask: 'Is there, in all republics, this inherent and fatal weakness? Must a government, of necessity, be too strong for the liberties of its own people, or too weak to maintain its own existence?' The reply given to this question by the glorious President [Lincoln], in theory and in practice, is known to all."[56] Agranat spoke as a son of the state of Illinois. In his youth he had spent many hours studying the Civil War.[57] President Lincoln had been his hero, and he was familiar with Lincoln's many speeches long before he became aware of the Arab question. For him, the Civil War was the paradigm of a just war. It was only natural that, as his mind searched in the late hours of the night for justifications for upholding the ban, the Civil War and Lincoln would be invoked. Only one steeped in American culture and history could draw an analogy between the leaders of the Confederacy and the Palestinians or equate Israel with the Union. In his anxiety about the balance he was striking, Agranat found comfort in Lincoln's powerful rhetoric. "The glorious President" helped him see the conflict as one between the republic and its detractors, not as a conflict between two nations claiming the same homeland. Thus he could wrap the Zionist narrative in the flag of democracy and avoid the painful truth that, in the Jewish state, some were less equal than others. It was a comforting argument, and he was content to make it the last paragraph of his opinion.

There was one more, unmentioned yet present, reason to be anxious, for which Lincoln could also provide a model. Like Lincoln, he was a new president (of the Court) whose leadership was being tested as he was facing a major constitutional crisis. In interview he told me that he thought he had done "what the people wanted." In reality, he deferred to his fellow justices, to the Knesset (the Central Elections Committee, which represented the entire spectrum of parties), and to the executive branch. Deep in his heart he, too, wished to be a glorious president; and protecting the Jewish state, avoiding risk, and retaining solidarity on the Court seemed to him to be the right steps for a leader not yet six months in office. Thus understood, the *Yeredor* case had as much to do with Agranat's new role as chief justice and the tension between religion and the state as with the Arab–Israeli conflict.

CONTINUITY AND CHANGE: THE COURT'S FUTURE

The celebration of the Zionist narrative was not only a reaction to the appearance of the Palestinian narrative in Al-Ard's platform. Agranat was now chief justice—president of the court. Like most people who ascend to high office, he experienced an emotional upheaval. On one hand, he felt enormously proud and gratified. The Jewish people had a state of their own, with a judiciary of their own, and he, the boy from Chicago, now led this distinguished institution. The High Holidays only added to the festive feeling of gratitude and wonderment at all that he and the young nation had accomplished. In this state of elation, feeling a deep identification with his people and his state, there is little wonder that Agranat was moved to celebrate the Zionist narrative, at the expense of the Palestinian right of collective representation, if need be. In the crucial part of his *Yeredor* opinion he discussed the "continuity—and if you wish: 'the immortality—of the state of Israel [as] a fundamental constitutional premise'" that no organ of the state could deny.[58] He might as well have been talking about "the continuity and immortality" of the Court. By adhering to the earlier judgments against Al-Ard, he was signaling, first and foremost to his brethren on the Court, his resolve to opt for continuity. It may well be that he was also signaling to the government and the security establishment that, regardless of his "Progressive opinions" in *Kol ha-Am* and *Qardosh,* the interests of the state would be well protected under his leadership.

Thus the explanation for Agranat's opinion in *Yeredor* is a complex amalgam of the various antinomies within Zionist thought as well as the peculiar circumstances of October 1965. *Eichmann* sharpened Agranat's focus on the perils of survival, thereby marginalizing the ideological emphasis on social reform.[59] The crisis related to the Golan report exacerbated the tensions between religion and state. The Arab–Israeli conflict accentuated the tension between democracy and the Jewish state. All of these coalesced to shape Agranat's perception of his role as chief justice. One may well imagine that his determination to succeed coexisted with a fear of failure. That fear animated his thoughts is evident from the first paragraph of the opinion, in which he described Justice Cohn's dissent: "I read with great interest the instructive—and if I may add: the courageous opinion of my colleague Justice Cohn. But it is not in my hands to agree to the final conclusion."[60] He knew that his own opinion was timid. But when in doubt, he had followed the maxim that caution is the better part of valor, and so he did in *Yeredor.* This caution, the care not to deviate too far from what he perceived as the national consensus, would be the main thrust of his judicial opinions as chief justice.[61]

At about the same time as *Yeredor* was pending before the Court, Israel's government was reviewing plans to terminate the regime of military rule over Israeli Arabs. Military rule was abolished in 1966.[62] But Israeli Arabs did not have a chance to ponder peacefully the question of who is a Palestinian-Israeli-Arab. The Six Day War brought the Palestinian population of the West Bank and Gaza under Israeli rule, thereby highlighting most forcefully both the Arab–Israeli conflict and the tension between the Zionist and Palestinian narratives. Meanwhile, the volatile marriage between religion and state was again placed on the Court's agenda. A perennial problem, which smoldered throughout the 1960s, appeared to tear the Zionist consensus from within. It came to be known as the question of "Who Is a Jew."

CHAPTER 12

Who Is a Jew?
The Split Revisited

WHY DOES IT MATTER?

In only one aspect were the Shalits—father Benjamin, mother Anne, and the children, Oren and Galia—different from their Israeli friends: Anne Shalit was not Jewish. To the secular and modern Shalits this difference was meaningless; religion played no role in their conception of self- and collective identity. Their sense of identity—Benjamin's by birth and Anne's by choice—was rooted in Israeli culture and nationhood. To the minister of the interior, leader of MAFDAL, however, Anne's difference made all the difference. The minister followed the halakhic rule that one was Jewish only if one's mother was Jewish or if one converted to Judaism. When the children were born, the Shalits learned that the category "religion" on their birth certificates would remain blank (as the Shalits had indeed desired) and that the category "nationality" would say "father Jewish, mother non-Jewish." The official refusal to register the children's nationality as Jewish precipitated the crisis known as "Who Is a Jew."[1]

Following a long correspondence with the Ministry of the Interior, Shalit decided to appeal to the high court of justice for relief. It must have been the cunning of history that caused his petition to arrive before the Court on the heels of the stunning victory of 1967 and the judicial deliberations, which erupted in unprecedented divisiveness, to take place as the 1960s came to a close. The case brought to a head the struggle for Israeli national identity that had reverberated throughout the decade. In the 1962 Eichmann trial, Israelis came to terms with the Holocaust as an integral part of their collective history; the *Yeredor* case focused on yet another enemy—the Palestinian Arab—and the dilemma of reconciling Israel's commitment to egalitarianism with the fear of annihilation, a fear that would be used to justify the suppression of rights. In *Shalit,* public attention turned from the anti-Semite and the Arab to the essence of Jewishness: is one Jewish because one feels and acts Jewish, or is one's Jewishness determined by external, halakhic rules? The question of the impact of interfaith marriages on Israeli nationality inflamed the controversy.

At the core was a struggle between Zionism and Judaism. From the perspective of secular Zionism, a central precondition for the liberation of the Jewish people was the separation of religion and state. From Independence to the Six Day War the majority of the Yishuv, as well as the cultural elite of Israel, were secular men and women who opposed the incorporation of religious tenets into the public sphere. Religious Jews split into those who integrated Zionism into their worldview and those who treated it as utter heresy.[2] As soon as Israel became a sovereign state, the secular and religious camps achieved a cease-fire, known as the status quo. The agreement delineated the spheres in which religious and secular principles, respectively, would dominate the Israeli polity. One question left unresolved by the status quo was whether a civic nationalism, neutral to religion, should be fostered, or whether the only conceivable nationalism was Jewish, resting on religious foundations. In his petition, Shalit asserted that Israeli nationalism was civic, not religious, and that self-determination, not Jewish law, should determine whether the nationality of his children was Jewish.

The Six Day War added fuel to the flames. On one hand, the victory epitomized the transformation of the Jew from a meek, subservient person in exile, shackled by both anti-Semitic regimes and premodern religious commands, to a strong, fearless, freedom-loving Israeli, psychologically robust, able to defend his home and state.[3] From this perspective, Jewish normality also required that the state be Liberal, founded on universal values, not on Jewish particularism and religious principles.

On the other hand, the Six Day War reawakened the sleeping giant of religious nationalism. The unification of Jerusalem, the tears shed by tough and secular paratroopers at the liberated Western Wall, the "return to the cradle of our civilization,"[4] and the miraculous nature of the victory itself were perceived as clear signs of the coming of the Messiah and of impending redemption, or *geulah.* From the perspective of the religious nationalists, these signals, pointing to divine intervention, proved the intrinsic value of the halakhah in the life of the Jewish collective, in Israel and elsewhere.[5]

These themes clashed before the Court, pitting its members against each other. In the end, a majority of five voted in favor of Shalit's self-determination. His children could be registered as Jewish because his belief that they were Jewish was sincere. The state had no business imposing religious principles on a citizen's self-determination. Agranat was among the four dissenters.

As expected, a governmental crisis followed, precipitated by MAFDAL's threat to resign from the coalition. Also as expected, the Knesset quickly overruled the Court.[6] Shalit's children were the only halakhically non-Jewish persons ever to be listed as Jewish in Israel's population registrar.[7] Almost twenty-five years later, it seems that the *Shalit* case had little effect on the status quo between the secular and religious camps. A combination of the rise of Jewish nationalism, accompanied by the rise of the right-wing Likud to power in 1977 and the transfer of MAFDAL's loyalty from MAPAI to Likud, the blow dealt to the secular wing of the Court by the quick repeal of its holding by the Knesset, and the appointment of religious or more moderate justices to replace the aging secular justices made *Shalit* one of the last victories of secular Zionism in the post-1967 era.[8]

Agranat himself designated *Shalit* as the most difficult case in his entire judicial career. He was torn between the yearning to honor universalism, individualism, freedom of conscience on one hand and the urge to protect some essence of Jewishness on the other. The dark menace of a split weighed heavy on his heart: a split between religion and nationality, between Judaism and Zionism, between religious and secular Jews, between his brethren, with some of whom he had served for almost twenty years. It brought back the bitter taste of the Split of 1921, between Brandeis and Weizmann, and the threat of a split between himself and his father. Was there a bridge between modernity and Jewishness?

The crisis was triggered by a peculiar Israeli requirement, dating back to Independence, that nationality and religion be listed in separate columns on the identification forms issued by the population registrar. Ironically, this bifurcation was rooted more in the desire to know who was an Arab, ostensibly for security reasons, than in the question of who was a Jew. A relatively convenient way to tell Arab from Jew was to make people state their religion and have that affiliation appear on the identity card, which all residents were required to carry. Here the proudly secular government of the late 1940s confronted the unwanted consequences of its own ideology. If, as its secular ideology held, religion was a relic of *galut,* then secular Jews could be expected to declare themselves irreligious. Arabs could do the same. Hence the category "religion" might not assist in telling an Arab from a Jew, as both might declare themselves atheistic. An alternative means was needed, and it was decided that the designation of "nationality" should be added. All residents were required to list both their religious affiliation and their nationality.

The information thus inscribed had no legal consequences. It affected neither one's right to citizenship nor one's eligibility to marry or divorce.[9] But the Shalits were principled people, or perhaps secular ideologues. As atheists they were happy to leave the "religion" column empty; yet they were deeply offended by the official refusal to assign their children the nationality of their choice. Benjamin Shalit, along with mainstream secular Zionists, believed that Jewish misery came from the pathologically dominant role of religion in their lives.[10] The purging of the religious factor from Israeli identity would bring Israel one step closer to normality. Nationality in the Jewish state should not differ from nationality in England or France.

Shalit's demand, grounded in his right to freedom of conscience as guaranteed by Israel's Declaration of Independence, reopened a ten-year-old controversy.[11] Meanwhile, as a result of the Six Day War, Israel came to be ruled by a national unity government. For the first time in Israeli history, MAPAI shared power with the right-wing opposition. Menachem Begin, leader of the nationalist Herut, was now a cabinet minister and enthusiastically defended the halakhah as an integral part of Jewish life, thereby forging an alliance with the MAFDAL. It was the beginning of a political and ideological affair between religion and nationalism that would come to dominate Israeli politics less than a decade later.[12]

Shalit's correspondence with the government began in the spring of 1967, before the Six Day War. He filed a petition in the winter of 1968,[13] as Israel was struggling with the meaning of its victory, with the addition of one million Palestinians to its population, and with deep questions about national identity: Was Israel a victim of aggression or was it an imperial power; a liberator of its ancient homeland or an occupier of another people's land?

LAW AND POLITICS

The first difficult question Agranat had to face was related to the composition of the judicial panel. The Court ordinarily sat in panels of three, and it was clear that the choice of any three would predetermine the result in the case. The avowed secularists on the Court would lean one way; the traditionalists and the religious, another way. Agranat decided to include nine in the panel. Never before had so many justices participated in the resolution of one case. The obvious explanation for this number was that at the time the Court had ten justices, and having the largest uneven number would make a panel of nine; the number nine thus indicated that, mindful of the public controversy, Agranat wished to involve as many justices as possible in the decision.[14] Still, the similarity to the nine-member U.S. Supreme Court is a striking reminder of his attachment to his native culture, even when he came to decide who was a Jew.

After oral argument, Agranat grew more distressed about the prospects of deciding the case. The divisions within the Court alarmed him. Furthermore, his reflections on the case convinced him that it had no legal solution. Not all of the justices agreed, but all would welcome an escape, relieving them of the duty to decide. On a Friday afternoon, after the parties had concluded their arguments before a courtroom packed with reporters and spectators, Chief Justice Agranat addressed Attorney General Meir Shamgar.

Shamgar, a tall and handsome man who, in his youth, had been deported by the British to Eritrea for membership in the outlawed Irgun, had only recently been appointed to his position, after having served as the military advocate general. He was the first attorney general after the crisis of 1962 to reinvigorate the office.[15] In ten years he would become Israel's chief justice. Now Shamgar was urging the Court to recognize Judaism's peculiar tie between religion and nationality and warning that other options would split the house of Israel. The press reported that Shamgar was astounded as he heard Agranat declare that the issue was not legal but ideological, that a pragmatic rather than a principled approach was appropriate, and that, therefore, it would be better if the government dissolved the crisis by initiating legislation that would drop the designation "nationality" from the registry.[16] It was a solution best suited to a Liberal state—a state neutral toward its citizen's ethnicity—that respected religious principles while honoring Shalit's autonomy. Within three days the government rejected Agranat's proposal. Tormenting the Court was a small price to pay compared to the evident gains of deflecting a coalition crisis. For some in the cabinet, the issue was still security and the need to know who was an Arab.[17] The religio-nationalists warned that they would not sit in a government that did not treat Israeli nationality as Jewish. Rumors spread that if the Court failed to rule for the government, the law would be amended to reflect the halakhah.

The ball was back in Agranat's Court. "My suggestion to the government was summarily dismissed after a telephone consultation. There was no deliberation. I was incensed," Agranat recalled, conceding that he could not bring himself to write an opinion. By custom the chief designated the justice who would write the first opinion for the Court, but time passed and Agranat did nothing. He told those who approached him to wait, that he wanted to be the first to write. But weeks went by, and there was no indication that he was working on an opinion. Much to Agranat's chagrin, Justice Cohn broke the impasse. Cohn told Agranat that his opinion was ready and that it favored Shalit. The "shofar of dissonant tunes" began to blow.[18] Shortly thereafter, Justice Silberg filed a blustery rebuttal. One by one the justices submitted separate opinions, until it became clear that a majority of five would grant Shalit relief. Agranat was next to last to write an opinion, which placed him in the dissenting camp. Only Justice Berinson waited to read the chief's opinion before he wrote his concurrence.[19] The realization that he lost the tactical advantage of being the first to write, the multiplicity of opinions, and the feeling that his authority as chief was impaired all deepened Agranat's anxiety. Fifty years after the Split, the *Shalit* case reawakened the trauma of the Brandeis–Weizmann dispute. Silberg, short, warm, humorous, and full of *yiddishkeit*, stood for Weizmann and, vicariously, for Agranat's father. Cohn, Sussman, and Witkon, with their German accents and secular, Liberal bent, could be associated with Brandeis. During the 1921 Split, Ussishkin observed that the Eastern European Jews had *yiddische herzen,* whereas American Jews had *goyische kops.* The Silberg-Cohn feud fit the same description: Silberg's opinion was all heart; Cohn's was utterly cerebral. This was the situation that Agranat dreaded most: caught between Cohn and Silberg, he twisted slowly above that deep and unbridgeable chasm.

SUBJECTIVE AND OBJECTIVE TESTS

Haim Cohn, who had been attorney general during the authoritarian 1950s and had precipitated the *Kasztner* debacle, had become a champion of the separation of religion and state. Cohn, a tall, impressively bald man with imperial manners, had a particular ax to grind with the Orthodox camp. Born and raised in an ultra-Orthodox home and groomed under the tutelage of Rav Kook in Jerusalem in the 1920s, Cohn severed his ties with Orthodoxy and became thoroughly secular. In 1966 he defied strict halakhic rules by marrying a divorcée (Michal, the daughter of Israel's first chief justice, Moshe Smoira), causing wrath and indignation among the Orthodox. Cohn was the subject of several Knesset debates, in which the MAFDAL demanded that he resign his judicial position or at least recuse himself from judicial panels dealing with religious matters. Agranat had always defended Cohn, refusing to bow to religious pressures. In the late 1950s Cohn authored the regulations for the Ministry of the Interior pertaining to "Who Is a Jew." Cohn's criteria for self-determination precipitated the crisis that led Prime Minister Ben-Gurion to seek the counsel of fifty intellectuals in the matter, yet the matter has never been resolved.[20] The story is told that when Cohn read his opinion to the assembled justices in a meeting convened to discuss the case, Justice Silberg lost his temper and, pounding on the table, thundered, "[T]his shall not be the opinion of an Israeli Court!" The meeting was adjourned.

Cohn himself described the Lithuanian-born, sometimes hypersensitive Silberg as his "arch rival."[21] If Cohn represented the cool, aristocratic demeanor associated with upper-class German Jewry, Silberg was the embodiment of the earthy Eastern European Jew. If Cohn's jurisprudence represented the effort to shape Israel in the image of the Liberal, Western polity, Silberg's jurisprudence sought unity between synagogue and state in the spirit of a Progressive, yet Jewish, law.

The confrontation between the two took the form of a clash between subjective and objective legal standards. The narrow legal question concerned statutory interpretation: how much power did the law confer on the government official in charge of processing identification forms? Did the law expect the official to accept the subjective determination of the applicant, or did the law require an objective test, hard, tough, and neutral to personal circumstances? If the official applied the subjective test, he or she would have to accept the personal definition of Jewishness supplied by the applicant. If the objective test were applied, then halakhah would obtain.[22] Cohn applied a subjective test; Silberg, an objective one. Ironically, the reverse was true of their arguments. Cohn, endorsing the subjective test, applied a thoroughly formalistic jurisprudence. Silberg, upholding the objective test, was most passionate, often polemical, and certainly not detached in his reasoning.

Agranat was in agony. His liberal instincts led him to side with the secular Zionists. From the perspective of administrative law, he was always in favor of delimiting the bureaucracy's power to intervene in the affairs of individuals. As a Zionist and a disciple of Ahad ha-Am, he believed that the establishment of the state would transform the Jewish people, so that the national and cultural components of Judaism would henceforth form the essence of Jewish life. In this sense, he empathized with Shalit and agreed with the majority. However, his legal consciousness revolted against the majority's reductive approach. With public opinion in turmoil and Silberg declaring the issue the most important question ever to come before an Israeli court, it simply felt wrong to announce that "who is a Jew is not the question."[23] Agranat found the majority's arguments thin, legalistic, and almost escapist in their avoidance of the substantive problem. At the same time, the dissent embraced too tightly Jewish particularism and was too insensitive to self-determination or to the power of history to change social reality.

US AND THEM: SITUATING THE JEW IN THE GALLERY OF OTHERS

Jewish identity and Israeli identity had always been tied to the perception of the other. The *Eichmann* case brought forth the Nazi; the *Yeredor* case involved the Palestinian Arab; in *Shalit,* both the Nazi and the Arab were present, but the gallery was enlarged, first with "a Jewish other"—the "disloyal" or "bad" Jew—and then with the non-Jewish woman.

A Jewish other emerged in *Shalit,* unmasking the particular Jewish self-perception of the speaking justice and revealing the futility of the search for a Jewish essence. Shalit himself distinguished between modern and Orthodox Jews. He felt so disconnected from these "other" Jews that he was prepared to drop the designation "Jewish" altogether, if only the government allowed him to register his children as "Hebrew" or "Israeli." Thus he aligned himself with the early Zionists, who appropriated the term *Hebrew* to distinguish themselves—seekers of political and cultural renewal—from the "Jew" of *galut,* whom they stereotyped as bound by halakhic shackles and cowed by anti-Semitic regimes. The government refused to accept Shalit's proposal, presumably because it was trying to maintain an appearance of Jewish unity.

Similarly, some of the justices deployed their particular interpretation of Zionism in order to distinguish the authentic Jew from other Jews. Justice Landau, a secular man rooted in nationalist Zionism, accepted the halakhic definition but gave it a Zionist spin by distinguishing the good Orthodox from the bad. Good Orthodox were those who accepted the basic Zionist premise of the necessity of Jewish sovereignty. With the ultra-Orthodox, he continued, the "denigrators from within" who "do not recognize the state 'de jure,' . . . we have no discourse on matters of state and religion."[24] Justice Silberg, who also associated (in italics) legitimate Jewishness with the state, gave Zionism a religious spin: "whoever disconnects Jewish nationality from its religious foundations strikes at the heart of our political claim to the land of Israel [Erets Yisrael]. Such disconnection is tantamount to the very act of treason."[25] Adding rightwing spice to his attack, Silberg pointed an accusing finger at "the perverse Jewish New Left in the universities of [the] Western United States."[26] For Silberg, secular Jews who sought to purge the religious content of their conception of the Jewish self, who disavowed Jewishness as altogether irrelevant to modern life or who vilified Israel for acquiring the territories were the incarnation of evil, traitors to the nation.

Silberg might have been talking about the American Jewish New Left and thinking of Shalit himself, maybe even of Justice Cohn. The New Left and Shalit both denounced the halakhic definition of Jewish as too similar to the Nuremberg laws. Both the Nazi Nuremberg laws and the halakhah relied on biological descent in determining individual identity. In his opinion, Justice Cohn attacked the dissent for its negative approach, describing it as concerned only with the "purity of the Jewish people."[27] Nonsense, retorted a furious Silberg. Judaism knows not the concept of racial inferiority and is not concerned with racial purity. All Judaism requires of the non-Jew is conversion. "A convert becomes a son of the Jewish people . . . even if he is a descendant of Blacks or Native Indians."[28]

The introduction of the Nazis into the discourse brought forth the quintessential other in Jewish history: the anti-Semite. Jews were the target of persecution wherever they went, regardless of whether they were halakhically Jewish. Political Zionism aimed at ending the helplessness a Jew felt in the presence of the anti-Semite. "My children are Jewish," Shalit claimed, "because the enemies of Israel are their enemies, and they will grow up to defend the State against them." Thus whoever identified with the cause of Israel was also Jewish. The dissent deployed the anti-Semite differently: the secret of Jewish survival, which gave the Jews the courage to continue against all odds through centuries of persecution and which in the modern era prevented extinction through assimilation was the halakhah. Now, in sovereign Israel, should Jews discard the halakhic shield that alone guaranteed their existence in *galut*? For Silberg the question was plainly rhetorical. In Israel Jews were still surrounded by Arab enemies intent on their destruction (and the events that precipitated the Six

Day War, said Silberg, only proved that too well). Hence Jews should remain loyal to the rule that preserved them historically.[29]

The Arab as the contemporary reincarnation of the anti-Semite only complicated further the question of "Who Is a Jew." Shalit, an officer in the Israeli army, had a live example of the halakhic failure to tell friend from foe: a member of the Palestine Liberation Organization (PLO) recently captured in East Jerusalem turned out to have been born of a Jewish mother. Justice Berinson, concurring with the majority, introduced Kamal Nimri: "[T]he commander of the terrorists from East Jerusalem, son of a Jewish woman and a Moslem man, who dedicated himself to kill, destroy and annihilate the State of Israel, will be considered a fellow Jew and a member of the Jewish nation; whereas the son and daughter of the Jewish officer fighting the wars of Israel will be considered as lacking Jewish nationality. The mind is horrified by imagining such a result."[30]

Relentless, Silberg redivided the camps, this time between good Jews and good Gentiles on one hand and bad Jews and bad Gentiles on the other: "The son of the Jewish mother . . . is a wicked and evil Jew, like many of the members of the Jewish New Left. The children of the petitioner, on the other hand, are poor, lovely non-Jewish children, who did not get an entry ticket to the Jewish nation because of the stubborn opposition of their parents."[31]

The matter, thus put, reduced the problem to another "other": the non-Jewish woman. From Silberg's perspective, Benjamin Shalit was a "bad Jew," first because he married a non-Jewish woman and second because he did not insist on the conversion of his children to Judaism. Anne Shalit, though not necessarily a bad Gentile, was a bad wife and mother. Had she abandoned her atheism ("stubbornness") and converted, the problem would have melted away. Thus understood, the question was not really who was a Jew, but who was a good Jew; not who was a friend, but who was friendly enough to accept the rules of good Jews about who was a Jew.

THE NON-JEWISH WOMAN

Agranat carefully avoided the labyrinth of friend and foe inside and outside the Jewish world. In his analysis, only the non-Jewish woman remained a significant other. More than the anti-Semite, the non-Jewish woman was feared in Jewish culture.[32] Volumes were written about her seductive sex appeal and about the danger that she would lure her (Jewish) man away from God and family. Agranat described this stereotype while discussing the reasons for the halakhic definition of a Jew. The insistence that the mother be Jewish, he observed, related to the prohibition of mixed marriages. From the times of Ezra and Nehemia, the Torah's strict prohibition of mixed marriages was interpreted rigidly. Agranat expressed doubts about the reason for the prohibition. Why is it, he asked, that the child of a Jewish mother and a Gentile father was Jewish but that the child of a Jewish father and a Gentile mother was not? "Perhaps . . . the idea is that when the child is still young, he is educated primarily by the mother, and therefore also in light of her religious beliefs."[33] Alternatively, he said, the fixation on the mother might be grounded in the search for genetic certainty, a certainty unavailable in the father-child relationship.[34]

Clearly Anne Shalit did not fit this description. She had moved to Israel after her marriage to Benjamin, had assimilated into his culture, and was raising her children as Israelis. Also, the example of the PLO leader disproved the ancient presumption against non-Jewish women: Kamal Nimri's mother was Jewish, yet she raised her son as a Palestinian, hostile to Israel. The non-Jewish Anne was raising her children as Jews. Agranat might have remembered the night he had spent in Chicago in 1953, imploring his aunt and uncle to accept the marriage of his cousin to a non-Jewish woman. The aunt and uncle, thoroughly secular and nonobservant, adamantly opposed the marriage. Agranat urged tolerance. Years later, he marveled at how she, the non-Jew, became a beloved daughter-in-law. He had the capacity to transcend stereotypes, and he addressed the plight of Anne and her children: "[T]he refusal to [register] . . . as Jewish . . . the child of the Jewish father may breed feelings of unjust discrimination vis-à-vis the child of the Jewish mother and . . . create feelings of inferiority in relation to his status in the Jewish-Israeli society, where he had integrated from the secular-social-political perspectives."[35]

Agranat also understood well the irrational basis of the hostility toward the non-Jewish woman and the need to let the new generation take control of its own life:[36] "[T]he present generation is equal to the generations of the past, and therefore is not bound by the entirety of the rules [*mitsvot*] held by previous generations, because the present has its own dynamics and . . . is free to act in accordance with its views and in consideration of the newly developed needs."[37] Yet he could not join the majority in instructing the registry to register the children as Jewish. Unlike his brethren, his reasons were not related to the perception of the Jew and the "other." For him, the focus was the historical meaning of being Jewish.

"TORAH AND ISRAEL ARE ONE AND THE SAME": THE JEWISH PEOPLE AS A RELIGIO-NATION

Agranat was well aware of the turmoil within his judicial family.[38] After nearly twenty years of camaraderie on the bench, the justices had become like family, socializing, celebrating, and grieving together. Now the question of "Who Is a Jew" exposed fundamental and irreconcilable differences. Agranat thus opened his discussion of *Shalit* with an emphasis on unity as the "fundamental factor" defining families and nations. It seemed that the more unity eluded public opinion, the government, the Knesset, and the Court, the more Agranat clung to its powerful allure: he insisted that "the . . . unity of the national community is the primary fact."[39] The retreat into the familistic was also evident in his methodology. The sources he used were predominantly Jewish: of the twenty-two, only two were authored by Gentiles; and all of the sources dealing with the nature of Jewish nationality had one or another connection to his immediate family.[40]

Agranat opened with a meditation on the nature of the Jewish people. Was Jewishness, as Shalit had argued, socially constructed, dependent on one's identification with one's own history and community, and independent of religious content? Or was it, as the government had argued, essentialist and biologically determined, as required by the halakhah?

The concept of a nation, he began, "is complex and complicated," varying with the particular nation, historical period, and philosophical outlook. One common characteristic, however, applied to all definitions— "the feeling of unity among the members of the national unit, stemming from mutual participation in the various aspects of its culture . . . from their positive attitude toward [it] . . . and from the will to share a destiny and future aspirations."[41]

What are the foundations on which the unity, essential for nationhood, is built? Often, Agranat observed, ethnic or blood relations, as well as a common religion, provide for such a bonding. A nation, he explained, is like a large family. Just as the family is made up of blood relations and is extended by marriage, so is the nation. And how could a Jew maintain such a view, given the fact that these were the foundations of Nazi race theory? Although the perverse application of these principles by the Nazis should be rejected, he said, their kernel of truth might be preserved. Common ethnicity did play a part in the making of nations. Still, he hastened to qualify: "to avoid misunderstanding, I must clarify the two following points": (1) the ethnic bonding is a necessary but not sufficient factor— "[a] common culture, that is, a common language signifying and expressing the ethnic bonding, is required"; and (2) the common ethnicity may retain its power as a preservative even after a full national culture has been developed. A common religion, he proceeded, may also affect national bonding, and he pointed to the significance of Catholicism in Polish and Irish nationhood and of Islam and Greek Orthodoxy in the Pakistani and Russian national identities.[42]

Having thus set up the framework for the definition of nationhood, all that remained was to show how well it fit Judaism. This analysis had a circular quality: the definition was distilled from the Jewish experience and in turn fit perfectly the Jewish phenomenon. For a brief moment Agranat conceded an awareness that his argument was somewhat self-referential: "I saw fit to emphasize the two characteristics [the ethnic bonding and the common religion] . . . because in the history of the Jewish people—also an ancient nation— . . . the racial-national motif and the religious motif influenced and fed each other." Yet logic quickly gave way to the powerful forces of history and faith: until the Enlightenment, Jews had retained their distinctive religious consciousness, and although it had weakened in modern times, this consciousness was still alive.

Agranat sought to give meaning to his conclusion that "throughout the long history of the Jewish people, and at least until the modern period, [halakhah] had the characteristic of a nation-religion." He listed three halakhic characteristics that, in his opinion, reflected the religio-national essence of Jewishness. First, a Jew is a person born to Jewish parents. Thus the preservation of the common origin from generation to generation is simultaneously ethnic and religious. Also, interfaith marriages are prohibited. Agranat was not prepared to commit himself to the justification for this rule, but he did endorse the position that this prohibition has guaranteed Jewish survival. "This prohibition is founded not on the plain will to distinguish between the Jews and other peoples, but . . . on the desire to prevent the religious assimilation of the Jews. . . . I have no doubt that the rootedness of this prohibition in Judaism was instrumental . . . in preserving the separate existence of the Jewish people."[43] This prohibition, he argued, was proof of the interrelationship between religion and ethnicity in Judaism. The religious rule was designed to, and in fact did, preserve the people as a separate entity. Finally, Agranat observed that the availability of conversion proved that "Judaism never feared the introduction of foreign blood." The purpose of the halakhah was not to maintain racial purity but to emphasize loyalty to the unique religious and yet universal message of monotheism.[44] Hence, he concluded, the halakhic structure emphasized the historical position of Judaism that nation and religion are one indivisible unity.[45]

Agranat's analysis had a decisively Zionist flavor. Unlike Justices Silberg and Kister, whose outrage stemmed from their belief that the halakhah was a body of divine commands based on the covenant between God and the Jewish people, Agranat's position was decisively modern. He demystified the halakhah by explaining its social basis and deemphasized the divine covenant in favor of the historic aspiration for unity as well as the common desire to share a future. This brought him to yet another disagreement with the dissent: for Silberg and Kister, religion (halakhah) dominated past, present, and future. In disagreement with both Orthodoxy and religious Zionism, Agranat accepted as inevitable the secularism of the modern age and its pivotal role in enabling the Jews to take charge of their future. Yet this approach only exacerbated the problem: from the modern vantage point, what was the actual relevance of religion?

BETWEEN JUDAISM AND MODERNITY

Twelve pages into his opinion Agranat identified the legal problem the case presented. Given the instrumental role played by the rule against interfaith marriages in guaranteeing Jewish survival, should this rule be accepted as a "permanent value, obliging the present as well," or should the Court recognize that "Jewish society in Israel is, fundamentally, a secular-dynamic community, in which religion does not play a general or decisive role"?[46] Modernity entailed secularization, the separation of religion and state, making the answer to the question of "Who Is a Jew" a matter of personal conscience, not of dictates from the state.

Agranat next presented the diverse approaches to this question within Zionism. The "purely national camp" considered religion a matter of the premodern past and the secular nation-state to be the core of the present. Rooted in Liberalism, it held freedom of religion and freedom of conscience as precious principles well worth fighting for. The Orthodox-Zionist camp insisted on continuity between past and present, which required loyalty to the halakhah, not to Liberalism, as the organizing principle of the nation-state. In between these camps, Cohn's and Silberg's, respectively, stood Agranat's camp. Agranat did not hesitate to assert that most Israelis belonged in his camp, even though his opinion was a lone dissent. His camp, he said, sought the reconstruction of Jewish culture in the nation-state of Israel. It taught that Israeli culture, revived after two millennia of exile, should not simply adhere to Liberal universal values but should, rather, reconstruct Jewish heritage by discarding the archaic and nurturing the valuable. This rendition of the moderate camp replicated quite closely Agranat's effort as a young man in Chicago to harmonize the theories of Herzl and Ahad ha-Am.[47] And yet he had to admit that his camp did not have a united view of Jewish identity. Some, like Ahad ha-Am, argued that Jewish survival was precarious and that a Jew should "sacrifice personal happiness" and avoid interfaith marriage. Others considered Jewish life in Israel to be sufficiently liberating and empowering to render the halakhic test obsolete.[48] Agranat's camp, then, was as split between a historical approach and a modern approach as were the country and the Court.

It was a sad moment. The strategy of dividing Zionism into camps and placing himself in the middle to represent national consensus, though designed to advance Agranat toward a solution, proved futile. The memory of the 1921 Split was at least one reason why the American Jewish community figured so prominently in his arguments favoring what he called "the historical position."[49]

THE AMERICAN JEWISH COMMUNITY AS AN ARGUMENT IN FAVOR OF CONTINUITY

How did the American Jewish community become relevant to the debate? One should learn from the experience of the Jewish communities in modern, Liberal states, said Agranat. If they, liberated and free, remained loyal to the halakhic definition of a Jew, so should the state of Israel.

Agranat observed two features distinguishing the American Jewish community from non-Jewish society. First, American Jews had a concrete affiliation with traditional Judaism, reflected in the fact that many of them were religiously organized, that many others visited the synagogues, at least on the High Holidays, and that many observed some of the religious principles and symbols in their private and social lives. Indeed, Agranat hastened to admit, there were other Jews whose religious identity was vague, "but when the subject matter is the cultural distinctiveness of the general Jewish community, then . . . those Jews who adhere to some traditional-religious form are at the center of that distinctiveness."[50] He then gave the religious affiliation of American Jews a Zionist spin: "they [did not] see themselves as a religious sect, since the memory of the Holocaust . . . and the impact of the establishment of the State of Israel and its struggles to survive" shaped their consciousness as a "religio-national group."[51]

Second, Agranat explained, American Jews in general avoided interfaith marriage, and all the Jewish religious movements—Orthodox, Conservative, Reform, and Reconstructive—adhered to the halakhic definition of a Jew. Agranat was probably aware that his last statement reflected less of the reality and more of his wishful thinking. Conceding that the number of interfaith marriages was rising, he added that "it should not be surmised that a fundamental change [in this matter] has taken place." Rather, American Jews displayed "a strong will to keep the separate existence of the . . . community and prevent its assimilation in the non-Jewish population."[52]

How was the Jewish consciousness of American Jewry relevant to the historical position against Shalit's claim? It introduced, for the first time in Agranat's analysis, the threat of a split. The argument that any deviation from the halakhah would split the Jewish people had been a major argument among apologists for the status quo. It featured prominently during the early 1950s in the debate about the Law of Marriage and Divorce.[53] The argument put forth by the religious parties and accepted by the Knesset was that a split between Jews would occur because of "inevitable" halakhic complications: a married woman who obtained a civil divorce remained halakhically married and was therefore prohibited to all men. Her subsequent (second and civil) marriage was illegal, and therefore—this was the crucial point—her children from the second marriage were halakhically bastards.[54] The halakhah prohibited marriage between bastards and Jews. Observant Jews, wherever they were, would avoid marrying Jews who had failed to observe the halakhah, for fear of violating either the prohibition against interfaith marriage or the prohibition against marrying a bastard. Any modification of the rules in Israel could encourage similar relaxation among American Jews and could result in deeper assimilation. Agranat concluded: "Any deviation from the Halakhic definition of 'Who is a Jew' might sow deep ideological divisions among the people in Israel and diaspora Jews or cause confusion and a weakening of the tendency to avoid interfaith marriages and assimilation as a result. We in Israel should not ignore such possibilities if we believe . . . [with Ben-Gurion] that the people of Israel . . . have a deep sense of unity and solidarity with the rest of world Jewry."[55]

Agranat was talking not about the American Jewish community as it actually was in the late 1960s (not one mention was made of the American Jewish New Left that featured so prominently in Silberg's opinion) but, rather, of his community—friends, relatives, and acquaintances who remained dear and close despite the distance in time and place. They were his America, and he made them representatives of the entire community. He portrayed them as they were when he left in 1930—not observant and yet traditionally attached to Jewish religious symbols—and assumed that their consciousness had been shaped by the same events and feelings that had shaped him—the Holocaust, pride in the Jewish state, and concern about its survival. He looked at the American Jewish community and saw himself; the idea of weakening the bridge between Washington and Jerusalem seemed all the more unbearable.[56] Ironically, two decades later the firm opposition of the American Jewish community would dissuade Israel's Knesset from making one further concession to the religious parties by making mandatory the Orthodox ritual of conversion.[57]

The reformative, Progressive fire that burned in Agranat in the early 1920s was no longer there. Sixty-six years old, his daughters Zilla and Yael (Didi) recently married, he was growing more attached to the old ways. Benjamin Shalit and Agranat's own oldest son, Israel, had been born in the same week, in the same hospital in Haifa. Psychologically astute, Agranat must have understood the conflict also as one between fathers and sons. In arguing for the historical approach, he captured his fatherly attachment to continuity, but he also expressed his feelings as an immigrant: he did not and could not forget where he came from. His American Jewish roots mattered, and the sense of solidarity was real. But he understood that for Shalit, as well as for his own children, the only recognizable roots were in Israel. Their parents' world—the particular Jewishness of the "old country"—were a matter of history. In the next section of his opinion, in which he rebutted the historical approach, the old fire was momentarily rekindled: Agranat the father became an eloquent and passionate advocate of the sons' claim to a right to mold the future in their own image.

THE MODERN APPROACH

Agranat opened the argument with a ringing assertion of the desirability and inevitability of change: "The present has its own dynamic, and the present generation is free to behave in accordance with its own world view and in keeping with developing new needs."[58] He then listed specific arguments in favor of Shalit. First, the Population Registry Law was a secular statute and had to be interpreted in a secular way. Agranat considered both Shalit's sincere, subjective opinion that his children were Jewish and the objective expectation that a child rooted in Israeli culture would develop a Jewish identity, regardless of the mother's formal religious affiliation. Second, the refusal to register the children as Jewish would breed a sense of inferiority in their hearts. Third, insistence on the halakhah would itself create a split in the modern Jewish world: if ever the gates of the Soviet Union opened, Israel would face a large immigrant population whose Jewishness did not meet halakhic standards. Fourth, the threat of a split was hollow. Israel did not permit interfaith marriages. If the Shalit children wished to marry, they would either have to convert or marry abroad. Their registration as Jews would not affect matters of marriage and divorce.

THE RESULT: CONSERVATIVE OR RADICALLY SUBVERSIVE?

In the end, Agranat realized he could not choose between the approaches. He concluded that it was not within the powers of any of the branches of government to make such a determination. Only society, in due course, could resolve the issue.

Agranat's approach to religion was free of both secular and religious fanaticism. He neither condemned religion as a conspiracy to keep the Jews in bondage nor praised it as the lifeblood of the people. His view was complex and shaped by his American upbringing, in which religion was perceived as a positive and private element of social life. Orthodoxy was not a part of his worldview. With the death of his father, whom he adored and who had become more observant in old age, he ignored the rule of going unshaven for thirty days; after the shivah, he reported to work clean shaven. He sent his children to secular schools, and for most of his adult life he worked with the tiny, Conservative Jewish movement in Jerusalem, the anathema of the powerful Orthodox establishment. Yet he always felt attached to traditional Judaism. He attended religious services on the High Holidays, observed the Sabbath at home with a family dinner and a *kidush,* and enjoyed an occasional reading in religious Jewish sources. He had sympathy for Silberg's raging admonition that Israel without Jewish religion would simply be a "small democracy, impoverished, *dull and mute* which has nothing *of itself* to say."[59]

In the realm of politics and ideology Agranat was confident of the right result. The category of "nationality" should be dropped from the registry, and people would no longer be officially labeled. Society would choose, with no coercion from above and at its own pace, how it wished to treat the religious element of Judaism. Such a solution was not within his power to impose, however. The cabinet had already rejected this idea. The second-best solution, he concluded, was to refrain from deciding. The statutory power of the Court was couched in terms that allowed it to avoid intervention. In light of the unfolding social strife, he said, justice would not be served by judicial intervention.[60]

The question is whether his dissenting opinion in fact supported the status quo. Did he avert his eyes from the fact that the Court's abstention would permit religious coercion and deny self-determination?

Had Agranat persuaded a majority to join his result, the practical consequence would have been the preservation of the halakhic rules in matters of nationality. The idea of the separation of religion and state would have received a further blow—a blow which, in fact, it did receive a few weeks later when the Knesset overruled *Shalit* by amending the law. From this vantage point, Agranat's was a Conservative opinion, which sided more with Silberg than with Cohn, more with fathers than with sons. It went well with his emphasis on continuity since his appointment as chief justice. It is perfectly possible to argue that just as in *Yeredor* he had believed that the political right to election should be sacrificed for the preservation of the Jewish state, so in *Shalit* he believed that freedom of conscience should be sacrificed to preserve some idealized Jewish unity. Still, it is possible to argue that his Conservative result in *Shalit* concealed a radically subversive strategy.

A hint of this strategy appears toward the end of the opinion. As he argued that only time would resolve the issue, he alluded to Ahad ha-Am's article, "Between the Two Jurisdictions."[61] In this article, Ahad ha-Am, the noted Zionist intellectual, discussed the phenomenon of social consciousness—its history and the conditions for its transformation. Ahad ha-Am maintained that the collective consciousness was socially constructed but that often its roots in the mind were so deep as to appear natural, external, and independent of social preferences. Agranat quoted Ahad ha-Am's description of the way social change made its mark, a description that used the metaphor of aliens knocking at the heart's gates. After much inspection and hesitation, the aliens were reluctantly let in and incrementally developed a base from which to gain power and prominence: "they [the aliens, representatives of the new spirit] gradually sap the strength of these creatures [representatives of the past] until they become dry bones, and then the breath of any breeze can at once blow them utterly off the path of life."[62] Detached from its original context, the quotation is ambiguous. It either warns the Orthodox not to let the secularists in, or it hints that the secularists are destined to win this battle. The parable could be taken as yet another indication of Agranat's ambivalence. But Ahad ha-Am aimed to show the best strategy to defeat the Orthodox, and it is quite possible that Agranat, too, was advising the secular camp to avoid a confrontation and thereby assure secular victory.

In "Between the Two Jurisdictions" Ahad ha-Am explored two means of bringing about a social transformation, one involving confrontation, the other a slow process of incubation. Ahad ha-Am dwelt on the church's attack on Galileo's scientific discoveries. The Enlightenment's frontal attack on religion resulted in compartmentalization or, in his words, "two jurisdictions." Neither the church nor science won the battle. A social consciousness developed in which religious beliefs dwelled in one compartment of the human mind and a scientific outlook in the other; the two coexisted, each oblivious to the other. Such compartmentalization, Ahad ha-Am argued, guaranteed the survival of the "old way" and revealed the perils of the strategy of frontal confrontation. The desired transformation of social consciousness was undermined as the "old way" immunized itself through society's compartmentalization. When one seeks a deep transformation and is fighting against formidable and deeply rooted beliefs, one is better off resorting to the strategy of slow incubation. Ahad ha-Am counseled: "The priests of the present, who wish to annul the past, should attempt . . . to delay any open confrontation, until the present completes its work secretly, until the power of the past weakens in the hearts enough to bring about its total collapse."[63]

Agranat may have recognized in himself the compartmentalized mind, on one hand Liberal and universalist and on the other, particularist and deferential to the collective. It is conceivable that, foreseeing the futility of open confrontation, he decided that the secularist strategy of confrontation would fail, that a true transformation of Israeli social consciousness would grow only out of a slow and steady process that would weaken Orthodox resistance by pretending to accept it.

Ahad ha-Am cautioned that this strategy was less heroic and required enormous reservoirs of patience.[64] It is reminiscent of Agranat's advice in his editorial in *The Herzlite* after the 1921 Split to "be patient till the last." It is at least arguable that, as in the Brandeis–Weizmann dispute, he was, as Shakespeare put it, "with himself at war," determined to assist those whom he did not dare help openly.[65]

And yet, in one way he himself was a "priest of the present." There was something innovative about his legal approach in this case. Usually a judge is not permitted to avoid a decision. Agranat's stubborn refusal to take sides had to be legally rationalized. His form of rationalization was the adoption of "process jurisprudence," a jurisprudence that had already gained considerable ground in his native United States and was beginning to take root in Israel as well.

THE RISE OF PROCESS JURISPRUDENCE
AND JUDICIAL RESTRAINT

Process jurisprudence, or legal process, developed in the United States during the 1950s. Its emphasis was on the process by which legal and constitutional decisions were made, as distinct from the substance of such decisions. Its aim was to find an alternative to the two jurisprudential giants that had struggled throughout the first half of the century: legal formalism and progressive jurisprudence.[66] The generation of the 1950s was uncomfortable with progressive jurisprudence and its enfant terrible, legal realism, for emphasizing the links between law and politics and between theory and practice. At the same time, this generation had internalized the critique of legal formalism advanced by Cardozo, Pound, and Llewellyn. In keeping with the spirit of the New Deal, which stressed the need for the judiciary to let the legislature—the people's representatives—make policy decisions, these judges and academics developed a jurisprudence that emphasized the virtue of judicial restraint.[67] At the heart of their theories was the belief that the expertise of the lawyer resided in his or her ability to decide which institution was most competent to make a particular decision. Herein lay the distinction between process and substance: lawyers were not skilled in making substantive decisions; for example, they could not decide who is a Jew. They were good at deciding which institution was most competent to make the decision.

Agranat never studied legal process as such, never read Hart and Sacks's famous collection of legal materials on the subject, and may not have given extensive thought to the tension between legal process and progressive jurisprudence. Agranat's intellectual sympathies were, however, rooted in the same legal soil that produced, simultaneously, progressive jurisprudence and a preference for judicial restraint. As a young man he was exposed to both the attack on legal formalism and the argument that excessive judicial activism stymied social reform. In the 1950s and early 1960s, Agranat employed sociological jurisprudence to steer Israel's legal system in the direction of the Progressive image. Now, approaching the end of his judicial career, he responded more approvingly to the other prong of New Deal jurisprudence—judicial restraint. He had heard about process jurisprudence, which emphasized judicial caution and modesty, from a number of sources. In 1967 two young Israeli lecturers, Aharon Barak and Itzhak Zamir, returned from Harvard Law School, the temple of legal process, with youthful enthusiasm about the "new approach."[68] Justice Moshe Landau, a close friend of Agranat, was a devoted disciple of judicial restraint even though he, too, was unfamiliar with the details of legal process as a school of thought.[69] The idea that judicial restraint was preferable to activism was very much in the air.

And so, whereas the majority employed legal formalism in their arguments in Shalit's favor, Agranat deployed sociological jurisprudence to analyze the problem and legal process to justify restraint. In exercising restraint and in simultaneously justifying it theoretically, Agranat introduced process jurisprudence into Israeli law: "When the judge encounters a problem . . . about which the opinions of the enlightened public are fundamentally divided so that between them there is a deep abyss— . . . it would be better for the judge to refrain from expressing his private opinion, . . . provided that he has a legal outlet which enables him to do so."[70] In *Shalit* there was a legal outlet: the Court was not obliged to review all cases but, rather, had discretion to intervene only when the circumstances required activism in order to advance the cause of justice. In the absence of a legal rule or a social consensus to guide the Court,[71] Agranat felt legally justified to refrain from making a decision.

THE AFTERMATH

From the moment the Court announced its decision, Israel felt like a society on the brink of civil war. The principle of the separation of religion and state, which *Shalit* came to symbolize, was as dear to the secular camp as it was odious to the religious camp. Immediately, the chief rabbinate issued an halakhic injunction (*isur torah*) prohibiting the registration of anyone as Jewish if it were known that they failed to meet the halakhic criteria. Irrelevant from the perspective of Israeli constitutional law, the injunction was directed at the Orthodox minister of the interior and his religiously observant personnel. It forced on Orthodox civil servants a confrontation they had always dreaded, between the halakhah and secular law. MAFDAL denounced the Court's decision, warning that it would destroy the coalition government unless a legislative amendment overruled its holding.

Belligerent and indignant, the secular camp admonished that Israel was about to revert to the Middle Ages and to oppression by the clergy. The mainstream press hailed *Shalit* as a great Liberal victory and urged the government to uphold the rule of law and obey the Court. Secular Knesset members frantically tried to persuade the legislative body, which was mainly secular, to follow their Liberal convictions rather than power politics. In a newspaper article, David Ben-Gurion, Israel's founder, now eighty-four years old and out of power, objected to Agranat's assertion that the designation of nationality should be dropped. Ben-Gurion thought that "the Jewish people in Israel [are] a part . . . of the greater Jewish people, and the elimination of the designation nationality . . . is the beginning of severing the ties between us and the Jewish people."[72] Ben-Gurion maintained, however, that Shalit was correct in insisting that his children were members of the Jewish people.

The Court, meanwhile, was experiencing the frailty of the least dangerous branch. The justices suspected that the religious minister of the interior would not implement their decree, thereby holding both the principle of the rule of law and the Court in open contempt. Some justices were even prepared to escalate the confrontation. Five days after *Shalit* the Court held that the registrar might not register Jewish children as Jewish if their parents objected to that designation. It was a further assertion of the right of self-determination, a further rejection of halakhic rules.[73] Agranat was receiving daily visits from his brethren, tense and worried, who urged him to deploy all of his weight as chief justice to ensure immediate implementation of *Shalit*. When Agranat met with the Minister of Justice Jacob S. Shapiro, he heard that the cabinet was still wavering and that "coercing the minister of the interior to abide by *Shalit* would amount to bloodshed."

A package deal to resolve the crisis was concluded after six days of intensive negotiations. The cabinet agreed to amend the law to incorporate the halakhic definition of a Jew.[74] Simultaneously, a majority of the cabinet refused to submit a bill to the Knesset that would declare the law retroactive and thereby annul the Court's decision. Party discipline was imposed to ensure a majority for the legislative amendment. In the Knesset, national-security grounds (the need to identify Arabs) combined with arguments of Jewish nationalism. In the end, the grand victory separating religion from state collapsed into an ad hoc administrative decision. The minister of the interior did obey the Court, but the decision was confined to the *Shalit* case. Oren and Galia Shalit were the first and last Israelis to be non-Jews according to the halakhah yet be registered as Jews.

The aftermath for the Shalit family itself looks like a Rorschach test of the trials and tribulations of Zionism. Within eight years Benjamin Shalit was caught in an embarrassing personal dispute with the army and emigrated to Sweden. His children grew up with a strong sense of a binational identity as Israeli Swedes. His son served in the Swedish army. Whether the children decided to make a home in Israel is unclear.

From the political perspective, the aftermath of the *Shalit* crisis was symbolic of the post-1967 climate. Amid the War of Attrition in the Sinai, the war against terrorism, and the deep political division over the fate of the occupied territories, Israelis were losing their appetite for yet another rift over religious orthodoxy. Perhaps the compartmentalization observed by Ahad ha-Am was already in place. The Court, shaken by its own divisiveness and traumatized by the decisive political blow to its holding, adjusted to the new reality.

Process jurisprudence provided the rationalization for the ever-so-subtle change in position. In the next six months the Court rejected two highly publicized petitions that dealt with issues at the heart of the secular-religious struggle. The first concerned the exemption from universal conscription granted to Yeshivah students. The administrative (not statutory) exemption touched a raw nerve in Zionism: the ultra-Orthodox, enjoying generous public financial support, would neither recognize the Jewish state nor send their sons and daughters to fight for its defense. The petition challenged the legality of that exemption. The second petition implicated the core of religious values: the sanctity of the Sabbath. After the Six Day War, prosperity brought television to Israel. The question was whether providing televised entertainment on the Sabbath was a legal exception to the general prohibition of work on the day of rest.[75]

In two separate opinions, one written by the fiercely secular members of the *Shalit* majority, the other written by Agranat and supported by members of the *Shalit* dissent, the Court rejected both petitions. The reason for the rejections was a narrow interpretation of the right of standing. The Court thus signaled its unwillingness to intervene in the political arena and built the foundation for what came to typify the Court of the 1970s, a deferential, cautious approach and an unwillingness to take a stand in matters of constitutional values.[76]

For Agranat these were difficult times. His leadership as chief justice had been challenged. The cabinet had declined to accept his proposal to resolve the crisis without litigation. His brethren had not waited for his written opinion before they wrote theirs, five of them had rejected his arguments, he had been charged with excessive ambivalence and an inability to decide, and the Knesset had promptly overruled his Court.

In the formalist, rather self-righteous, legal climate of Israel, few were willing or able to appreciate the nuanced, highly intellectual, and sensitive analysis Agranat provided to show that this problem should not be resolved by the Court. Still, he loved the Court, and he continued to find enormous satisfaction in his work as a judge. When, in late 1972, his old friend, Minister of Justice Shapiro, approached him about the possibility of his being Prime Minister Golda Meir's nominee as president of Israel, he experienced little hesitation in declining. Not only family considerations made him resist the temptation; the most compelling reason was his love for his work as a judge. He knew that under the Judges Law he would have to retire at age seventy, and he did not wish to forgo a few more years on the bench, not even for the prestige and honor associated with the presidency of the state. Little did he know that in the following year he would find himself at the center of the most bitter controversy Israel has ever had and that national unity, so dear to his heart, would explode in his face. Had he accepted the offer of the presidency, Carmel ruefully mused, he could have spared himself that terrible ordeal.

PART VI

THE YOM KIPPUR WAR

CHAPTER 13

War and the Agranat Commission

"YOU ATE THE PREJUDICES OF THE REST OF THE CROWD"

The Agranat Commission, appointed by the cabinet to investigate the debacle of the Yom Kippur War, catapulted Agranat into the center of Israel's gravest crisis. He became the target of one of the most acrimonious and caustic torrents of criticism the country has ever known. The Agranat Commission's reports were ferociously debated on the front pages of newspapers, on radio and television, by every cab driver and shopkeeper across the country. Every Israeli had—still has—a definite opinion about its findings.

Agranat came to experience the impetuous nature of public opinion. From the relatively secluded, venerated position of chief justice, he suddenly found himself dressed as a collaborator, charged with participating in a cover-up designed to exonerate the government, and accused of partiality and partisanship. He bore the attacks with dignity and reserve, but the suffering was excruciating and his wounds never healed. To his last day, he became visibly upset at the mere mention of the commission and vehemently insisted that he had been grossly misunderstood.

We came to discuss the Agranat Commission, more than ten years after the events, late in our series of interviews. By then we had a friendly relationship, but the very mention of the Agranat Commission would trigger a change in the atmosphere. Agranat would puff on his pipe for a longer time and would answer questions defensively, generally by reading aloud from the official report and reiterating its statements, a glimmer of suspicion in his eyes. At one point, as I probed, he retorted, switching to English: "You ate the prejudices of the rest of the crowd." I thought then, and continue to believe, that Agranat did not compromise his integrity and that whatever conclusions and recommendations he reached were based on what he believed was best for the country. And yet I do disagree with parts of the reports. I hope this chapter will do him justice.

THE FLOWERS THAT BLOOM IN THE SPRING

"And so we parted, he to the war and I to the synagogue." Agranat was telling the story of that Day of Awe, early afternoon on Yom Kippur, 6 October 1973. Ronnie, his youngest son, who had recently been discharged from active duty and was about to begin his university studies, was ready to report back to his unit. Father and son said good-bye. Tension hung in the air, but no one could foresee the impending calamity.

At two o'clock in the afternoon the wail of sirens launched the most cataclysmic event in Israeli history since Independence: a simultaneous, well-planned, and well-executed surprise attack on Israel by both Syria and Egypt. Within three weeks, more than 2,500 Israeli soldiers lay dead, more than 3,000 were wounded, and nearly 300 were taken prisoner. Israel had suffered its first defeat. True, by the war's end it had managed to recover most of its territorial losses and reestablish its military superiority, but the smug sense of invincibility, the pride of being a regional power, melted away. The euphoria of the victory of 1967 gave way to renewed fears of another Holocaust.

For two days following Yom Kippur, Israel's government misled itself and its people into expecting the miracle of 1967 to repeat itself, confident that the Arabs would pay dearly and decisively for their misguided impertinence. Only on the eve of 8 October was some of the truth cautiously disclosed: the army was suffering serious losses on both fronts.[1]

Like most households in Israel, the Agranats sat in their darkened home in a community of women, children, and the elderly (all able men were mobilized), thirsty for every bit of news. But it is one thing to be collectively worried and another to be a parent of a combat soldier. The parent dreads less the official broadcast than the telephone call, the knock on the door, the personal message. Was Ronnie alive?

Agranat knew that Ronnie was fighting in the Golan. He also knew that the battles were fierce and the carnage great. Never before had he so worried about one of his children. It was then that the *Yurman* case came before the Court.[2] In several interviews, Agranat described the context of that case. He wrote the opinion and resolved to cling to its arguments "no matter what." "It was irrational," he recalled, and "somehow connected to Ronnie," as if keeping the argument alive would also preserve the son. Justice Sussman tried to persuade him that his argument was wrong; Justice Kahan gently intervened. But it was to no avail. "A line from Gilbert and Sullivan was stuck in my mind," he recalled. "The flowers that bloom in the spring, tra-la, have nothing to do with the case." The next day he learned that Ronnie had been wounded.[3]

The *Yurman* case concerned a procedural point related to tort law. A woman had been injured by a truck. She sued both the truck driver and his insurance company. At issue was whether a judgment, given ex parte against the driver, could bind the insurance company. Agranat thought that, except for special circumstances, the insurance company was bound by such a judgment. Sussman and Kahan disagreed, finding that the insurance company could not be bound by a judgment against the driver. The disagreement did not change the result, as Agranat found special circumstances in this case.[4]

It is a tribute to him that he was both aware of his inner turbulence at the time and willing to relate the story later. It stands to reason that in other cases he was similarly self-conscious and that this incident of permitting superstition to control an argument (but not the result) must have been exceptional. Superstition was not part of his worldview. Carmel had her share of superstitions, and his respect and love for her made him tolerate the practice, but he himself was too much of a rationalist to allow them space in his own life. His inability to abandon superstition in this case—his unyielding refusal to drop an argument, as if this would somehow save his son—bespeaks his anxiety. Falling into dark despair, this tenacious attachment to the argument provided a string by which he was clinging to hope.

Yurman makes clear that the "front" dominated his thinking. Six times he repeated his assertion that the insurance company was entitled to raise all arguments "across the front," a phrase the majority did not use. His opinion ended with the words "In support of my solution . . . I drew sustenance," perhaps conceding that the entire exercise of writing the opinion was aimed at somehow providing him sustenance. One wonders whether the particular facts of the case had any bearing on his behavior. The case involved an Arab who had inflicted injury and an insurance company now held responsible. The father could be projecting his yearning for "insurance" that the son be saved onto the insurance company in the case at bar.[5]

Still, there could be a deeper meaning to the phrase that reverberated in his mind as he defended his argument: "The flowers that bloom in the spring, tra-la, have nothing to do with the case." The refrain very likely had less to do with the distance between an argument and a result than with flowers. Agranat's mind was on Ronnie. The associations of soldiers with flowers, and of the aftermath of war with bloom, were common in Israeli popular culture.[6] The fate of the nation's sons had nothing to do with the technical disagreement between the plaintiff and the insurance company. Could it be tied to the trials and tribulations of Zionism?

After the Six Day War, Zionism seemed fulfilled. Jewish sovereignty had emerged triumphant and powerful. Arab wishes and concerns hardly mattered. Israel would retain the territories it had conquered until the Arabs accepted Israeli conditions for peace. Moshe Dayan, the charismatic, widely admired minister of defense, coined the phrase "better Sharm-al-Sheik without peace than peace without Sharm-al-Sheik."[7] Zionism was transformed into an ideology of pride and power. Were the sons now to pay the price for their fathers' conceit? Did these "flowers" have nothing to do with "the case" of retaining the territories, of undervaluing peace and compromise? Were the fathers following in the footsteps of Abraham, sacrificing their sons at the altar, not to God but to ideology? Could it be that now, with Zionism fulfilled, Israel had become the most dangerous place in the world for young Jews?

The dramatic appeal of this explanation might yield to a more conventional, pragmatic interpretation: as the war went on, it became clearer and clearer that some terrible technical miscalculations had been made. There had been enough indications of Egypt's and Syria's preparations for war. Israel's leadership failed to give these indications credibility. It was inconceivable that the Arabs would start a war. The quotation Agranat used to end *Yurman,* which "lent [him] sustenance," suggests a yearning for the status quo ante: "In this case . . . the Court is fortunately able to cure the slips and errors that have been made in practice upon terms which will prevent the possibility of injustice and will place the parties in the position in which they would have stood and ought to have stood but for technical mistakes."[8] Agranat could not know that by the time this opinion was officially signed and sealed, he would be assigned the burden of reviewing governmental mistakes, striving to realize the promise of the *Yurman* quotation, to "place [Israel] . . . in the position in which [she] would have stood and ought to have stood."

THE AGRANAT COMMISSION: INVESTIGATING
THE MISHAP

As the cease-fires began to take hold, public anxiety became anger. The more people learned about the war, the more indignant they became. Anger manifested itself as a demand for accountability. Who was responsible for Israel's failure to foresee the attack, and what price should they pay? The daily reports about Richard Nixon, the American president who would shortly resign as a result of the Watergate scandal, may have strengthened the conviction about the pivotal role of accountability.[9]

But Golda Meir's cabinet stood still. Meir, who had succeeded Eshkol as prime minister, was known as champion of the status quo. In an embarrassing spectacle Meir and Dayan refused to accept responsibility for Israel's unpreparedness and resign. Many reasons could explain this state of affairs, from considerations of *raison d'état* to a fear that there was no satisfactory replacement for the leadership, to a desperate effort to deny guilt, and to personal cowardice.[10] Whatever the reasons, the cabinet would not bring itself to concede collective responsibility. Only Minister of Justice Jacob S. Shapiro submitted his resignation, after failing to persuade Dayan that he should assume responsibility and resign. These events precipitated the appointment of the Agranat Commission. Israeli law empowered the cabinet to appoint a commission of inquiry, possessing judicial powers, to conduct investigations.[11] After much hesitation, Golda Meir decided to embark on that route.

On 18 November 1973, Attorney General Shamgar completed the consultations about the language of the mandate vesting power in the commission. By coincidence, on the same day David Ben-Gurion, Israel's founder and first prime minister, suffered a fatal cerebral hemorrhage.[12] The Yom Kippur War thus signified the end of an era, the closure of a chapter in Zionist history.

The law provided that once the cabinet decided to appoint a commission of inquiry, the chief justice would choose its members. Unlike the cabinet ministers, Agranat did not shirk responsibility. He could appoint another person as chairman. Rather than spare himself the trouble, Agranat viewed the very gravity of the situation as the most compelling reason to serve.

Agranat decided on a commission of five members. His recent and dramatic reckoning with the fragility of human life led him to seek someone who could replace him in case he became incapacitated. He chose Justice Moshe Landau, his colleague and confidant since their days on the Haifa magistrate court. Landau had shared his views in *Kol ha-Am*, *Yeredor*, and *Shalit*. To Landau he added Yitzhak Nebenzahl, then state comptroller general, a man known for his objectivity and integrity and who, by virtue of his position, had some expertise in military oversight. None of the three had actual military experience. To them Agranat added two decorated generals, Yigael Yadin, a professor of archeology and Israel's second chief of staff, and Haim Laskov, Israel's fifth chief of staff, who then served as the army's ombudsman. In time, after the commission reached its conclusions, the two generals would be accused of turning the tide in favor of Dayan and against Chief of Staff David Elazar.[13] Yet when Agranat announced his choice, the media and the politicians lavished him with praise. *Ha-Arets* opined that the commission gave Israel "a chance that the painful blow we have suffered will turn into an invigorating act." *Ha-Arets* also commented that it was unlikely that the commission would have enough time to draw any conclusions before the upcoming elections for the Knesset, on 31 December 1973.[14]

Because of the war, the Knesset had postponed the elections, which had been scheduled to take place in October 1973. Yet the December elections were held as if the war had never happened. Labor (the Alliance) headed its list of candidates with Golda Meir and members of the war cabinet, including Minister of Defense Moshe Dayan. Labor won, and Menachem Begin's Likud party remained in the opposition.[15] Was this an expression of the public's confidence in the old leadership? A symptom of numbness and confusion? A reluctance to further destabilize the ship of state? Or were the election results an expression of confidence that the leadership would receive its comeuppance from the Agranat Commission and that the people themselves could avoid responsibility?[16] Whatever the explanation, the elections did not calm the public fury. Dayan was frequently met with shouts of "Murderer!" Golda Meir, too, took her share of verbal abuse. Demonstrators continued to insist on the principle of ministerial responsibility and demanded Dayan's removal from public office, at least from security-related responsibility. Golda Meir clung to the status quo.[17]

Meanwhile, Agranat, who had temporarily left the Court and was devoting all of his attention to the commission, discovered the extraordinary difficulties of conducting the investigation. He came to learn that chairing a commission of inquiry was very different from presiding over a court. The Court certainly had its share of prima donnas, but the judicial structure had ways of accommodating strong egos and eccentrics. Judges were at liberty to file either a dissenting opinion or a concurring one, thereby retaining their own voice. Here, rumor had it that the two generals, Yadin and Laskov, were particularly opinionated and controlling and expected deference to their views on military matters. Indeed, photographs of the commission show Agranat, Landau, and Nebenzahl seated at the center, with a general on each side, like two lions guarding the gates of judgment. Agranat made his task particularly difficult when he set his heart on unanimity in the commission's report. He, who never feared filing a dissent, whose best opinions were written in solitude, consulting his texts and listening to his conscience, now succumbed to the magnetic allure of solidarity. The result was an unbearable tension among the members that only the secrecy imposed on the commission's deliberations helped hide from the public eye—and significant compromises.

The commission issued three reports. Each came in two parts, one long, detailed, and classified top secret;[18] the other, rather short, available to the public. The commission submitted its first round of recommendations on 1 April 1974, detonating a public uproar that shook the nation, dismantled the government, and exposed Agranat and his commission to vitriolic public criticism. Overnight, he and the commission that bore his name fell from the revered status of savior of the nation to a group of "eccentrics" who exercised "unacceptable favoritism."[19]

PURGE OF THE MILITARY COMMAND: WAS THE GOVERNMENT EXCULPATED?

Recommendations

The commission considered two distinct loci of responsibility: the government and the military command. With regard to the government, the commission addressed the question of parliamentary responsibility. Did Golda Meir and Moshe Dayan bear parliamentary responsibility because of their failure to expect an attack? The commission decided that the question did not fall within its jurisdiction. The question of parliamentary responsibility, the commission held, was a political question, and only the political institutions—the Knesset, the political parties, and the cabinet—were empowered to decide it. Thus the commission declined to decide whether the state leadership was accountable for the mishap and left it to the people and their representatives to be the judges.[20]

But the commission did not decline to review all matters related to the responsibility of the political leadership. Distinguishing between parliamentary and personal responsibility, it undertook the task of deciding whether either Prime Minister Meir or Minister of Defense Dayan was personally responsible for Israel's failure to anticipate the attack. The legal question in this context was whether Meir and Dayan were negligent in the discharge of their official duties in the days preceding the war. The commission concluded that neither was negligent. Because the commission declined to pass judgment on the question of parliamentary responsibility and did not find personal responsibility, the net result was that neither Meir nor Dayan was found responsible.

The military command was not so fortunate. Because the military officers were governmental employees, rather than elected representatives like Meir and Dayan, the commission had no problem passing judgment on their behavior. The judgment was clear and unequivocal: the chief of staff, two brigadier generals, and several lower officers were found responsible for the mishap, and the commission recommended their discharge.[21] The commission noted that the military command had all the information necessary to foresee the attack. The generals failed to read the writing on the wall, said the commission, because of a prevailing "conception," the premises that guided their interpretation of the facts. "The conception" posited that Egypt would not go to war until its air power matched Israel's, that other Arab countries would not go to war without Egypt, and that given Israel's post-1967 expanded borders and its military superiority, the regular army could absorb an attack quite efficiently until its reserves mobilized. To these factors was added an almost religious faith in the ability of the intelligence branch to give the chief of staff adequate warning. The Yom Kippur War refuted each of these propositions.[22] Because they allowed themselves to be blinded by "the conception," the commission held, the generals had to go. Compared with the commission's indictment against the military command, its decisions concerning the government appeared overly lenient. The public and many commentators had trouble comprehending how the cabinet could get away with such a colossal disaster, letting the military command alone take the blame. This basic intuition, that the result was grossly unfair, and a feeling that a double standard must have been applied ignited the public wrath.[23]

But the public fire was also fueled by the oil of politics. Within Labor there had been an intense rivalry between Moshe Dayan and the deputy prime minister, Yigal Allon. Neither Allon nor Dayan, representatives of different factions in the Alliance, hid his ambition to ascend to the prime ministership after Golda Meir's retirement. With his supporters, Allon, a former mentor of David Elazar, fed the press with negative evaluations of the commission's finding, highlighting the injustice done to the military command. Thus the public fury was partially fed by the power struggle within the Labor movement itself.[24] Yet to the untrained eye the criticism appeared to be based purely on considerations of due process and justice.

Criticism

Why did many commentators condemn the report as flawed, distorted, and fundamentally unfair?[25] The criticism was both general and specific, and it contained political and legal arguments.

The general criticism blamed the war not on the specific failure to foresee the attack but, rather, on the worldview that had materialized from the post-1967 euphoria. The stunning victory bred smugness and arrogance. Israelis developed a self-image as strong, resourceful, and efficient beings, complemented by an image of Arabs as weak, helpless, and incompetent.[26] Public opinion viewed the status quo as beneficial for Israel and change as welcome only if and when the Arabs came to accept Israel's conditions for peace. This approach precluded Israel's leadership from understanding that, just like Jews, Arabs could resolve to take destiny into their own hands; that if the Jews of *galut* could transform themselves into "new Israelis," the Arabs could change as well. Israelis gave little credibility to Egyptian President Anwar Sadat's resolve to restore Arab honor and ignored his statements that only a war would shake the status quo and create the momentum for negotiations.[27] Sadat failed to communicate his strategy because Golda Meir's cabinet was prisoner of its own conception. The Meir-Dayan conception, said the critics, was the mother of all conceptions and gave birth to the "military conception" denounced by the commission. The commission failed, so said the critics, because it did not identify those who were truly responsible for the post-1967 euphoria, without which the generals could not have developed their military conception.[28]

Many, but by no means all, of the critics believed that it was the commission's duty to highlight this state of affairs and to have advised the government to accept responsibility. But the criticism did not end there. Critics made much of the commission's finding that neither Meir nor Dayan, particularly Dayan, was negligent prior to the war.

In analyzing the issue of personal responsibility, the commission started with a question: what should the appropriate standard of review be? Should the commission take into consideration the fact that Dayan was himself a military expert, a war hero admired by Israelis since the establishment of the state? Or should the commission ignore Dayan's special qualifications and apply to him the standard of a "reasonable minister of defense"? The commission chose the latter path and applied to Dayan the criterion of "reasonable behavior."[29] To critics this smacked of excessive legalism, a manipulation of semantic technicalities designed to set Dayan free. People failed to understand how the commission could ignore the very military expertise that had brought Dayan the ministry of defense in 1967.[30] Furthermore, in the context of Dayan's well-known personal involvement in the daily operations of the army prior to the war (he did develop a low profile afterward), the commission's decision to abstract him into a faceless "reasonable minister of defense" appeared more like legalistic wizardry than any genuine attempt to do substantive justice.

There was more to the criticism. Even conceding that the commission's standard of "reasonable behavior" was proper, people believed that it was inappropriately applied. Indeed, Dayan formally told the military command that it should prepare for war in the second half of 1973,[31] but this was only part of the truth. The fact was that Dayan issued contradictory statements. Although he predicted a war in the spring of 1973, he also made statements that Israel's borders were secure and that the possibility of war was remote. In the summer of 1973, Dayan approved important structural changes that belied any genuine belief that war was imminent. Chief among them was his decision to replace the experienced general Ariel Sharon with the inexperienced Shmuel Gonen as head of the Southern Command. If Dayan believed that war was at hand, why would he assign the most dangerous border to an inexperienced officer?[32]

This line of criticism revealed the deep sense of betrayal that afflicted the upper echelons of the military after the commission released its first report. The officers, who looked up to Dayan as a role model, expected the man to stand with them as the commission scrutinized their behavior.[33] They were flabbergasted to learn that Dayan was developing a separate legal defense, which portrayed him as an innocent civilian misled by his team of military experts. The officers believed that whereas they followed a code of honor and appeared before the commission to tell the truth, the wily Dayan employed brilliant counselors to manipulate the evidence and escape responsibility.[34] They believed that Dayan had managed to charm the members of the commission, just as he had managed to charm the army in years past. In particular, they were convinced that the two former generals on the commission—Yadin and Laskov—favored

Dayan. The rage against Dayan for this act of self-preservation was also directed at the commission. Shocked and confused by the fury, the commission huddled behind the closed doors of its headquarters and blamed the media for its woes.

Agranat's Response

Agranat believed strongly that the commission's distinction between the civilian and the military levels was correct, important, and misunderstood. The cardinal principle, he held, was that an appointed commission should not decide whether the cabinet should or should not continue to serve the people. This task fell primarily to the Knesset and secondarily to the political parties represented therein. On this issue, Agranat believed, he was on solid ground. The English position in this matter was perfectly clear: parliamentary responsibility should be monitored by parliament.[35] In interview, he also emphasized that the same situation obtained in the United States. The president of the United States cannot be removed by a commission of inquiry. Only the process of impeachment, involving the two houses of Congress, may accomplish such an awesome task. Revered principles of separation of powers required no less than the commission's restraint.

Agranat failed to mention Richard Nixon, whose impeachment process had started during the commission's deliberations. But he did mention Abraham Lincoln. The president he most admired, commander in chief during the Civil War, suffered many defeats in battle and a good number of skirmishes and disagreements with his generals. Yet only the generals could be removed; Lincoln stayed on. Similarly here, Agranat believed, Meir and Dayan could only be removed through the political process. His position was strongly consistent with the legal-process jurisprudence he had come to embrace in the final stage of his judicial career.[36] Relying on legal-process thought, Agranat postulated that only the political branches of government, by virtue of their accountability to the people, had the authority to make substantive decisions. The presence of fellow commissioner Justice Landau, a staunch believer in judicial restraint, and of other members of the commission, with their strong positivist inclinations, reinforced Agranat's philosophy. Agranat reasoned that the commission's mandate did not authorize it to judge the political performance of the civilian leadership. Only the electorate could do that.

Agranat insisted, however, that it was wrong to assert, as many had done, that the commission had "exculpated" the civilian level. To the contrary, he maintained, a careful reading of the report would show that the commission directed a fair amount of criticism at the political level. The report highlighted a series of constitutional and structural deficiencies in the civilian decision-making process that contributed mightily to the mishap. First, no law spelled out the division of authority between the minister of defense and the commander in chief; nor was it clear who was authorized to make security decisions in the event that the entire cabinet could not meet.[37] Second, no civilian authority was formally authorized to regularly review classified information and make security decisions. In practice, an ad hoc group of ministers (known collectively as "Golda's kitchen") assisted Meir, but this arrangement was devoid of legal authority. The informal arrangement impaired the government's power to make consequential security decisions.[38] Third, there was no constitutional provision for a war cabinet.[39] Fourth, the army's centralization of intelligence gathering and analysis encouraged uniformity of thought and chilled critical evaluations.[40]

As for the distinction between the direct responsibility of the military command and that of the minister of defense, Agranat conceded that the commission applied two different standards, but he insisted that these standards applied to very different situations. The standard applied to the chief of staff was essentially one of strict liability. Members of the commission believed that Israel could not, should not, face such an existential threat again. The commission hoped that if it set a very high standard, holding the chief of staff liable for any errors within his jurisdiction, then future chiefs of staff would be more vigilant, leaving Israel forever prepared.

It was not easy for Agranat to accept the commission's condemnation of David Elazar, the army's commander in chief. He was mindful of the very wide gap the commission left between the stern standard that led to Elazar's termination and the lax standard applied to Dayan. He recalled a sleepless night before adding his name to the commission's recommendations concerning Elazar. He worried that the harsh recommendation failed to recognize the successful military leadership demonstrated by Elazar throughout the war. But he found himself at odds with the majority of the commission and, given his resolve to maintain unanimity, he was reluctant to issue a dissenting opinion. He thus came to accept his colleagues' view that Elazar should go.

But Agranat thought it was wrong to adopt a standard that would take into account Dayan's military expertise. Agranat himself wrote this part of the report, penning: "[T]he good and correct constitutional order requires the application of a uniform standard, when one comes to determine the personal responsibility of a public official, and we should not use, for this purpose, a standard which changes with the particular attributes of the individual who serves in the particular position."[41] Fifteen years or more after the event, Agranat continued to insist not only that the standard of "a reasonable minister" was the only appropriate one but also that the commission applied it properly. He thought that Dayan, in fact, had behaved cautiously and carefully and that his reliance on his generals' underestimation of the probability of war was reasonable. Agranat felt wronged by the accusations that he, or any other member of the commission, consciously favored Dayan.

Interestingly, however, the commission's report twice refers to the "pull of the unconscious."[42] These references appear neither in the context of the distinction between the civilian and military authority nor with regard to the standard of negligence versus strict liability. But they do indicate an awareness that subtle forces pervaded the decision-making process, forces that were, perhaps, stronger than the cognitive powers of individual members.

Did the Agranat Commission Have "A Conception"?

The attribution of the mishap to "a conception," which led the military command to distort the facts and adjust them to preconceived values, was an important intellectual breakthrough. The relationships between facts and values, between ideology and reality, were exposed and illustrated in powerful and painful ways. But it is possible that the commission itself had a conception, which it neither articulated nor transcended but which explained its reluctance to take responsibility for a change in government.

The language of the report disclosed some of the deeper layers of the members' consciousness. The publicly released report was written in two styles. The actual discussion and analysis was delivered in dry, formal, and lean prose. One may assume that the commission was hoping thereby to signal its scientific detachment and legal objectivity. The prologue and the epilogue, however, invoked the familiar Israeli rhetoric of pathos and patriotism. The introduction to the final report read: "Many of those who fought on both fronts are no longer, and we shall never know the full testimony about the horror of war and the sacrifice of life. The Commission lowers its head before their heroic deeds and those of their comrades, which decided the battle."[43] The conclusion read: "As we walked the long way to the end of the investigation, we could relive—in as much as it is possible by hearing testimony—the experiences of our soldiers, their sacrifices and heroism. And this experience only strengthened within us the recognition that indeed, the performance of the assignment entrusted to us amounted not only to the fulfillment of a heavy public duty, but also was a great privilege."[44]

The fathers were identifying with the sons in battle and committing their heroism to memory. They gratefully recognized the sons' enormous sacrifice for the welfare of the collective. They were doing this out of deep communal solidarity, "looking forward to the future of Israel's Defense Forces and the state."[45] Agranat persuaded the commission to quote Churchill's aphorism that the commission's target was to "correct that which needed correction."[46] The quotation from the great English wartime leader suggested that the commission's members were themselves soldiers, albeit of a different kind. The rhetoric confirmed the essence of catastrophe Zionism, that Israel was a "nation in arms," in which each and every person, including middle-aged judges, professors, and civil servants, was forever mobilized to defend its survival, each serving according to his or her abilities.[47] Everyone's task was to help the state correct the errors that caught the nation unprepared. Loyal, dedicated soldiers, they were not summoned to, nor could they, question the greater framework; they were not equipped to step outside the boundaries of the polity and reflect on the Zionist narrative. Condemning the leadership in matters of national security was beyond the pale. One could only call to "correct that which needed correction" within the parameters of the Zionist narrative. In the final analysis, neither Agranat nor his colleagues understood the deep crisis of leadership that had been simmering since 1967 and that had now reached its boiling point.

The members of the commission clearly belonged to Israel's founding generation, who had subordinated themselves to the collective and obeyed their leaders in order to fulfill the task of establishing a state. They could not see that Israel was at a crossroads and that the post-1973 era would not be the same. This last point was better understood by the public, which eventually summoned up the courage—indeed, with the encouragement of the commission that refused to do the "dirty" work—to replace its rulers. But what the public failed to acknowledge, when it unleashed its wrath against the commission, was the pure and heartfelt love of nation expressed by these five elderly men. Post-1973 Israel was growing tired of its founders' worldview that not rocking the boat too much, standing together, and sacrificing the personal for the political were the key to preserving the Jewish state.

Israelis were not in the mood to listen to patriotic rhetoric or to appreciate the noble, if not altogether persuasive, motives of the commission. Nor were they able to acknowledge their own role in fostering the uncritical, arrogant, and hedonistic climate of the post-1967 era. What they wanted most was not reasoned analysis but the punishment of those who were responsible, and their frustration turned into self-righteous accusations hurled against the commission.[48]

In fact, the commission did explain itself rather clumsily. Through the months of investigation, the relationship between the commission and the media became increasingly strained. In the final report, a special section directed to the press expressed the commission's frustration and disappointment at the image it had acquired in the public eye. The report also contained recommendations to discipline the press that were starkly at odds with Agranat's lifelong views about the significance of a free press in a democratic society.

THE COMMISSION AND THE PRESS

The Yom Kippur War did not spare Israel's press, for it shattered journalists' perception of their political role. Until the war, journalists, like everyone else, perceived themselves as members of the "nation in arms" and frequently subordinated professional considerations to what they were told was in the public interest.[49] A critical stance was tolerated [the tolerance was rooted in Agranat's *Kol ha-Am* opinion]—but never encouraged—and was constrained by both military censorship and a general view that open criticism might undermine Israeli interests. Because of their pivotal role as communicators, journalists were admonished to put their loyalty to the greater interests of Israel above their duty to monitor the government.

The Yom Kippur War brought home the fact that journalists had served as a vehicle to trumpet the view that "Israel never had it so good."[50] In the period immediately preceding Yom Kippur, the press had deliberately refrained from questioning the official line about the low probability of war.

Feeling guilty and ashamed, perhaps mindful of the sharp contrast between themselves and the American media, which was basking in the glory of its role in uncovering both the Pentagon Papers and Watergate, Israeli journalists were undergoing a rapid change of heart. A new resolve to perform their responsibility as members of the fourth estate found an ideal subject in the Agranat Commission. From the publication of its first report until the appearance of its final report a year later, the commission became the target of unrelenting, rancorous, and scathing coverage.

With the fall of Golda Meir's government, Yitzhak Rabin, architect of the victory in the Six Day War, became the first sabra to hold the high office of prime minister. Rabin disapproved of the commission's initial findings and had a difficult time concealing his low opinion of its work. The attacks on the commission took a particularly ugly turn. The press did not spare Rabin but, reflexively sensitive to governmental signals, understood that the commission would be easy prey. It could display a critical stance while pleasing the powers that be.[51] As a result, the commission felt more and more besieged. The fact that under its mandate, the commission was required to hold its hearings behind closed doors and that it was dealing with sensitive, classified information created a vicious circle. The commission sometimes exaggerated the need for secrecy, in order to protect itself from the increasingly aggressive press.[52] At the same time, its members also believed that the very rules governing judicial proceedings, coupled with the cloak of mandatory secrecy, prevented them from refuting the attacks.[53] Also, unversed in the art of public relations, commission members did not bother to hide their resentment of reporters.

Rebuffed and mishandled, the press escalated its attack. Matters between the press and the commission were so bad that when the reports were issued the commission failed to distribute advance copies to journalists. The press had to simultaneously digest and report on the most important news of the day. The more the press retaliated, the more the commission withdrew, viewing itself as the victim of a hostile government and an irresponsible press.

Reports of the period describe Agranat's silently passing by reporters, refusing to respond to questions, puffing his pipe incessantly.[54] His demeanor revealed extreme stress. He was particularly hurt by the fact that his family was not spared the public exposure. Because the name Agranat is unusual, his sons and daughters, and occasionally a grandchild, were identified and reproached, sometimes harassed, about the commission's performance. He was also pressured by his colleagues on the commission. All were bruised by the press coverage, and three of the four insisted that he use his status and clout to protect them against the barrage of accusations. The stress seemed to have weakened Agranat's commitment to freedom of the press. He agreed to ask the attorney general to take steps to restrain the press. More significant, the commission's final report opened with a section on the media, recommending steps for whipping the press into shape: "When in April 1974 we permitted the publication of the first interim Report . . . there were people, among them public figures and journalists, who did not agree with some of our conclusions and recommendations and who based their public negative criticism not on substantive arguments—and substantive, decent criticism is of course permitted and desirable and is a part of the democratic process—but accused the members of the Commission of having been 'partial' and having applied 'double standards.'"[55] These accusations of partiality and double standards (put in quotations to indicate the author's rejection of the charge), the report noted, were published in violation of Israeli law. Agranat highlighted three such violations.

First, the law equated commissions of inquiry with courts. Israel's Criminal Code prohibited the publication of invectives against both judges and members of commissions: "Clearly, just as the attribution to a judge of 'partiality' and 'double standards' is one of the most injurious things, likely to poison the public atmosphere, so it is when such marring language is used against members of a commission."[56]

Second, Israeli law prohibits the publication of materials which are sub judice. The press is enjoined from publishing its own conclusions about any matter under judicial consideration, in order to avoid undue influence on judges in their deliberations and to avoid prejudicing the public. These rules apply with equal force to a commission of inquiry, and the press had violated them: "We do not mean that it was prohibited to say anything about these subjects, but it was not permitted to include . . . decisive assertions . . . in [these] controversial matters, prior to the release of the Commission's own conclusions—or to provide factual descriptions which implicitly contain such assertions."[57]

Third, "the publications . . . included . . . irresponsible stories which amounted to a violation of the vital requirements of . . . national security . . . and which contained inaccuracies and distortions."[58] The commission did not explain the relationship between its complaint and the fact that the publications were presumably cleared by the military censor, in charge of protecting the nation against the inadvertent disclosure of vital information. The report only commented that "this phenomenon . . . disturbed the quiet work of the Commission, while the Commission was prevented from disclosing the actual truth to the public."[59]

A footnote to these admonitions signifies a crack in the seemingly unanimous facade of the commission's report. The footnote criticized the Ministry of Justice's long-standing policy of refraining from prosecuting journalists for violations of the sub judice rule. It was time to reconsider this policy, the footnote insisted. The argument that the public interest required a free and uninhibited press coverage of these vital political issues was of no avail, the footnote observed, because the law had already decided that the protection of the judicial process trumped press freedom.[60]

One commission member dissented from this view, and he was not Agranat. Yitzhak Nebenzahl broke the unanimity by holding that one needed to balance the public harm in such publications against the advantages of free expression. "[I]f the balance cannot be maintained," he argued, "it is better to decide in favor of freedom." Nebenzahl's dissent pointed out that given the crucial importance of the war, public discussion was unavoidable. Criminal trials of the media associated with the commission's work, Nebenzahl noted, would only deepen social strife just as the commission was endeavoring to heal the wounds.[61] In interview, Nebenzahl emphasized that Agranat could have joined his dissenting opinion but said "not one word about it."

What happened to the boy who had wanted to be a journalist? To the man whose 1953 *Kol ha-Am* opinion had laid the foundations of press freedom in Israel?[62] It could be his growing Conservatism, even though later in his life he still stood by his *Kol ha-Am* principles.[63] More likely, Agranat's personal involvement led to this momentary departure. Having himself experienced the pain of being pilloried by the press, he empathized all the more with his colleagues' indignation.

Agranat's personal suffering at the hands of the press weakened his ability to apply the *Kol ha-Am* principles to the case at hand. In interview, Agranat took responsibility for writing the text of the report related to the press but mentioned that the recommendation of applying the criminal law was penned by Justice Landau and was added only as a footnote. Even as he bowed to the pressure and agreed to recommend the muzzling of the press, he could not stomach such a recommendation in the text of the report itself. Two aspects of the text reflected his state of mind. First was a long quotation from his own opinion in the 1956 *Kasztner* case, admonishing the press to exercise more restraint. The *Kasztner* opinion stopped short of recommending legal measures against the press. The allusion to Kasztner, who had been assassinated on the heels of a caustic public controversy, hinted that Agranat too, felt ill-used by the press. Just before he quoted his *Kasztner* opinion, he invoked Justice Frankfurter's observation about the "strong pull of the unconscious."[64] He must have understood that this counterattack on the press was rooted in personal bitterness and disappointment and that neither he nor his colleagues had the detachment and distance required to reach a balanced judgment.

SOME PERSONAL REFLECTIONS

In his 1931 eulogy for Ephraim Chizik, Agranat celebrated the "new Jewish hero—the Gibbor" and buried the traditional Jewish martyr.[65] More than forty years later he came to experience the terrifying loss associated with military heroism, both as a father and as the commission chairman. Israel's heroes, Dayan and his generals, victors of Israel's wars from Independence to 1967, were reduced to their human proportions. Even the "hero" could be weak, fearful, manipulative, and shortsighted. Nor was the concept of martyrdom erased from the Zionist landscape. Agranat now felt himself martyred by vicious attacks after he had devoted his entire professional career to doing what was best for the state.

No other period in Agranat's career caused him as much agony as his service on the commission. The achievements of the commission, primarily its detailed study of the performance of the military during the initial phases of the war, were never sufficiently acknowledged. More significant, Israelis failed to give the commission credit for preserving and revitalizing democratic processes. In hindsight, the commission's insistence that the political process alone should resolve the question of parliamentary responsibility facilitated the healthy governmental transition. There is no doubt that the commission's refusal to make the decision forced Labor to act. In April 1974 Rabin's government showed Israelis that a change in leadership was possible and safe and would not imperil the state. It was a liberating step, which paid dividends three years later, when, for the first time, Labor lost and Menachem Begin's opposition party came to power. The Likud's reign heightened the appeal of catastrophe Zionism and purged the universalist core from utopian Zionism; but it also taught Israelis how to use the democratic process and vote for political change.

Although the report was partially written by Agranat and certainly received his approval, it was different from the typical Agranat product. The arguments were brief and declaratory. They lacked the lengthy, careful elaboration of the pros and cons of each issue, and they contained no reasoned rejection of the assertions by the other side. Indeed, Agranat himself commented on the irony that this report, which received more public attention than anything he had ever written, was so uncharacteristic of his writing style.

From a jurisprudential perspective, the report was internally incoherent. Some of its premises were grounded in pragmatism; others were rigidly formalistic. When the commission decided to deny the military officers due-process rights analogous to those vested in criminal defendants, it relied on pragmatic considerations.[66] Agranat repeated time and again that it would have been impossible to make progress if the inquiry had resembled a criminal trial. Against this pragmatic stance, the critical decision to ignore Moshe Dayan's military qualifications and judge him by standards of reasonable behavior was exceedingly formalistic.

Incoherence was also evident in the explication of democratic theory. The major premise of the commission, which drew most of the fire, focused on the political nature of parliamentary responsibility. This premise was built on the idea that in a democracy only the citizens could decide whether an elected official should continue to serve. Yet the strong democratic commitment was diluted in the discussion of the press. In order for the political process to bring about an informed decision concerning accountability, the press had to be free to criticize. It could not perform this function in a gentlemanly fashion, as the commission expected.

Several factors account for these characteristics. First, as Agranat insisted in interviews, the task was overwhelming. Never before or since has a quasi-judicial body been asked to investigate topics of such magnitude. The sheer volume could not but affect the quality of the report as a whole. Moreover, the sixty-eight-year old Agranat had never served in Israel's Defense Forces, and military matters were hardly a part of his professional expertise. But these factors were merely the tip of the iceberg. Chairing a commission meant intensive teamwork. This was not Agranat's general modus operandi. Although he was used to teamwork on the Court and had gained considerable insight into management by presiding over the judicial system during the past eight years, at heart he remained a loner. He worked best by himself, writing his most memorable opinions during the night in his small study at home. Chairing the commission forced him to deviate from his regular working habits. His lack of expertise in military matters pressured him to be unusually attentive and deferential to the views of the two retired generals on the commission. His perception that an awesome task was at hand, that the survival of the state was at stake, and that it was his responsibility to administer a remedy in matters of national security made him yearn for consensus. Yet he was not accustomed to imposing his views on others; nor was he adept at manipulating people to accept his position. Hence a consensus among the five members necessitated some suppression of his own inner voice about what was right and just. He failed to see that the Yom Kippur War had destroyed the national consensus about the meaning of Zionism and about what was in the best interests of the state. This is why the report was perceived as one more brick in the now controversial status quo ante.

A glimpse into Agranat's state of mind at this time in his life is provided by the books he was reading. Throughout the months of the investigation he immersed himself in the five volumes of Anthony Trollope's *The Palliser Saga*. From the American dramas of the Progressive Era—the favorite literature of his youth—he had now turned to nineteenth-century Victorian England. Trollope's masterful storytelling must have been a helpful palliative for his increasingly agitated nerves. He must have identified with the principled and decent Duke of Omnium, who wished for moderate, orderly social reform but who found himself devoured by the ferocious, impatient forces of politics. The grief of the fiercely private duke over the unfair treatment he received from London's budding modern press must have echoed in Agranat's heart. The difference between the authors Agranat preferred as a youth, such as Upton Sinclair, and Anthony Trollope is an apt metaphor for the long distance Agranat had traveled from Chicago in the 1920s to Jerusalem fifty years later.

When he resumed his duties as chief justice in early 1975 he was a distressed—some may say, even depressed—old man. All his life he strove for harmony and unity, to avoid a "split." Now he himself was responsible for national divisiveness. Worse, caught in the maelstrom was the institution dearest to his heart, the Supreme Court. Because the commission was perceived as a judicial body and because his reputation as chief justice was associated with it, the accusations of partiality and double standards were also leveled at the Court.[67] Some justices, unhappy about the developments, greeted Agranat's return with sullen faces. From Agranat's perspective, this effect on the reputation of the Court was the most hurtful of the consequences of the Agranat Commission. He braced himself and spent the next year, the last before his retirement, diligently devoting himself to his favorite activity, adjudication.

PART VII

JUDGING THE TRUTH TRUTHFULLY

CHAPTER 14

Retirement, 1976–1992

In the aftermath of the Agranat Commission, Agranat immersed himself in judicial work. The volumes of Israeli Supreme Court decisions in 1975 and 1976 are full of opinions bearing his trademark: long and learned, painstakingly sifting arguments and counterarguments.[1] This flurry of activity could well have represented Agranat's last embrace of judging before mandatory retirement would force his separation from the bench. But it may also have been his way of dealing with the other major event occurring at this stage in his life: the public controversy over the Agranat Commission's reports.

My impression from our interviews was that a certain melancholy had come over Agranat that related to his retirement on the heels of the controversy. His (and his family's) recollection of the actual events surrounding retirement could be attributed to the general sadness he was feeling in September 1976.

In 1965 Agranat introduced a formal way of bidding farewell to a retiring justice. On Chief Justice Olshan's last day at the Court, all of the justices sat on the bench to hear Olshan deliver his last opinion. When he finished reading, they paid tributes to his judicial legacy. Agranat was pleased with his innovation. He found the practice of saying farewell collectively, in the working habitat of the judge, surrounded by attorneys and litigants, a particularly appealing way to end a judicial career.[2] He acknowledged both Silberg's and Kister's retirements in that fashion, and he thought that he was creating a tradition. But on 5 September 1976, his seventieth birthday, only Carmel, his oldest son, Israel, and his daughter-in-law, Ilana, were present as his judicial tenure ended.[3] "It was pathetic," Israel recalled. As Agranat rose to leave the bench, an administrative clerk cried, "May you live a long life." Agranat remembered the clerk's indignant comment that the banality of the day was "a disgrace." Agranat's memory, perhaps inaccurate, reflected his feelings. He must have been deeply disappointed by the failure of his longtime colleagues to acknowledge his retirement on his last day on the bench.

Agranat was well aware of other plans to honor his retirement. Two days later a grand party would be held at the Knesset, with the prime minister, the cabinet, and the elite of the legal profession present, all paying tribute to his legacy. Justice Haim Cohn was planning yet another, more intimate party, at his home. The justices gave Agranat the rather expensive Hebrew encyclopedia, symbol of Jewish revival in Israel. The judges of the lower courts presented him with an impressive sterling-silver menorah, symbol of Jewish continuity. Warm speeches, full of praise, appreciation, and genuine affection, were given at the Knesset, but none of them brightened the memory of that lackluster final day on the Court. Agranat probably yearned for fraternity on the day before retirement, for brotherly recognition. He did not receive them.

In fairness to the justices, it should be noted that they did not share Agranat's recollections. Landau failed to remember any particular ritual associated with retirement. Cohn recalled that Sussman, the next chief justice, was preoccupied with the plans for the grand farewell party at the Knesset. It may well be, however, that the "tradition" that meant so much to Agranat was simply a trivial detail to his brethren. The incident is a comment not only on Agranat's state of mind but also on the transformation of Israel's social culture as it approached its thirtieth anniversary.

Agranat's last day on the bench was a far cry from his first day as a magistrate. When he first entered the courtroom in Haifa he was greeted by the president of the district court and by representatives of the bar. Thirty-five years later the Israeli legal profession was no longer a small family in which the workplace and the site of celebrations were one and the same. By 1976 a celebration meant a media event, an exclusive list of eminent invitees, a lavish reception. The party following Agranat's uneventful last day symbolized the transition that Israel was experiencing, from a small, close-knit community to a modern society.

After retirement Agranat devoted himself to part-time teaching and scholarly pursuits.[4] The man whose productivity was legendary, as evidenced by scores of dissertation-length opinions, produced relatively little in the next sixteen years.[5] This may well be typical of retired judges. It is one thing to write opinions based on a concrete case, stimulated by briefs and oral arguments and restrained by a deadline; it is quite another to write in the isolation of one's home, in the abstract, detached from one's natural community, and without secretarial services.

With the advent of the 1980s, as what came to be known as "Israel's constitutional revolution" gained momentum, a new appreciation of Agranat's legacy began to spread. The second generation of justices, eager to fortify Israel's legal system with a judicial bill of rights, discovered that Agranat's early opinions had already set the intellectual foundations as well as the legitimating methodology for their ambitious project. Agranat's opinion in *Kol ha-Am* soon became the most quoted of all opinions. He received several awards and honorary degrees acknowledging his distinct and distinguished contribution to Israeli law and to the jurisprudence of rights.[6]

Toward the end of Agranat's life the events of the early 1970s were put into perspective. The controversy receded into memory and became merely a small part of the whole of his life's work. When the subject of his legacy was mentioned, his growing contentment was clear. He had partaken in laying liberal foundations for Israel's legal system, and his judicial work was already canonized.

Aging was not similarly kind to Zionism, however. The years between the ill-fated Israeli invasion of Lebanon in 1982 and the return of Labor to power in 1992, after fifteen years of Likud governance, brought to the fore a combination of regional might, right-wing nationalism, and religious messianism which has so transfigured the face of Zionism that it barely resembles its image of yesteryear. As the regime of repression in the occupied territories grew fiercer, Agranat's disapproval of the means applied to retain control—particularly of house demolitions, which he considered inhumane—grew stronger. He saw with alarm the contempt for the rule of law on the part of the government, which was intent on harnessing all means to preserve the ideal of a Greater Israel. He worried about the politicization of the Ministry of Justice and fretted over the cynical dismissal of an attorney general who refused to bend the principle of the rule of law to considerations of *raison d'état*. He was appalled by the rise to prominence of fellow American Meir Kahane, whose Kach party platform trumpeted the incompatibility between democracy and the Jewish state.[7]

In 1992 Agranat cast his ballot for Labor and was content to see a government speaking the language of common sense and compromise come to power. He passed away two months later, three weeks before his eighty-sixth birthday.

Agranat died at home, with Carmel by his side, on 10 August 1992. Carmel had already determined that the funeral should be a private affair, unencumbered by the official symbolism of status and office. Hundreds assembled at the Sandhedriah Cemetery in Jerusalem, listening to the one man asked to bid Agranat farewell: his old friend, Justice Landau. In keeping with Jewish tradition, there was no coffin. Grandsons, relatives, and friends carried the stretcher on which Agranat's body lay, wrapped in a prayer shawl. Also in keeping with Orthodox tradition, only the sons, not the daughters, said the mourners' prayer, the kaddish. Agranat's daughters, daughters-in-law, and granddaughters surrounded Carmel, seeking shelter from the scorching sun under a lonely tree, while the sons performed the ceremonial rituals after the burial.

Witnessing this process, a wave of indignation shot through me: why should women be excluded from this important rite of passage? I have wondered many times since that day what Agranat would have chosen if he had confronted the option of the women in his life also saying kaddish after him. Reform or continuity? Inclusion or exclusion of women in public life? I suspect that in his old age he would have preferred continuity and tradition, that he would not have wished his funeral to be the site of innovation and reform.

His gravestone, elegant in its simplicity, is inscribed "Ha-Shofet Shimon Agranat, Dan Din Emet La-Amito." The approximate English translation is "Justice Simon Agranat, who judged the truth truthfully." The stone's invocation of the poignant Talmudic phrase symbolized the growth and transformation of Zionism. The idea that the Talmud and other religious sources were the product of the Jewish mind in exile and therefore unworthy of a liberated people returning to claim its land, so typical of early Zionist thought, had given way to a recognition that here lay a cultural treasure, the legacy of both religious and secular Zionists.[8] Agranat would have been pleased to see it. The inscription offers a literal, clear meaning: Agranat was a judge whose judgments reflected the essence of truth. The Talmud, however, gives a more complex interpretation: truth is an elusive concept, beyond the reach of any one individual. "To judge the truth truthfully" means to do justice to the best of one's abilities. That was certainly descriptive of Agranat. His work has captured the deep truth about truth's elusiveness. His worldview was a constant struggle with the multiplicity of meaning lurking behind every factual situation and every idea,[9] an effort to calibrate delicately the demands of principle and the needs of the public interest. One could not have chosen a better motto to capture his judicial work or his Zionism.

Epilogue

[W]ith the completion of the Supreme Court, Israel, a nation that has shown little architectural leadership, has produced a building that can stand as an example to the world of the potential of public works to reflect a culture's highest aspiration.
—PAUL GOLDBERGER, "Public Work That Ennobles as It Serves," *New York Times,* 13 August 1995, H30.

Becoming "an example to the world" was Agranat's youthful ambition for the Zionist project when, at the age of nineteen, he published his article "Concerning the Hebrew University." He would have loved the superlatives heaped on the new Court building by the *New York Times:* "majestic," "Israel's finest building," "combining a sense of monumentality with a sense of easy, inviting accessibility," "a remarkable and exhilarating balance between the concerns of daily life and the symbolism of the ages." He would have also drawn gratification from the deeper historical meaning the article ascribed to the building: "for too long [Israel] . . . was too poor and too beleaguered to think of buildings as doing much more than providing cover from the rain. But in the last decade, as Israel has become more certain of its continued existence, the notion of a permanent architecture has begun to take root—and nowhere to better result than in the new Supreme Court building, which marks a critical point in the architectural maturation of this country."[1]

Agranat, who saw the plans for the new building but did not live to see it in full splendor, had misgivings about the project, misgivings that themselves symbolize the changes Israel has undergone since its Supreme Court was inaugurated forty-five years earlier in the humble quarters of the Russian compound. Agranat disapproved of the fact that the building was yet another gift from the Rothschild family to the state of Israel—the Rothschilds had already financed the Knesset building. He regarded self-financing as a logical deduction of the Zionist principle of Hebrew labor—the idea that the nation could only be rebuilt through its own blood and sweat. During his tenure as chief justice he insisted, as Olshan had insisted before him, that Israel itself should finance the home for its highest court.[2] He disagreed with the wisdom of locating the Court next to the Knesset and the prime minister's office. He was troubled by its proximity to the center of politics. He wanted geography itself to express detachment from short-term, partisan considerations.[3]

But the torch has been passed to a new generation, for whom Agranat's concerns no longer seemed material. The inauguration of the building coincided with a critical development in the Court's history. Israel's Constitution, made up of a series of Basic Laws, has been fortified with some guarantees of fundamental rights and is almost complete.[4] At the same time, a new generation of justices has been boldly transforming the constitutional landscape. Justice Meir Shamgar, appointed in 1974, assumed the presidency of the Court in 1982. New justices were appointed, most significantly Justice Aharon Barak, who succeeded Shamgar as chief justice in 1995.[5] These two dedicated, ambitious, and politically sophisticated men resurrected Agranat's legacy of the 1950s and pushed its frontiers beyond Agranat's wildest imagination. The path of cautious continuity that characterized Agranat's tenure as chief justice and was also followed by his successors in the 1970s, was abandoned. Drawing on Agranat's *Kol ha-Am* opinion for guidance and legitimacy and inspired by American constitutional law, Shamgar and Barak led the Court in turning Israel's Declaration of Independence into a tool legitimating the judicial crafting of a jurisprudence of rights.[6] Understanding that neither a jurisprudence of legal formalism nor the theory of legal process would be helpful in achieving their goal, they returned to Agranat's original understanding of adjudication as partaking in the national dialogue about substantive values.[7]

The revival of themes from utopian Zionism, however, did not put catastrophe Zionism to rest. From the 1970s through the 1990s, the same new Court, which has developed a dazzling jurisprudence of rights, has also built a jurisprudence of repression, thereby legitimating Israel's attempt to maintain the regime of occupation in Gaza and the West Bank. The Court condoned a plethora of abusive policies, mainly in the occupied territories, but sometimes within the pre-1967 borders as well, all related to the Palestinian struggle for self-determination. Administrative detentions, house demolitions, deportations, and suppression of political expression have survived most challenges before the Court.[8]

In intricate ways, which I have tried to explore in this book, the question of national security affects, and is affected by, the question of the separation of religion and state. Both are informed by the presence of the Holocaust in Israeli collective memory. Israel's raison d'être is a Jewish state. Its national identity is intimately tied to Judaism. Its conception of itself as Jewish affects its comprehension of the Arab as the "other," the enemy who threatens the state's survival. But its conception of itself as Jewish also produces deep conflicts over the viability of religious pluralism, as well as over the viability of a secular lifestyle. Like its predecessors, the current Court is struggling with the meaning of Israel as a state that aspires to be at once democratic and Jewish.

In their endeavors to develop an Israeli jurisprudence for the twenty-first century, the justices may well take a clue from the architecture of their home. It is a structure that strives to weave the motifs of the past with the esthetics and needs of the present. Some of the motifs of this past are the subject of this book. Consulting the past while rebuilding the present was the spirit that pervaded the complex legacy of Simon Agranat.

Notes

PROLOGUE

1. Golda Meir (formerly Meirson) was born in Russia and brought up in the United States. Abba (Aubrey) Eban (known in Israel as Even) was born in South Africa and brought up in England.

2. The two exceptions were Justices Shneur Zalman Cheshin, appointed in 1948, and Eliyahu Mani, appointed in 1962.

3. C.A. 448/60, *Lev v. ha-Mashbir ha-Merkazi,* 16 P.D. 2688, 2699 (1962). Agranat wrote the majority opinion, with Justice Moshe Silberg dissenting.

4. This book draws heavily on interviews with Simon Agranat, conducted between 1983 and 1991. The quotations attributed to him in the text are based on the notes taken during those interviews. All the quotations from books, articles, and judicial opinions, which originally appeared in Hebrew, were translated by the author, following the conventional rules of transliteration.

5. Although a devout Zionist, he refused to hebraize his family name, unlike David Ben-Gurion (formerly Greenboim) or Golda Meir. He thereby rejected the Zionist notion that, in Israel, the Jew should shed all marks of *galut,* including the "foreign" family name, and insisted on retaining that part of his old identity. When Israel became a state, government policy required that public officials change their names into Hebrew. It is interesting that the majority of the Supreme Court justices would not comply.

CHAPTER 1

1. For the Agranat family genealogy, see Paula Agranat Hurwitz, *The Agranat Family: These Are the Generations* (Los Angeles, 1988), 43.

2. John M. Allswang, *A House for All Peoples: Ethnic Politics in Chicago, 1890–1936* (Lexington: University Press of Kentucky, 1971), 20.

3. Later in his life, Aaron gave a series of lectures in Haifa, on a diverse range of topics, from Maimonides, medical history, women in the Talmud, and Jewish liturgy, to the Jewish theater. Aaron Agranat, untitled, Agranat papers, Agranat family, Jerusalem.

4. Irving Howe, *World of Our Fathers* (New York: Harcourt Brace Jovanovich, 1976), 205.

5. Simon himself attributed his dread of sailing to Palestine to his fear of sailing across Lake Michigan to visit his grandmother in Milwaukee.

6. Dorothy Kurgeans Goldberg, interview by the author, Washington, D.C., November 1983.

7. *Von Humboldt Record* 3 (January 1919).

8. Esther Schour, interview by the author, Chicago, Illinois, March 1983; Mary Satinover, interview by the author, Chicago, Illinois, March 1983; Leo Wolf, interview by the author, Tucson, Arizona, March 1983; Ben Sackheim, interview by the author, Tucson, Arizona, March 1983.

9. Ben Sackheim, letter to the author, 14 January 1983.

10. Elias Canetti, *Crowds and Power,* trans. Carol Stewart (New York: Viking Press, 1962), 394–96.

11. Richard Hofstader, *The Age of Reform* (New York: Vintage Books, 1955), 5, 11; Arthur A. Ekirch Jr., *Progressivism in America* (New York: New Viewpoints, 1974), 72.

12. *Von Humboldt Record* 3 (January 1919).

13. Simon Agranat, "School Spirit," *Tuley High School Review* 28 (December 1921): 3. Agranat's emphasis.

14. *Von Humboldt Record* 3 (January 1919).

15. Kevin Tierney, *Darrow: A Biography* (New York: Thomas Y. Crowell, 1979), 203.

16. Upton Sinclair, ed., *The Cry for Justice: An Anthology of the Literature of Social Protest* (Philadelphia: John C. Winston, 1915; New York: L. Stuart, 1963), 22.

17. Ibid., 9.

18. Theodor Herzl (1860–1904) was the founding father of political Zionism. His pamphlet *The Jewish State* ([*Der Judenstaat*], trans. Harry Zohn [New York: Herzl Press, 1970]) argued that the Jewish question in Europe could not be resolved unless Jews had a state of their own. In 1897 he organized the World Zionist Congress and served as its first president.

19. Yonathan Shapiro, *Leadership of the American Zionist Organization, 1897–1930* (Urbana: University of Illinois Press, 1971), 52.

20. The source of inspiration for both the Conservative movement and Young Judea was Professor Israel Friedlaender. Baila R. Shargel, *Practical Dreamer: Israel Friedlaender and the Shaping of American Judaism* (New York: The Jewish Theological Seminary of America, 1985), 12. In 1933, Simon married Israel Friedlaender's daughter, Carmel. See discussion on p. 54.

21. *The Herzlite* (1921), a private publication in the author's files.

22. Ibid.

23. Ibid.

24. Simon played Major Spence, who defended the young man in his military trial. Another indication that the issue of American Jewish identity was on

Simon's mind is the fact that his speech at his bar mitzvah was about the difficulties of growing up Jewish in America.

25. Philippa Strum, *Louis D. Brandeis: Justice for the People* (Cambridge, Mass.: Harvard University Press, 1984), 266; Arthur Hertzberg, *The Jews in America: Four Centuries of an Uneasy Encounter: A History* (New York: Simon & Schuster, 1989), 222–25.

26. Zionist Organization of America, *Brandeis on Zionism: A Collection of Addresses and Statements by Louis D. Brandeis* (New York: H. Wolff, 1942), 29. Agranat invoked this formula, quoting Brandeis, in C.A. 630/70, *Tamarin v. State of Israel*, 26(1) P.D. 197, 205 (1972).

27. George L. Berlin, "The Brandeis-Weizmann Dispute," *American Jewish Historical Quarterly* 60 (1970–1971): 37, 40.

28. Shapiro, *Leadership*, 161–79; Melvin I. Urofsky, *American Zionism from Herzl to the Holocaust* (Garden City, N.Y.: Anchor Press, 1975).

29. Chaim Weizmann, *Trial and Error: The Autobiography of Chaim Weizmann* (Philadelphia: The Jewish Publication Society of America, 1949), vol. 2, 267.

30. Norman Rose, *Chaim Weizmann: A Biography* (New York: Viking Press, 1986), 210.

31. The distinction is Ussishkin's. Urofsky, *American Zionism*, 295; see also Urofsky's analysis of American and European culture on pp. 283–98.

32. *The Herzlite*. Emphasis added.

33. Strum, *Brandeis*, 256.

34. Harry Barnard, *The Forging of an American Jew: The Life and Times of Judge Julian W. Mack* (New York: Herzl Press, 1974), 281.

35. Shakespeare, *Julius Caesar*, Act V, Scene 5, line 68.

36. Ibid., Act I, Scene 2, line 169.

37. *The Herzlite*. Agranat's emphasis.

38. Wolf, interview.

39. Theodor Herzl, *Altneuland*, trans. Lotte Levensohn (New York: Herzl Press, 1987); *Rubin's Tel Aviv: A Salute to Tel Aviv on the Occasion of Its Seventy-Fifth Anniversary* (n.p., n.d.).

40. Weizmann, *Trial and Error*, vol. 2, 318–19.

41. Ibid., 238.

42. Simon Agranat, "Bublik Speech" (a lecture given at the Hebrew University, July 1979).

43. Simon Agranat, "Concerning the Hebrew University," *Chicago Yidisher Kuryer*, 4 April 1925, English section of the weekend edition.

44. Agranat, "Bublik Speech" (emphasis added). Agranat had a long and complex relationship with the Hebrew University. He had served as a professor of criminal law since a law faculty had been established and is universally recognized as the founder of modern Israeli criminal law. The university, however, was not consistently kind to him. When told that he could no longer offer courses, he was stunned to learn that despite more than fifteen years of teaching he was not entitled to any pension. A proud man, he kept his pain to himself, but during the Bublik ceremony he did not resist the temptation to gently chide the university: "In 1950 I was asked by the Dean . . . to teach criminal law. . . . This is a position of an adjunct professor, he said to me, limited to one year only. . . . Despite this

constraint I agreed, with no hesitation, to take the task upon myself. . . . [The search for my replacement] took a long time." This remark was characteristic, both because of its subtle humor and because it captured the man: he would not forget wrongs done to him, but he detested fights for personal material gain.

45. 1348 Y.B. Liber Assisarium.

46. Lawrence M. Friedman, *A History of American Law,* 2d ed. (New York: Simon & Schuster, 1985), 613.

47. Oscar Kraines, *The World and Ideas of Ernst Freund: The Search for General Principles of Legislation and Administrative Law* (University: University of Alabama Press, 1974). See also Frank L. Ellsworth, *Law on the Midway: The Founding of the University of Chicago Law School* (Chicago: Law School of the University of Chicago, 1977).

48. Agranat contrasted the closed and open legal system in the following manner: "[A] 'closed' legal system [is] . . . one requiring the answers to all legal questions to be logically deduced from a fixed number of prescribed rules. . . . It is thus distinct from an 'open' system, which permits the gradual filling of legal gaps in accordance with changing circumstances, by the application of general standards and with the help of principles of equity considerations and of public policy." Simon Agranat, "The Supreme Court in Action," *Jerusalem Post,* 6 May 1973.

49. Morton J. Horwitz, *The Transformation of American Law, 1870–1960: The Crisis of Legal Orthodoxy* (New York: Oxford University Press, 1992), 17; G. Edward White, *Patterns of American Legal Thought* (Indianapolis, Ind.: Bobbs-Merrill, 1978), 97–191. It is quite possible that in the University of Chicago the struggle was less manifest than it had been at Yale, Harvard, or Columbia. The Law School at the University of Chicago was established on an understanding that there was room for both approaches. See Ellsworth, *Law on the Midway,* 74–77. Most Chicago law professors tried to pay lip service to Freund's insistence on the interdisciplinary approach. James Parker Hall, for example, said:

The case method . . . which has achieved so complete a mastery of American legal education of the better sort, has certain unrivaled advantages in dealing with fundamental or difficult legal problems. . . . But, as has often been observed, it is a slow method, and in a given time [more] . . . ground can be covered . . . by . . . didactic, or descriptive, or informational [methods]. It is not so often perceived, however, that this is not so much a criticism of the case method as a statement . . . that there is no easy and rapid method of acquiring an adequate professional knowledge of . . . law. History, economics, politics, religion, and all the important emotional reactions of society have affected the reasoned processes by which its doctrines have been wrought. (James Parker Hall, "Some Observations on the Law School Curriculum," 5 *Am. Law School Rev.* 61 [1923].)

In addition, people like Hall had been influenced not only by the father of the case method, Christopher Columbus Langdell, but also by Roscoe Pound, one of the founders of sociological jurisprudence, and they imparted to their students the notion that legal rules reflected the balancing of interests.

50. This tendency, which became more pronounced in later years and typified his performance as a judge, could have also contributed to his failure in his first bar examination in 1929. See discussion on pp. 37, 69.

51. Until his last year of law school, Simon lived with his family in Albany Park, worked as a teacher in a Reform synagogue, and commuted to law school. Thus he was probably remote from the school's social life.

52. Benjamin L. Sacks, letter to the author, 14 February 1983.

53. "After the law school graduation ceremony, Simon wanted me to go to Palestine to practice law. He assured me that there were great opportunities for us in that country. He suggested, after studying Turkish and English laws, we would become successful lawyers in the Holy Land. I declined—he immigrated to Palestine. Simon did have the ability to look into the future and anticipate the possibilities in Palestine for our people." Samuel J. Benjamin, letter to the author, 3 April 1983.

54. Leon M. Despres, letter to the author, 14 February 1983.

55. Kraines, *Ernst Freund*, 154.

56. Joseph S. Shubow, "When We Lighted the Torch," *Avukah Annual* 5 (1930): 37, 38.

57. Ibid., 39. With the rise of European Fascism and anti-Semitism and the simultaneous collapse of the British commitment to the Jewish National Home, Avukah grew militant. It agitated in favor of a Jewish state, a "non-minority Jewish center in Palestine." It became a burden on the Zionist Organization of America (ZOA), which took a cautious diplomatic approach toward Britain and the future of Palestine and feared that Avukah was under Communist influence. By the end of 1941, the Executive Committee of the ZOA recommended that recognition of Avukah as the sole Zionist Junior Organization be rescinded. See *The Avukah Problem: A Special Report by the American Zionist Youth Commission* (New York: American Zionist Youth Commission, 1942), Jewish Archives, Cincinnati. Avukah closed down in 1943, after a majority of its membership had enlisted or been drafted into the armed forces. See Melvin I. Urofsky and David W. Levy, eds., *Letters of Louis D. Brandeis,* vol. 5 (Albany: State University of New York Press, 1978), 645.

58. Anita Shapira, *Herev ha-Yonah* [Land and Power] (Tel Aviv: Am Oved, 1992), 141–56. Shapira sees the events of Tel Hai as the first to form "the defensive ethos" in Zionist historiography, according to which the Yishuv was peace seeking and nonbelligerent but at the same time determined to defend its settlements against aggression. According to the myth, the last words of Yosef Trumpeldor, the commander of the small force in Tel Hai, who died in the battle, were, "It is good to die for our country." This statement has become a motto in Israeli education. For a more provocative historical interpretation, see Idith Zertal, "Ha-Meunim veha-Kdoshim: Kinunah shel Martirologiyah Leumit [The Tortured and the Saints: The Establishment of a National Martyrology]," *Zmanim* 48 (1994): 28; Yael Zerubavel, *Recovered Roots: Collective Memory and the Making of Israeli National Tradition* (Chicago: University of Chicago Press, 1995).

59. See A. D. Gordon, "On Labor," *Avukah Annual* 5 (1930): 128. The political sympathies of Avukah also lay with labor Zionism. Max Rhoade, the president of Avukah, observed that "[w]e have set for ourselves . . . the goal of bringing the living creative Palestine of today—Erets Yisrael ha-Ovedet—Laboring Palestine—to the Jewish Youth of America—insofar as we are unable to bring them to Erets Yisrael ha-Ovedet." Max Rhoade, "Avukah Convention," *New Palestine,* 2 November 1928, 345.

60. Simon appended to the proposal correspondence with the leadership of the Youth Movement in Palestine and with the Keren Kayemet (Jewish National Fund), inquiring about the viability of his project. The responses from Palestine were at best lukewarm.

61. Palestine Project for Avukah, *Avukah's Future* (Chicago: Chicago Chapter of Avukah, 1928).

62. Ibid., 7.

63. *New Palestine,* 11 November 1927, 379, announced that "on Dec. 4th Chicago Avukah will present a Forum and Musicale, the proceeds of which are to go toward the Avukah project in Palestine."

64. Ibid., 13–20 July 1928, 55.

65. *Annual Avukah Report,* Yivo Archives, New York, 1928.

66. Not only did the national leadership oppose them, but their correspondence with the institutions of the Yishuv made it clear that there was no enthusiasm for the project in Tel Aviv. Palestine Project for Avukah, *Avukah's Future*.

67. Shlomo Avinery, *Arlosoroff* (London: Weidenfeld & Nicolson, 1989), 11–59, 99–112.

68. Miriam Getter, *Hayim Arlozorov: Biyografyah Politit* [Chaim Arlosoroff: A Political Biography] (Tel Aviv: Ha-Kibuts ha-Meuhad, 1977), 176–81, 227.

69. Simon Agranat, letter to Louis and Mini Orloff, 26 January 1930, Agranat papers, Agranat family, Jerusalem.

70. Ibid.

71. "Shvirderlishe Shkhita in Tsfat, A Tsveyte Hevron, 22 Yiden Toit, Wilde Shvatim fun Siriyen Marshiren auyf Palestina," *Chicago Yidisher Kuryer,* 1 September 1929, 1.

72. "Ganze Yidishe Bafelkerung Antloyft fun Haifa," ibid., 10 September 1929, 1.

73. "Palestine Pool of Blood," *Sunday Jewish Courier,* English section of ibid., 8 September 1929, 1.

74. "The Ferment in Arabia," ibid., 1 September 1929, 1 (quoting the *Chicago Daily News*).

75. Agranat, letter to Louis and Mini Orloff, 26 January 1930.

76. Ibid.

77. Simon Agranat, letter to Louis and Mini Orloff, 23 February 1930, Agranat papers, Agranat family, Jerusalem.

CHAPTER 2

1. After 1948, when Israel gained sovereignty, stationery of Jews would rarely display information in Arabic.

2. Simon Agranat, letter to Louis and Mini Orloff, 10 April 1930, Agranat papers, Agranat family, Jerusalem. Agranat is referring here to the British restrictions on Jewish immigration to Palestine.

3. Simon Agranat, "A Modern Maccabean, The Life and Death of Ephraim Chizik," *Avukah Annual* 5 (1930): 106.

4. Ibid., 108.

5. Ibid., 106.

6. Ibid., 109.

7. This was up from 83 lawyers at the end of 1921. By 1936 the number jumped to 360. Of the 360, only 112 were Arabs, an indication of the influx of profes-

sional Jews coming to Palestine as a result of the British open-door policy and the rise of Fascism in Europe. See Gavriel Shtrasman, *Ote ha-Glima: Toldot Arikhat ha-Din be-Erets Yisrael* [Wearing the Robes: A History of the Legal Profession until 1962] (Tel Aviv: Hotsaat Lishkat Orkhe ha-Din be-Yisrael, 1984), 161.

8. Ya'acov Halevy (Simon's law partner in the 1930s), interview by the author, Givatayim, Israel, October 1984.

9. Simon Agranat, letter to the editor of *Ahdut ha-Avodah,* undated, Agranat papers, Agranat family, Jerusalem.

10. See Eli Shaltiel, *Pinhas Rutenberg: Aliyato u-Nefilato shel "Ish Hazak"* [Pinhas Rutenberg: Life and Times] (Tel Aviv: Am Oved, 1990).

11. The struggle took the British and Turkish governments before the International Court. See Permanent Court of International Justice, "The Mavrommatis Jerusalem Concessions," *Collection of Judgements,* ser. A, no. 5 (Leiden: A. W. Sijthoff, 1925).

12. "Simon Agranat Memorandum on the Rutenberg Concession," undated, Agranat papers, in the author's files.

13. Thorsten Sellin (editor-in-chief of the *Annals*), letter to Mordechai Eliash, 8 September 1932, Agranat papers, in the author's files.

14. Ibid.

15. Harry Viteles, letter to Mordechai Eliash, 18 September 1932, Agranat papers, Agranat family, Jerusalem. The volume was finally published as *Palestine: A Decade of Development,* Annals of the American Academy of Political Science, vol. 164 (Philadelphia: American Academy of Political and Social Science, 1932).

16. In Palestine, prominent lawyers always found themselves engaged in public affairs. When Simon joined his office, Eliash headed the delegation representing the Yishuv before the International Commission on the Status of the Western Wall.

17. It may well be that the "Yemenite male secretary," whom Simon remembered, later became Eliash's Yemenite law partner (Moshe Kehaty). Shtrasman, *Ote ha-Glima,* 26.

18. Ibid., 68.

19. Harry Sacher and Bernard Joseph, memorandum to the high commissioner, 10 December 1925, file P6/857, Bernard Joseph Archive, Israel State Archive.

20. Shtrasman, *Ote ha-Glima,* 39. Although Agnon was describing the dusk of the Ottoman period, his description is still telling of the beginning of the Mandatory era.

21. See Assaf Likhovski, "In Our Image: Colonial Discourse and the Anglicization of the Law of Mandatory Palestine," 29 *Is. L. Rev.* 291 (1995).

22. Moshe Silberg, *Bain Ke-Ehad: Asufat Dvarim shebe-Hagut uva-Halakhah* [In Inner Harmony: Essays and Articles] (Jerusalem: Magnes Press, 1981), 111.

23. Gad Frumkin, *Derekh Shofet Bi-Yerushalayim* [A Judge in Jerusalem] (Tel Aviv: Dvir, 1955), 275.

24. "The Jurisdiction of the Civil Courts shall be exercised in conformity with the Ottoman Law . . . and so far as the same shall not extend or apply, shall be exercised in conformity with the substance of the common law, and the doctrines of equity in force in England . . . [p]rovided always that the said . . . [English law] . . . shall be in force in Palestine so far only as the circumstances of Palestine

and its inhabitants . . . permit and subject to such qualification as local circumstances render necessary." Palestine Order in Council, 1922, art. 46, in *Laws of Palestine,* ed. R. Drayton, vol. 3 (London: Waterlow and Sons, 1934).

25. The case had a long trail of litigation. It started at the district court of Jaffa, then came before the Supreme Court of Palestine, from there to the Privy Council in London and back to the district court, and again on appeal to the Palestine Supreme Court in Jerusalem.

26. P.C.A. 1/35, *Faruqi v. Aiyub* [*sic*], 2 P.L.R. 390 (1935); C.A. 191/37, *Farouqi v. Ayoub,* 4 P.L.R. 331 (1937); P.C.A. 30/39, *Ayoub v. Farouqi,* 8 P.L.R. 116 (1941).

27. Margery Bentwich, *Lilian Ruth Friedlander: A Biography* (London: Routledge & Kegan Paul, 1957), 23.

28. Shargel, *Practical Dreamer.*

29. One of her close friends was the noted Zionist activist Henrietta Szold. Bentwich, *Lilian Ruth Friedlander,* 37.

30. Most of her friends advised her against the move. Cyrus Adler (the scholar and Jewish leader) wrote: "It is difficult to exercise one's judgment on a short visit to the Holy Land. . . . It is a ruined and not too friendly land, to be redeemed, if at all, by the sturdy pioneer amidst many hardships. . . . Judaism in America needs your brave soul and your children too." Ibid., 81. The children learned Hebrew, attended Ha-Re'ali Gimnasium in Haifa, and acquired higher education abroad. Carmel's older brothers studied in Chicago, and Carmel herself graduated from the Froebel Educational Institute in Roehampton, England. In 1936 Lilian founded Beit Daniel, a guest house for artists and musicians, and became a major force in the development of the music scene in Palestine. The *Encyclopaedia Judaica* does not devote an entry to Lilian (as it does to her father, brothers, and husband), but Leonard Bernstein, in his foreword to her biography, wrote: "Every infant needs a mother; and so does every infant State. Young Israel has had its doting fathers. . . . [T]he world knows these men of passion, pride and dignity. We have heard less about its mothers . . . Lilian Friedlander was such a mother . . . a woman whose great fountain of maternal love was trained on the land she adored. My memories of her are all bathed in a matriarchal glow: I remember a piercing facial beauty, a lofty simplicity, and a steady effluvium of strength and kindness." Bentwich, *Lilian Ruth Friedlander,* foreword.

31. "Papa's 'Tuntine' (sunshine) was his name for her, and she was the delight of Lilian's father, who called her Peg-o'-my-Heart." Bentwich, *Lilian Ruth Friedlander,* 37.

32. Simon had relied on one of Friedlaender's essays for a college paper. In 1970 Agranat paid tribute to his father-in-law, quoting from his work in his *Who Is a Jew* dissent (see discussion on p. 207).

33. The description of Friedlaender's work in the *Encyclopaedia Judaica* could apply with equal force to that of Agranat's: "His public activity, as well as his writings, were characterized by his ability to see the different sides of the same question and to mediate between them." *Encyclopaedia Judaica,* s.v. "Israel Friedlaender."

34. Bentwich, *Lilian Ruth Friedlander,* 112.

35. Ibid.

36. "The picture that remains uppermost, is the six bridesmaids, such lovely children, in Kate Greenaway dresses of organdy, all assembled in Nita's small room,

like a cloud of white and blue. Little Nita [Carmel's cousin] might have stepped out of a Botticelli picture, and Viola like nothing but her attractive self." Ibid., 112–13.

37. See, for example, Judah Magnes's speech at the opening of the Hebrew University's academic year 1929/1930: "One of the greatest cultural duties of the Jewish people is the attempt to enter the promised land, not by means of conquest as Joshua, but through peaceful and cultural means, through hard work, sacrifice, love and with a decision not to do anything which cannot be justified before the world conscience." *Encyclopaedia Judaica*, s.v. "Judah Magnes." Compare that entry with Agranat's elegy for Ephraim Chizik, written at about the same time.

38. Their first, Israel, was born in 1935; Zilla, in 1939; Hillel, in 1941; Yael (Didi), in 1942; and Ronnie, in 1951.

39. See his description of his fiftieth birthday party: "That event was celebrated 'en famille'—the highlights being a tape-recorded program given by the children, with Hillel orating (remarkably well and in the original) an Antonius speech from Shakespeare's Julius Caesar and Zillah playing beautifully two of my favorite (and sentimental) American songs on the piano. The deus ex machina behind all this was, as usual, the Good Lady Carmel." Simon Agranat, letter to Morris and Mary Schussheim, 24 December 1956, Agranat papers, Agranat family, Jerusalem.

40. Yitzhak Kahan, interview by the author, Haifa, June 1984.

41. Shoshana Klein, letter to Simon Agranat, 7 March 1965, in *Gvurot le-Shimon Agranat* [Essays in Honor of Simon Agranat], ed. Aharon Barak et al. (Jerusalem: Graf Press, 1986), unnumbered page.

42. Article 2 of the Mandate for Palestine provides, simultaneously, for a Jewish National Home and for safeguarding the rights of the Palestinian (native) population: "The mandatory shall be responsible for placing the country under such political administrative and economic conditions as will secure the establishment of the Jewish National Home . . . and also for safeguarding the civil and religious rights of the inhabitants of Palestine irrespective of race and religion." Max M. Laserson, ed., *On the Mandate: Documents, Statements, Laws and Judgements Relating to and Arising from the Mandate for Palestine* (Tel Aviv: Igereth, 1937), 41.

43. Chaim Weizmann recalled Lord Passfield's having told him, in 1930, that "there is not room to swing a cat in Palestine." Palestine Royal Commission, *Minutes of Evidence Heard at Public Sessions*, vol. 1 (London: H. M. Stationery Office, 1937), 36; Shabtai Teveth, *Ben-Gurion: The Burning Ground, 1886–1948* (Boston: Houghton Mifflin, 1987), 572.

44. Simon Agranat, letter to Louis and Mini Orloff, 22 May 1930, Agranat papers, Agranat family, Jerusalem.

45. Ha-Va'ad ha-Leumi. The local Jewish committee—Va'ad ha-Kehilah—was also involved. The lawyers were paid five English pounds per month, a small sum not sufficient to cover costs. They were expected and agreed to do the work as a national service. Most of the illegal immigrants in the Safed court were Syrian Jews. Yehuda Shachrour, letter to the author, 11 July 1995.

46. Ordinarily, the illegal immigrant would be sentenced to three months in jail. Next, the attorney would approach the chief of police and the head of the C.I.D. (the security services of Mandatory Palestine), who had discretion to release the prisoners on bail, pending deportation orders.

47. Ironically, Agranat himself was not a Palestinian citizen at the time. He

also recalled making ludicrously legalistic arguments, when the case seemed utterly hopeless. In one case, when the immigrant was caught close to the border and not far from a police station, he argued that one was not obliged to obtain a visa prior to arrival: "[I]t is perfectly conceivable that the defendant was heading toward the police station, after having crossed the border, in order to request a visa." To his astonishment, the court accepted the argument. But visa was denied, and the person was duly deported. "The operation was successful; the patient died," Agranat apologetically said in summation.

48. The high commissioner decided to free the detainees on a bail of 100 English pounds per person—an exorbitant amount. Members of the public volunteered to sign as collaterals. Simon, along with Moshe Goldberg, who owned an automobile, drove to the prison on a rainy Friday afternoon, just before the Sabbath began, to inform the prisoners that their release was imminent and that they should terminate their hunger strike.

49. Arlosoroff, head of the Political Department of the Jewish Agency, with whom Simon had crossed paths during the days of Avukah and in the debate over the legislative council for Palestine, was assassinated as he was strolling with his wife on the Tel Aviv beach. There followed an acrimonious upheaval, with the Left blaming the Right for the assassination. The question is still an open wound in Israel. See Shabtai Teveth, *Retsah Arlozorov* [The Murder of Arlosoroff] (Jerusalem: Schocken, 1982).

50. The other attorney was Zeev Argaman. Assisting the committee was Yitzhak Kahan, who later became Simon's clerk.

51. For historical background on Brit Shalom, see Aharon Kedar, "Brith Shalom—The Early Period (1925–1928)," in *Pirkey Mehkar be-Toldot ha-Tsiyonut* [Studies in the History of Zionism], ed. Yehuda Bauer, Moshe Davis, and Israel Kolatt (Jerusalem: Ha-Sifriyah ha-Tsiyonit, 1976), 224.

52. Babbitt was the conformist hero of Sinclair Lewis's novel *Babbitt* (New York: Harcourt Brace Jovanovich, 1922).

53. Palestine Royal Commission, *Report: Presented by the Secretary of State for the Colonies to Parliament by Command of His Majesty, July 1937* (London: H. M. Stationery Office, 1937), 120. "[A]bout 43 per cent of the qualified population were not Palestinian citizens. The Jews have not availed themselves readily of the opportunity . . . and this is accounted for by the fact that their chief interest is in the Jewish community itself and allegiance to Palestine and its Government are minor considerations to many of them" (p. 332).

54. "The Department of State in Washington has informed the Consulate General that you lost the nationality of the United States on March 17, 1941 . . . by acquiring Palestine citizenship on that date. A certificate of Loss of Nationality was . . . approved by the Department of State on September 20, 1941." American Consul in Jerusalem, letter to Simon Agranat, Agranat papers, Agranat family, Jerusalem. Until the 1960s, loss of citizenship occurred automatically once it was established that a citizen had obtained naturalization in a foreign state. Since that time, a consensus has evolved that American citizens have a constitutional right to remain citizens unless they voluntarily assent to expatriation. See, generally, Alan G. James, "Expatriation in the United States: Precept and Practice Today and Yesterday," 27 *San Diego L. Rev.* 853 (1990). The American-born Carmel did retain her American citizenship, but Simon's expatriation could have been in-

terpreted as casting doubts on the validity of her citizenship because she was now married to a foreign national, an act that also entailed expatriation, according to American law at the time.

55. Arthur Koestler, *Thieves in the Night: Chronicle of an Experiment* (New York: Macmillan, 1946), 235. Agranat directed my attention to this description. It was common knowledge in Haifa legal circles at the time that Koestler was describing the courtroom in which Agranat and Landau held trials.

56. "Shoftey Shalom 'Britim' ve-Yehudim ['British' and Jewish Magistrates]," 2 *Ha-Praklit* 98 (1945); "Shoftim Britim ve-Erets Yisraelim [British and Palestinian Judges]," 3 *Ha-Praklit* 164 (1946). In the 1940s there were a number of changes in the jurisdiction of Palestinian magistrates. See, generally, "Harhavat Samkhutam Shel Shoftey ha-Shalom ha-Erets Yisraeliim [Wider Jurisdiction for Palestinian Magistrates]," *Ha-Praklit*, April 1944, at 5; "Bitul ha-Zkhut le-Berur Shoftim [The Abolition of the Right to Choose Judges]," 4 *Ha-Praklit* 197 (1947).

57. At the insistence of Carmel's mother the family moved to Zikhron Ya'acov, to escape the bombing. They were joined by the families of Agranat's two good friends, Naftali Lifshits and Jacob S. Shapiro. The men commuted between Haifa and Zikhron Ya'acov.

58. Agranat and his colleague, Moshe Landau, served as privates. Jacob Solomon, another Jewish lawyer, was bombardier, and Jacob S. Shapiro was lance bombardier.

59. The Court could thereby save the cost of interpreting the opinions in order to make them accessible to the English- and Arab-speaking members of the legal community.

60. For a sample of Agranat's unpublished opinions as a magistrate, see C.A. 6776/40, *Abramowitz v. Argamann;* C.A. 4261/41, *Gorodisky v. Shwartzbord;* C.A. 1152/42 (names of parties not mentioned); C.A. 2704/43, *Dayan v. "Haver";* C.A. 2853/43, *Dikstein v. Glazer,* Agranat papers, Agranat family, Jerusalem.

61. "In the paper which Cohen delivered at the first Conference of Legal and Social Philosophy, he demonstrated—to my mind, effectively—the falsity of what he called 'the phonograph theory of the judicial function,' according to which 'the judge merely repeats the words that the law has spoken to him'. . . . [T]oday most jurists would, I think, look upon that thesis as commonplace, yet at the time when Cohen advanced it, it was anathema to legal orthodoxy." Simon Agranat, "The Philosophy of Morris R. Cohen, A Symposium: Reflections on the Man and His Work," 16 *Is. L. Rev.* 282, 287 (1981). For an analysis of the challenge to legal orthodoxy in the United States, see Horwitz, *Transformation.*

62. "I remember that . . . he was unable to obtain a copy of Holmes' Common Law [in Palestine] and I found a copy and sent it to him." Fred H. Mandel, letter to the author, 8 February 1983.

63. Felix Cohen, "Transcendental Nonsense and the Functional Approach," 35 *Colum. L. Rev.* 809 (1935). See also Agranat's 1973 characterization of the Mandatory legal system as a "closed system," Simon Agranat, "The Supreme Court in Action," *Jerusalem Post,* 6 May 1973.

64. The fact that he continued to write long opinions after his elevation to the top of the judicial pyramid does not necessarily cast doubt on this explanation. It may well be that by then the practice had become second nature to him, difficult if not impossible to shed.

65. "Shwartz v. Hoiser," 10 *P.L.R.* 170, 172 (1943). "How do you like my excessive modesty?" Agranat asked, after showing me the quotation. "I don't brag about myself, but I admit that I am good."

66. The program, announced in the Biltmore Hotel in New York, included the opening of the gates of Palestine to mass Jewish immigration, an active role in the Palestine economy for the Jewish Agency, and the eventual establishment of a Jewish commonwealth in a part of Palestine.

67. *Palestine Gazette,* Supp. 2, 1055 (1945).

68. Yehoshua Porath and Yaacov Shavit, eds., *Ha-Historyah shel Erets Yisrael: Ha-Mandat Veha-Bayit ha-Leumi* [The History of Palestine: The British Mandate and the Jewish National Home] (Jerusalem: Keter, 1981), 76; Joseph Heller, "Meha-Shabat ha-Shhorah la-Halukah, Kayits 1946 ki-Nekudat mifne be-Toldot ha-Tsiyonut [From the 'Black Sabbath' to Partition (Summer 1946 as a Turning Point in the History of Zionist Policy)]," *Zion* 43 (1978): 314, 331–38.

69. "Mi-Yom le-Yom [From Day to Day]," *Ha-Arets,* 2 July 1946, 2.

70. See chap. 6, n. 14, and chap. 10, n. 8.

71. The British generally refrained from utilizing native judges in their effort to crush the rebellion. Native judges could not be trusted to side with British interests in such matters. Agranat was seldom called on to preside over trials of a political nature and hence did not experience the dilemma between justice and law in its most acute form.

72. Benny Morris, *The Birth of the Palestinian Refugee Problem, 1947–1949* (Cambridge, England: Cambridge University Press, 1987), 19–23; Simha Flapan, *The Birth of Israel: Myth and Realities* (New York: Pantheon Books, 1987), 187–99; Ilan Pappe, *The Making of the Arab-Israeli Conflict, 1947–1951* (London: I. B. Tauris, 1992), 102–34. For a description from the Palestinian perspective, see Walid Khalidi, "The Fall of Haifa," *Middle East Forum* 35 (1959): 22.

73. United States, Department of State, *Foreign Relations of the United States 1947,* vol. 5, *The Near East and Africa* (Washington, D.C.: U.S. Government Printing Office, 1971), 1327.

74. "Mevakshim Hahashat Berur Mishpatim Lifney Ha-Pinuy [Requests for Expedited Trials before the Evacuation]," *Ha-Arets,* 23 October 1947, 3.

75. "According to British Military Intelligence, 'the hurried departure of Ahmad Bey Khalil . . . is a very significant illustration of the opinion of the local Arabs as to the outcome of an extensive Jewish operations at present.'" Morris, *Palestinian Refugee Problem,* 77.

76. Cable from the foreign minister of Egypt to the U.N. Security Council, 15 May 1948: "Egyptian forces entered Palestine for the purpose of restoring security and order." Shmuel Ettinger, *Toldot Am Yisrael* [History of the Jewish People], ed. H. Ben-Sasson, vol. 3 (Tel Aviv: Dvir, 1969), 335.

CHAPTER 3

1. Moshe Landau, "Al ha-Shofet Shimon Agranat: Be-Nimah Ishit" [About Justice Simon Agranat: A Personal Recollection], in Barak et al., *Gvurot,* 1, 2.

2. See Ruth Bondy, *Felix: Pinhas Rozen u-Zmano* [Felix: Pinchas Rosen and His Time] (Tel Aviv: Zmora-Bitan, 1990), 385–86, 417–18.

3. Jerusalem became a center of political activity only later. At the time, Hebrew Jerusalem was under Jordanian siege, and all government business centered in Tel Aviv. The Partition Resolution designated Jerusalem as an international city. See, generally, Motti Golani, "Zionism without Zion: The Jerusalem Question, 1947–1949," *Journal of Israeli History* 16 (1995): 39.

4. Jacob S. Shapiro, interview by the author, Tel Aviv, January 1984.

5. "Ha-Yakum Bet ha-Din ha-Elyon ha-Kavua al Yedei Moetset ha-Memshalah ha-Zmanit? [Will the Provisional Government Establish a High Court?]," *Al ha-Mishmar,* 15 July 1948, 1; "Herkev Bet ha-Din ha-Elyon Huavar le-Va'adat ha-Va'adot [Composition of the Supreme Court Forwarded to the Steering Committee]," *Ha-Arets,* 11 July 1948, 1; Protocols of the provisional government, 14 July 1948, pp. 44–45, on file with the author.

6. The list of five candidates included three prominent lawyers (Moshe Smoira, Menachem Dunkleblum, and Isaac Olshan), one representative of the religious sector (Simha Assaf, who did not have a law degree), and one judge (Agranat). Of the three lawyers, two (Olshan and Smoira) had close ties to MAPAI, and one (Dunkleblum, chairman of the Jewish Bar Association of Palestine) was a centrist. The insistence on Judge Cheshin's appointment could be attributed either to the fact that he was a more senior and experienced judge than Agranat or to his reputation as a nationalist (thereby making the list more politically balanced)—or both.

7. The proceedings against Shams are themselves indicative of the turmoil that overtook Israeli society at that point. The judge was put on trial by the Haganah. Obviously, considerations of the separation of powers and the integrity of the judiciary were not yet a part of the public ethics in Israel. Agranat, who told me the story, remembered objecting to this process. Azoulai was promoted to the presidency of the district court once Agranat had left for the Supreme Court. It is widely thought that the only Sephardi minister in the government, Bechor Shetreet, had held hostage the permanent appointment of Justice Moshe Silberg to the Supreme Court until the government agreed to Azoulai's promotion.

8. The red ribbons signaled the wearer's competence to adjudicate murder trials. The custom of wearing a gown was preserved in Israel, but the red ribbons had been removed.

9. "Nesi Bet ha-Din ha-Mehozi Mevatel Psak Din Briti [The President of the District Court Invalidates a British Decision]," *Ha-Arets,* 31 August 1948, 4.

10. It is, however, quite likely that once the other branches of the government were firmly established in Jerusalem, the Court would have naturally followed suit. The point here is that given the uncertain status of Jerusalem at the time, the justices preferred the Tel Aviv location, and they would have had it had the Court been higher on the government's priority list.

11. Pnina Lahav, "The Supreme Court of Israel: Formative Years, 1948–1955," *Studies in Zionism* 11 (1990): 45, 49.

12. Ibid.

13. "We declare that . . . until the establishment of . . . the Constitution which shall be adopted . . . not later than 1 October 1948, the People's Council shall act as a Provisional Council of State." Declaration of the Establishment of the State of Israel, 14 May 1948, 1 L.S.I. 3.

14. Isaac Olshan, *Din u-Dvarim: Zikhronot* [Memoirs] (Jerusalem: Schocken, 1978), 213.

15. This was a temporary appointment. Agranat became a permanent member on 28 December 1949.

16. Knesset Members (Immunity, Rights and Duties) Law, 5711–1951, 5 L.S.I. 149.

17. Judges Law, 5713–1953, 7 L.S.I. 124.

18. Olshan, *Din u-Dvarim,* 241–42, 349–53.

19. For a development of this thesis, see Ehud Sprinzak, *Ish ha-Yashar be-Enav: Illegalizm ba-Hevrah ha-Yisraelit* [Every Man Whatsoever Is Right in His Own Eyes: Illegalism in Israeli Society] (Tel Aviv: Sifriyat Poalim, 1986).

20. Yosef Heller, *LEHI: Idiologyah u-Politikah 1940–1949* [LEHI: Ideology and Politics, 1940–1949], vol. 2 (Jerusalem: Keter, 1989), 435–62.

21. There was also fear that, following the assassination, Bernadotte's plan would acquire more power because it would be viewed as the late count's will.

22. In June 1948, when the *Altalena,* an Irgun ship loaded with arms and ammunition, arrived, Ben-Gurion insisted that the shipment be handed over to the Israel Defense Forces (IDF). He interpreted the arrival of the *Altalena* as "a threat to his authority and the legitimacy of the new government." Amos Perlmutter, *The Life and Times of Menachem Begin* (Garden City, N.Y.: Doubleday, 1987), 233. Indeed, it seems that a putsch was contemplated by certain quarters at both the Irgun and the LEHI (Stern Gang) leadership (ibid., 232). After nerve-wracking negotiations between the IDF and Menachem Begin, the Irgun's chief commander, the *Altalena* was hit by cannon fire and burst into flames. The Irgun was subsequently dissolved, and its members joined the IDF as individuals (ibid., 233). Toward the end of September 1948, Ben-Gurion had also accomplished the controversial dissolution of the Palmah, the kibbutz movement's ideologically left-leaning elite combat units, for fear that the Palmah would not be unequivocally loyal to Israel's civilian government under his leadership. Anita Shapira, *Mi-Piture ha-Rama ad Peruk ha-Palmah: Sugiyot ba-Maavak al ha-Hanhagah ha-Bithonit* [The Army Controversy, 1948: Ben Gurion's Struggle for Control] (Tel Aviv: Ha-Kibbutz ha-Meuhad, 1985), 50–57.

23. "Camps of LEHI in Jerusalem were surrounded and occupied, persons found in camps were arrested and substantial quantities of arms and ammunition were confiscated." "Conclusions of the Commission to Assess the Report Submitted by the Solicitor General to the Government of Sweden in the Matter of the Assassination of Count Folke Bernadotte," *Bernadotte Report,* 1, in the author's files.

24. Ibid.

25. Prevention of Terrorism Ordinance, 5708–1948, 1 L.S.I. 76.

26. Ironically, when the right-wing Likud (descendant of the Irgun and LEHI) came to power, its leaders cleared the dust off the antiterrorism ordinance and turned it into a weapon against the Palestine Liberation Organization (PLO). Prevention of Terrorism Ordinance (Amendment) Law, 5740–1980, 34 L.S.I. 211; Hok le-Tikun Pkudat Meni'at Teror (Mispar 2), 5746–1986 [Amendment to the Prevention of Terrorism Law (No. 2)], 1985/6 S.H. 219.

27. *Mo'etset ha-Medinah ha-Zmanit* [Provisional State Council], vol. 1, 19th session at 17 (23 September 1948).

28. *Bernadotte Report,* 28, 42, 55, 62. The report is also discussed in Kati Marton, *A Death in Jerusalem* (New York: Pantheon Books, 1994), 246–50.

29. For a discussion of the relationship between Israel's government and LEHI in the summer of 1948, see Ilan Amitzur, *Bernadotte in Palestine, 1948: A Study in Contemporary Humanitarian Knight-Errantry* (London: Macmillan, 1989), 210–11. At the time, there was a feeling that the government did not do all it could to bring the perpetrators to justice. See Gideon Rafael, *Destination Peace: Three Decades of Israeli Foreign Policy: A Personal Memoir* (New York: Stein & Day, 1981), 18. In the recently released cabinet protocols from this period, the sections pertaining to the cabinet's discussions of the Bernadotte affair are censored, thereby implying that "the government is concealing information about the matter. A few items mentioned in this context about LEHI were also censored. Question: did the cabinet know who assassinated Bernadotte and did it conceal it?" Tom Segev, "Ha-Sodot ha-Rishonim [The First Secrets]," *Ha-Arets,* 3 February 1995, 35.

30. This conclusion was supported by another member of the commission, Justice Haim Cohn (then solicitor general), interview by the author, Jerusalem, June 1984.

31. See also Yonathan Shapiro, *Ilit le-Lo Mamshikhim: Dorot Manhigim ba-Hevrah ha-Yisraelit* [An Elite without Successors: Generations of Political Leaders in Israel] (Tel Aviv: Sifriyat Poalim, 1984), 107–25.

CHAPTER 4

1. H.C. 16/48, *Brun v. Prime Minister and Minister of Defense,* 1 P.D. 109, 112 (1948). Emphasis added. On the panel with Smoira sat Olshan and Dunkleblum; the three were the troika that led the Court.

2. Dan Horowitz and Moshe Lissak, *Origins of the Israeli Polity: Palestine under the Mandate,* trans. Charles Hoffman (Chicago: University of Chicago Press, 1978), 131.

3. The confiscation was limited and did not include passage of title. Among those who benefited from the confiscations were the attorney general and a few judges. In interview, Agranat emphasized that he loathed the procedure and was determined not to resort to it, even though the Ministry of Justice did indicate that he could benefit from it should he need housing when he moved from Haifa to Jerusalem. The issue of confiscation of Arab land should not be confused with the one discussed here. Ian Lustick, *Arabs in the Jewish State: Israel's Control of a National Minority* (Austin: University of Texas Press, 1980), 173; David Kretzmer, *The Legal Status of the Arabs in Israel* (Boulder, Colo.: Westview Press, 1990), 49–69.

4. H.C. 10/48, *Zeev v. Gubernik,* 1 P.D. 85, 88–89 (1948); "The provisional state council is the superior institution in whose jurisdiction lies the discretion to prefer the needs of public security over individual rights," *Brun,* 112. See also *Marbury v. Madison,* 5 U.S. 137 (1803).

5. Amnon Rubinstein, *Ha-Mishpat ha-Konstitutsyoni shel Medinat Yisrael* [The Constitutional Law of the State of Israel] (Jerusalem: Schocken, 1991), 44–45; Ruth Gavison, "The Controversy over Israel's Bill of Rights," 15 *Israel Yearbook on Human Rights* 113 (1985).

6. Prevention of Terrorism Ordinance, 5708–1948, 1 L.S.I. 76.

7. See for example, Itzhak Zamir, "Labour and Social Security," in *Studies in Israel Legislative Problems,* ed. Gad Tedeschi and Uri Yadin, *Scripta Hierosolymitana* (Jerusalem: Magnes Press, Hebrew University, 1966), 298.

8. The very first case to be decided by the Court was the appeal of an Englishman who had been convicted of spying. The hearing took place in a charged and volatile atmosphere, hypersensitive to "spies and traitors." The acquittal, a direct rejection of the position of the government, was accomplished through a narrow reading of the Criminal Code and a meticulous evaluation of the evidence. This methodology set the boundaries of judicial intervention. See Cr.A. 1/48, *Sylvester v. Attorney General,* 1 P.D. 5 (1948).

Later, the Court overturned the government's decision to end the institution of "petition writers," which deprived a whole group of people of their livelihood. The government's decision was well intentioned and typical of the period. The "petition writers," a part of the oriental landscape, were a go-between the citizenry and the bureaucracy. Their elimination thus signified planning and modernization, an end to the age of undue influence. The Court held that the "right to pursue an occupation" was a "natural right" that could not be taken away from a citizen without an authorizing statute, through administrative fiat. See H.C. 1/49, *Bezerano v. Minister of Police,* 2 P.D. 80 (1949). See also H.C. 144/50, *Sheib v. Minister of Defense,* 5 P.D. 399 (1951), where the Court invalidated the dismissal of Israel Eldad Sheib, a LEHI leader, from his position as an educator, by Prime Minister and Secretary of Defense Ben-Gurion.

9. Olshan had been a partner at Eliash's law firm, where Agranat had clerked in the early 1930s. See discussion on p. 49.

10. In one of Agranat's first opinions, decided 28 February 1949, he expressed an understanding for the need to use emergency powers in violation of civil rights and refused to interfere with a confiscation order:

Everyone knows that when this [emergency] statute was enacted (May 1948) it was a few days after we declared independence—when the state was fighting to defend itself against enemy armies which had attacked it from almost all sides. It was, in fact, a situation of emergency in the full sense of the term. Section 9 was designed . . . to invest full authority in the . . . [executive] to act in order to defend the state, the public security and the . . . essential services, without facing any obstacle or hindrance. . . . [I]t would be a serious harm to the above purpose—to the point of foolishness—if we [gave the statute a narrow interpretation]. (H.C. 9/48, *Selinger v. Commander of the Dan Region,* 2 P.D. 190, 195 [1949]).

In H.C. 37/49, *Goldstein v. Custodian of Property of Missing Persons,* 2 P.D. 716, 729 (1949), decided 11 September 1949, Agranat held that a governmental entity can evacuate a person from property only through legal means, even if that person took hold of that property through illegal means. The above is a sample of Agranat's opinions during the period under discussion.

11. H.C. 95/49, *Al-Couri v. Chief of Staff,* 4 P.D. 34A (1950).

12. "Two Jews were killed and one is missing as a result of Arab attacks in the Gaza area today. A truck on the way to Negba settlement from Gath was ambushed and Ernst Miller, an immigrant from Chile, was killed and another reported missing. Later, a party that set out from Negba to search for the missing man was en-

gaged by an Arab band and Moshe Litvak was killed." "Two Killed in Attack in South," *Palestine Post,* 7 December 1947, 1.

13. *Al-Couri,* 41–46.

14. Ibid., 46–47.

15. Ibid., 37.

16. Ibid.

17. Ibid.

18. Ibid.

19. Amos Shapira, "Judicial Review without a Constitution: The Israeli Paradox," 56 *Temple L. Q.* 405, 417–26 (1983).

20. Karl Llewellyn's distinction between formal- and grand-style opinions and their respective role in the development of the law is relevant here. Israeli Supreme Court opinions of the 1950s were written in the formal, not the grand, style. Agranat's opinions, written in the grand style, were clearly exceptional in the Israeli judicial landscape. See Karl N. Llewellyn, *The Common Law Tradition: Deciding Appeals* (Boston: Little, Brown, 1960), 62.

21. Protocol in the author's files.

22. On 17 February 1952, one day before Cr.A. 95, 99/51, *Podamsky v. Attorney General,* 6 P.D. 341 (1952) was argued and six weeks before the *Podamsky* opinion was delivered, Justice Olshan rebuked the government for having repealed a license previously granted to open an ice-cream factory, on the ground that such a factory was not vital to the state: "I doubt whether members of the civil service in our state . . . understand their [responsibility]. . . . [T]hey have to follow certain principles, tantamount to first principles, such as: every citizen is innocent until *otherwise proven* [guilty], justice should be done and also seen. . . . [E]lementary justice requires that before a decision is reached the citizen be granted the opportunity to explain so as to remove doubts. We are convinced that in this case this was not done." Olshan's emphasis. The Court, however, only partially granted the petition. See H.C. 113/52, *Sax v. Minister of Trade and Industry,* 6 P.D. 696, 703 (1952).

Agranat had personal reasons for being aggravated with the bureaucracy as well. On 16 April 1954 he wrote the following letter (on file with the author) to the customs officials:

[L]ast Saturday we celebrated my son Hillel's Bar Mizvah. At the same time, I received a notice . . . that a parcel containing a Parker fountain pen 51, and a mechanical pen, sent to him by my uncle . . . a Chicago resident . . . has arrived, and that I should pay duty in the sum of 39.305 Israeli pounds. All would agree that this sum is much higher than the value of the gift. Indeed, it is a wonder that when an American Jew sends his relative here a Bar Mizvah gift, he [should pay such a high fee]. . . . It is hard to accept the thought that the authorities in the state of Israel shall turn their back to this typical Jewish institute [the Bar Mitzvah] and require a sum so high as to force me to return the gift to its sender. I hope that your honor will exempt the parcel from the above said taxes.

23. *Podamsky.*

24. Wesley Newcomb Hohfeld, "Some Fundamental Legal Conceptions as Applied in Judicial Reasoning," 23 *Yale L. J.* 16 (1913); Wesley Newcomb Hohfeld, "Fundamental Legal Conceptions as Applied in Judicial Reasoning," 26 *Yale*

L. J. 710 (1917). Hohfeld's work was incorporated into John William Salmond, *Jurisprudence,* 10th ed. (London: Sweet and Maxwell, 1947), 238.

25. The judge issuing the detention order on 1 September 1950 had jurisdiction to detain the prisoners for a period of only fifteen days. Hence, by 15 October (the day these events took place) the detention order had expired, and the prisoners were free men. *Podamsky,* 346.

26. The problem of law enforcement was so acute that Prime Minister Ben-Gurion, in a broadcast speech to the nation on the occasion of Israel's first anniversary, devoted a whole paragraph to it, emphasizing the need to change national attitudes toward the judge and the policeman: "In exile, and for a long time in our own land, we saw the alien judge and policeman—as a hostile enemy. With independence, we have the opportunity to . . . see in the agents of the law and its guardians loyal friends of the people. . . . In particular, a difficult and heavy responsibility rests on the young police force." *Luah ha-Arets li-Shnat Tashay* [Ha-Arets Yearbook, 1949], 300. The program of austerity and rationing, introduced by the government in an effort to rebuild the economy, caused a black market to flourish and an almost universal violation of the austerity laws. In addition, the large influx of immigrants, embattled and disoriented, caused significant law-enforcement problems. See Tom Segev, *1949: The First Israelis* (New York: Free Press, 1986), 297–323.

27. Criminal Code Ordinance, 1936, *Palestine Gazette,* 1936, Supp. 1, 285, 316–17.

28. *Podamsky,* 353.

29. Justices Cheshin and Assaf concurred. The Court also overturned the conviction for carrying a weapon without license. In the indictment the appellants were charged not with this offense but rather with a violation of section 66(a) of the Criminal Code (carrying a weapon for the purposes of committing treason against the government). The district court decided that even though section 66(a) did not apply, it had jurisdiction to convict the appellants of carrying a weapon without a license. The Court held that section 66(a) had already been held as implicitly repealed by a new law and that the district court could not substitute a valid offense for one which was void. Ibid., 346–50.

30. Ibid., 354.

31. In Hebrew this second category appeared as "liberty rights"; that is, the term right was used for this category as well as for the first one.

32. *Podamsky,* 354. Agranat's emphasis.

33. Ibid.

34. Ibid., 355.

35. Ibid., 357.

36. Ibid.

37. "A homeowner empowering another to sell his house invests in him the power to deny the homeowner's right in the property." Ibid.

38. Ibid. The significance of this statement lies in its emphasis on the premise of the coequality of the branches of the government and the concomitant assumptions that executive actions not warranted by law are ultra vires. These should be read in the context of the attack on judges in the Knesset that took place at about the same time.

39. Ibid., 359.

40. It is important, however, to reemphasize that the appeal was partially successful, in that the Court overturned the conviction for holding weapons without a license. Thus, even in terms of the result alone, the case cannot be seen as a straight triumph for the police.

41. *Sax,* 703.

42. "It should be clear that in our discussion we [relied on] . . . a few principles which are relevant to our subject matter and which were derived from . . . writings of authoritative legal scholars—as follows:—Salmond, *Jurisprudence,* 10th ed. chapter 10; Paton, *Jurisprudence* (1946) part III chapter 10; the article Legal analysis and Terminology by Corbin, published in *Hall's Readings in Jurisprudence,* p. 471." *Podamsky,* 354.

43. Hence Agranat's dictum that had they petitioned the Court for habeas corpus they probably would have won their freedom through legal means. Ibid., 361.

44. Ibid.

45. Mitchell Cohen, *Zion and State: Nation, Class and the Shaping of Modern Israel* (New York: Basil-Blackwell, 1987), 201.

46. This is amply clear when one looks at the sources that inspired the model and also at the various examples offered by Agranat, mostly related to issues of private law.

47. Joseph W. Singer, "The Legal Rights Debate in Analytical Jurisprudence from Bentham to Hohfeld," 1982 *Wis. L. Rev.* 975, 1057.

48. Ibid., 984.

49. I am indebted to Morton J. Horwitz for helping me clarify this relationship between *Podamsky* and American law.

50. For a discussion of Israeli legal education in its formative period, see Asher D. Grunis, "Legal Education in Israel: The Experience of Tel-Aviv Law School," 27 *J. Legal Ed.* 203 (1975).

51. There were, however, legal consequences to the categorization of the policemen's actions as liberty. It precluded a criminal or civil charge against the police for such actions. It should also be mentioned that the Israeli legal academy was enchanted by Hohfeld, whose model was taught extensively in introductory courses in jurisprudence as the epitome of legal philosophy.

52. It may well be that the pragmatic Israelis had no patience with the highly analytical concepts embedded in the opinion. Shortly thereafter, when Israeli Supreme Court opinions were proudly translated into English to show the world the fruit of Israeli judicial labor, *Podamsky* was not included.

53. Indeed, Agranat himself returned to his *Podamsky* opinion in 1956 and introduced to Israel's legal landscape the fourth category put forward by Hohfeld, immunities. C.A. 22/56, *Cohen v. Ministry of Defense,* 10(2) P.D. 1375 (1956).

54. Other Agranat opinions related to civil liberties at this time concerned Israeli Arabs, particularly their right to stay in Israel and their freedom of movement, and the government's often rough treatment of the right wing and of free speech. For example, in H.C. 112/52, *Khalf and Issa Halil Khalf v. Minister of Interior,* 7 P.D. 185 (1953), Agranat rejected a challenge to a deportation order. He did, however, urge the minister of the interior to let the petitioner stay in Israel. The petitioner, a seventeen-year-old, had been a student in Lebanon during the 1948 war, had no relatives in Lebanon, and had a large family in Israel. In H.C.

46/50, *Al-Ayoubi v. Minister of Defense,* 4 P.D. 222 (1950), Agranat sustained an order limiting the right to travel of an Israeli Arab. The petitioner asserted that he was sick and in need of relocating to Jaffa, where he could obtain medical treatment. Agranat held that the military governor had acted within his powers when he decided to confine the petitioner to his village on the grounds of danger to the public peace and that the governor was not obliged to disclose his reasons in court. Agranat, however, recommended that the governor reconsider his order. But in H.C. 183/52, *Abu Gosh v. Minister of Interior,* 6 P.D. 862 (1952), Agranat dissented from a decision to sustain a deportation order on the ground that the petitioner left during the war "out of his own free will." Agranat held that there was no free will, because the petitioner, being known for his help to the Israeli forces, was in real danger of retribution. Similarly, in H.C. 8/52, *Moustafa Saad Bader v. Minister of Interior,* 7 P.D. 366 (1953), Agranat held three deportation orders against an Israeli Arab as invalid on grounds of due process and deployment of irrelevant considerations.

In Cr.A. 37/50, *Sternhal v. Attorney General,* 6 P.D. 119 (1952), Agranat upheld a conviction for contempt of court. Appellant Sternhal was convicted for having written in a letter to the minister of justice that, "because there is in the Supreme Court an atmosphere of fear of lawyers, there must be [a greater fear] of [judges in the rabbinical courts] because they have a connection to the court in Heaven." In Cr.A. 139/52, *Attorney General v. Amos Keynan,* 7 P.D. 619 (1953), Agranat rejected the prosecution's appeal of the acquittal of a defendant who was known as a former member of LEHI. The appellee was charged with placing a time bomb near the residence of former Minister of Transportation David Zvi Pinkas on 22 June 1952. Agranat spoke at length about the significance of the right to remain silent and then, refusing to interfere with the holding of the district court that the appellee, a journalist, did not have to testify about a telephone message he had received concerning the bomb, explaining that it was "a professional secret, that he should not divulge to others, including to the police." It was, probably, the first recognition of a reporter's privilege in Israel. Ibid., 644–48. The above is a sample of Agranat's opinions during this period.

55. A bill on the judiciary was presented to the Knesset on 26 February 1951, 8 *Divre ha-Knesset* [Israeli Parliamentary Protocol], 1176 (1951). It was passed to the Constitution, Statutes and Law Committee.

56. From its inception and until 8 October 1951, the Ministry of Justice was in the hands of the Progressive Party. A crisis related to a disagreement between the government and the Knesset about elementary-school education led to the organization of a new government in which the Progressive Party did not participate. During this period Bernard Joseph, known in Israel by his Hebrew name, Dov Yoseph, served as minister of justice. The Progressive Party returned to the government on 23 December 1952, and the Ministry of Justice was returned to Pinhas Rosen, who had held it previously. See Gad Yaacobi, *Ha-Memshalah* [The Government] (Tel Aviv: Am Oved & Zmorah, Bitan, Modan, 1980), 341.

57. 11 *Divre ha-Knesset,* 1115–29 (1952).

58. Ibid.

59. Ibid., 1116.

60. After observing that Israel's press is licentious and is damaging the inter-

ests of the state, Joseph continued: "It is true that our financial situation is bad, but it is not necessary to publicize it so that the enemy will know." "Ha-Hok al Tkifat Shotrim Hu'avar la-Va'adah [The Law of Assault on Policemen Was Transferred to the Committee]," *Ha-Arets,* 25 June 1952, 2.

61. Olshan, *Din u-Dvarim,* 244.

62. Elyakim Rubinstein, *Shoftey Erets* [Judges of the Land] (Jerusalem: Schocken, 1980), 98.

63. On grounds of separation of powers. Ibid.

64. 11 *Divre ha-Knesset,* 1146 (1952).

65. "Sar ha-Mishpatim etsel Nesi Bet ha-Mishpat ha-Elyon [The Minister of Justice Visited the Chief Justice]," *Ha-Arets,* 5 March 1952, 10.

66. Simon Agranat, "Trumatah shel ha-Rashut ha-Shofetet le-Mifal ha-Hakikah [The Contribution of the Judiciary to the Legislative Endeavor]," 10 *Iyune Mishpat* 233, 234 (1984).

67. Judges Law, 5713–1953, 9 L.S.I. 124, sec. 13.

68. Smoira was in bed with a stroke, and Justices Olshan and Silberg were not on speaking terms. In addition, the Court was in the midst of a confrontation with the Ministry of Foreign Affairs, which had refused to issue the justices diplomatic passports. Agranat's travel on an ordinary passport was viewed as a setback in this struggle. There were also some personal considerations against traveling: a fifth child had just been added to the family.

69. *Durham v. United States,* 214 F.2d 862 (1954).

70. Bartley C. Crum was a partner in the law firm of Hays, Podell, Algase, Crum & Feuer in New York City. He had been a member of the Anglo-American Committee of Inquiry on Palestine in 1946, an experience that turned him into a staunch supporter of the Jewish state, as he revealed in his book, *Behind the Silken Curtain: A Personal Account of Anglo-American Diplomacy in Palestine and the Middle East* (New York: Simon & Schuster, 1947).

71. Simon Agranat, letter to Dr. Arthur Fishzohn, 30 October 1953, Agranat papers, Agranat family, Jerusalem, acknowledging receipt of books and ink.

72. H.C. 73/53, 87/53, *Kol ha-Am v. Minister of the Interior,* 7 P.D. 871 (1953) (Hebrew), 1 Selected Judgments of the Supreme Court of Israel 90 (1948–1953) (English) (known as *Kol ha-Am*).

73. *Dennis v. United States,* 341 U.S. 494 (1951).

74. See *Abrams v. United States,* 250 U.S. 616 (1919); *Gitlow v. New York,* 268 U.S. 652 (1925); *Whitney v. California,* 274 U.S. 357 (1927) (concurrence).

75. *Terminiello v. Chicago,* 337 U.S. 1 (1949).

CHAPTER 5

1. S. N. Eisenstadt, *The Transformation of Israeli Society* (Boulder, Colo.: Westview, 1985), 177–78. At the same time, Agranat was also involved in a number of cases related to the suppression of right-wing extremists. Notable among these was the trial of the Zriffin underground. After a series of terrorist attacks on the Czech and Soviet embassies in Tel Aviv in 1952, the police arrested a number of right-wing activists and sympathizers and charged them with membership in a

terrorist organization. The group was tried before a military court. Ben-Gurion suggested that Agranat be the judge in the trial, but Agranat refused on grounds of separation of powers. A district court judge, Benjamin Halevy, accepted the military appointment. Agranat then reluctantly accepted an appointment as appellate judge.

Agranat's confidential memorandum to the minister of defense recommended that the sentences be reduced considerably. Agranat rejected the military court's position that no proof of intent (mens rea) was necessary for a finding that the group formed a terrorist organization. Such an approach, he said, based on a literal reading of the law, imposed strict liability on the defendants and collided with the most basic principles of criminal law. Furthermore, he overruled the military court's holding that the confessions of two defendants could be used as recriminating evidence against other defendants. (Two of the defendants confessed to having been involved in the bombings, declined to testify, and were not cross-examined.) He differed substantially when it came to the teenaged defendants. The military court "impose[d] such [heavy] sentences as [would] constitute an effective deterrent against such deeds." Agranat disagreed: the guiding principle should be rehabilitation, not deterrence. "They did what they did out of light-headedness or because of adult influence, [imprisonment] might damage them deeply, destroy their future, nurse a sense of bitterness toward the state and even turn them into dangerous . . . criminals." Instead of jail sentences, he recommended individual attention and education.

Agranat's opinion helped cool the heated atmosphere. It brought the messianic zealots down from their high ladder (the movement's newspaper was called *Sulam* [Ladder]) and yet sheltered them from the paranoic wrath of the government. It was another brick in the legacy Agranat had already began to build—his determination that the rule of law was not only about ends but also about means. Simon Agranat, Memorandum to the Minister of Defense, 16 September 1953, Agranat papers, Agranat family, Jerusalem.

Pinhas Lavon (replacing Ben-Gurion, who was still on leave) accepted fully the Agranat recommendations. On 24 April 1955, Ben-Gurion, again minister of defense, pardoned the members of the group who remained in jail. See Isser Harel, *Ha-Emet al Retsah Kastner: Teror Yehudi be-Medinat Yisrael* [The Truth about the Kasztner Murder] (Jerusalem: Idanim, 1985), 72; Cr.A. 49/58, *Heruti v. Attorney General,* 12 P.D. 1541 (1958).

2. Between 11 and 18 July 1952 twenty-three of the Soviet Union's most senior Jewish intellectuals were tried and sentenced to death. On 13 January 1953 nine physicians, seven of whom were Jewish, were accused of an attempt to poison the Soviet leadership. In the Jewish world these events were interpreted not only as anti-Semitic but also as a campaign to crush Jewish consciousness in the Soviet Union. See Benjamin Pinkus, *The Soviet Government and the Jews, 1948–1967: A Documented Study* (Cambridge, England: Cambridge University Press, 1984), 195–201; Bernard D. Weinryb, "Antisemitism in Soviet Russia," in *The Jews in Soviet Russia since 1917,* 3rd ed., ed. Lionel Kochan (Oxford: Oxford University Press, 1978), 300, 322–23.

3. *Kol ha-Am,* 875 (Hebrew), 94 (English).

4. H.C. 25/53, *Kol ha-Am v. Minister of the Interior,* 7 P.D. 165 (1953) (known

as the *First Kol ha-Am*). This *First Kol ha-Am* was written by Justice Olshan, with Justices Agranat and Silberg concurring. Agranat did not mention this case in his own *Kol ha-Am* opinion. Why Agranat joined the majority in the *First Kol ha-Am* and why he failed to distinguish it in his own opinion remain unknown. In interviews, Agranat was not helpful in shedding light on the episode. Because the Court was not bound by its own opinions, Agranat was free to ignore the *First Kol ha-Am*. One explanation could be that Agranat joined Olshan and Silberg because he did not wish to single himself out as "too Progressive," knowing that both Olshan and Silberg were unsympathetic to the idea of broad press freedoms and that he was waiting for a more sympathetic panel to help him voice his views on free speech as a majority opinion. Also, because Olshan, as deputy chief justice, had the power to decide who would sit on the panels, Agranat could expect that Olshan might not assign him to future press cases if he expressed a "Radical" commitment to press freedom. The combination of a more supportive panel of justices (Landau and Sussman), his trip to the United States, and a less strenuous relationship between Israel and the Soviet Union could explain his seminal opinion in *Kol ha-Am*.

For attempts to explain the conflict between the two *Kol ha-Am* cases, see Abraham Shapiro, "Ha-Risun ha-Atsmi shel Bet ha-Mishpat ha-Elyon ve-Havtahat Zekhuyot ha-Ezrah [Self Restraint of the Supreme Court and the Preservation of Civil Liberties]," 2 *Iyune Mishpat* 640 (1973); Pnina Lahav, "American Influence on Israel's Jurisprudence of Free Speech," 9 *Hastings Const. L. Q.* 21, 30 (1981); Pnina Lahav, "Kavim le-Hashkafat ha-Olam ha-Mishpatit shel ha-Shofet Agranat [The Jurisprudence of Chief Justice Simon Agranat]," in Barak et al., *Gvurot*, 9.

5. See Lahav, "American Influence," 37–69.

6. Ibid., 46–61.

7. See discussion on p. 30.

8. *Kol ha-Am*, 876 (Hebrew), 94 (English).

9. Ibid., 876 (Hebrew), 95 (English).

10. Ibid.

11. Ibid., 877 (Hebrew), 96 (English).

12. Ibid.

13. Ibid., 879 (Hebrew), 99 (English).

14. Citing *Schenck v. United States*, 249 U.S. 47 (1919); *Whitney*.

15. *Kol ha-Am*, 880 (Hebrew), 100 (English).

16. Ibid.

17. Ibid., 881 (Hebrew), 101 (English).

18. He could resort to the charter of the Mandate or the King's Order in Council; both were still good law in Israel, but they were not authentic Israeli documents, and it would be too much of a paradox to speak of democracy and self-rule and then rely on norms imposed on the polity from without. See the Palestine Order in Council, 1922, in Drayton, *Laws of Palestine*, 2569.

19. *Zeev*.

20. *Kol ha-Am*, 884 (Hebrew), 105 (English).

21. The declaration had taken root as the source of constitutional rights in Israel and was frequently being invoked by the Supreme Court. See Aharon Barak,

Parshanut ba-Mishpat [Interpretation in Law], vol. 2 (Jerusalem: Nevo, 1993), 425–27 and references therein. In 1994 the Declaration of Independence was recognized as a guiding interpretive tool by two Basic Laws recognizing human rights.

22. Defense (Emergency) Regulations, *Palestine Gazette*, 1945, Supp. 2, 1055. For example, Regulation 94 regulates the issuance of permits to publish newspapers thus: "The District Commissioner, in his discretion and without assigning any reason therefore, may grant or refuse any . . . permit."

23. "The High Commissioner [now replaced by the minister of interior] . . . may (a) if any matter appearing in a newspaper is, in the opinion of the High Commissioner . . . likely to endanger the public peace, . . . suspend the publication . . . for such a period as he may think fit." Sec. 19(2), Press Ordinance, 1933, in Drayton, *Laws of Palestine*, 1225.

24. *Kol ha-Am*, 892 (Hebrew), 115 (English).

25. When discussing political and civil liberties in Israel, commentators uniformly hail *Kol ha-Am* as proof of the commitment of the Court to basic notions of liberty. See, for example, Joseph Laufer, "Israel's Supreme Court: The First Decade," 17 *J. Legal Ed.* 43, 52–53 (1964); Aharon Barak, "Ha-Nasi Agranat: 'Kol ha-Am': Kolo shel ha-Am [Chief Justice Agranat: 'Kol ha-Am': The People's Voice]," in Barak et al., *Gvurot*, 129; Asher Maoz, "Defending Civil Liberties without a Constitution: The Israeli Experience," 16 *Melb. U. L. Rev.* 815, 820 (1988).

CHAPTER 6

1. Cr.A. 118/53, *Mandelbrot v. Attorney General*, 10(1) P.D. 281 (1956) (Hebrew), 2 Selected Judgments of the Supreme Court of Israel (1954–1958), 116 (English).

2. Ibid., 298 (Hebrew), 138 (English).

3. For discussion of the history of the act, see Yoram Shachar, "Mekorotehah shel Pkudat ha-Hok ha-Plili [The Sources of the Criminal Code Ordinance, 1936]," 7 *Iyune Mishpat* 75 (1979).

4. See, generally, *Dine Onshin: reshimot Le-fi Hartsaot S. Agranat* [Criminal Law: Notes of S. Agranat's Lectures], ed. Mordekhai Lemberg and Shabat Levi (Jerusalem: Mifal ha-Shikhpul, 1964). For an assessment of Agranat's contribution to Israeli criminal law, see Mordechai Kremnitzer, "Le-Zikhro shel ha-Shofet Agranat [In Memoriam: Justice Agranat]," 22 *Mishpatim* 5 (1992).

5. It is also interesting to note that in crafting the Durham opinion, Judge Bazelon relied heavily on a brief by a brilliant Progressivist Jewish lawyer (later Supreme Court justice), Abe Fortas. See Laura Kalman, *Abe Fortas: A Biography* (New Haven, Conn.: Yale University Press, 1990), 177–80. See also Sheldon S. Glueck, *Mental Disorder and the Criminal Law: A Study in Medico-Sociological Jurisprudence* (Boston: Little, Brown, 1925), 215–16.

6. *Mandelbrot*, 346 (Hebrew), 203 (English).

7. "I would consider it highly improper to usurp the place of the Knesset and myself lay down the law. . . . [W]e must not allow ourselves to be beguiled into giving decisions that undermine the legal edifice. We are subject to the law as it is and not as we would wish to see it." Ibid., 345 (Hebrew), 201 (English). In a

eulogy for Justice Goitein, Agranat quoted him as saying that in some of Israel's decisional law, "English conservatism won a victory over Israel-American liberalism." Simon Agranat, "In Memoriam: Mr. Justice Goitein," *Jerusalem Post,* 28 August 1961, 4. This statement, which in reverse could be applied to *Mandelbrot,* indicates that both Agranat and his brethren understood the jurisprudential tension to be between Conservatism and Liberalism, England and America, respectively.

8. Section 11 (Intention, Motive) of the Criminal Code Ordinance reads:

(1) Subject to the express provisions of this Code relating to negligent acts and omissions, a person is not criminally responsible for an act or omission which occurs independently of the exercise of his will, or for an event which occurs by accident.

(2) Unless the intention to cause a particular result is expressly declared to be an element of the offence constituted, in whole or in part, by an act or omission, the result intended to be caused by an act or omission is immaterial.

(3) Unless otherwise expressly declared, the motive by which a person is induced to do or omit to do an act, or to form an intention, is immaterial so far as regards criminal responsibility.

Section 14 (Insanity) reads:

A person is not criminally responsible for an act or omission if at the time of doing the act or making the omission he is through any disease affecting his mind incapable of understanding what he is doing, or of knowing that he ought not to do the act or make the omission. But a person may be criminally responsible for an act or omission, although his mind is affected by disease, if such disease does not in fact produce upon his mind one or other of the effects above mentioned in reference to that act or omission.

9. See Glueck, *Mental Disorder,* 215–16.

10. "The view of the subject of rights embraced by the seventeenth-century contract theorists is usually termed Cartesian. It assumes that the individual will is the cause of all actions, individual and collective; it ascribes decisive epistemic and, hence, moral authority, to the individual over his actions, on the grounds that he has privileged access to the contents of his own mind. For this reason individual consent becomes vital to the whole idea of political activity." Ian Shapiro, *The Evolution of Rights in Liberal Theory* (Cambridge, England: Cambridge University Press, 1986), 275.

11. *Mandelbrot,* 323 (Hebrew), 170 (English).

12. Ibid., 293–94 (Hebrew), 131 (English).

13. Ibid., 311 (Hebrew), 156 (English). See also his reference to "a sense of justice and fairness," ibid., 311 (Hebrew), 155 (English).

14. Ibid., 313 (Hebrew), 158 (English) (emphasis added).

15. See discussion on p. 91.

16. See chap. 4, n. 42.

17. In *Kol ha-Am,* 887 (Hebrew), 108 (English), he interpreted the term *likely* to incorporate the Vinson/Hand formula of *Dennis.* In *Mandelbrot* he interpreted Section 11 to include the insanity defense.

18. *Mandelbrot,* 328 (Hebrew), 177 (English). In Cr.A. 186/55, *Meysan v. Attorney General,* 11 P.D. 769 (1955), a majority of the Court accepted Agranat's opinion in *Mandelbrot,* and it has been followed ever since. Interestingly, it was the

prosecution which argued in *Meysan* that the Agranat position should be endorsed as reflective of the positive law. See Miriam Ben-Porat, "Zikhronot Me-Nivhe He-Avar [Memories of the Past]," in Barak et al., *Gvurot*, 5. For a discussion, see Yuval Levy and Eliezer Lederman, *Ikarim be-Ahrayut Plilit* [Principles of Criminal Responsibility] (Tel Aviv: Ramot, 1981), 266–75.

19. Other opinions of the period confirm Agranat's resolve to lay solid foundations for a judicial bill of rights. Typically, the opinions concerned bureaucratic excesses, Israeli Arabs, or governmental treatment of dissent. In several cases Agranat structured and limited the powers of the executive to deny licenses to individuals; see, for example, H.C. 180/57, *Nahisi v. Herzliya*, 12 P.D. 272 (1958); H.C. 212 /57, *Aurbach v. Director of Customs*, 12 P.D. 780 (1958); H.C. 20/58, *Geffen v. Regional Council of Ashkelon*, 12 P.D. 1306 (1958).

In Cr.A. 40/58, *Attorney General v. Taufik Ziad*, 12 P.D. 1358 (1958), an Israeli Arab and political activist was imprisoned after a military court convicted him of breaching the peace. In prison he refused an order to sweep his cell, and, after an argument, he attacked his guard, was convicted of battery, and appealed. Agranat sustained the conviction, but *in dicta* he set down the rules concerning police behavior. The police could order a prisoner to do only things that were expressly permitted by law, and these did not include sweeping cells. Otherwise, he explained, vesting drastic powers in the police might lead to police abuse, for example, by "torturing the prisoners who are within their jurisdiction and treating them tyrannically" (p. 1365).

In another important opinion, *Heruti*, which should be read as a companion case to *Kol ha-Am*, Agranat limited the powers of emergency legislation to curb freedom of association. Jacob Heruti, a LEHI activist who was suspected of close ties to right-wing extremists, appealed his convictions of contempt of court and membership in a terrorist organization, pursuant to the Prevention of Terrorism Ordinance. Agranat sustained the conviction for contempt of court where, following a Jerusalem lower-court acquittal of Kasztner of perjury (chapter 7), Heruti published a pamphlet in which he wrote, "Citizens, even the Israeli courts are joining the defense of war criminals."

Speaking for a majority of three, with two justices dissenting, Agranat sustained the defendant's acquittal of the charge of membership in a terrorist organization. The significance of this opinion lies in the guidelines Agranat laid down for the evidentiary rules required for proof of membership in terrorist organizations, with Justices Landau and Sussman concurring. In order to prove the existence of a terrorist organization, Agranat held, it was not enough to show conspiracy. Proof should be submitted that "the defendants passed from the stage of preparation to the stage of [violent] action." Agranat also held that no proof was submitted that "the members of the organization continued to believe in violence as a means that should be used in the *present* or in the near future" (Agranat's emphasis) and that the government's declaration that the organization is a terrorist organization was not dispositive, for otherwise the trial would be a "show trial, in which the court will decide the fate of a defendant solely on the basis of a document which is traced to an act of the executive without more." In so holding, Agranat expressly narrowed the reach of *Brun*. Agranat also narrowed considerably the meaning of the offense of sedition. *Heruti*, 1556, 1559, 1562–63.

Finally, in Cr.A. 63/58, *Najim Ajami, Eliyahu Shalom et al. v. Attorney General,* 13 P.D. 421 (1959), Agranat defended the autonomy and dignity of women. The appellant, who was convicted of organizing an invasion of his estranged wife's bedroom in order to obtain proof of her adultery, argued that he was justified as a husband attempting to vindicate his marriage rights. Agranat responded: "The meaning of [the defendant's] argument is that the husband is entitled to instruct strangers . . . to treat his wife's body as an object abandoned in their hands, so long as they do not use excessive force against her; as if the end justifies these foul means. Clearly this is an intolerable view which should be absolutely rejected, and I can only express my indignation at the phenomenon that an attorney in the state of Israel saw fit to make such an argument and ask these courts to endorse it" (p. 436). The above is a sample of Agranat's opinions during this period.

CHAPTER 7

1. Yehiam Weitz, *Ha-Ish she-Nirtsah Paamayim* [The Man Who Was Murdered Twice] (Jerusalem: Keter, 1995), 60.

2. Kasztner was not elected, but his inclusion in the list shows his political clout within MAPAI circles.

3. Shalom Rosenfeld, *Tik Plili 124: Mishpat Gruenvald-Kastner* [Criminal Trial 124—The Gruenvald-Kasztner Trial] (Tel Aviv: Karni, 1955), 16–17.

4. The phrase "converted from Orthodoxy to Zionism" is Haim Cohn's. Michael Shashar, *Hayim Cohn, Shofet Elyon: Sihot im Michael Shashar* [Haim H. Cohn, Supreme Court Judge: Talks with Michael Shashar] (Jerusalem: Keter, 1989), 49. He used it to describe the ideological conversion of his cousin, Azriel Karlibach, founder of the evening daily newspaper, *Maariv.* The description fits both cousins.

5. In his memoirs, Bernard Joseph denied that he had urged Kasztner to press a libel charge or resign and claimed that it was Cohn who had put pressure on Kasztner. Dov Joseph, *Yonah va-Herev* [In Quest of Peace] (Givatayim: Masada, 1975), 321–22. Joel and Hansi Brand, in their book, remember that it was Joseph who had applied the pressure. Joel and Hansi Brand, *Ha-Satan veha-Nefesh* [Satan and the Soul], ed. Benjamin Gepner (Tel Aviv: Ladori, 1960), 115.

6. Yonathan Shapiro, *Le-Shilton Behartanu: Darkah shel Tenuat ha-Herut: Hesber Sotsyologi-Politi* [Chosen to Command: The Road to Power: The Herut Party in Israel: A Socio-Political Interpretation] (Tel Aviv: Am Oved, 1989), 93–94. In 1952 Tamir resigned from Begin's Herut because "the Party has given up the war to decimate the criminal and corrupt . . . regime." Ibid.

7. Halevy was president of the district court. He sat alone, rather than in a panel of three judges (Israel has no jury), failing to anticipate the developments in the trial. His opinion was published only ten years later, in *Attorney General v. Gruenvald,* 44 P.M. 3 (1965).

8. Cr.A. 11/58, *Menkes v. Attorney General,* 12(3) P.D. 1905 (1958). Kasztner's assassins were pardoned in 1963. Zeev Ekstein, one of the assassins, acknowledged the strong influence that extreme right-wing ideology (LEHI circles) had on his thinking about Kasztner, denied the theory that he was recruited to kill, and said,

"[T]he moment I understood the psychology of this man [Kasztner] this country could not bear both of us." Yair Sheleg, "Rotsho shel Kastner Medaber [Kasztner's Assassin Speaks]," *Kol ha-Ir,* 13 August 1993, 38, 94. See Harel, *Ha-Emet,* arguing that extremist right-wing circles were behind the assassination.

9. "Halevy's opinion looks more like the final argument by the prosecutor." "Mi-Yom le-Yom [Day to Day]," *Ha-Arets,* 25 June 1955, 2.

10. Tom Segev, *The Seventh Million: The Israelis and the Holocaust,* trans. Haim Watzman (New York: Hill & Wang, 1993), 292–93.

11. In particular, Agranat became acquainted with Yohanan Bader, a leader of Herut and a close friend of Menachem Begin. He found Bader to be "a charming, cultured, and a reasonable man," one not at all fitting MAPAI's image of a nationalist, irresponsible, and demagogic Herut. Agranat recalled beginning to doubt the good sense in Ben-Gurion's famous dictum that he would not form a coalition with either Herut or the Communist Party.

12. See also "Sar ha-Pnim Kore le-Hishtatfut mele'ah [The Minister of the Interior Calls for Full Participation]," *Ha-Arets,* 26 July 1955, 1, reporting Agranat to have concluded: "This is a holiday, where we demonstrate at home and abroad that the previous elections were not an aberration and that our state is a freedom loving state whose foundations are democratic."

13. See discussion on pp. 41–43.

14. See discussion on pp. 73–74.

15. Yehuda Bauer, *Ha-Shoah: Hebetim Historiyim* [The Holocaust—Some Historical Aspects] (Tel Aviv: Sifriyat Poalim, 1982), 134–218; Dina Porat, *Hanhagah Be-Milkud* [An Entangled Leadership] (Tel Aviv: Am Oved, 1986), 385–91; Michael R. Marrus, *The Holocaust in History* (Hanover, N.H.: University Press of New England, 1987), 185–92.

16. Cr.A. 232/55, *Attorney General v. Gruenvald,* 12(3) P.D. 2017, 2021 (1958). Ten years later Agranat denounced violence as a means of settling political controversy. In Cr.A. 255/68, *State of Israel v. Ben-Moshe,* 22(2) P.D. 427 (1968), decided a year after the Six Day War, a Holocaust survivor and army veteran stabbed Meir Vilner, leader of Israel's Communist Party. The defendant justified his act as an attempt to alert public opinion to the evil inherent in Vilner's criticism of Israeli policy concerning the occupied territories. In arguing against leniency in such cases, Agranat emphasized the significance of safeguarding the freedom of speech of politicians: "[T]he right of a member of the Knesset to voice, within or outside of this forum, his world view about current political questions without fear or suspicion that he might be hurt by someone, who disapproves of these views or is convinced that they are dangerous to the people—this right is the mirror image of the strong link between the principle of freedom of expression and debate and the . . . democratic process" (p. 435).

17. *Gruenvald,* 2215.

18. Shalom Rosenfeld, "Ha-Shofet Agranat Mezake Et Kasztner [Justice Agranat Acquits Kasztner]," *Maariv,* 16 January 1958, 2. Another telling aspect of the trial was the logistics of producing the opinion. The Court did not have the resources to reproduce multiple copies and arranged for Akademon, the student organization of the Hebrew University, to oversee the operation. Agranat remembered that the justices were proud that, in contrast to the government, which

hardly managed to prevent leaks, a complete veil of secrecy shrouded the entire process of publication. "Emtsa'ey Bitahon Likrat Psak ha-Din be-Irur Kasztner [Security Measures in Anticipation of Kasztner's Verdict]," *Yediot Aharonot,* 14 January 1958, 1.

19. *Gruenvald,* 2022.

20. See discussion on p. 108.

21. *Gruenvald,* 2065.

22. Ibid., 2084.

23. Nazi and Nazi Collaborators (Punishment) Law, 5710–1950, 4 L.S.I. 154.

24. *Gruenvald,* 2084–85.

25. Rosenfeld, *Tik Plili,* 312.

26. Ibid., 5. Rosenfeld, declaring in his introduction that his 451-page book aims at assisting in the discovery of truth, failed to mention one fact: that an appeal against the decision of the lower court was pending before the Supreme Court of Israel.

27. He cited George Macaulay Trevelyan, "Bias in History," in *An Autobiography and Other Essays* (London: Longmans, 1949), 68; Isaiah Berlin, *Historical Inevitability* (London: Oxford University Press, 1954). *Gruenvald,* 2055.

28. Agranat cited Justice Felix Frankfurter, *Of Law and Men: Papers and Addresses of Felix Frankfurter, 1939–1956, ed. Philip Elman* (New York: Harcourt Brace, 1956). *Gruenvald,* 2056.

29. Ibid., 2058.

30. Ibid., 2060.

31. Rosenfeld, *Tik Plili,* 371.

32. Roscoe Pound, "Mechanical Jurisprudence," 8 *Colum. L. Rev.* 605 (1908).

33. Sheldon Glueck, *Crime and Justice* (Boston: Little, Brown, 1936), 97 (citing Roscoe Pound).

34. *Gruenvald,* 2043, 2076.

35. Ibid., 2076.

36. In accordance with the Law against the Nazis and Nazi Collaborators. An implicit criticism of the trial judge could also be discerned in the present analysis, in which Agranat commented that, even though Halevy decided that Kasztner's behavior did "not differ morally, publicly and even *legally* from handing over most Jews to their murderers," he failed to refer to any substantive criminal offense in Israel's criminal code. *Gruenvald,* 2067. Agranat's emphasis.

37. Ibid., 2069 (quoting Glanville Williams).

38. Ibid., 2071.

39. Idith Zertal, "The Poisoned Heart: The Jews of Palestine and the Holocaust," *Tikkun* 2 (1987): 79. Yitzhak (Antek) Zuckerman, one of the leaders of the Warsaw Ghetto uprising, told Claude Lanzmann, creator of the film *Shoah,* that "If you could lick my heart, it would poison you to death." Ibid.

40. *Gruenvald,* 2073.

41. Ibid., 2076–77.

42. See, for example, Herbert Wechsler and Jerome Michael, "A Rationale for the Law of Homicide," 37 *Colum. L. Rev.* 701, 1281 (1937).

43. Otto Kirchheimer, "Criminal Omissions," 55 *Harv. L. Rev.* 615, 636 (1942), quoted by Agranat in *Gruenvald,* 2077. This analysis rejected the fiction that a man

is presumed to intend the natural consequences of his actions, applied by the lower court in the *Kasztner* case. Ibid., 2076.

44. Ibid., 2082.

45. Ibid., 2179.

46. Ibid.

47. Ibid., 2080.

48. Ibid.

49. Ibid., 2121.

50. Ibid., 2033, 2046, discussing the Strashof-Vienna plan.

51. Ibid., 2098.

52. Much of the evidence in the trial tried to show that MAPAI's leadership during the early and middle 1940s had collaborated with the British by self-censoring news about the Holocaust, by condemning the Irgun's violence against the British (which, Tamir claimed, could have brought about earlier independence, thereby providing a haven for the persecuted Jews), and by failing to encourage the Jews in occupied Europe to organize armed resistance. The attitude of MA-PAI's leadership and the Jewish population in Palestine toward the Holocaust is the subject of extensive debate among Israeli historians. See Dalia Ofer, *Escaping the Holocaust: Illegal Immigration to the Land of Israel, 1939–1944* (New York: Oxford University Press, 1990); Hava Eshkoli, *Elem: Mapai le-nokhah ha-Shoah, 1939–1942* [Silence: MAPAI and the Holocaust, 1939–1942] (Jerusalem: Yad Izhak Ben-Zvi, 1994); Idith Zertal, *Zehavam Shel ha-Yehudim* [From Catastrophe to Power] (Tel Aviv: Am Oved, 1996).

53. See Zertal, "Poisoned Heart."

54. This line was also followed by the leadership of MAPAI. See Nathan Alterman, *Al Shete ha-Derakhim: Dapim min ha-Pinkas* [Between Two Roads: Sections From a Diary], ed. Dan Laor (Tel Aviv: Ha-Kibbuts ha-Meuhad, 1989).

55. Rosenfeld, *Tik Plili*, 91–2.

56. *Gruenvald*, 2265. Silberg concludes his discussion of *Kasztner* in this paragraph: "I searched behind this fantastic language ['we paid less'] to find some bitter irony, a pinch of 'gallows humor,' but in vain! The careful financial calculations, the apologetic language, prove conclusively that Kasztner spoke in absolute earnestness. Indeed, here is egocentrism and its reward."

57. See discussion on p. 42.

58. *Gruenvald*, 2176. Emphasis added.

59. Michael Shagrir, "Be-Shulei ha-Psika" [Comments on Judicial Opinions]," *Al-ha-Mishmar*, 18 January 1958, 4.

CHAPTER 8

1. Israel did not actively search for Eichmann until 1957, when it received information from Germany concerning his whereabouts. Segev, *Seventh Million*, 324–25. The *Kasztner* case, then pending on appeal, probably spurred the government to undertake the daring operation to abduct Eichmann from Argentina.

2. *Gruenvald*, 2280–81.

3. Olshan, *Din u-Dvarim*, 312–24.

4. See American Jewish Committee, *The Eichmann Case in the American Press* (New York: Institute of Human Relations Press, 1962); Pnina Lahav, "The Eichmann Trial, the Jewish Question, and the American-Jewish Intelligentsia," 72 *B. U. L. Rev.* 555 (1992).

5. The initial plan was to exclude Halevy from the trial altogether, but Herut opposed the move, and in order to preserve political unity a compromise was reached whereby Halevy would serve on but not chair the panel. Olshan, *Din u-Dvarim,* 315–17.

6. Even Hannah Arendt, critical of the trial, praised Justice Landau's performance. Hannah Arendt, *Eichmann in Jerusalem: A Report on the Banality of Evil* (New York: Penguin, 1965), 4–5.

7. Cr.A. 336/61, *Eichmann v. Attorney General,* 16(3) P.D. 2033, 2084 (1962). *Eichmann* Supreme Court opinion, III–1 (English, mimeographed, in the author's files).

8. Gideon Hausner, *Ha-Shoah bi-Re'i ha-Mishpat* [Holocaust on Trial] (Tel Aviv: Am Oved, 1988), 8–9.

9. Susan Sontag, "Reflections on The Deputy," in *The Storm over The Deputy,* ed. Eric Bentley (New York: Grove Press, 1964), 118–23.

10. Carmel attended one of the sessions, a grueling experience. Her identification with the Jewish plight had nourished a strong aversion to Germans long before Eichmann's abduction. The catharsis offered during the Eichmann trial did not change her views. Throughout Agranat's service as chief justice she would shun any official ceremonies involving Germans. Years later, while returning from Liberia, the Agranats realized that their aircraft would make an emergency landing in Dusseldorf. The passengers were to stay in Germany overnight, but Carmel would not hear of it. She insisted that they leave immediately. After intensive nocturnal negotiations, the Agranats rode in the van that drove the crew across the border to Amsterdam, where the Israeli Consulate prepared accommodations for them.

11. "The world understood that it could not escape confrontation with its yesterday." Hausner, *Ha-Shoah,* 6.

12. Michael A. Musmanno, "The Objections in Limine to the Eichmann Trial," 35 *Temp. L. Q.* 1, 2 (1961). See also Yosal Rogat, *The Eichmann Trial and the Rule of Law* (Santa Barbara, Calif.: Center for the Study of Democratic Institutions, 1961); Dominik Lasok, "The Eichmann Trial," 11 *Int'l & Comp. L. Q.* 355 (1962); Herbert Wechsler, *The Nation's Future* (audiotape of NBC Radio debate, 8 April 1961). There were, however, scholars who did support the legality of the trial. See, for example, Hans W. Baade, "The Eichmann Trial: Some Legal Aspects," *Duke L. J.* 400 (1961).

13. Aviezer Golan, "Servatius Lo Hitsliah Lahafokh Le-Drama Maarekhet Ha-sium shel Mishpat Eichmann [Servatius Failed to Dramatize the Final Act in the Eichmann Trial]," *Yediot Aharonot,* 23 March 1962, 2.

14. Aviezer Golan, "Ha-Yo'ets ha-Mishpati Mazkir Nishkahot le-Eichmann [The Attorney General Makes Eichmann Remember]," ibid., 25 March 1962, 3.

15. On the tension between universalism and particularism, see Jacob Talmon, *Ahdut ve-Yihud: Masot be-Hagut Historit* [The Unique and the Universal] (Jerusalem: Schocken, 1965), 209–358.

16. The factor of "lawlessness" connecting the raid in Nukeib and the Eichmann trial was not overlooked by Israelis. See, for example, Moshe Prager, "Nekudat hà-Moked shel ha-Mishpat ha-Histori [The Focus of the Historic Trial]," *Davar,* 30 March 1962, 2.

17. *Eichmann,* 2039 (Hebrew), I–4 (English).

18. Ibid., 2047 (Hebrew), I–17 (English).

19. See chap. 7, n. 23.

20. *Eichmann,* 2039 (Hebrew), I–5 (English).

21. Lahav, "Eichmann Trial," 559–65.

22. "Before [the state] was established, Chaim Weizmann, then president of the World Jewish Congress . . . , asked in vain to appear before the Nuremberg Tribunal and testify . . . about the Jewish catastrophe. . . . In the State of Israel we could decide by ourselves what was preferred from the perspective of the Jewish interest." Hausner, *Ha-Shoah,* 8–9.

23. See discussion on p. 151.

24. *Eichmann,* 2048 (Hebrew), I–18 (English).

25. Ibid., 2048 (Hebrew), I–19 (English).

26. Ibid., 2049 (Hebrew), I–21 (English).

27. Ibid., 2051 (Hebrew), I–23 (English).

28. Ibid., 2052 (Hebrew), I–25 (English).

29. Ibid., 2053 (Hebrew), I–25 (English).

30. Ibid., 2061 (Hebrew), I–38 (English).

31. Ibid., 2066 (Hebrew), I–44 (English).

32. Ibid., 2067 (Hebrew), I–46 (English).

33. Ibid., 2070, 2075 (Hebrew), I–53, I–60 (English).

34. Agranat quoted at length from Sheldon Glueck, "The Nuremberg Trial and Aggressive War," 59 *Harv. L. Rev.* 396, 419–30 (1946), and from Quincy Wright, "The Law of the Nuremberg Trial," 41 *Amer. J. of Int'l L.* 38, 70–71 (1947).

35. *Eichmann,* 2075 (Hebrew), I–60 (English). Agranat's emphasis. The words "thereby absolving the executioners" were omitted from the English translation.

36. Ibid., 2080 (Hebrew), I–70 (English). The words "at all times and in all seasons" do not appear in the English translation.

37. And: "We could easily and in very few words dismiss all these contentions by saying that even a small cog, even an insignificant operator, is liable, under our criminal law, to become an accomplice. . . . But we shall not follow this facile and convenient path." Ibid., 2085 (Hebrew), III–3 (English).

38. "Now that the Eichmann trial has ended and the world has seen with what decorum, punctilio and meticulous observance of internationally recognized legal procedure the trial was conducted, the fears entertained by many honest-minded critics have been dissipated." Musmanno, "Objections," 2.

39. *Eichmann,* 2040 (Hebrew), I–6 (English).

40. *Gruenvald,* 2025.

41. *Eichmann,* 2081 (Hebrew), I–71 (English).

42. Ibid., 2100 (Hebrew), III–34–35 (English).

43. Hayim N. Bialik, "On the Slaughter," in *The Penguin Book of Hebrew Verse,* ed. T. Carmi (New York: Viking Press, 1981), 512–13.

44. "Hayiti Ed Reiya la-Tliya [I Witnessed the Execution]," *Yediot Aharonot,*

1 June 1962, 2; "Ha-Tguva ba-Olam: Naasa Din Tsedek [The Reaction in the World: Justice Was Done]," *Davar*, 3 June 1962, 1; "Ha-Tguvot ba-Olam al Tliyat ha-Tsorer: 'Naasa din Tzedek' [The Reactions in the World to the Hanging of the Enemy: Justice Was Done]," *Herut*, 3 June 1962, 1. Eichmann was hung on Thursday, minutes before midnight. That explains why *Yediot Aharonot* made the announcement the next Friday, whereas the morning newspapers had to wait until Sunday because in Israel newspapers do not appear on Saturday.

45. See discussion of the Bernadotte Report on p. 88.

CHAPTER 9

1. Yehuda Gotthilf, "E-Nahat ba-Hevrah ha-Yisraelit—Al shum Ma? [Restlessness in Israeli Society—Why?]," *Davar*, 7 June 1962, 2; Aharon Polonski, "Maamad Orekh ha-Din ba-Medinah uva-Hevra [The Status of the Lawyer in the State and in Society]," 18 *Ha-Praklit* 169 (1961).

2. "Bar-Or Hushaa me-Tafkido [Bar-Or Suspended from Office]," *Ha-Arets*, 1 June 1962, 8.

3. Mitchell Cohen, "Israel: The Lavon Affair," in *The Politics of Scandal, Power and Process in Liberal Democracies*, ed. Andrei S. Markovits and Mark Silverstein (New York: Holmes & Meier, 1988), 230.

4. In an interview, Hausner expressed the belief that at that time Ben-Gurion had decided to revive the issue of the mishap and, fearing that Hausner as attorney general might not assist him, decided to replace him. Yechiel Gutman, *Ha-Yoets ha-Mishpati Neged ha-Memshalah* [The Attorney General versus the Government] (Jerusalem: Idanim, 1981), 130, 167.

5. Ben-Gurion, however, kept insisting on a judicial resolution of the affair, thereby trying to involve the courts in the resolution of the political crisis. M. Cohen, "Lavon Affair," 234–35; Gutman, *Ha-Yoets*, 166–79.

6. See Gutman, *Ha-Yoets*, 130–36.

7. Ibid. (quoting Yohanan Bader, Herut's representative in the Knesset).

8. The Ministry of Justice did retain the position of solicitor general, who was generally expected to exercise professional judgment and be insulated from politics.

9. Ben-Gurion's letter of 26 June 1962 instructed the commission to consider three questions:

1. (a) What are the powers of the attorney general concerning appeals, termination of legal proceedings and indictments?

   (b) Are his powers exclusive?

   (c) Is he obliged to consult the minister of justice, especially in matters related to defense, political implications or matters related to the public interest?

2. If the minister of justice does not accept the opinion of the attorney general—may he take over these powers?

3. If the minister and the attorney general contradict each other in the cabinet meeting—whose interpretation of the law is correct?

10. *Robert Soblen v. United States*, 370 U.S. 944 (1962).

11. There could be a tangible reason for Israel's hasty deportation of Soblen.

That same week Yosseleh Shuhmacker, an Israeli child abducted by his ultra-Orthodox grandfather, who had been missing for more than a year, was located in New York. Yosseleh's disappearance was a matter of intense concern for the government, which believed that the Orthodox establishment was defying its authority by shielding the abductors. Yosseleh was located by the Mossad on 27 June 1962. It may well be that Israel feared that the American government would not cooperate in releasing Yosseleh if Israel withheld cooperation in the Soblen matter. For an account of the Mossad's search for Yosseleh, see Isser Harel, *Mivtsa Yossel'eh* [Operation Yossel'eh] (Jerusalem: Idanim, 1982).

12. "Cabinet Today Rules on Soblen's Fate," *Jerusalem Post*, 1 July 1962, 1; "High Court Rejects Order Nisi; Appeal by Soblen's Lawyer," ibid., 4 July 1962, 1. The neutralization of the attorney general during the Soblen affair is also discussed in Gutman, *Ha-Yoets*, 142.

13. H.C. 156/56, *Schor v. Attorney General*, 11(1) P.D. 285 (1957). Schor sued a lawyer for defamation (in a criminal procedure, which a private party could initiate), claiming that she had fabricated a suicide attempt in order to prevent her eviction. The attorney general has the power to halt criminal proceedings if he or she thinks they are not in the public interest. Agranat declined to intervene, holding that there was a legal presumption that the attorney general had acted in good faith and in the public interest.

14. The report, issued unanimously and written by Agranat, reviewed three powers vested in the attorney general: the power to indict, the power to invalidate decisions of the district attorneys, and the power to halt proceedings. Agranat observed that all three powers have this in common: they deal with the power of the attorney general "to activate the judicial branch in order to punish a person for having committed a certain offence." Inherent in such jurisdiction was "legal discretion" to decide how law should be applied to a particular set of facts and whether considerations of justice or the public interest required that legal proceedings be halted. "Doh Va'adat ha-Mishpetanim bi-Dvar Samkhuyot ha-Yoets ha-Mishpati la-Memshalah [Jurists' Report about the Powers of the Attorney General]," in *Sefer Klinghoffer Al ha-Mishpat ha-Tsiburi* [Klinghoffer Book on Public Law], ed. Itzhak Zamir (Jerusalem: Institute for Legislative Research and Comparative Law, 1993), 421. Hereafter cited as Jurists' Report.

15. Ibid., 432.

16. Ibid., 427–28.

17. He was thus conceding implicitly that legal training alone could not necessarily capture the essence of the decision making involved.

18. Jurists' Report, 428.

19. Ibid., 433.

20. Ibid., 435.

21. Indeed, that was Pinhas Rosen's view. See Gutman, *Ha-Yoets*, 141.

22. The responsibility of the government before the Knesset for actions of the attorney general is rather narrow. The government does not have parliamentary responsibility for an actual action taken by the attorney general in executing his responsibilities. If the attorney general takes an action against the recommendation of the cabinet, the cabinet is responsible to the Knesset only in the narrow sense of not firing him for his action. Jurists' Report, 444–45.

23. It is true that the result of this analysis means that the "supervisory pow-ers of the Knesset over the attorney general are also limited" (in the same way that the responsibility of the cabinet toward the Knesset in this regard is limited). But "this is a low 'price' to 'pay' for the wish to invest in an a-political organ . . . the responsibility of safeguarding the public interest in matters of the criminal law." Ibid., 447.

24. Gutman, *Ha-Yoets,* 140.

25. Ibid., 156.

26. Olshan, *Din u-Dvarim,* 357.

CHAPTER 10

1. "Justice Agranat Receives His Notice of Appointment as President of the Supreme Court," *Jerusalem Post,* 19 March 1965, 8.

2. The regulations concerning the appointment of a chief justice were set in the early 1950s and were largely a product of the personal and political circum-stances of the time. Smoira, the much-admired chief justice, suffered a stroke and became increasingly incapable of discharging his duties. His retirement, however, was postponed until the proper arrangements for his pension were solidified. Meanwhile, Olshan took over Smoira's responsibilities. The Court came to con-sider the question of how a new chief justice would be selected in a climate of political partisanship, shortly after the judicial crisis of 1953. It is in this context that one should understand the justices' recommendation to apply the principle of seniority. The recommendation was endorsed by the government, and on 5 Au-gust 1954 Olshan was appointed chief justice.

3. In his memoirs, Olshan denied these rumors categorically (*Din u-Dvarim,* 367).

4. The appointment of the deputy chief justice represented an even more difficult hurdle. By seniority, Moshe Silberg was to ascend to the position. But Bernard Joseph, the minister of justice, feared that should Agranat become inca-pable of fulfilling his duties, Silberg would become chief justice. After a bitter ar-gument, the Appointment Committee adjourned without making a decision. Joseph, not accustomed to having his judgment overruled, was angry; Shmuel Tamir, now a member of the committee, threatened to make the issue public. Agranat remembered several conversations with Joseph, during which he even-tually managed to persuade the minister to remove his objections. Shalom Co-hen, "Agranat Is Nominated Supreme Court Head," *Jerusalem Post,* 4 March 1965, 1. Why Joseph opposed Silberg is not too difficult to fathom. An Orthodox Jew who believed that Jewish law should and could govern the Jewish state could eas-ily appear to Joseph as more representative of *galut* than of the nation reborn. It may well be that Joseph was eager to have secular leadership for the Court, em-blematic of the Zionist dream of joining other Western democracies in form as well as substance.

5. Smoira was reputed to have called Olshan "Pahad Yitzhak"—the fear of Isaac—implying that he instilled fear in those close to him. Others called Olshan "the evil dwarf" (because he was rather short).

6. In his opening remarks Agranat said: "Judicial and legal jurisprudence is not expressed and reduced to a mechanical application of laws and decisions. . . . [W]e all know . . . that a judicial decision contains what is generally called a value judgment, an ethical judgment . . . and the making of such a judgment depends, of course, first on the legal and general philosophy of the judge, on his world-view, but also on his character and the measure of responsibility he feels toward his role, not only from the perspective of the purpose to do justice in the particular case, but also from the perspective of his judicial work generally; from the perspective of efficiency . . . and other perspectives." *Protocol of the Opening Session of the Judges Conference,* 13 October 1965, 4–5, Agranat papers, Agranat family, Jerusalem.

7. "This conference is meant for judicial self-criticism. We must examine ourselves, our judicial activity in general, not the judicial activity of any particular judge. All the topics we chose for discussion . . . [have in common] the theme of judicial policy generally; since judicial policy, even if it is not written in the law books, is capable of influencing the judicial substance." Ibid.

8. In the summer of 1965, Agranat wrote two opinions that had a Conservative flavor. In C.A. 54/65, *Mekitan v. Mekitan,* 19(2) P.D. 651 (1965), Agranat wrote a concurring opinion in order to "refute . . . the claim that we are sitting as an appellate jurisdiction to review the judgment of the rabbinical court" (p. 666). In Cr.A. 94/65, *Turjeman v. Attorney General,* 19(3) P.D. 57 (1965), Agranat, with Silberg and Mani, and against the dissenting opinion of Justices Sussman and Landau, decided that the criminal law, which prohibited the "holding or administering of a place for prostitution," also applied to a place that was used by the prostitute for the dual purposes of work and residence. The case was particularly painful for Agranat because Sussman criticized Agranat's literal interpretation, calling it excessively formalistic. It appears that Agranat's formalism was designed to reach the Conservative conclusion that would permit the expansion of the war against prostitution.

After *Yeredor* the Conservative trend continued. See, for example, H.C. 130/66, *Segev v. Rabbinical Court,* 21(2) P.D. 505 (1967). Israeli Jews, married in a private ceremony, petitioned the Court to order the rabbinical courts to make a declaratory judgment about their marital status. Agranat held that because the petitioners did not exhaust their alternative remedies, the Court should not intervene. Agranat further said: "[T]his Court cannot be used—after the legislator in 1953 decided in favor of religious marriages as an exclusive option—as a forum where the struggle in favor of this reform shall be conducted" (p. 541).

To this list should be added an opinion classified as secret, upholding the government's power to censor a publication based on data obtained during an author's years in government service. Agranat, with Justices Silberg and Landau, held that the government may prohibit the publication of Isser Harel's (former Mossad chief) memoirs concerning the Eichmann abduction. The book, Isser Harel, *Ha-Bayit bi-Rehov Garibaldi* [The House on Garibaldi Street] (Tel Aviv: Sifriyat Maariv, 1974/1975), has since been published, but the opinion remains classified. This information is based on an untitled essay in honor of Simon Agranat written by Moshe Ben-Ze'ev (in the Agranat papers, Agranat family, Jerusalem).

However, while Agranat tilted toward a more Conservative judicial stance, his judicial work as chief justice still contained the reformist elements that had characterized his earlier work. One of the most significant cases of his tenure as chief justice was the first case in which the Court exercised judicial review and invalidated a Knesset law. In H.C. 98/69, *Bergman v. Minister of Treasury,* 23(1) P.D. 693 (1969), a unanimous Court invalidated a campaign-financing law on the grounds that it violated the equal-protection guarantee of Basic Law: The Knesset, without meeting the procedural requirements that would validate such a violation. Agranat recalled that Justice Landau, who wrote the opinion for the Court, declined his advice to make Bergman an anonymous per curiam opinion. Another indication of his reformist inclinations is an announcement that "[t]he conference of Supreme Court justices decided that henceforth the Court will follow the principle that the fact that an attorney's fees were not paid on time should not be a justification for recusing the defense attorney from the obligation to represent his client on appeal." Simon Agranat, *"Hoda'a—Se'if 15" [Announcement—Section 15 of the Criminal Procedure Law 5725–1965],* 22(1) P.D. 308 (1968).

See also *Ben-Moshe;* Cr.A. 281/69, *Bar Shalom v. State of Israel,* 23(2) P.D. 85 (1969), where Agranat overruled a conviction for violation of a traffic sign, holding that drivers should not be required to ponder the meaning of vague traffic signs; and chap. 12, n. 76.

9. The ministry was in the hands of Chaim Moshe Shapira, leader of MAFDAL. But Shapira, who also served as minister of religious affairs, left the Health Ministry in the hands of his close associate, Raphael.

10. The "contribution" of 220,000 Israeli pounds was to be paid to two institutions: The Rav Kook Institute and a Yeshivah named after Rav Maimon. Both Raphael and Spiegel were involved in the affairs of these institutions. Moshe Golan, *Doh Va'adat Hakira* [Report of the Commission of Inquiry], 7 March 1965, 6, 33, in the author's files.

11. Levy Eshkol became prime minister in 1963 after Ben-Gurion, angry and frustrated by MAPAI's failure to heed his demands concerning "The Affair," left the government and later the party.

12. M. Golan, *Doh,* 33. Although the report's conclusions were made public, the report itself remained classified, thus feeding speculations and innuendo. In October 1965 the report was released as a part of the governmental effort to assuage the crisis.

13. "Ha-MAFDAL Yitba Limnoa Kfiyat Hizakekut le-Shiput Hiloni [MAFDAL Will Demand the Prevention of Coercive Secular Judicial Jurisdiction]," *Ha-Arets,* 23 September 1965, 3; "Raphael Says N.R.P. for Jurisdiction to Religious Courts," *Jerusalem Post,* 24 September 1965, 8. The rabbinical courts of Israel have exclusive jurisdiction in matters of marriage and divorce among Jews in Israel. In some other matters (personal status and succession, for example) the rabbinical courts have concurrent jurisdiction, conditioned upon the consent of all parties. Criminal law is within the exclusive jurisdiction of the secular courts. Rabbinical Courts Jurisdiction (Marriage and Divorce) Law, 5713–1953, 7 L.S.I. 139 (1952/1953).

14. "Lishkat Orche ha-Din Megalah Herdatah al Divre Yitzhak Raphael" [The Bar States Alarm at Raphael's Speech], *Davar,* 1 October 1965, 2.

15. See discussion on p. 103.

16. See also "Rejecting Raphael," *Jerusalem Post,* 8 October 1965, 9. Indeed,

within ten years MAFDAL would break its "historic alliance" with MAPAI and form a coalition with Likud. The roots of this major political shift could be found in the affair of Tel Giborim.

17. Aryeh Tsimuki, "Me-Hashash le-Hitpatrut ha-Shoftim ha-Elyonim Pursam Doh Golan [The Golan Report Was Published for Fear of the Resignation of the Justices]," *Yediot Aharonot*, 4 October 1965, 1; "Yefursam Gam Kovets ha-Eduyot she-Nimseru bifne ha-Shofet Golan [The Evidence Heard by Judge Golan Will Also Be Published]," *Ha-Arets*, 5 October 1965, 1, 3; Yosef Harif, "Ma Garam le-Pirsum ha-Doh ha-Maleh [What Caused the Publication of the Full Report]," *Maariv*, 4 October 1965, 11.

18. The "Agreement to Maintain the Status Quo"—that is, to maintain public religious observance (for example, shutting down transportation on the Sabbath)—was the result of fierce negotiations between Rabbi Leib Fishman Maimon, leader of MAFDAL, and Ben-Gurion in 1948. From Independence onward, secular Israelis challenged the legality of the status quo. See Rubinstein, *Ha-Mishpat ha-Konstitutsyoni*, 260. Rubinstein's book, the leading textbook on Israeli constitutional law, takes a decidedly secular position and is reflective of the view of mainstream secular Israelis on the issue.

19. See Justice Haim Cohn's statement in affirming Spiegel's conviction: "[The reporting of Spiegel to the police] was an exemplary act of good citizenship . . . that every law-abiding citizen and every conscientious citizen with a whiff of public responsibility is bound to make." Cr.A. 316/64, 325/64, *Spiegel v. Attorney General* 18(4) P.D. 7, 35 (1964). For a discussion of *mamlakhtiyut*, see M. Cohen, *Zion and State*, 228.

20. For a sample of these cases, see: H.C. 155/60, *Elazar v. Mayor of Bat Yam*, 14 P.D. 1511 (1960) (denying a license in order to promote a religious purpose violates the law); H.C. 262/62, *Perets v. Kfar Shmaryahu*, 16 P.D. 2101 (1962) (invalidating the refusal of a local community to rent a hall to Reform Jews to hold a religious service); H.C. 143/62, *Funk Schlesinger v. Minister of Interior*, 17 P.D. 225 (1963) (the ministry must register as married all Israeli Jews who were married abroad, regardless of the halakhic validity of the marriage); H.C. 231/63, *Retef v. Minister of Trade and Industry*, 17 P.D. 2730 (1963) (the Ministry of Trade and Industry cannot condition issuing an import license on the presentation of a kosher certificate from the rabbinate); H.C. 301/63, *Streit v. Chief Rabbi*, 18(1) P.D. 598 (1964) (the chief rabbinate cannot use the statutory exemption from bigamy [the permission to marry a second wife] as a means to coerce the first wife to agree to a divorce; this opinion was overruled in 1969 by Agranat, F.H. 10/69, *Burnovski v. Chief Rabbis*, 25[1] P.D. 7 [1971]); H.C. 195/64, *Ha-Hevrah ha-Dromit and Marbek v. Chief Rabbinical Council*, 18(2) P.D. 324 (1964) (despite protestations by the rabbinical council that it is not subject to judicial review, the Court held that it would intervene when the rabbinate acted ultra vires).

21. "Shapira: Be-Inyan Raphael Paal Eshkol Tahat Lahats u-Mitoh Pahad ma Yihtevu [Shapira: In the Matter of Raphael, Eshkol Acted under Pressure and out of Fear of Public Opinion]," *Yediot Aharonot*, 22 October 1965, 2.

22. Agranat had started his efforts to heal the rift between the religious and the secular as soon as he was appointed chief justice. The staunchly secular Olshan was replaced by Yitzhak Kister, a devoutly religious judge. It was the first nomination

of a religious judge since the appointment of Justice Silberg to the bench in 1949. Kister's appointment raised the number of religious judges to two out of nine. The decidedly secular composition of the Court explains its willingness to expand the principle of the separation of church and state in the 1960s. During Agranat's tenure as chief justice, more moderate justices were appointed, thereby steering the Court away from contentious rulings on this issue. See also chap. 12, n. 8. In Israel, judges are appointed by a committee composed of members of the Supreme Court, the executive, the Knesset, and the bar, but the chief justice does have considerable influence on the decisions. See, generally, Shimon Shetreet, "Developments in Constitutional Law: Selected Topics," 24 *Is. L. Rev.* 368 (1990).

23. See discussion on p. 191.

24. Agranat, *Judges Conference*, 12–13. The remarks appear to have been made spontaneously.

CHAPTER 11

1. Since 1948 Israelis have used various terms to designate the Palestinian Arabs who remained within Israeli territory: Israel's Arabs, Israeli Arabs, Palestinian Israelis, Falastini Israelis. See, generally, Dani Rabinowitz, "Nostalgiyah Mizrahit [Oriental Nostalgia]," *Teoryah u-Vikoret* 4 (1993): 141; Uzi Benziman and Atallah Mansour, *Dayare Mishneh* [Subtenants] (Jerusalem: Keter, 1992).

2. E.A. 1/65, *Yeredor v. Chairman of the Central Elections Commission*, 19(3) P.D. 365 (1965).

3. See Lustick, *Arabs in the Jewish State;* Benziman and Mansour, *Dayare Mishneh;* Sabri Jiryis, *The Arabs in Israel,* trans. Inea Bushnaq (New York: Monthly Review Press, 1976); Jacob M. Landau, *The Arabs in Israel: A Political Study* (London: Oxford University Press, 1969). For an analysis of the legal status of Israeli Arabs, see Kretzmer, *Legal Status.* In the Kafr Kassem incident of 1956, forty-seven Israeli Arabs, including fifteen women and eleven children, were massacred by members of the border police. A military court presided over by Judge Benjamin Halevy convicted eight and acquitted three of the accused. The incident fed the anger and increased the demoralization among Israeli Arabs. See Yigal Elam, *Memaley ha-Pkudot* [The Executors] (Jerusalem: Keter, 1990), 53–70.

4. "We also call upon the government to halt the persecution of Arabs in Israel and recognize the Arab Giant currently awaking and the peoples of Asia and Africa as the light towards which it should turn." *Kifakh Al-Ard* [The Struggle of Al-Ard], 7 December 1959, in the author's files.

5. H.C. 241/60, *Qardosh v. Registrar of Companies*, 15(2) P.D. 1151, 1154 (1961); 4 Selected Judgments of the Supreme Court of Israel 7 (1961–1962).

6. Cr.A. 228/60, *Qahwaji v. Attorney General*, 14(3) P.D. 1929 (1960). Qahwaji was a poet and schoolteacher. He was later dismissed from his teaching position. Al-Ard did apply for a permit to publish, but the government took its time pondering how to respond, and Al-Ard decided to publish while the application was pending. The publications contained polemical criticisms of Israel and were later used as evidence of Al-Ard's intentions. The opinion was written by Justice Landau. Agranat concurred.

7. *Qardosh*, 1169. In the further hearing Agranat's majority prevailed. F.H. 16/61, *Registrar of Companies v. Qardosh*, 16(2) P.D. 1209 (1962); 4 Selected Judgments of the Supreme Court of Israel 32 (1961/2). One can discern an interesting pattern of increasing recognition of Israel by Al-Ard. In 1958 Al-Ard urged Arab voters to boycott the elections and thereby deny Israel legitimacy. By petitioning the Court in *Qardosh*, Al-Ard was signaling its readiness to offer Israeli institutions some recognition. The pattern peaked in the *Yeredor* case, when Al-Ard's members wished to run for the Knesset.

8. According to Jacob M. Landau, Al-Ard increased its capital from 1,500 to 120,000 English pounds. When the group was outlawed, a Haifa district court put the Al-Ard corporation out of business. See Landau, *Arabs in Israel*, 97, 100, 106.

9. See Jiryis, *Arabs in Israel*, 188; Landau, *Arabs in Israel*, 92–107.

10. H.C. 253/64, *Jiryis v. Supervisor of Haifa District*, 18(4) P.D. 673 (1964).

11. In 1961 and 1964 they attempted to attract international attention to their plight by protesting to the United Nations and foreign embassies in Israel about the "military government, expropriation of land, and the condition of Arab culture in Israel" (Landau, *Arabs in Israel*, 97–98). That, too, could not have endeared them to the Israeli authorities.

12. It is also possible that the Communist Party, which correctly understood Al-Ard's potential as a competitor for Arab votes, encouraged the Central Elections Committee to ban the party.

13. *Yeredor*, 371–73.

14. The irony of this result from the perspective of Zionism is striking. In the aftermath of the emancipation of French Jews, the slogan was "to the Jews as a nation—nothing, to the Jews as individuals—everything." In response, the Zionist movement insisted on the national rights of the Jewish people. Now the sovereign Jewish state was applying the same French slogan to the Palestinian Arabs.

15. See discussion on p. 93.

16. In interview, Agranat recalled that had he opposed efforts by the military governors to stifle Arab political speech by closing down Arab cafés under the pretext that heated discussions might cause a breach of the peace. In one case, he recalled, he ordered the reopening of such a café.

17. See discussion on p. 108.

18. *Qardosh*. Qardosh was the leader of Al-Ard. Agranat did, however, concur in the conviction of another Al-Ard leader. See *Qahwaji*. When asked about this case, Agranat said that his hands were tied because the violation of the law was so clear. Agranat's liberal view toward Arabs, however, was always tempered by the Zionist ethos. See, for example, Yoram Shachar, "Ha-Shimush be-Koah Katlani le-Bitsua ha-Din: Gold bi-Rei ha-Historyah [The Use of Lethal Force to Enforce the Law: Gold in Historical Perspective]," in Barak et al., *Gvurot*, 275.

19. Cohn said that the company registrar's decision was valid "whether reasonable or unreasonable, to the point or not to the point—I fear that even arbitrariness cannot suffice to invalidate such discretion." He tied this interpretation to judicial restraint, holding that the Knesset is free to change the contours of the discretion. *Qardosh*, 1172–73.

20. When the black-letter law served to suppress freedom, Agranat sought to

soften it through an interpretation that subordinated the language to the higher goals mentioned in Israel's Declaration of Independence. This was his view in both *Al Couri* and *Kol ha-Am*.

21. *Qardosh*, 1162.

22. Ibid., 1167.

23. Ibid., 1168–69. On the same page, he added: "My view is that to the extent that the legislature made specific and explicit arrangements, in which it vested in the executive branch the powers of 'prior' restraints on freedom of expression . . . , it is essential to insist that such powers be employed only pursuant to the conditions appearing in these arrangements through—and this is the crucial point—the administrative agencies designated to execute this difficult and delicate function, and through them alone" (p. 1169).

24. Further hearing, *Qardosh*, 1228. Olshan's reasoning centered on the fact that Agranat's limitation of the registrar's discretion reflected the Companies' Law as it obtained in Britain, not in Israel, and therefore amounted to judicial legislation.

25. Under Olshan's leadership, the chief justice retained complete control over the assignment of justices to the various panels. There is little question that this discretion enabled Olshan to manipulate the results of cases. Under Agranat's leadership, the system slowly shifted, and the panels were randomly composed by the Court's registrar. However, the chief justice still retains the privilege of assigning justices to particularly important cases.

26. The fact that Israel was the Jewish state was repeated twice in the section in which Agranat held that the "immortality—of the State of Israel—is a fundamental constitutional premise." *Yeredor*, 385–86.

27. Yaacov Yeredor, the petitioner, was a Jewish attorney and a member of a new leftist group, Ha-Peulah ha-Shemit (Semitic Action), dedicated to cooperation between Arabs and Jews. He started his political activity in the 1930s, as a supporter of the extreme nationalist leader Abba Ahi-Meir. During Israel's struggle for independence he was an active member of LEHI. In the 1950s, LEHI membership was split between the left and the right. Yeredor belonged to the leftist camp, which believed in a binational state. Later, his son, Reuven Yeredor, served as commander of Israel's high-security intelligence unit. The story is emblematic of the diverse roads to security, all in the family. Yossi Melman, "Yehidah Sodit Beyoter [A Top Secret Unit]," *Ha-Arets*, 14 April 1995, B4.

28. In *Qardosh*, 1172–73.

29. But he was too secular and modern to observe the other cardinal rule of orthodox Sabbath observance—refraining from travel. Occasionally, he would take trips to visit family and friends.

30. Sussman filed a concurring opinion, relying on the Weimar experience and on the constitutional law of the Federal German Republic. Insisting that "life experience requires that we do not repeat the same mistake that we were all witness to [the fall of Weimar]," Sussman relied on the concept of "a fighting democracy" in the Basic Law of Germany and on a holding by the German Constitutional Court that certain principles are so sacred as to bind the Constitution itself. *Yeredor*, 389–90.

Sussman, born in Poland and raised in Germany, was a young *referendar* (clerk) in the *Ausgericht* Berlin—Pankow—the magistrate court of Berlin, when the Nazis came to power. Days later, the chief magistrate assembled the clerks: "I have a letter here which applies to the Jews among you," he said. The letter ordered the immediate suspension of all Jewish personnel. Within three months Sussman found himself in Tel Aviv. Dr. Wulf Cegla, interview by the author, Tel Aviv, March 1984.

The comparison of Agranat's and Sussman's opinions is a fascinating illustration of the material that forms Israeli constitutional jurisprudence. Sussman wove German constitutional law into the *Yeredor* opinion. Agranat wove American law and experience. Thus both the fall of Weimar and the American Civil War came to influence a result related to the Palestinian–Israeli conflict in the Middle East.

31. *Yeredor*, 386.

32. Ibid., 387.

33. *Jiryis*, 192.

34. Quoted in Justice Cohn's dissent: "We do not sit here as a court of law, and therefore we do not require the strenuous proof required by the law of evidence. We may be satisfied with less than would be required in a legal suit." *Yeredor*, 372.

35. Ibid., 370.

36. However, some of the leaders of Al-Ard left Israel after 1965 and participated in the Arab struggle against Israel. Habib Qahwaji joined the Syrian intelligence services and was rumored to be the mastermind behind the Arab Jewish spy ring in the early 1970s. His wife, Naif Akala, was convicted in Israel for spying for Jordan. Sabri Jiryis joined the PLO and became a scholar of the Arab–Israeli conflict. See Benziman and Mansour, *Dayare Mishneh*, 25.

37. *Jiryis*, 675. The full text of Article I reads: "To raise the educational, scientific, physical, economic and political level of all its members."

38. The reference to the "contemporary political dictionary" is Justice Landau's in ibid., 680. The classic analysis of the Palestinian discourse as one containing multilayered meaning is found in Yehoshafat Harkabi, *Arab Attitudes to Israel* (Jerusalem: Keter, 1972).

39. Dani Rabinowitz, discussing the complex connotations attached to any term describing Israeli Arabs (or Palestinians who are Israeli citizens, which is the term he prefers) observes that in the 1950s and 1960s the term *Arab* "connoted a demonic and dangerous conglomerate of persons and nations . . . ready and able to coordinate powers and effort at any moment, so long as the target is inflicting an injury upon Israel. This disturbing feeling is an inseparable part of my childhood memories." Rabinowitz, "Nostalgiyah," 145.

40. I use the Arabic term here, to distinguish it from Mandatory Palestine.

41. *Yeredor*, 386. In interview, Agranat defended his ruling by saying, "I did what the people wanted," by which I think he meant that the cardinal precepts of Zionism had to be upheld.

42. And which Chafee himself borrowed from English legal historian Frederic William Maitland. Zechariah Chafee, *Free Speech in the United States* (Cambridge, Mass.: Harvard University Press, 1964), 20.

43. *Yeredor*, 386.

44. Ibid., 385–86, for the proposition that the Declaration of Independence has normative validity.

45. Ibid., 386.

46. "It may be that Eichmann's trial will help to ferret out other Nazis—for example, the connection between Nazis and some Arab rulers. From what we hear on the Egyptian radio, some Egyptian propaganda is conducted on purely Nazi lines. . . . I have no doubt that the Egyptian dictatorship is being instructed by the large number of Nazis who are there." David Ben-Gurion, "The Eichmann Case as Seen by Ben-Gurion," *New York Times Magazine,* 18 December 1960, 7, 62.

47. It is important to note that Agranat did not altogether deny Arabs the right of representation. In a dictum he emphasized that the Declaration of Independence stated that Arabs should be adequately represented in all government institutions. *Yeredor,* 386.

48. "No free regime would assist and recognize a movement which strives to annihilate the same regime." Ibid., 388, quoting Justice Witkon in *Jiryis,* 679.

49. Ibid.

50. See Segev, *Seventh Million,* 373.

51. Indeed, that was the theme which animated Justice Sussman's concurrence in *Yeredor,* 389.

52. Golda Meir, then Israel's foreign minister, said in the Knesset: "The strong connection between Hitler's regime and Cairo is known since Hitler's days. . . . [E]ighteen years after [the Holocaust] . . . the sons of this people [the Germans] reappear to partake in activity designed to destroy the state of Israel, where the Holocaust survivors have assembled." Segev, *Seventh Million,* 373.

53. Sir Ernst Barker, *Reflections on Government* (London: Oxford University Press, 1942), 405, quoted in *Yeredor,* 388.

54. *Dennis.*

55. In addition, in the early 1960s, Israel's security services had uncovered a few Soviet moles working within the Israeli security establishment. Their convictions, upheld by the Court, acquainted the justices with Soviet involvement in Israeli affairs. See, for example, Cr.A. 45/61, *Cite v. Attorney General,* 15 P.D. 1373 (1961); Michael Bar-Zohar, *Ha-Memuneh* [Isser Harel and Israel's Security Services] (Jerusalem: Weidenfeld and Nicolson, 1971), 179 (discussing the conviction of Yisrael Baer, a senior analyst in the Ministry of Defense who was convicted of espionage in 1962); Cr.A. 28/62, *Ploni v. Attorney General,* 16 P.D. 2305 (1962).

56. *State Papers by Abraham Lincoln* (1907): 9, quoted by Agranat, *Yeredor,* 388. Recall that Agranat wrote the entire opinion on a Saturday night. The fact that he kept a volume of Lincoln's speeches in his personal library made the insertion of the quotation in the opinion possible.

57. In his last year, he was thrilled to watch Ken Burns's epic on *The Civil War* on videotape.

58. *Yeredor,* 386.

59. In a curious way, the Eichmann trial and the heightened awareness of the Holocaust, which were meant to empower the Israelis, in fact paralyzed them. Fear for the Jewish state made it impossible to take risks or to think about the meaning of life other than in terms of mere survival. Thus the Court lost an opportunity to encourage a dialogue between Israeli Arabs and Jews.

60. *Yeredor,* 384. An article by a rabbi and retired professor of Hebrew, Louis Isaac Rabinowitz, in the right-wing newspaper *Herut* tied together the three events

in October—the final phase of the Tel Giborim scandal, Al-Ard, and the Judges Conference in an interesting way. The article challenged the idea that judicial decision making was objective and advised the readers that textual deconstruction could well explain the justices' worldview and thereby facilitate the prediction of results. Agranat and Sussman, the author observed, were devoted to the Jewish cause; hence their decision to sustain the ban on Al-Ard. Justice Cohn was not so devoted; hence his decision to invalidate the ban. Louis Isaac Rabinowitz, "Hakayemet Bikhlal Obyektiviyut ba-Mishpat [Is Law Objective?]," *Herut,* 22 October 1965, 3. The characterization of Cohn as a "bad Jew" was based on Cohn's commitment to the principle of the separation between church and state. Cohn's opinion in *Spiegel* and his comments, the previous year, that "because of an ancient Talmudic rule, racist-Nazi principles became law in the State of Israel" particularly enraged religious Jews. See H.C. 4/64, *Vagnar v. Attorney General* 18(1) P.D. 29 (1964), in which the Court rejected a petition challenging the decision not to open criminal proceedings against Justice Cohn.

61. One landmark opinion, however, stands out in this period: *Bergman.*

62. Benziman and Mansour, *Dayare Mishneh,* 111.

CHAPTER 12

1. H.C. 58/68, *Shalit v. the Minister of the Interior and the Population Registrar,* 23(2) P.D. 477 (1969). Selected Judgments of the Supreme Court of Israel (Special Volume, 1971), 35.

2. Horowitz and Lissak, *Origins,* 51–64; Boas Evron, *Jewish State or Israeli Nation?* (Bloomington: Indiana University Press, 1995), 172–204; Ehud Luz, *Parallels Meet: Religion and Nationalism in the Early Zionist Movement (1882–1904)* (Philadelphia: Jewish Publication Society, 1988).

3. David Vital, *The Future of the Jews* (Cambridge, Mass.: Harvard University Press, 1990), 81.

4. Ehud Sprinzak, *The Ascendance of Israel's Radical Right* (New York: Oxford University Press, 1991), 40 (quoting Moshe Dayan).

5. For a discussion, see Menachem Friedman, "The State of Israel as a Theological Dilemma," in *The Israeli State and Society,* ed. Baruch Kimmerling (New York: State University of New York Press, 1989), 203.

6. Law of Return (Amendment No. 2) 5370–1970, 24 L.S.I. 28 (1970). See Asher Maoz, "Mihu Yehudi: Rov Mehuma al lo Meuma [Who Is a Jew: Much Ado about Nothing]," 31 *Ha-Praklit* 271 (1978).

7. When, in 1972, Shalit petitioned the Court to register his third child, Tomer, as Jewish or, in the alternative, as "Hebrew," a unanimous panel of justices (Berinson, Kister, and Kahan) denied him relief, holding that that was an impermissible way to dodge the 1970 Amendment. H.C. 18/72 *Shalit v. Minister of Interior,* 26(1) P.D. 334 (1972) (the second *Shalit*).

8. The Orthodox Justice Yitzhak Kahan replaced the retiring Justice Halevy. Justice Moshe Etzioni, replacing Justice Silberg, though not Orthodox, was not an avowed secularist either. See, for example, his concurring opinion in C.A. 450/70, *Rogozinsky v. State of Israel,* 26(1) P.D. 129, 137 (1972) (denying a petition

by atheist kibbutz members to recognize their "common-law" marriage ["(W)ith all the empathy I have for the conscientious argument of petitioners, I feel wholeheartedly offended by the idea that the uniform objective test of who is a Jew shall be sacrificed at the altar of freedom of conscience."]) There is no doubt that Agranat supported the elevation of these two Haifa district court judges to the Court. In 1982, Justice Kahan became the first Orthodox chief justice of Israel. See also discussion on p. 179.

9. Under Israeli law, matters of marriage and divorce are adjudicated by the religious courts, which are not bound by the data of the population registry and may make their own determination as to the religious identity of persons appearing before them. For a detailed critique of the relationship between rabbinical and secular law in matters of marriage and divorce, see Ariel Rosen-Zvi, *Dine ha-Mishpahah be-Yisrael: Ben Kodesh le-Hol* [Israeli Family Law: The Sacred and the Secular] (Tel Aviv: Papirus, 1990).

10. For an elaboration of this view, see A. B. Yehoshua, *Between Right and Right*, trans. Arnold Schwartz (Garden City, N.Y.: Doubleday, 1981), 64–68.

11. The Court first confronted the issue in the Brother Raphael matter, H.C. 72/62, *Rufeisen v. Minister of Interior*, 16 P.D. 2428 (1962). A Jewish Holocaust survivor who had converted to Catholicism and became a monk came to live in Israel and petitioned the Court to recognize him as Jewish under the Law of Return and grant him citizenship. All agreed that under the halakhah he remained Jewish despite his conversion. Rejecting his petition, the Court opined that the meaning of "Jewish" under the Law of Return is popular, not halakhic. Agranat did not participate in the *Rufeisen* panel.

12. See, generally, Sprinzak, *Ascendance*.

13. Galia Shalit was born on 11 February 1967. There followed lengthy correspondence between Shalit and the Ministry of Interior. Shalit filed his petition on 25 February 1968.

14. Initially, Justice Halevy, who sat in the district court during the Kasztner and Eichmann trials, was included in the panel, but he resigned in order to run for the Knesset under the Likud ticket, and the Orthodox Justice Kister took his place.

15. See discussion on p. 171.

16. Gideon Reicher, "Ish Fatah she-Imo Yehudiyah Rashai le-Herashem ke-Yehudi, va-Ani, Yelid ha-Arets, Eneni Yakhol Lirshom et Yeladay ke-Yehudim? [A Fatah Man Whose Mother Is Jewish May Be Registered as Jewish and I, Native Born, Cannot Register My Children as Jewish?]," *Yediot Aharonot*, 22 November 1968, 2. The headline here is particularly interesting, because the newspaper makes a distinction between the native-born man (who is Jewish) and the "other" Fatah man, thereby ignoring the fact that the Palestinians are also native born.

17. "In view of our special circumstances, when there is no practical way to supervise . . . all the borders . . . against infiltrators . . . who are a source of continuous grave danger to the state and its residents, it is essential that a legal resident in Israel will always be able to identify himself by an identity card." J. S. Shapiro, presenting the amendment in the Knesset, 56 *Divre ha-Knesset* 723, 725 (1970). In Hebrew, *infiltrators* (*mistanenim*) is a euphemism for Palestinian refugees.

18. *Shalit,* 521 (per Justice Landau).

19. Justice Eliyahu Mani gave the majority its fifth vote. It is interesting that he, the only Sephardi justice on the Court, sided with its more Liberal camp. It is generally considered that Sephardi Jews have a more relaxed view of religion. Agranat, however, recalled that he had expected Mani to vote with him and was very disappointed at Mani's decision. Because Mani's opinions were typically cryptic, as was his *Shalit* opinion, not divulging any reasoning, it is difficult to assess his role as the first Sephardi justice on the Court.

20. Rubinstein, *Ha-Mishpat ha-Konstitutsyoni,* 89.

21. Cohn, *Sihot,* 118.

22. None of the parties to the dispute challenged the assumption that an objective test and the halakhic test were one and the same or submitted a different "objective" criterion (for example, a secular one).

23. See *Shalit,* 505 (per Justice Sussman), 492 (per Justice Silberg).

24. Ibid., 518.

25. Ibid., 498.

26. Ibid., 501.

27. Ibid., 490.

28. Ibid., 501.

29. Ibid.

30. Ibid., 606.

31. Ibid., 502.

32. The contemporary explorer of this theme is Philip Roth. The theme harks back to Proverbs 6: 24–25: "To keep thee from the evil woman, from the flattery of the tongue of a strange woman. Lust not after her beauty in thine heart; neither let her take thee with her eyelids."

33. *Shalit,* 584.

34. Ibid.

35. Ibid., 596, 599.

36. "Today pure logic denies the [discriminatory] distinction against the other [the child of the Jewish father]." Ibid., 595.

37. Ibid.

38. The phrase "Torah and Israel . . . " is Agranat's. Ibid., 580.

39. Ibid., 576 (quoting Ernst Barker).

40. In the library of his late father, Aaron Agranat, he found Yehezkel Kaufmann's monumental work, *Golah ve-Nekhar* [Exile and Alienation] (Tel Aviv: Dvir, 1929–1932), and Chaim Tchernowitz's (Rav Tsa'ir) classic, *Toldot ha-Halakhah* [The History of the Halakhah] (New York, 1934). He quoted at length from his father-in-law's book, Israel Friedlaender, *Past and Present: Selected Essays* (New York: Burning Bush Press, 1961). Carmel's uncle, Eugen Meyer, contributed Ernst Barker, *Principles of Social and Political Theory* (Oxford: Clarendon Press, 1951). From his son-in-law, Oved Cohen (who the previous year had married his daughter Yael [Didi]), he borrowed S. N. Eisenstadt, *Israeli Society* (New York: Basic Books, 1967). His daughter Zilla, married in 1967, received from Carmel's uncle his books, Louis Finkelstein, ed., *The Jews: Their History, Culture and Religion* (Philadelphia: Jewish Publication Society of America, 3d ed., 1966) as a wedding gift; he now borrowed them to use in the opinion. From his son, Hillel, then a student of philosophy at the Hebrew University, he borrowed Nathan Roten-

streich, *Ha-Mahshavah ha-Yehudit ba-Et ha-Hadasha* [Jewish Thought in Modern Times] (Tel Aviv: Am Oved, 1945), and from his neighbor, Shimon Herman, he received Herbert Kelman's article, Herbert C. Kelman, "Patterns of Personal Involvement in the National System: A Social-Psychological Analysis of Political Legitimacy," in *International Politics and Foreign Policy,* ed. James N. Rosenau (New York: Free Press, 1969), 276.

41. *Shalit,* 577.

42. Ibid., 580.

43. Ibid., 585.

44. In support of these propositions he returned to the scholars Yehezkel Kaufmann and Rav Tsa'ir and quoted their analyses of the peculiar particularist and yet universal nature of Judaism. The Jewish people are the guardians of the Torah; in this sense they are bound to preserve its particularity. But the content of the Torah is universalist, and it is applicable to all people. Ibid., 585, 586.

45. Ibid., 586.

46. Ibid.

47. See discussion on p. 25.

48. *Shalit,* 589.

49. Ibid., 592–93.

50. Ibid., 592.

51. Ibid. Agranat then proceeded to quote Max Lerner for the proposition that, after World War II, one sees a trend within American Jewry "away from assimilationism and toward . . . assertion of their uniqueness and separateness as a historical community." Max Lerner, *America as a Civilization: Life and Thought in the United States Today* (New York: Simon & Schuster, 1957), 510. See also *Shalit,* 593. Agranat then quoted Melville J. Herskovits, "Who Are the Jews?" in *The Jews: Their History, Culture & Religion,* ed. Louis Finkelstein, 3d ed., vol. 2 (New York: Harper, 1960), 1493, who quoted Raymond Kennedy's assertion that American Jewry has both national and religious traits, which qualify them as a "religionational group." *Shalit,* 593.

52. *Shalit,* 594.

53. Rabbinical Courts Jurisdiction (Marriage and Divorce) Law, 5713–1953, 7 L.S.I. 135 (1952/1953), invested the rabbinical courts with a monopoly in matters of the marriage and divorce of Jews in Israel.

54. The concept of bastards under Jewish law applies to incestual, not to out-of-wedlock, relationships. A bastard cannot marry a Jew. See, generally, Ben Zion Schereschewsky, *Dine Mishpahah* [Family Law in Israel], 4th ed. (Jerusalem: Reuben Mass, 1992), 353–55.

55. *Shalit,* 394.

56. In C.A. 630/70, *Tamarin v. State of Israel,* 26 (1) P.D. 197 (1972), the petitioner stated that upon immigrating to Israel he felt both Croatian and Jewish. That gave Agranat another occasion to discuss the American Jewish community: "I only wish to state that it is not necessary that a person with two ethnic identities, will feel in certain situations that these identities conflict, but it is quite possible that their influences will coincide or affect him through mutual interaction, so that he might behave without feeling a conflict." And he quoted L. D. Brandeis: "[T]o be good Americans we must be good Jews, and to be good Jews we must be Zionists." Ibid., 205.

57. Amending the law to validate only conversions that are recognized by the halakhah or by Orthodox Jewry would deny recognition of the Conservative and Reform conversions in the United States. Rubinstein, *Ha-Mishpat ha-Konstitutsyoni*, 183–87. See also note 74 below.

58. *Shalit*, 595.

59. Ibid., 503. Silberg's emphasis.

60. Ibid., 600.

61. Ahad ha-Am, *Al Parashat Drakhim: Kovets Maamarim* [At the Crossroads: Collected Essays], 2d ed., vol. 1 (Jerusalem: Dvir, 1949), 151.

62. *Shalit*, 598.

63. Ahad ha-Am, *Parashat Drakhim*, 158. Emphasis deleted.

64. Ibid., 159.

65. See discussion on p. 19. The phrases "Be patient till the last" and "with himself at war" come from Shakespeare, *Julius Caesar*, Act I, Scene 2, line 45 and Act I, Scene 2, line 169, respectively. See also discussion on p. 21. Within two years, in *Tamarin*, Agranat, speaking for the Court, rejected a petition to register an Israeli born in Croatia as Israeli rather than Jewish, arguing that the emerging Israeli identity should retain a religious element, but that there is room within the Jewish nation for a secular perspective, and that Israel is built on "Liberal-secular elements" which will enable the petitioner to fight for his views in the political process. *Tamarin*, 222.

66. Horwitz, *Transformation*, 253. See also White, *Patterns*, 144; Henry M. Hart and Albert M. Sacks, *The Legal Process: Basic Problems in the Making and Application of Law*, prepared for publication by and containing an introductory essay by William N. Eskridge Jr. and Philip P. Frickey (Westbury, N.Y.: Foundation Press, 1994).

67. Alexander M. Bickel, *The Least Dangerous Branch: The Supreme Court at the Bar of Politics* (Indianapolis, Ind.: Bobbs-Merrill, 1962).

68. Barak is now chief justice, and Zamir an associate justice, on Israel's Supreme Court. As a law student at the Hebrew University at the time, I still remember the enthusiasm of Barak and Zamir about this "new approach." In 1970 Zamir published an article recommending the repeal of the word *justice* in the statute defining the Court's jurisdiction, so that judicial considerations would be purely objective. See Itzhak Zamir, "Al ha-Tsedek be-Vet ha-Mishpat ha-Gavohah le-Tsedek [On Justice at the High Court of Justice]," 26 *Ha-Praklit* 212 (1970). But this was not the only trend in Israeli law at the time. Amnon Rubinstein, then a young lecturer at Tel Aviv Law School, published an article calling on the legal profession to recognize the difference between formal and substantive justice and not to ignore the latter. See Amnon Rubinstein, "Shilton ha-Hok: ha-Tfisah ha-Formalit veha-Mahutit [The Rule of Law: Formalistic versus Substantive Approach]," 22 *Ha-Praklit* 453 (1966). Rubinstein's call was heeded fifteen years later, after Barak had joined the Supreme Court and adopted a more substantive, less processual approach to decisional law.

69. Moshe Landau, "Koho shel Bet ha-Mishpat u-Migbalotav [The Court's Power and Its Limitations]," 10 *Mishpatim* 196 (1979/80).

70. *Shalit*, 600.

71. *Consensus* was another term brought to esteem as a justifying construct for

judicial review by adherents of the school of legal process. See Harry H. Wellington, "Common Law Rules and Constitutional Double Standards: Some Notes on Adjudication," 83 *Yale L. J.* 221, 284 (1973).

72. David Ben-Gurion, "Hahlatat ha-Memshalah be-Inyan mihu Yehudi: Maaseh ha-Noged ofya shel Medinatenu [The Government's 'Who Is a Jew' Decision: An Act Which Is Contrary to the Character of Our State]," *Maariv,* 6 February 1970, 11.

73. H.C. 4/69, *Ben-Menashe v. Minister of Interior,* 24(1) P.D. 105, 106 (1970), decided on 28 January 1970.

74. But there was no majority for requiring that conversion be performed "in accordance to the halakhah." That meant that conversion in accordance with the Reform or Conservative movements could be recognized as valid. More than a decade later, Yitzhak Shamir's government was about to conclude another deal with the religious parties and add the words "in accordance with the halakhah" to the law. The bill was defeated, largely because of the solid opposition of the American Jewish community. Ari L. Goldman, "21 Jewish Groups Deplore Israeli Bill," *New York Times,* 15 January 1985, 6; Thomas L. Friedman, "Israel Assembly, 62 to 51, Rejects Move to Redefine 'Who Is a Jew,'" ibid., 16 January 1985, 1.

75. H.C. 40/70, *Becker v. Minister of Defense,* 24(1) P.D. 238 (1970); H.C. 287/69, *Miron v. Minister of Labour and Broadcast Authority,* 24(1) P.D. 337 (1970).

76. The Court again refused to intervene in the matter of Saturday broadcasting in H.C. 80/70, *Elizur v. Broadcasting Service,* P.D. 24(2) 649 (1970).

In H.C. 161/70, *Zaksh v. Mayor of Petach Tikva,* P.D. 24(1) 698 (1970), Agranat denied a petition by a rabbi to shut movie and entertainment establishments on Saturday nights because they violated the freedom of exercise of religion of Orthodox Jews, on the grounds of no standing. In H.C. 222/68, *Hugim Leumiyim v. Minister of the Police,* 24(2) P.D. 141 (1970), a five-member panel rejected a petition to order the police to refrain from preventing petitioners from praying on the Temple Mount and to order the police to provide protection for petitioners as they exercised their religious practices. The issue was extremely volatile because it threatened to escalate the potent conflict between Jews and Muslims over the holy places. Agranat held that the Court lacked jurisdiction in this matter and that the issue was not justiciable.

In H.C. 243/71, *Shik v. Minister of Interior,* 26(2) P.D. 33 (1972), Agranat denied a woman's petition to change her name to the name of her companion, with whom she had established a home and had had two children. The petitioner stated that she was philosophically opposed to religious marriage, the only form of marriage available in Israel. Writing for the Court, Agranat let stand the government's position that the change might mislead the public to assume the couple was married.

In H.C. 442/71, *Lansky v. Minister of Interior,* 26(2) P.D. 337 (1972), Agranat, speaking for a unanimous five-member panel, held that the minister of the interior could invoke section 2 of the Law of Return to deny the petitioner, who was linked to organized crime in the United States, an immigrant visa, for fear that he might endanger the public peace.

In H.C. 89/71, *Fauzi Al-Asmar v. Chief of the Central Command,* 25(2) P.D. 197 (1971), Agranat denied a petition by an Israeli-Arab author and journalist, a former member of the outlawed Al-Ard, against a restraining order confining him to the town of Lod. Al-Asmar argued that he could only make a living and socialize in Tel Aviv. Speaking for the Court, Agranat declined to interfere with the judgment of the military commander who had imposed the order.

In H.C. 148/73, *Kaniel v. Minister of Justice,* 27(1) P.D. 794 (1973), the Court rejected, per curiam (with Agranat on the panel), a challenge to an amendment to the elections law as violating the equality principle in section 4 of Basic Law: The Knesset, thereby refusing to extend the *Bergman* precedent to substantive violations that did meet the formal legislative requirements (61 votes). See also *Tamarin.*

In 1971 Agranat, overruling an important precedent and urging judicial restraint in statutory interpretation, held that the rabbinical authorities had the power to allow a married man to marry a second wife without violating the bigamy laws. Justices Sussman, Berinson, and Mani, members of the *Shalit* majority, joined Agranat with Justice Haim Cohn in dissent. F.H. 10/69, *Burnovski v. Chief Rabbi,* 25(1) P.D. 7 (1971). The case enabled the rabbis to overcome the problem of recalcitrant wives. The plight of *agunot* (anchored women) remains unresolved.

However, in Marriage Dissolution Petition 13/70, *Rivkin v. Rivkin,* 25(1) P.D. 309 (1971), Agranat criticized action by the rabbinical court in a matter concerning the divorce of a Jew and a non-Jew who had been married by a reform rabbi in New York, holding that the (secular) district court had jurisdiction. In H.C. 1/72, *In re Holzman,* 26(2) P.D. 85, 90 (1972), in a dictum, Agranat opined that Reform conversions in the United States were valid. Agranat also retained his Liberal attitude in matters of criminal procedure. In C.A. 44/72, *Shimshi v. State of Israel,* 26(1) P.D. 654, 657 (1972), Agranat emphasized the limits on the powers of policemen and insisted that in a criminal trial, the subject of which is personal liberty, an appellant should not be prevented from making a significant legal argument only because he or his attorney had failed to make that argument at the court below.

CHAPTER 13

1. Robert Slater, *Warrior Statesman: The Life of Moshe Dayan* (New York: St. Martin's Press, 1991), 352–66.

2. C.A. 604/72, *Yurman v. "Hasneh" Insurance,* 28(1) P.D. 141 (1974).

3. Ronnie recovered, completed his studies, and joined the Physics Department at the Hebrew University in Jerusalem. The *Yurman* decision was signed by the Court on 26 November 1973. Ronnie had been wounded on 16 October. It appears that Agranat had circulated his opinion during the war and that in the intervening weeks Justices Sussman and Kahan had completed their majority opinion. Retired Chief Justice Olshan, whose only child, Yoram, died in the aftermath of the Yom Kippur War while serving as a reservist, wrote about the pain of a parent whose child died in war: "I always thought that I could feel the pain of these parents . . . that with time . . . the wound heals, and I believed that logic and persuasion could help in keeping the depression under control. But my misfortune taught me that it is a mistake for one who never experienced this to think that he can understand and feel . . . what transpires in the heart of the . . . parent. . . .

[E]xcept for when I sleep, not even a moment passes without my seeing Yoram before me." Olshan, *Din u-Dvarim*, 378–79.

4. Agranat held that the Court had jurisdiction to amend the decision against the driver to include a proviso that the judgment should not affect the insurance company's defense. *Yurman*, 153.

5. The Hebrew words *bituah* (insurance) and *bitahon* (security) have the same root.

6. As represented most forcefully in Haim Goury, *Pirhey Esh* [Flowers of Fire], the most popular collection of poems published after the War of Independence. See Dan Miron, *Mul ha-Ah ha-Shotek* [Facing the Silent Brother] (Jerusalem: Keter, 1992), 199–234.

7. William B. Quandt, *Camp David: Peacemaking and Politics* (Washington, D.C.: Brookings Institution, 1986), 112. Sharm-al-Sheik, returned to Egypt under the peace treaty, was conquered by Israel in the Six Day War.

8. *Yurman*, 153.

9. The watershed event in the Watergate scandal, known as the Saturday Night Massacre, when President Nixon fired Special Prosecutor Archibald Cox, reported that Attorney General Elliot Richardson and his deputy, William Ruckelshaus, had resigned, and announced that the Office of the Special Prosecutor was being abolished, occurred on 20 October 1973. In the preceding days the media had focused simultaneously on Nixon's negotiations with the special prosecutor and his handling of the raging war in the Middle East. Richard Nixon, *The Memoirs of Richard Nixon* (New York: Grosset & Dunlap, 1978), 920–42.

10. Fighting, particularly on the Syrian front, erupted frequently. Israel, Egypt, and Syria were negotiating disengagement agreements. Henry Kissinger, who launched his shuttle diplomacy then, did not make a secret of his preference for dealing with Meir and Dayan. Any of these reasons militated in favor of stability. See, for example, Golda Meir, *My Life* (London: Weidenfeld & Nicolson, 1976), 378–81; Moshe Dayan, *Avne Derekh* [Story of My Life] (Jerusalem: Idanim, 1976), 724–35; Abba Eban, *Personal Witness: Israel through My Eyes* (New York: G. P. Putnam's, 1992), 554–55, 562–63.

11. See, generally, Zeev Segal, "The Power to Probe into Matters of Vital Public Importance," 58 *Tulane L. Rev.* 941 (1984).

12. Matti Golan, "Vaadat Hakira Mamlakhtit Turkav ba-Yamim ha-Krovim [A Commission of Inquiry Will Be Established Shortly]," *Ha-Arets*, 19 November 1973, 1. The news about Ben-Gurion appeared on the same page. Ben-Gurion died on 1 December 1973.

13. The argument about favoritism rested on the fact that in 1967 Yadin, as advisor to Prime Minister Eshkol, had strongly lobbied to appoint Dayan minister of defense. Dan Hanegbi, "Yadin," *Yediot Aharonot Magazine: Yamim,* 6 July 1984, 12–13. Laskov was appointed military ombudsman by Dayan after two years of unemployment. Mordecai Naor, *Laskov* (Jerusalem: Keter, 1988), 334, 337. See also Slater, *Warrior,* 380.

14. Editorial, "Herkev Meule [Excellent Composition]," *Ha-Arets*, 23 November 1973, 5. For praise from public figures, see Haviv Kenaan, "Reactions," ibid., 22 November 1973, 2.

15. Of the 120 seats in the Knesset, the Alliance won 51 (down from 56), and

the Likud 39 (up from 33). RATZ, a new party founded by Shulamit Aloni, won 3 seats, and MAFDAL held onto its 10 seats.

16. Indeed, it may well be that during the elections of 31 December 1973 the people did not have the courage to perform the task and were hoping that the commission would do it for them. It could also be that the commission interpreted the popular vote in favor of Golda Meir's government as an indication that the people still trusted its leadership. A poll taken during the last week of November 1973 reflected the public confusion. Almost 56 percent of the respondents believed that some leaders should draw personal conclusions (a euphemism for resignation); slightly more than 24 percent believed that personal conclusions should not be drawn; and just under 20 percent had no opinion. More than 50 percent of those who favored personal conclusions could not decide which leaders should be required to resign; 73 percent believed that Dayan should not be replaced. *Ha-Arets,* 23 November 1973, 1–2.

17. For a description of public anger expressed at Dayan, see, for example, Slater, *Warrior,* 378; "Waterloo Be-Bar-Ilan [Waterloo at Bar-Ilan]," *Ha-Olam ha-Zeh,* 25 December 1974, 15. For a discussion of the protest movements, see Gad Barzilai, *Demokratyah be-Milhamot* [A Democracy in Wartime] (Tel Aviv: Sifriat Poalim, 1992), 163–73.

18. The full reports were declassified following a petition to the Court by *Maariv.* See "Bagats Maariv: ha-Nimukim ha-Ikariyim [The Maariv Petition: The Main Arguments]," *Maariv Magazine,* 24 September 1993, 11.

19. The quotes are from Eban, *Personal Witness,* 564. The following is a sample of the criticism after the report had been submitted: in the cabinet meeting, Yitzhak Rabin, then minister of labor, called the report "fundamentally defective" and suggested that it be returned to the commission (Yosef Harif, "Tsfouyim Za-azouim ba-Memshalah uva-Maarakh be-Ikvot ha-Tviot le-Hadahat Moshe Dayan [Shake-ups Expected in the Cabinet and the Alliance following the Demands to Impeach Moshe Dayan]," *Maariv,* 4 April 1974, 1); a front page editorial in *Davar* accused the report of applying a double standard ("Doh Agranat: Tsarikh le-Vatsea, u-Mutar le-Vaker [The Agranat Report: Must Be Implemented and Can Be Criticized]," *Davar,* 3 April 1974, 1); Yitzhak Ben-Aharon, Labor's venerated leader, called the day the report was submitted "a dark day for Israeli law" (quoted in Eliyahu Salpeter, "Mehol ha-shedim [Dance Macabre]," *Ha-Arets,* 5 April 1974, 16); the Moked Party in the Knesset (left wing) condemned the report as a part of a cover-up ("Moked: Doh Agranat Meavet u-Mehape [Moked: The Agranat Report Distorts and Covers Up]," *Maariv,* 4 April 1974, 2); Amnon Rubinstein, Israel's leading constitutional law expert, opined that the report was flawed because it ignored a whole body of Israeli law related to the powers of the minister of defense ("Doh Agranat: He'arot Mishpatiyot [The Agranat Report: Legal Comments]," *Ha-Arets,* 9 April 1974, 11).

Although public condemnation was widespread, there were also voices of caution, defending the commission: Editorial, "Vaadat Agranat veha-Politikah [The Agranat Commission and Politics]," *Ha-Arets,* 5 April 1974, 15; Shalom Rosenfeld, "Medinat Mishpat oh Medinat Lintch? [A State of Law or a State of Lynching?]," *Maariv,* 5 April 1974, 13–4.

20. Vaadat Agranat, *Din ve-Heshbon Vaadat Agranat: Vaadat ha-Hakira Mil-*

hemet Yom ha-Kippurim [Agranat Commission Report: Report of the Commission of Inquiry, the Yom Kippur War] (Tel Aviv: Am Oved, 1975), 44.

21. Ibid., 34–43. The commission recommended that the head of the intelligence services and other intelligence officers no longer serve in the intelligence branch, that the chief of the Southern Command be suspended, and that the service of the chief of staff be terminated.

22. Ibid., 19–21.

23. The Kahan Commission, appointed in 1983 to investigate Israeli involvement in the massacre at Sabra and Shatila, was bolder in its evaluation of the responsibility of the civilian leadership. While retaining the approach taken by the Agranat Commission, it gave a broader interpretation to the notion of "personal responsibility" and found that Minister of Defense Ariel Sharon was so responsible. But even the Kahan Commission was cautious not to intervene too heavily in political affairs and couched its recommendations in ambiguous language. Sharon was removed from his position as minister of defense but remained in the cabinet as minister without portfolio. See Segal, *Power to Probe*, 969–70.

24. Yaacov Hisdai, "Pirsum ha-Doh Tsoreh Leumi [Publication of the Report Is a National Imperative]," *Maariv Magazine*, 24 September 1993, 12–13.

25. See n. 19 above.

26. Zvi Lanir, *Ha-Haftaah ha-Bsisit: Modiin be-Mashber* [Fundamental Surprise: The National Intelligence Crisis] (Tel Aviv: Ha-Kibbutz ha-Meuhad, 1983), 55–59.

27. See, for example, Meron Medzini, *Ha-Yehudia ha-Gea: Golda Meir va-Hazon Yisrael: Biyografyah politit* [The Proud Jewess: Golda Meir and the Vision of Israel] (Jerusalem: Idanim, 1990), 359–409; Eban, *Personal Witness*, 492–555; Henry Kissinger, *Years of Upheaval* (London: Weidenfeld and Nicolson, 1982), 459.

28. See, for example, Lanir, *Ha-Haftaah*, 55–59; Uri Milstein, *Krisah ve-Likhah: mi-Sadat le-Arafat* [The Lesson of a Collapse: From Sadat to Arafat] (Kiron: Seridut, 1993), 96–98.

29. Vaadat Agranat, *Din ve-Heshbon*, 49.

30. See, for example, David Elazar's letter of resignation: "I refute the fundamental approach of the Commission regarding the respective jurisdictions of the minister of defense and the chief of staff. . . . In reality . . . the minister of defense was an operational authority above the chief of staff and all the operational and tactical plans before the war were submitted for his approval." Ibid., 146.

31. Ibid., 46, quoting Dayan's speech to the General Command on 21 May 1973: "I am now speaking as the representative of the government, also on the basis of information. We, the cabinet, say to the general command, gentlemen, please get ready for war where those threatening to open it are Egypt and Syria."

32. See Eli Zeira, *Milhemet Yom Ha-Kippurim: Mitos mul Metsiut* [The October '73 War: Myth against Reality] (Tel Aviv: Yediot Aharonot, 1993), 106–7.

33. Ibid., 242–43.

34. Dayan's legal advisor was Elyakim Rubinstein, who later played important roles in the Camp David accords and the peace treaty with Jordan. Zeira claimed that Agranat himself advised him not to be represented by an attorney. Ibid., 190. David Elazar also said that he did not consult an attorney. Yaacov Erez, "Daddo: Ani lo Kofer be-Ahrayut ha-Ramatkal [Daddo: I Do Not Deny the Responsibility of the Chief of Staff]," *Maariv*, 5 April 1974, 1.

35. Agranat relied on several sources, among them S. A. de Smith, *Judicial Review of Administrative Law,* 2d ed. (London: Stevens, 1968), 170–71, and Ivor Jennings, *The British Constitution,* 5th ed. (Cambridge, England: Cambridge University Press, 1968), 153–54. Vaadat Agranat, *Din ve-Heshbon,* 44.

36. See discussion on p. 216.

37. Vaadat Agranat, *Din ve-Heshbon,* 26.

38. The report's description of Meir's government can only be read as criticism: the commission described how the institution previously in charge of security matters—the Ministerial Committee for Security Affairs—was expanded to include almost all members of the cabinet "for the sole purpose of guaranteeing thereby the secrecy of its deliberations" and thus to cure the problem of leakages. As a result, the committee ceased to perform its original function—serious deliberation of national security. This task, in turn, was vested in the "kitchen." Members of the "kitchen" who did not live in Tel Aviv did not take part in the critical decisions made on Yom Kippur. Ibid., 27.

39. Ibid., 28. The commission recommended that during war the government should authorize the prime minister to establish a war cabinet of not more than five persons who would make decisions related to the war, thereby permitting other ministers to continue to attend to other important matters.

40. Ibid., 30. The commission recommended the appointment of a national security council in the prime minister's office. The commission fell short of censuring the government for having failed to implement similar recommendations made in 1963.

41. Ibid., 45.

42. Ibid., 63, 80.

43. Ibid., 58.

44. Ibid., 95.

45. Ibid., 94.

46. Ibid.

47. See Uri Ben-Eliezer, "Uma be-Madim u-Milhama: Yisrael bi-Shnotehah ha-Rishonot [The Nation-in-Arms and War: Israel in Its First Years]," *Zmanim* 59 (1994): 50; Baruch Kimmerling, "Al Militarism be-Yisrael [Militarism in Israeli Society]," *Teoryah u-Vikoret* 4 (1993): 123.

48. This was also true about the feelings in the army. See Zeev Schiff, "Retia Psihologit be-Tsahal Midoh Agranat [A Psychological Reaction in the Army against the Agranat Report]," *Ha-Arets,* 2 February 1975, 3.

49. See Moshe Negbi, *Namer shel Neyar* [Paper Tiger: The Struggle for Press Freedom in Israel] (Tel Aviv: Sifriat Poalim, 1985), 37–40.

50. The Alliance's slogan during the 1973 election campaign, before the war.

51. See n. 19 above.

52. See, for example, Uzi Benziman, "Sodiyut Mugzemet [Exaggerated Secrecy]," *Ha-Arets,* 11 December 1973, 9.

53. "As we mention these phenomena, it has not been our aim to ask for correction of a personal wrong. Our main aim is to explain that the tense—and oftentimes foul—atmosphere . . . could have impaired the credibility of the . . . [commission], and turned our very onerous mission almost unbearable." Vaadat Agranat, *Din ve-Heshbon,* 63.

54. See, for example, Gaby Baron, "Keshe-Hitbakesh ha-Shofet Agranat Lehagiv al ha-Doh Histapek Etmol be-Hafrahat Anney-Ashan mi-Miktarto [When Justice Agranat Was Asked Yesterday to React to the Report, He Only Puffed His Pipe]," *Yediot Aharonot,* 31 January 1975, 1.

55. Vaadat Agranat, *Din ve-Heshbon,* 61.

56. Ibid., 62.

57. Ibid.

58. Ibid., 63.

59. Ibid.

60. "Journalists and publishers who take the liberty to publish such things cannot argue that it is in the public interest. The Law decides what is permissible and what is forbidden in the public interest, and once the legislature has spoken all arguments about the public interest are terminated." Ibid., 64.

61. Ibid.

62. See discussion on pp. 11, 112.

63. But see his classified opinion, in the late 1960s, sustaining the censorship of a book on Eichmann's abduction, discussed in chap. 10, n. 8.

64. Vaadat Agranat, *Din ve-Heshbon,* 62–63.

65. See discussion on p. 42.

66. The commission had to decide whether it would allow the officers to conduct cross-examinations of witnesses and bring evidence to refute charges against them. At stake were sections 15(a) and (b) of the Commissions of Inquiry Law (1968), which stated that persons who might be damaged by the inquiry could defend themselves before the commission, through the presentation of evidence or through cross-examination. See Commissions of Inquiry Law, 23 L.S.I. 32 (1968) as amended 26 L.S.I. 30 (1972) and 33 L.S.I. (1979). The commission decided that a literal application of these sections would "absolutely undermine the inquiry, by irreparable entanglement of its processes" and gave the law an excessively narrow interpretation that denied the right to conduct a cross-examination or bring evidence, when the commission intended to rest its conclusions on the officer's own testimony or on documents to which he had been a party. Vaadat Agranat, *Din ve-Heshbon,* 15–16. General Shmuel Gonen, chief of the Southern Command during the war, who was suspended by the commission, petitioned the Court twice, arguing that this interpretation violated his rights and the statutory language. The Court denied his petitions, reasoning that justice did not require judicial intervention. H.C. 128/74, *Shmuel Gonen v. Vaadat ha-Hakirah,* 28(2) P.D. 80 (1974); H.C. 469/74, *Shmuel Gonen v. Vaadat ha-Hakirah,* 29(1) P.D. 635 (1975).

67. This was so both because two of the Court's most senior justices were members of the commission and because the public perceived the denial of Gonen's petition as an effort by the Court to assist the commission.

CHAPTER 14

1. See, for example, F.H. 30/75, *Koby v. State of Israel,* 30(2) P.D. 757 (1976); Cr.A. 515/75, *Katz v. State of Israel,* 30(3) P.D. 673 (1975). The only opinion related to constitutional law in these volumes is H.C. 549/75, *Noah Films Ltd. v. Film and*

Theatre Censorship Board, 30(1) P.D. 757 (1975), reversing the board's decision to deny a permit to show the film *Guardian of the Night.* The board reversed its decision to grant the permit on the ground that the film might hurt the feelings of Holocaust survivors.

2. Agranat learned about the practice from Sir Leon Radzinowicz's account of James Fitzjames Stephen's retirement from England's High Court. See Leon Radzinowicz, *Sir James Fitzjames Stephen: Selden Society Lectures* (Menston, England: Scolar Press, 1975), 42–43. I am indebted to David Seipp for tracing this information for me.

3. The last reported case with Agranat as a panel member is C.A. 44/76, *ATA Textile Company v. Schwartz,* 30(3) P.D. 785 (1976). This decision is dated 5 September 1976. Justice Shamgar wrote the opinion, with Justices Agranat and Landau concurring. Agranat's very last opinion, in which he sat as a single judge, was not published.

4. For several years he taught a seminar at Bar-Ilan University Law School. Agranat also taught at Yeshiva University in New York and at Santa Clara University School of Law in California as a visiting professor of law.

5. Agranat's major writings during this period were: "The Philosophy of Morris R. Cohen: A Symposium"; "The Madrid Conference Demonstration Trial: Opinion in Rescue of Hostages Case," 16 *Is. L. Rev.* 142 (1981); "Trumatah shel ha-Rashut ha-Shofetet le-Mifaal ha-Hakikah [The Contribution of the Judiciary to the Legislative Endeavor]," 10 *Iyune Mishpat* 233 (1984); "Hitpathuyot ba-Mishpat ha-Plili [Developments in the Criminal Law]," 11 *Iyune Mishpat* 33 (1985).

6. Among these prizes were honorary degrees from the Jewish Theological Seminary, from Ben-Gurion University, and from the Hebrew University. In 1986 he received the Sussman Prize, for—among other things—his "Life work of truth and justice" and "For the example he set, in theory and in practice, to the future generations." In 1990 he was recognized by the bar for "being among the founders of democracy in Israel, for his unique contribution to laying down the principles of the rule of law, for his judicial opinions that shaped the principles of political and human rights, and for educating generations of law students." Agranat papers, Agranat family, Jerusalem.

7. See, generally, Moshe Negbi, *Me'al la-Hok: Mashber Shilton ha-Hok be-Yisrael* [Above the Law: The Constitutional Crisis in Israel] (Tel Aviv: Am Oved, 1987); Pnina Lahav, "A Barrel without Hoops: The Impact of Counterterrorism on Israel's Legal Culture," 10 *Cardozo L. Rev.* 529 (1988); Dan Simon, "The Demolition of Houses in the Israeli Occupied Territories," 19 *Yale J. Int'l L.* 1 (1994); Sprinzak, *Ascendance.* In 1988 Agranat agreed to serve as president of the Israeli Association of Civil Rights (ACRI), thereby lending the young organization his prestige and authority. This was a significant step on Agranat's part, and it attests to his commitment to political and civil rights. The legal establishment frowned on his decision, and some members of his family advised him against it, because ACRI was constantly challenging human-rights violations, thereby causing embarrassment to the government and to the Court. Agranat's decision to assist ACRI is another indication that his prudent approach during his service as chief justice stemmed more from his conception of his position than from a change of heart about the need to protect rights in and by the Israeli polity.

8. Compare with Agranat's own 1925 dismissal of the Talmud in "Concerning the Hebrew University."

9. The phrase was suggested to the family by Justice Cohn, who had contributed an article on the subject to the Festschrift published in honor of Agranat's eightieth birthday. See Haim Cohn, "Din Emet La-Amito," in Barak et al., *Gvurot*, 35. The Talmud explains that "[t]he one who judges the truth truthfully is like an accomplice to the Lord in the Creation." And "a truthful judgment is when the truth inheres in the heart of the judge; judging the truth truthfully means that that truth has accomplished its mission, a just judgment." Ibid., 86.

EPILOGUE

1. Paul Goldberger, "Public Work That Ennobles as It Serves," *New York Times,* 13 August 1995, H30.

2. After 1967 Agranat declined to move the Supreme Court to East Jerusalem. In response to my question, "Why?" he said, cryptically, "There are enough good places in Hebrew Jerusalem."

3. In 1973 Agranat participated in a ceremony to lay the foundations for a Supreme Court building on Mount Scopus. Golda Meir's government pledged to underwrite the building, but the Yom Kippur War brought about the suspension of these plans.

4. Basic Law: Freedom of Occupation (5752–1992), S.H. 114, as amended (5752–1994), S.H. 90; Basic Law: Human Dignity and Freedom (5754–1992), S.H. 150. See Aeyal Gross, "Theories and Discourses of Rights and Democracy: A Comparative Inquiry" (S.J.D. diss., Harvard Law School, 1996).

5. On his last day in Court, Agranat sat on a panel with the recently appointed Justice Shamgar. The occasion was poetically symbolic, for in that case Agranat and Shamgar joined forces in limiting the power of film censorship in Israel. See *Noah Films Ltd. v. Film and Theatre Censorship Board.*

6. Aharon Barak, "Ha-Mahapekhah Ha-Hukatit [The Constitutional Revolution: Protected Human Rights]," 1 *Mishpat U-Mimshal* 9 (1992–1993); Gary J. Jacobsohn, *Apple of Gold: Constitutionalism in Israel and the United States* (Princeton, N.J.: Princeton University Press, 1993).

7. Menahem Mauntner, *Yeridat ha-Formalizm va-Aliyat ha-Arakhim ba-Mishpat ha-Yisraeli* [The Decline of Formalism and the Rise of Values in Israeli Law] (Tel Aviv: Maagele Daat, 1993).

8. See, for example, David Kretzmer, "Akhifata U-Ferusha shel Amanat Geneva IV [The Supreme Court and the Fourth Geneva Convention: Domestic Enforcement and Interpretation]," 26 *Mishpatim* 49 (1995); Simon, "Demolition of Houses"; Ronen Shamir, "'Landmark Cases' and the Reproduction of Legitimacy: The Case of Israel's High Court of Justice," 24 *Law and Society Rev.* 781 (1990); Gad Barzilai, "Political Institutions and Conflict Resolution: The Israeli Supreme Court and the Peace Process," in *The Middle East Peace Process: Interdisciplinary Approaches,* ed. Ilan Peleg (New York: State University of New York Press, forthcoming).

Glossary

Al-Ard	A pan-Arab Israeli movement
Anschluss	The annexation of Austria by Nazi Germany in 1938
Balfour Declaration	The pledge by Foreign Secretary Lord Arthur James Balfour of British aid to establish a Jewish National Home in Palestine, delivered on 2 November 1917
Brit Shalom	Peace Alliance; a Jewish group in Palestine committed to Jewish–Arab coexistence
Erets Yisrael	Land of Israel; Palestine
Galut	Exile; the history and consciousness of the Jewish people after the destruction of the Second Temple in the first century A.D.
Geulah	Redemption
Herut	Nationalist political party; established in 1948 by members of the Irgun
Histadrut (Ha-Histadrut ha-Klalit shel ha-Ovdim be-Erets Yisrael)	General federation of labor
Irgun (Irgun Tsva'i Le'umi)	National Military Organization; a Jewish military group founded in 1931
Jewish Agency	The executive arm of the World Zionist Organization
Knesset	Israel's parliament
Labor Zionism	The Socialist wing of the Zionist movement
LEHI (Lohame Herut Yisrael)	Israel Freedom Fighters; a Jewish military group in Palestine; also called the "Stern Gang"

Likud	An Israeli political party formed by a merger of Herut and the centrist General Zionists
Maccabees	Leaders of the Jewish revolt against Syria in the second century B.C.
MAFDAL (Miflagah Datit Le'umit)	National Religious Party
Mamlakhtiyut	A variation of etatism developed in the early years of Israeli statehood
MAPAI (Mifleget Po'ale Erets Yisrael)	Jewish Socialist Party
MAPAM (Mifleget ha-Po'alim ha-Me'uhedet)	United Workers Party, a left-wing Jewish party
Mitnagged	Ultra-Orthodox Jews; historically the Mitnagdim were opposed to the Hasidic movement
Mossad (Ha-Mosad le-Modi'in ule-Tafkidim Meyuhadim)	The Israeli Secret Service
Peel Commission	A British commission appointed to investigate the causes of the 1936 Arab rebellion in Palestine
Revisionists	A right-wing Zionist movement
Six Day War	Arab–Israeli war, June 1967
Stern Gang	See LEHI
Succot	The seven-day festival which commemorates the tabernacles or booths in which the children of Israel dwelled in the wilderness after the Exodus from Egypt
Tel Hai	A Jewish settlement in the Upper Galilee; site of a battle between Jewish settlers and Arabs in 1920
Yiddishkeit	Eastern European Jewish culture
Yom Kippur War	Arab–Israeli war, October 1973
Young Judea	American Zionist youth organization

Index

Table of Cases

Designer:	Nola Burger
Compositor:	Integrated Composition Systems
Text:	Galliard
Display:	Bernhard/Galliard
Printer:	Thomson Shore
Binder:	Thomson Shore